Recent Advances in the Analysis of Competition Policy and Regulation

 **CRESSE 2011 GOLD SPONSORS**
(in alphabetical order)

Bank of Greece

Charles River Associates

Hellenic Gas Transmission
System Operator S.A.

Microsoft

Public Power Corporation

Recent Advances in the Analysis of Competition Policy and Regulation

Edited by

Joseph E. Harrington Jr

Professor of Economics, Johns Hopkins University, USA

Yannis Katsoulacos

Professor of Economics, Athens University of Economics and Business, Greece

Edward Elgar

Cheltenham, UK • Northampton, MA, USA

Published by
Edward Elgar Publishing Limited
The Lypiatts
15 Lansdown Road
Cheltenham
Glos GL50 2JA
UK

Edward Elgar Publishing, Inc.
William Pratt House
9 Dewey Court
Northampton
Massachusetts 01060
USA

A catalogue record for this book
is available from the British Library

Library of Congress Control Number: 2012930626

ISBN 978 1 78100 568 2

Typeset by Servis Filmsetting Ltd, Stockport, Cheshire
Printed and bound by MPG Books Group, UK

Contents

Contributors

Per J. Agrell, Louvain School of Management and CORE, Université catholique de Louvain, Belgium.

Kern Alexander, Professorial Chair in Law and Finance, the University of Zurich Law Faculty, Switzerland. Member of the European Parliament's Expert Panel on Financial Services and Specialist Adviser to the British Parliament's Select Committee on the Draft Financial Services Bill.

Gary Biglaiser, University of North Carolina, USA.

Emilio Calvano, IGIER and Department of Economics, Bocconi University, Italy.

Carlo Cambini, Politecnico di Torino and EUI, Italy.

Jacques Crémer, Toulouse School of Economics (TSE), France.

Xeni Dassiou, Department of Economics, City University London, UK.

George Deltas, University of Illinois at Urbana-Champaign, USA.

Federico Etro, Department of Economics, University of Venice, Ca' Foscari, Italy.

Lapo Filistrucchi, CentER, TILEC, Tilburg University and University of Florence, Italy.

Raffaele Fiocco, Institute for Microeconomic Theory, Humboldt Universität zu Berlin, Germany.

Adelino Fortunato, University of Coimbra, Portugal.

Panagiotis N. Fotis, Hellenic Competition Commission, General Directorate of Competition, Director, B′ Directorate of Economic Analysis and University of Central Greece, Department of Regional and Economic Development, Greece.

Axel Gautier, HEC, University of Liège and CORE, Belgium.

Mario Gilli, Department of Economics, Bicocca University, Italy.

Dionysius Glycopantis, Department of Economics, City University London, UK.

Joseph E. Harrington Jr, Department of Economics, Johns Hopkins University, USA.

Thomas F. Huertas, Member, Executive Committee, Financial Services Authority, UK and Alternate Chair, European Banking Authority. Currently a partner in the risk practice at Ernst & Young.

Marc Ivaldi, Toulouse School of Economics (TSE), France.

Bruno Jullien, Toulouse School of Economics (TSE), France.

Yannis Katsoulacos, Athens University of Economics and Business, Greece.

Tobias J. Klein, CentER, TILEC, Tilburg University, the Netherlands.

Johannes Koenen, University of Bonn, Germany.

Vítor Marques, Portuguese Energy Regulatory Authority (ERSE), Portugal.

Thomas O. Michielsen, CentER, TSC, Tilburg University, the Netherlands.

Sébastien Mitraille, Toulouse Business School, University of Toulouse, France.

Catherine Muller, Toulouse School of Economics (TSE), France.

Martin Peitz, University of Mannheim, Germany.

Laura Rondi, Politecnico di Torino, Italy.

Alberto Salvo, Northwestern University (KSM), USA.

Isabel Soares, University of Porto, CEP UP, Portugal.

Yossi Spiegel, Tel Aviv University, CEPR and ZEW, Israel.

Emanuele Tarantino, Department of Economics, University of Bologna, Italy.

Helder Vasconcelos, Faculdade de Economia do Porto and CEF UP, Portugal.

Geoffrey Wood, Professor Emeritus of Economics, Cass Business School and Professor Emeritus of Monetary Economics, University of Buckingham, UK.

Introduction

Joseph E. Harrington Jr and Yannis Katsoulacos

The Competition and Regulation European Summer School and Conference (CRESSE) is an informal network of academics and professionals with an interest in competition policy and sectoral regulation. It was initiated by Yannis Katsoulacos (Athens University of Economics and Business) in 2005. The annual conference organized by CRESSE has since grown to become an important event in the competition and regulation conferences calendar with the support of Joe Harrington (Johns Hopkins University), Massimo Motta (Barcelona Graduate School), Patrick Rey (University of Toulouse), Pierre Régibeau (University of Essex), and David Ulph (University of St Andrews). The objective is to provide a forum in which the latest research in the areas of competition and regulation is presented and discussed. Presentations in the three-day annual conference include 3–5 invited papers and a limited number of papers selected from those submitted following a call in the major IO journals and the conference website (http://www.cresse.info). The annual CRESSE Conference is organized in early July in Greece, the institution responsible for the organization being the Athens University of Economics and Business.

CRESSE also organizes an annual Summer School in which visiting faculty from a large number of European and US universities provide high quality training to practitioners of competition policy and sectoral regulation that wish to be acquainted with the most recent economic and legal developments. It is also active in disseminating research in the areas of competition policy and regulation and in contributing to the field through the organization of special policy sessions and roundtables that deliver public debates on topical policy issues.

The Sixth CRESSE Annual Conference took place in Rhodes on 1–3 July 2011, on 'Advances in the Analysis of Competition Policy and Regulation'. There were two Keynote Lectures:

- The Jean-Jacques Laffont Lecture was presented by Professor Mike Whinston (Northwestern University) on the topic of 'Horizontal merger policy: new work on an old problem'.

- The CRESSE Conference Policy Lecture was presented by Professor Jacques Crémer (Toulouse School of Economics) on the topic of 'Switching costs and network effects in competition policy'.

There were also two special policy sessions: one on 'Financial regulation' and one on 'Online search and advertising'.

This volume contains papers that were presented at the 2011 CRESSE Conference and which were selected from a large number of papers submitted for inclusion in the volume. We have categorized the selected papers into four parts. In Part I there are chapters on competition policy/ antitrust and some related issues, while in Part II there are chapters on 'Online search, advertising and two-sided markets'. In Part III there are chapters on regulation and finally, Part IV contains the papers presented in the special policy session on Financial Regulation. The vast majority of chapters present original research rather than being review papers, and contain important new theoretical and/or empirical results.

PART I: COMPETITION POLICY AND RELATED ISSUES

With the exception of the chapter by Johannes Koenen and Martin Peitz on 'The economics of pending patents' all chapters in Part I contain analyses of various aspects of competition policy. In particular, the chapters contained in Part I address issues concerning the implications of switching costs and network effects in competition policy, the effects of leniency programmes, the identification of maverick firms, the implications of competition policy on the share value of infringed firms, optimal bundling and the analysis of a case of social welfare-enhancing collusion.

The chapter on 'Switching costs and network effects in competition policy' by Jacques Crémer and Gary Biglaiser builds on a series of papers – Biglaiser et al. (2011) and Biglaiser and Cremer (2011a, 2011b) – with the aim of discussing the similarities and differences between the strategic consequences of switching costs and network effects. The chapter reviews a number of recent results on the economics of competition with network effects and switching costs and highlights several which have important consequences for antitrust and regulatory policy. Crémer and Biglaiser show that the distribution of switching costs and network effects in the population is important for the dynamics of markets. Second, despite the impressive amount of work on these effects in the literature (see Farrell and Klemperer, 2007), there is still much which is not understood at the most fundamental theoretical level about the dynamics of these industries.

Third, although it is true that switching costs and network effects have some similarities, there are also many differences. In particular, our understanding of the value of incumbency is on much more solid ground for switching costs than for network effects. Finally, it is noted that studying switching costs and network effects in isolation could be misleading. Given the importance of markets where they co-exist, much more effort should be spent on understanding their interaction.

In the chapter 'Corporate leniency with private information: an exploratory example', Joseph E. Harrington Jr examines corporate leniency programmes that provide relief from government penalties to the first member of a cartel to come forward and cooperate with the authorities. The chapter explores the incentives to apply for leniency when each cartel member has private information as to the likelihood that the competition authority will be able to convict them without a cooperating firm. A firm may apply for leniency because it fears being convicted or because it fears another firm will apply. An example is provided which suggests that leniency programmes are significantly more effective when firms have private information.

In the chapter on 'The economics of pending patents', Johannes Koenen and Martin Peitz provide a treatment of a number of questions pertaining to pending patents – a subject that has so far mainly been discussed *en passant* in the existing literature. They present the underlying institutional and legal framework that governs pending patents and some basic facts related to them. Koenen and Peitz focus on the strategic considerations of firms in the earliest stage of the patenting process and the interplay with the patent office. This is followed by a consideration of the perspective of the patent and trademark offices (PTOs) and, in particular, acknowledging the limited resources that are available to PTOs. Finally, Koenen and Peitz investigate the potential abuse of pending patents and the role of reputation of patenting firms.

In 'Testing for the presence of a maverick in the French audit industry', Marc Ivaldi, Sébastien Mitraille and Catherine Muller propose an original test for identifying a maverick firm which is part of the assessment of the risks of collective dominance according to the so-called Airtours criteria used by the European competition authorities. First, they study the French legal and institutional background – whose main feature is to require large- and medium-size firms to be annually audited by a pair of auditors – and in particular they investigate the applicability of the three cumulative Airtours criteria. Second, they implement a test of the presence of a maverick by fitting a supply equation to an original dataset that was collected over the period 2004 to 2006 that contains all the fees paid to audit committees by the 120 companies with the largest market capitalizations of the French marketplace (the SBF120). Their results indicate that there is no evidence of a maverick in this market and that the Airtours criteria might be met.

The chapter on 'Optimal decisions in two-stage bundling' by Xeni Dassiou and Dionysius Glycopantis develops a generalized framework for pure bundling where buyer tastes for two goods are assumed to follow a normal distribution. In the previous literature, optimal bundling decisions have been considered under the assumption that the weights of the two goods are fixed and equal, which has the implication that the only consideration is to choose the profit maximizing optimal price. The approach adopted by Dassiou and Glycopantis is different and more realistic. The monopolist first decides on the optimal weights of the two goods and in the second stage derives the profit maximizing bundle price. The authors derive welfare and policy implications and provide comparisons to results obtained by the fixed weights approach.

In 'Competition policy and firm's damages', Panagiotis N. Fotis evaluates the impact of major antitrust and abuse of dominant position investigations on a firm's share value. For this purpose, he divides the period of each competition case into two sub-periods: the 'Investigation period', which begins from the outset of the investigation and ends when the competition authority issues its final decision to the infringed firms, and the 'Deterrence period', which follows the 'Investigation period' and ends with the final judgment of the Court of Appeal. He uses the aggregate regression-based approach to estimate the average and cumulative average residuals of the firms that infringe Articles 1 and 2 of Greek Competition Law. The empirical results support the hypothesis that the release of the final decisions of the Hellenic Competition Commission and the Court of Appeal negatively affect the share value of the infringed firms.

In 'Social-welfare-enhancing collusion and trade', George Deltas, Alberto Salvo and Helder Vasconcelos extend Deltas et al. (2011) that examines the welfare implications of collusion (or merger to monopoly) in a model of geographically separated markets with differentiated goods. Their original paper showed how restricting trade relative to duopolistic competition can be beneficial for society and consumers. In this chapter, they show that a social planner would further restrict trade than the perfect cartel would, and also how the socially optimal market allocation can be induced through a system of taxes and subsidies, or through 'anti-dumping' regulation. They generalize the model to allow for home-biased consumer tastes and show that their original analysis is robust. They also consider whether autarky can improve social welfare over market-based trade regimes, in the spirit of Brander and Krugman (1983).

PART II: ONLINE SEARCH, ADVERTISING AND TWO-SIDED MARKETS

Part II starts with 'A note on vertical search engines' foreclosure' by Emanuele Tarantino which offers a brief review of online searches and their relation to competition policy issues. The chapter discusses the functioning of the Internet search intermediation market and then examines general search engines' incentives to bias search results so as to favour integrated websites. Two forms of manipulating practices are considered – organic search manipulation and sponsored search manipulation – and the main trade-offs are discussed.

'Issues in online advertising and competition policy: a two-sided market perspective' by Emilio Calvano and Bruno Jullien shifts the focus to issues related to online advertising. They emphasize the relevance of theories of competition between two-sided platforms noting that, although theories of platform competition are not specific to the Internet, they shed light on most of the basic trade-offs faced by Internet platforms. These theories contrast market outcomes with welfare-maximizing outcomes under various market configurations and governance structures. In the chapter, the authors first discuss competition policy issues specific to two-sided intermediation that are relevant for advertising markets in general, and then turn to those aspects inherent to the online world that they consider can potentially lead to new intuitions or deserve specific treatment.

The chapter 'Assessing unilateral merger effects in the Dutch daily newspaper market' by Lapo Filistrucchi, Tobias J. Klein and Thomas O. Michielsen compares different methods for assessing unilateral merger effects in a two-sided market by applying them to a hypothetical merger in the Dutch newspaper industry. For this purpose, the authors first specify and estimate a structural model of demand for differentiated products on both the readership and the advertising side of the market. This allows them to recover price elasticities and indirect network effects. Following Filistrucchi et al. (2010), marginal costs are then recovered from an oligopoly model of the supply side. They use these estimates of price elasticities, network effects and marginal costs to compare different methods that can be used to evaluate merger effects. Specifically, they perform a concentration analysis based on the Herfindahl Hirschmann Index, a small but significant non-transitory increase in price test, measure upward pricing pressure and conduct a full merger simulation.

'Leadership in multi-sided markets and dominance in online advertising' by Federico Etro analyses the role of leadership in multi-sided markets. Etro argues that search and display advertising are better characterized by quantity and price competition, respectively, with leadership by a dominant firm and few followers. A platform that reached dominance in search advertising may have an incentive to limit services to consumers that are aggressive with the advertisers, or may be more likely to exploit its scale in search advertising to build barriers to entry and to adopt click-weighted auctions to manipulate the pricing of sponsored links. A dominant platform in display advertising may increase the rewards of content providers to increase prices on advertisers, or may adopt exclusive clauses to predate on other platforms. The author discusses how this creates the potential for various antitrust abuses.

PART III: REGULATION

'Bargaining and collusion in a regulatory model' by Raffaele Fiocco and Mario Gilli considers a standard three-tier regulatory model, in which a benevolent principal delegates to a regulatory agency two tasks: the supervision of the firm's (two-type) costs and the arrangement of a pricing mechanism. The agency may have an incentive to manipulate information to the principal to share the gains of collusion with the firm. The novelty of this chapter is that both the regulatory mechanism and the side contracting between the agency and the firm are modelled as a bargaining process. While as usual the inefficient firm does not have any interest in cost manipulation, the authors find that the efficient firm has an incentive to collude only if the agency's bargaining power is high enough, and the total gains of collusion are now lower than what the two partners would appropriate if the agency could make a take it or leave it offer. They then focus on the optimal institutional responses to the possibility of collusion. In a setting where the incompleteness of contracts prevents the principal from designing a screening mechanism and thus Tirole's equivalence principle does not apply, they show how the players' bargaining powers crucially drive the optimal response to collusion.

The chapter 'Investment and the strategic role of capital structure in regulated industries: theory and evidence' by Carlo Cambini, Laura Rondi and Yossi Spiegel provides a summary and synthesis of results from an ongoing research project on the effect of privatization and the establishment of Independent Regulatory Authorities (IRAs) on the capital structure and investments of regulated firms and on regulated prices. The theoretical model yields the following predictions: (1) regulated firms should become more leveraged and should invest more when they are subject to regulation by IRAs; (2) regulated firms should become more leveraged and should invest more when they are more privatized (the state holds a smaller stake in the firm); and (3) higher financial leverage should lead to higher regulated prices. Based on evidence from the 15 European Union (EU) countries, the authors provide strong support for hypotheses (1) and (3), but much weaker support for hypothesis (2). Their results indicate that the increase in the leverage of many EU regulated firms since the early 1990s, often referred to as the 'dash for debt' phenomenon, is a natural response of regulated firms to the privatization process and the establishment of independent regulatory agencies. The results also indicate that while the 'dash for debt' is associated with higher regulated prices, it is also associated with higher investments and hence may be welfare enhancing.

In 'Rethinking regulatory capture', Per J. Agrell and Axel Gautier note that conventional capture models rely on the idea that the regulator is induced to be lenient with respect to the regulated firm through offers of monetary transfers (the bribery model) or future employment (the revolving doors model). To avoid socially costly capture, the political principal should then either implement collusion-proof mechanisms through the delegation of welfare gains, or severely restrict the career paths of regulatory staff. The paradox of capture is that neither of the two modes of capture, nor the remedy are commonly found in practice. This chapter proposes a rethink of capture based on the widespread use of industry commissioned consultants, experts and lobbyists that produce information for regulatory and policy use. A model (Agrell and Gautier, 2010) introduces a 'soft capture' concept based on self-enforced collusion between the firm and regulator, linked to the role of the regulator as information-processing intermediary for the political principal. The firm puts processed but biased information at the free disposal of the regulator who can then either use the submitted information or produce more accurate information at a cost. Under a set of mild conditions, the equilibrium involves soft capture and the regulator uses the submitted information, leading to some distortions in welfare. A case study of the US Occupational Safety and Health Administration (OSHA) serves to motivate and illustrate the model.

In 'Can structural models be useful to understand the electricity wholesale markets? An application to Spain', Vítor Marques, Adelino Fortunato and Isabel Soares aim to analyse the behaviour of agents in highly concentrated and strongly regulated electricity wholesale markets with rigid demand. A structural estimation is performed on the former Spanish electricity generation market during January 1999 to June 2007. Despite the characteristics of this market, the chapter suggests that the average high markups observed in the period were very likely due to the implementation of anti-competitive strategies. Therefore, the authors conclude that the opening of a wholesale electricity market without the prior increase in the number of market players does not prevent, by itself, the manipulation of the market, even when the market is strongly regulated.

PART IV: FINANCIAL REGULATION

Part IV contains the three papers presented in the conference special policy session on financial regulation.

In 'Rebuilding international financial regulation and Basel III', Kern Alexander considers the effectiveness of the Basel Capital Accord in influencing states to regulate their banks and how international financial regulation should be rebuilt post the financial crisis. Basel II embodied some of the major weaknesses with the current international financial standard-setting approach because the standards failed to protect the broader financial system against systemic risk. Effective international regulatory reform will require a more macro-prudential approach to regulation, supervision and crisis management that will necessarily require enhanced measures to control excessive risk-taking.

In 'The shock of the old: the first financial crisis of the twenty-first century', Geoffrey Wood notes that at the end of the twentieth century the world seemed to be booming, and this boom seemed set to continue for many years. Yet, in less than a decade, the world had been ravaged by banking crises. This was particularly striking in Britain, where the previous banking crisis had been in 1866. This chapter considers what had changed between 1866 and the twenty-first century to allow an individual bank failure to turn into a crisis, and how to undo the effects of these changes. So far as Britain goes, Wood suggests, the answers are straightforward. All that is needed to restore stability, through allowing the nineteenth-century approach of providing general liquidity and not bailing out individual institutions, is to improve deposit protection and have a special insolvency regime for banks. But there are also international problems. A market system cannot function unless it is possible for firms to fail, but this failure must be orderly. Hence, only when there is a system to allow orderly closure of banks, including large ones, international ones and investment banks, is there minimal danger of chaotic bailouts again in the future.

In 'Fixing finance: are we there yet?', Thomas F. Huertas, after briefly reviewing the huge cost caused by the post-2008 financial crisis, argues that policymakers have put in place a comprehensive programme (better regulation, better deposit guarantee schemes, better supervision and better resolution) that should not only make banks less likely to fail, but also safe to fail. If implemented, this programme will limit the risk that the financial sector will cause crises in the future. However, reform to the financial system must also be accompanied by steps to prevent other shocks (such as might be posed by Eurozone sovereign debt), if crises are to become a thing of the past.

REFERENCES

Agrell, P.J. and A. Gautier (2010), 'A theory of soft capture', Discussion Paper 2010/84, CORE, Université catholique de Louvain.

Biglaiser, G. and J. Crémer (2011a), 'Equilibria in an infinite horizon game with an incumbent, entry and switching costs', *International Journal of Economic Theory*, **7**, 65–76.

Biglaiser, G. and J. Crémer (2011b), 'The value of incumbency in heterogenous networks', available at http://cremeronline.com/research/BCD (accessed February 2012).

Biglaiser, G., J. Crémer and G. Dobos (2011), 'The value of switching costs', available at http://cremeronline.com/research/BCD (accessed February 2012).

Brander, J.A. and P.R. Krugman (1983), 'A reciprocal dumping model of international trade', *Journal of International Economics*, **15**, 313–21.

Deltas, G., A. Salvo and H. Vasconcelos (2011), 'Consumer-surplus-enhancing collusion and trade', Manuscript.

Farrell, J. and P. Klemperer (2007), 'Coordination and lock-in: competition with switching costs and network effects', in M. Armstrong and R. Porter (eds), *Handbook of Industrial Organization*, Vol. 3, Amsterdam: North-Holland, pp. 1967–2072.

Filistrucchi, L., T.J. Klein and T. Michielsen (2010), 'Merger simulation in a two-sided market: the case of the Dutch daily newspapers', NET Institute Working Paper No. 10-15.

PART I

Competition policy and related issues

1. Switching costs and network effects in competition policy

Jacques Crémer and Gary Biglaiser[1]

In their traditional definition switching costs refer to real, concrete, 'hard' costs that consumers or firms must bear when changing suppliers. There is no switching cost, or very little, when you switch from one baker to another; there is some switching cost when you change the brand of car you are driving as you need to relearn how to program the radio; there are substantial switching costs when a firm changes consumer relationship management (CRM) software. As a consequence, incumbent suppliers have a strategic advantage: they can, within limits, charge a higher price than entrants and 'keep' their customers.

Network effects refer to the fact that, for some types of goods, individuals or firms prefer to consume the same good as others. Using a social networking site that does not have any other users does not increase one's utility. Economists have stressed the fact that network effects lead to strategic effects which are very similar to those induced by switching costs. Consumers will hesitate to 'leave' an incumbent, even to migrate to an entrant which offers lower prices and/or better quality, as they fear that they will lose the benefits of the network effects.

This analogy is so ingrained in the collective wisdom of economists that they sometimes speak of network effects as 'collective switching costs.' For instance, in his lectures at Berkeley on 'Strategic Computing and Communications Technology'[2] Hal Varian states 'network effects lead to substantial collective switching costs and lock-in,' which are 'even worse than individual switching costs due to coordination costs.' However, because switching costs are physical whereas network effects are the consequences of defective coordination between customers we should take this analogy with a grain of salt. The aim of this chapter is to build on a series of papers, Biglaiser et al. (2012) and Biglaiser and Crémer (2011a, 2011b) to discuss the similarities and differences between the strategic consequences of switching costs and network effects.[3]

In many markets, switching costs and network effects are both present. As Levin (2011) puts it

In traditional industries with network effects, high switching costs are often an important compounding factor. Consider the case of operating systems, where switching costs can be relatively high for individual users and for firms with large computer installations. Switching between internet platforms or using multiple platforms can be considerably easier. That is, one can shop on Amazon and eBay, or be a Facebook user and try Twitter. At least in some cases, the combination of low switching costs and low costs to creating new platforms might mitigate traditional concerns about lock-in and dynamic inefficiency.

In Section 1.3, we will comment on the interactions between switching costs and network effects and describe some of the research issues which they raise.

The main four themes which we will tackle are therefore:

- How do switching cost models and network models differ?
- How do we model inertia in networks?
- What are the consequences of heterogeneity of consumers in dynamic models of both types?
- How do switching cost and network effects mix?

1.1   THE SIMPLEST POSSIBLE MODELS

1.1.1   One Period Models

Let us first turn our attention to a model with switching cost. As in the rest of the chapter, we will assume that there is at the start an incumbent who has sold in the past to all the consumers. The market is opening, and there is free entry, with many potential entrants.[4] For instance, a patent which protected the incumbent has just expired. There is a continuum of mass α of consumers and, to make our life simpler, we will assume that all of them must buy a unit of the product in each period. All the consumers have a switching cost equal to σ (we will introduce heterogeneity in switching costs later in Section 1.2). Therefore when a consumer purchases from the incumbent who charges p_I his total cost is p_I whereas when he purchases from an entrant who charges p_E his total cost is $p_E + \sigma$. He will choose to purchase from the incumbent whenever $p_I - p_E < \sigma$ and from one of the entrants (assuming it is one of the lowest price entrants) if $p_I - p_E > \sigma$.

Figure 1.1 shows the order of moves in the simplest one period game that we consider.

Notice that we are assuming a Stackelberg game in which the incumbent chooses its price before the entrants do. Most of our results hold true if we

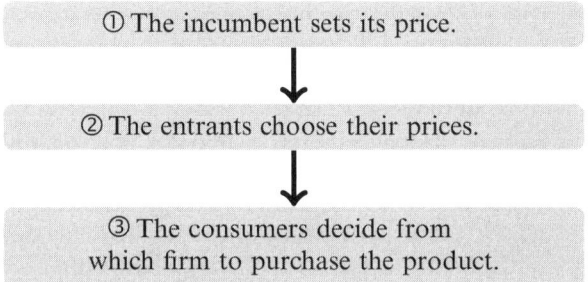

Figure 1.1   The basic model used in the chapter

assume that the entrants and the incumbent announce their prices simultaneously, but the analysis can be more complicated and involve mixed strategies. We treat this problem in detail in Biglaiser et al. (2011).

We assume constant returns to scale in production, and, without loss of generality, that the cost of production is equal to 0.[5] It is then clear that the incumbent will sell to all the consumers whenever it chooses a price strictly less than σ and will have zero sales whenever it prices strictly above that level. The unique equilibrium outcome of the game is therefore for the incumbent to choose a price equal to σ and for all the consumers to choose to purchase from the incumbent when the entrants charge a non-negative price. The profit of the incumbent is equal to $\alpha \times \sigma$.

Let us now compare the analysis of this switching cost game with that of a similar network effect game. There is still an incumbent, and the market opens up. We can imagine that a firm has created a new social network platform which has attracted many users – once it is known that there is a demand for this type of platform, other firms find it relatively easy to copy its features. We assume once again that consumers must join one platform and that their utility is equal to

$$v \times \text{mass of consumers on the same platform} - \text{price},$$

where v is the intensity of preference for the presence of other consumers.

Assume here again that costs are equal to zero, and that we have the same game form as in Figure 1.1, where the incumbent is a Stackelberg leader.

Informally we can analyse the game in the following way (we will discuss some of the formalities in Subsection 1.1.3). If the difference between the price charged by the incumbent, p_I, and the price charged by the lowest price entrant, p_E, is less than $\alpha \times v$, then no consumer will choose to 'leave' the incumbent for an entrant and the same limit pricing reasoning as above shows that the incumbent will choose a price equal to $\alpha \times v$, that the consumers will purchase from the incumbent when the entrants charge 0, and therefore that the profit of the incumbent will be equal to $\alpha \times (\alpha \times v) = \alpha^2 v$.

It is on the basis of this type of analysis that competition authorities are worried about the potential for long-term monopolization of industries with network effects. And it is also on this basis that we can say that network effects are similar to collective switching costs: they play the same role, but in the case of network effects the cost is the cost of abandoning the benefits of having joined the same network as the other consumers. Of course, there is one important difference between markets with switching costs and markets with network effects: in the latter case profits are proportional to the square of the number of consumers; in the former they are linear in α.

What about social welfare? In both the switching cost and the network effect setups, the resulting allocation is efficient, but for different reasons. With network effects any allocation of consumers between suppliers is efficient, as long as they join the same platform. With switching costs, the only efficient allocation is for the consumers to all purchase from the incumbent. There is certainly an underlying feeling that in the case of network effects the profits of the incumbent are coming out of thin air as it is benefiting from the fact that the consumers are reluctant to migrate to one of its rivals, when there would be no social cost from them doing so, but we are not aware of any way to express this more formally.[6]

The consequences for social welfare can also be illustrated by assuming that the incumbent offers a (large) stand-alone utility W, whereas the entrants offer a stand-alone utility of $W + \varepsilon$, with ε, as usual, strictly positive but 'small.' Using the game form of Figure 1.1, in a switching cost model, consumers purchase from the incumbent who charges $\sigma - \varepsilon$; efficiency is preserved. In a network effects model, consumers also purchase from the incumbent and pay $\alpha v - \varepsilon$. In this case, the equilibrium is inefficient. It would seem that network effects are more conducive to the presence of inefficient equilibria than switching costs.

Of course, our analysis of the game played by the consumers when they must choose which network to join requires discussion and, as promised, we will discuss it below. Before doing so, we would like to point out that the cost of monopoly is actually less important than the results obtained so far would make one believe.

1.1.2   Elementary Repeated Games with Homogeneous Consumers

The analysis of Subsection 1.1.1 would seem to indicate that the incumbent has touched a jackpot. It can grab for itself the whole value of the reluctance of consumers to change suppliers. This explains, we believe, the close supervision by competition authorities of industries with large network effects and/or large switching costs: they feel that the incentives for monopolization are extremely high.

However, it is a common theme in the switching cost literature that large switching costs protect incumbents but also make entrants more aggressive as capturing consumers yields larger future profits – this is the 'bargains followed by ripoffs' feature discussed by Farrell and Klemperer (2007, section 2.3.1). For instance, using a a two period model with consumers unattached at the beginning of the first period, Klemperer (1987) has shown that competition between firms will induce them to price below cost in the first period in such a way that their profits will be equal to 0 (if they all have the same cost).

In our set up with free entry, this phenomenon will show itself through an increased aggressiveness of entrants in dynamic models, as attracting consumers will yield profits not only in the current period but also in future periods. To illustrate this assumes that the game of Figure 1.1 is expanded to include a second period. In the second period, there can be several incumbents if the consumers have not all decided to buy from the same firm in the first period (this will not happen on the equilibrium path). Let δ be the discount factor.

We will assume that the firms cannot price discriminate between consumers on the basis of their past purchasing history. It is therefore impossible to offer lower prices to consumers of other firms. Depending on the industry and the product, this hypothesis is or is not reasonable.

Consider first the switching cost model. In the second period, the analysis of the one period model carries: any incumbent charges σ and consumers do not switch firms. Therefore, any entrant who has attracted consumers in the first period will have second period profits equal to σ times the mass of consumers it has attracted. In the first period, entrants are therefore willing to price 'down to' $-\delta\sigma$. The consumers, knowing that the price they will pay in the second period is independent of the identity of firm from which they purchase in the first period, will use the same rule in the first period as they do in the static model of Subsection 1.1.1, and purchase from the incumbent whenever the price difference is smaller than σ.

Therefore in order to 'keep' its consumers the incumbent can charge at most $-\delta\sigma + \sigma$ in the first period. Its first period profit will be $\alpha \times (-\delta\sigma + \sigma)$, its second period profit will be $\alpha \times \sigma$, and its discounted profit over two periods will be

$$\alpha \times (-\delta\sigma + \sigma) + \delta \times \alpha \times \sigma = \sigma,$$

the same profit as in the one period model! Competition from entrants ensures that the profits over two periods is the same as the one period profit. The incumbent 'cashes' the switching costs only once. Although this result is very easy to prove, we are not aware that it had been noticed in the literature before Dobos (2005).

Let us now turn to the network effect model. The hardest consumer to attract is the first consumer who 'leaves' a platform: he abandons larger network effects than subsequent leavers and joins a platform with fewer (zero) participants. Therefore, if an entrant attracts one[7] consumer in the first period, it attracts them all. This implies that at the beginning of the second period there will be only one incumbent, and by the reasoning of Subsection 1.1.1, the second period profit of this incumbent will be $\alpha^2 v$. Therefore the smallest price $\underline{p}_E$ that an entrant will be willing to charge in the first period to attract consumers will satisfy

$$\alpha \underline{p}_E + \delta \alpha^2 v = 0 \Leftrightarrow \underline{p}_E = -\delta \alpha v.$$

Let us now examine the choice of a platform by a consumer in the first period. He knows that in the second period he can switch platform at no cost. Furthermore, because he is atomistic, his choice of platform does not affect the second period equilibrium. It is therefore optimal for the consumer to choose his first period platform simply by maximizing his first period utility and the same analysis as in Subsection 1.1.1 implies that an entrant can attract consumers only by charging at least αv less than the incumbent. Therefore, the incumbent will protect its client base by charging a price at most equal to the lowest price that entrants are willing to charge plus the price difference that consumers are willing to accept, that is

$$-\delta \times \alpha v + \alpha v = (1 - \delta)\alpha v,$$

and its discounted profit over two periods will be

$$\underbrace{\alpha \times (1 - \delta)\alpha v +}_{\text{1st period profit}} \underbrace{\delta \alpha^2 v}_{\text{2nd period profit}} = \alpha^2 v,$$

again the same profit as in the one period model. As with switching costs, network effects do not generate a jackpot that you can cash in every period.

For both the switching cost and the network effect models, the results that we have presented extend with no difficulty for any *finite* number of periods: whatever the number of periods the total discounted profit of the incumbent is equal to the one period profit. With an infinite number of periods, the results depend on stationarity assumptions. Biglaiser and Crémer (2011a) discuss this issue at greater length and characterize the whole set of equilibria in the infinite horizon switching cost model.

As we will see in Section 1.2, the results that we have obtained must be qualified when consumers are heterogeneous, with different σs or different vs. This is the reason for the qualifier 'with homogeneous consumers' in the title of this subsection.

1.1.3   Modeling Collective Switching Cost

Although the results that we have obtained show very strong similarities between the strategic implications of switching costs and network effects, there are two subtle differences which we would like to stress. These differences have important consequences when we enrich the model as we shall do below.

First, if the reader turns back to the reasonings that we have made in the two cases, she will notice that the cognitive burden that the consumers must bear in the switching costs case is much heavier than in the network effects case. With switching costs, consumers must understand the game well enough to be able to compute the prices charged by firms in the second period and understand that all the firms will charge the same price. In contrast, with network effects consumers can simply reason 'in the second period, I will join whatever network offers me the highest utility; I can choose myopically without worrying at all about the second period.' If the reader thinks that we are splitting hairs, she should know that with heterogeneous consumers, firms and platforms do, depending on the parameters of the game, charge different prices in the second period and this difference is substantial. Of course, the within-period game that the consumers play is much simpler in the switching costs case, as they do not face a coordination problem.

The second issue is also a difference between the fundamental economic forces at play behind similar looking results. In both our frameworks, all the consumers purchase from the incumbent. However, in the network effect model, this is a consequence of the way in which we think about coordination between the consumers in the third stage of the game of Figure 1.1; we do not need to know anything about the other stages of the game in order to make this prediction. In the switching cost model, it is a consequence of the limit pricing argument that along the only equilibrium path of the game, in the third stage, the consumers have to choose to all purchase from the incumbent when they are indifferent.[8]

The third issue that we would like to discuss is our modeling of the incumbency advantage in the network effect case. It is quite common for economists when faced with difficulties arising from a multiplicity of equilbria to assume that the agents will coordinate on the Pareto optimal equilibrium (or one of them if there are several Pareto optimal equilibria). In models of network effects, this should imply that the consumers would purchase from the network that proposes the lowest price,[9] and would prevent us from modeling the inertia that experience and intuition tell us is prevalent in these markets.

Different authors have proposed different ways of tackling this problem. For instance, Crémer et al. (2000) studied the consequences of a merger in the market for Internet backbone services. In order to model the incumbency advantage, they assumed that there existed a mass of 'trapped' consumers who had signed long-term contracts with the incumbent and could not change supplier. Although this modeling strategy was appropriate for the applied theory exercise which the paper was tackling, it is not a general solution to the problem.

In their classical 'chicken and egg' paper, Caillaud and Jullien (2003) study 'dominant-firm equilibria', that is, equilibria that 'involve only one active matchmaker [i.e., platform] on the equilibrium path.' They show that such an equilibrium 'can always be sustained by a 'bad-expectation' (or pessimistic) market allocation against E [the entrant]' (p. 314): 'after any price deviation by E, users coordinate on an equilibrium distribution with zero market share for E, whenever possible (p. 314).' Therefore, Caillaud and Jullien select an equilibrium by looking at the properties of the allocation of consumers between the networks.

In Biglaiser and Crémer (2011b), we propose another solution for selecting equilibria. For given prices announced by the networks, we first define 'nomadic consumers equilibria,' which are standard equilibria for models with network externalities: no consumer would be better off moving by himself from the network he has joined to another one. We call them 'nomadic consumers' equilibria because they assume that there are no impediments for consumers to move from one network to the other. Among these equilibria, we select 'sedentary consumers' equilibria, whose definition depend on the initial allocation of consumers among the networks: a nomadic consumers equilibrium is a sedentary consumers equilibrium if and only if there exists a sequence of migration of small masses of consumers from the initial allocation to the equilibrium allocation such that at every step of the sequence it is some of the consumers with the highest gain from migration who change networks.[10]

The precise definition is notationally heavy, so let us consider two examples. Let $\alpha = 3$ and $v = 2$. Assume first that there is one incumbent network which charges 6 and which all consumers had previously joined. The net utility of a consumer from joining this network is $\alpha \times v = 6$. If the entrants charge a non-negative price, no small mass of consumers would strictly increase its utility from migrating, and the initial equilibrium is both a nomadic and a sedentary consumers equilibrium. On the other hand, if both entrants charge -2, consumers will find it profitable to move. The first group of consumers who migrate will choose one of the entrants, let us say E_2. Once the first group has migrated, the second group will choose to migrate to the same entrant, E_2, and actually has greater incentives to migrate. The reasoning can be continued to show that all consumers will join E_2. More generally, the only 'sedentary consumers' equilibrium is for the consumers to all purchase from the same entrant.

On the other hand, if we assume that in the initial allocation there is a mass 1 of consumers for incumbent 1 who charges p_1 and a mass 2 for incumbent 2 who charges p_2, all the consumers will join an entrant who charges $p_E < -\max\{2 - p_1, 4 - p_2\}$, and network 1, for instance, if

$$2 - p_1 > 4 - p_2 \text{ and } 2 - p_1 \geq -p_E.$$

If $2 - p_1 = 4 - p_2$ and p_E is not too small, then the consumers will not migrate. Notice that there exist no prices charged by the incumbents and the entrants such that the consumers would strictly prefer to stay with their platforms. With switching costs, on the other hand, it is possible to find such prices.

1.2 HETEROGENEOUS CONSUMERS

The result which we have discussed above, that the discounted profit over several periods is equal to the discounted profit in a one period model, breaks down when consumers are different from each other. Furthermore, the dynamics of the switching cost and network effects models are quite different. In this section, we explore this fact in a simplified model and explain at the end of the section how they generalize.

Let us first consider a switching cost model, and assume that there are α_H H-consumers with a *H*igh switching cost equal to σ_H, and α_L L-consumers have a *L*ow switching cost equal to σ_L. We assume that σ_L is substantially smaller than σ_H.[11] Because σ_L is small, in the one period model, the best the incumbent can do is to charge σ_H and to sell only to the H-consumer which yields profits equal to α_H.

In a network effects model, we assume that the utility of the H-consumers when they join a network is equal to v_H times the number of H-consumers on the same network minus the price charged by the network, whereas the L-consumers derive a utility equal to v_L times the number of L-consumers from the presence of other consumers. Then, the incumbent's profit maximizing strategy is to charge $\alpha_H \times v_H$ which yields a profit equal to $\alpha_H^2 v_H$, if we assume that v_L is small enough. (All the L-consumers purchase from one of the entrants.)

Turning to the dynamic extension of the model, we get very different results depending on the values of σ_L and v_L. If they are equal to zero, our two setups generate similar results. Take the switching cost model. If an entrant attracted all the consumers it would make profits equal to $\alpha_H \sigma_H$ in the second period. Therefore, the lowest price p_E that it would be willing to charge in the first period satisfies

$$(\alpha_H + \alpha_L)p_E + \delta\alpha_H\sigma_H = 0 \Rightarrow p_E = -\delta\frac{\alpha_H\sigma_H}{\alpha_H + \alpha_L}.$$

H-consumers will not purchase from the entrant if the first period price charged by the incumbent is at most $p_E + \sigma_H$ and therefore the profit of the incumbent is

$$\alpha_H \times \left(-\delta\frac{\alpha_H\sigma_H}{\alpha_H + \alpha_L} + \sigma_H + \delta\sigma_H \right) = \alpha_H\sigma_H \times \left(1 + \delta - \delta\frac{\alpha_H}{\alpha_H + \alpha_L} \right).$$

Biglaiser et al.(2011) provide a complete description of the economic lessons one can derive from this equation. For the purpose of the present chapter, we will stress two of them. First, the profit of the incumbent is greater than the one period profit, but smaller than a discounted flow of one period profits. Second, an increase in the number of L-consumers increases the profit of the incumbent, even though it never sells to any of them. Indeed, the presence of more L-consumers makes the entrants less aggressive: in order to attract the profitable H-consumers they need to throw away more money to unprofitable L-consumers. As a consequence, p_E is an increasing function of α_L.

It is worthwhile noticing that along the equilibrium path, no entrant charges p_E: it would attract only the L-consumers and would not be able to recover in the second period the rebate they received in the first. Competition between the entrants in the second stage for the first period game will bring the price down to 0.[12]

Exactly the same formulas hold with a network effect model if we replace α_H by $\alpha_H v$. Hence, as in the switching cost model, the two period profit is equal to the one period profit multiplied by $1 + \delta - \delta\alpha_H/(\alpha_H + \alpha_L)$, and we can draw the same economic lessons as above.

The situation changes drastically if σ_L and v_L are strictly positive. A full analysis would take us too far afield and we refer the reader to Biglaiser et al. (2011) and Biglaiser and Crémer (2011b) for further details; we shall only sketch the main economic difference here. With the network effect model, in equilibrium all the H-consumers purchase from the incumbent in the first period and all the L-consumers purchase from an entrant. The equilibrium is more complicated in the switching cost case. Indeed, if an entrant attracted only L-consumers in the first period, it would charge σ_L in the second period. More generally, any entrant whose first period clientele included a proportion γ of H-consumers which satisfies

$$(1 + \gamma)\sigma_L > \gamma\sigma_H \Leftrightarrow \gamma < \bar{\gamma} \overset{\text{def}}{=} \sigma_L/(\sigma_H - \sigma_L)$$

would certainly charge σ_L in the second period. It can be shown that along the equilibrium path if an entrant is predicted to charge σ_L in the first period, then an individual H-consumer, who, by himself, does not affect the price charged by the entrant in the second period, would gain by accepting to incur the switching cost in the first period and purchase from the entrant. Therefore at equilibrium enough H-consumers purchase from entrants that they are a proportion $\bar{\gamma}$ of their consumers and the entrants use a mixed strategy in the second period, charging either σ_L or σ_H. Consumers with high switching cost try to 'hide' among consumers with low switching cost.

Therefore, the dynamics of erosion of market share are very different with switching costs and with network effects. With switching costs, the incumbent loses some of the 'profitable' consumers, whereas with network effects all of these consumers continue to purchase from the incumbent. This again illustrates our discussion of the beginning of Subsection 1.1.3: with network effects, consumers can maximize period per period; with switching costs, they need to deploy a sophisticated dynamic reasoning.[13]

In Biglaiser and Crémer (2011b) we analyse the case where there are positive network effects between groups. Despite the fact that it is then efficient for all the consumers to join the same platform, there exist parameters for which two networks emerge in equilibrium. Somewhat surprisingly, the number of networks is not necessarily monotone on the discount factor δ.

1.3   MARKETS WITH BOTH NETWORK EFFECTS AND SWITCHING COSTS

As Jon Levin's citation at the beginning of this chapter points out, in most markets of interest both switching costs and network effects are present.

However, there is surprisingly little literature on the interactions between them (we are only aware of Suleymanova and Wey, 2011). The aim of this section is to show, through a very simple example, that switching costs and network effects together can affect the profits of the incumbent in unexpected ways.

Consider a very simple static model, with the structure presented in Figure 1.1. Assume first that all the consumers have switching costs σ and that they also value network effects as above, obtaining a utility of v times the number of consumers in the same network. Combining the analyses of Subsection 1.1.1, it is easy to show that the incumbent will charge $\sigma + \alpha v$: indeed, entrants will be ready to charge 0 and a consumer who would migrate to one of the entrants would lose the benefits of the presence of other consumers, which it values at αv, and incur the switching cost σ. Its profits, $\alpha \sigma + \alpha^2 v$, will be the sum of its profits in the pure network effect model and in the pure switching cost model.

So far, combining our two models has not generated much interesting results. Assume now that the consumers are heterogeneous. They all have the same taste for the presence of others, represented by the parameter v, but half of them (that is, a mass $\alpha/2$) have a switching cost σ while the other half have a switching cost equal to zero. If there were only switching costs, the incumbent would have profits equal to $\alpha\sigma/2$.

Let us first consider the case where network effects are more important than switching costs:

$$\sigma < \alpha v. \tag{1.1}$$

If the incumbent charges $p_I > \alpha v$, the low switching cost consumers will find that they derive a negative utility from purchasing from the incumbent, and will therefore purchase from one of the entrants at a price equal to zero. Once they have all migrated, the high switching cost consumers will face the choice between a utility of $\alpha v/2 - p_I < -\alpha v/2$ if they purchase from the incumbent, and a utility of $-\sigma + \alpha v/2$, which, by Equation (1.1), is strictly greater than $\alpha v/2$, if they purchase from the entrant. They will therefore choose to purchase from the entrant and the profit of the incumbent will be equal to zero. Therefore, the incumbent maximizes its profits by charging αv, and selling to all the consumers for a profit of $\alpha^2 v$. It generates no benefit from the presence of switching costs and the additivity of the switching cost and the network effect profits disappear.

If $\sigma > \alpha v$, with $p_I > \alpha v$ the incumbent will sell to the high switching cost consumers if it provides them with a higher net utility than does the entrant, that is, if

$$\alpha \frac{v}{2} - p_I \geq \alpha \frac{v}{2} - \sigma \Leftrightarrow p_I \leq \sigma.$$

If it charges σ, the incumbent has profits of $\alpha\sigma/2$, which are greater than the profits $\alpha^2 v$ which it can generate by selling to all the consumers only if $\sigma > 2\alpha v$. Whatever the optimal price, additivity does not hold.

We are planning work to expand on these intuitions to help us understand better the interactions between switching costs and network effects.

1.4 CONCLUSIONS

In this chapter, we have reviewed a certain number of recent results on the economics of competition with network effects and switching costs and tried to highlight a number of them that we believe have important consequences for antitrust and regulatory policy.

First, the distribution of switching costs and network effects in the population is important for the dynamics of the market. It is not enough to make general statements about the fact that these effects are important on average. Close attention to the specificities of the industry is required. In particular, we have shown that even consumers who never purchase from the incumbent can have an important influence on its profits.

Second, despite the impressive amount of work on these effects in the literature (see Farrell and Klemperer, 2007), there is still much that is not understood at the most fundamental theoretical level about the dynamics of these industries. For instance, we have not been able to characterize the equilibrium with switching costs in an infinite horizon model.

Third, although it is true that switching costs and network effects have some similarities, there are also many differences in the economic analyses. In particular, our understanding of the value of incumbency is in a much more solid foundation for switching costs than for network effects: in this latter case the stickiness is due to mis-coordination between the consumers. Expressions such as 'collective switching cost' should be used with caution.

Finally, studying switching costs and network effects in isolation could be misleading. Given the importance of markets where they co-exist much more effort should be spent on their interaction.

NOTES

1. This chapter is derived from Jacques Crémer's keynote lecture at the sixth CRESSE Annual Conference in Rhodes, Greece, 2 July 2011. We thank the organizers of the

conference for giving us the opportunity to think about the issues and the participants for comments.

2. http://people.ischool.berkeley.edu/~hal/Courses/StratTech09/Lectures/Networks/networks.ppt.

3. Farrell and Klemperer (2007) provide a recent and up to date survey of the literatures on switching cost and network effect.

4. Much of what we will say is true even with one entrant. However, when we turn to models with more than one period, we will assume that there are potential new entrants in every period – in this case it makes more sense to assume that entry is easy, and that there are lots of entrants. In Biglaiser et al. (2011), we discuss the consequences of allowing entry costs.

5. We will allow for negative prices, so that rebates below the marginal cost are possible. In some markets the impossibility of charging negative prices can put binding constraints on the size of these rebates; see Chen and Xie (2007) for an exploration of some of the issues raised by this constraint.

6. Of course, if we added a small switching cost to the network effects model, it would be efficient for all the consumers to purchase from the incumbent. However, the profits of the incumbent would still be much larger than the loss of social welfare that would be caused by a migration to an entrant. See Section 1.3 for more discussion of the relationship between switching costs and network effects.

7. Of course, with a continuum of consumers 'one' should be understood metaphorically. A more correct statement would be 'Therefore, if an entrant attracts a mass $\varepsilon > 0$ of consumers, . . .' See Biglaiser and Crémer (2011b) for more discussion of this point. Note also that the same line of reasoning implies that if 'one' consumer leaves the incumbent to purchase from an entrant, all the consumers will purchase from the same entrant.

8. Alternatively, we could have chosen to assume that the consumers purchase from the incumbent when they are indifferent. See Tirole (1988, chapter 5) for a discussion of this issue.

9. Of course, if we take into account the welfare of the firms, all the equilibria are Pareto-efficient, but we believe that in most cases economists would apply this selection criterion at each stage.

10. The same results should obtain if we make the weaker assumption that the probability that a group of consumers migrate is an increasing function of their gain of utility from so doing.

11. More precisely, we require

$$\sigma_L \times (\alpha_H + \alpha_L) < \sigma_H \times \alpha_H.$$

It is less profitable to sell to all the consumers at price σ_L than to all the consumers at price σ_H.

12. The analysis is more complex in the case of Bertrand competition, as the equilibrium strategies are mixed strategies. But the incumbent profits are as in the text.

13. This would presumably imply that the predictions of the theory are more sensitive to the presence of bounded rationality in the switching cost case.

REFERENCES

Biglaiser, G. and J. Crémer (2011a), 'Equilibria in an infinite horizon game with an incumbent, entry and switching costs', *International Journal of Economic Theory*, **7**, 65–76.

Biglaiser, G. and J. Crémer (2011b), 'The value of incumbency in heterogeneous networks', available at http://cremeronline.com/research/BCD.

Biglaiser, G., J. Crémer and G. Dobos (2011), 'The value of switching costs', available at http://cremeronline.com/research/BCD.

Caillaud, B. and B. Jullien (2003), 'Chicken and egg: competition among intermediation service providers', *RAND Journal of Economics*, **34**, 521–52.

Chen, Y. and J. Xie (2007), 'Cross-market network effect with asymmetric customer loyalty: implications for competitive advantage', *Marketing Science*, **26**, 52–66.

Crémer, J., P. Rey and J. Tirole (2000), 'Connectivity in the commercial internet', *Journal of Industrial Economics*, **48**, 433–72.

Dobos, G. (2005), 'Switching costs and competition', PhD Thesis, Université de Toulouse.

Farrell, J. and P. Klemperer (2007), 'Coordination and lock-in competition with switching costs and network effects', in M. Armstrong and R. Porter (eds), *Handbook of Industrial Organization*, Vol. 3, Amsterdam: North-Holland, pp. 1967–2072.

Klemperer, P.D. (1987), 'Markets with consumer switching costs', *Quarterly Journal of Economics*, **102**, 375–94.

Levin, J. (2012), 'The economics of internet markets', in D. Acemoglu, M. Arellano and E. Deckel (eds), Stanford University and NBER *Advances in Economics and Econometrics*, forthcoming, available at http://www.stanford.edu/~jdlevin/research.htm (accessed 8 February 2012).

Suleymanova, I. and C. Wey (2011), 'Bertrand competition in markets with network effects and switching costs', *B.E. Journal of Economic Analysis and Policy*, **11** (1) (contributions), Article 56.

Tirole, J. (1988), *The Theory of Industrial Organization*, Cambridge, MA: MIT Press.

2. Corporate leniency with private information: an exploratory example

Joseph E. Harrington Jr[1]

2.1 INTRODUCTION

One of the most important policy developments in US antitrust policy in recent decades is the 1993 revision of the Corporate Leniency Program by the Department of Justice (DOJ). Originally created in 1978, this program allows corporations, who are engaging in illegal antitrust activity (such as price-fixing), to receive amnesty from government penalties if they come forward and cooperate. The 1993 revision made it possible for amnesty to be awarded even when an investigation had been started and made it a condition that the DOJ 'has not received information about the illegal activity being reported from any other source.' This means that amnesty is limited to one firm per cartel. The appeal of these programs for discovering cartels and acquiring the evidence to effectively prosecute them has resulted in the adoption of some form of a corporate leniency program by more than 50 countries and jurisdictions.

In light of the importance of leniency programs in practice, there has been a considerable amount of research exploring how leniency programs affect the incentives to collude and to report cartels. Beginning with the pioneering paper of Motta and Polo (2003), the primary force in theoretical analyses is that the competition authority may catch the colluding firms and, in anticipation of that prospect, firms may apply for leniency; this I will refer to as the 'prosecution effect.' For example, in Harrington (2008), the probability of the competition authority discovering and successfully prosecuting the cartel varies over time and when it is sufficiently high, collusion collapses and all firms race for leniency. While the threat of the competition authority catching the cartel is indeed critical, there is another first-order effect which is absent in previous analyses. Referring to it as the 'pre-emption effect,' this is when a firm – which doesn't necessarily believe the competition authority is likely to catch the cartel – is still concerned that another cartel member may apply for leniency and, because of that concern, applies itself. The threat is not being caught by the competition authority but instead a rival firm turning witness. Indeed, in practice, it is typical that one firm pre–empts its rivals by applying for leniency, as opposed to multiple firms racing for leniency. This outcome – whereby a single firm turns in its fellow colluders – runs contrary to the prediction of all previous models which is that either all or no firms apply.

The presence of the pre-emption effect is documented in recent experiments which measure the impact of a leniency program on collusion (Bigoni et al., 2010). Two subjects interact in a price game with the possibility of communication. Prior to selecting price, they each decide whether to press a button that signals a desire to communicate. If both press the button then they are permitted to communicate about price though this also makes them liable for penalties. After their communication, firms simultaneously choose price and decide whether to apply for leniency. If they did communicate and neither firm applied for leniency then there is a fixed probability p that each is assessed a penalty F. Various values of (p, F) are considered. Let us define 'collusion' as when both firms press the communicate button. The experimental findings show that, for the same expected penalty from the competition authority (that is, holding pF fixed), the frequency of collusion is lower when F is higher (and thus p is lower so that pF is unchanged). This effect is consistent with concerns that a rival will apply for leniency, holding fixed the threat posed by the competition authority, and thus with the presence of a pre-emption effect.[2]

The objective of this research project is to develop and explore a model that encompasses the pre-emption effect in order to both better understand the incentives of firms in an environment with a leniency program and to investigate how the competition authority can manipulate those incentives through ancillary instruments in order to make a leniency program more effective. Obviously, the key modeling modification is to allow cartel members to have private information regarding the likelihood that the competition authority may be able to effectively prosecute them. As the introduction of private information is a substantive complication, I explore its role in the post-cartel environment; that is, the cartel has collapsed for internal reasons and the objective of each firm is to minimize its expected penalties. Future work will consider embedding this setting into an infinitely repeated game so that the impact of the leniency program on the stability of collusion can be explored. In the current chapter, a simple example is investigated to highlight a few properties, while more general results are available in Harrington (2011).

2.2   GENERAL MODEL

While the focus in this chapter is on a highly structured example, I begin with a description of the more general model that is explored in Harrington (2011). The additional structure of the example is provided in Section 2.6.

Consider a cartel composed of two firms for which collusion has ended and firms are independently deciding whether or not to apply for leniency. If a firm is convicted without having received leniency, it pays a fine $F > 0$, while if it receives leniency then its fine is θF where $\theta \in [0, 1)$, so more leniency is associated with a lower value of θ. A firm's only decision is whether or not to apply for leniency and its objective is to minimize expected penalties.

Regarding the decision to apply for leniency, a primary source of uncertainty for a firm is the likelihood that it will be prosecuted and convicted by the competition authority (CA) when no firm has cooperated through the leniency program; that is, enforcement without assistance of the leniency program. Let ρ denote the probability of a conviction when no firm has applied for leniency. ρ is a random variable from the perspective of firms and, prior to making a leniency decision, firm i receives a private signal $s_i \in [\underline{s}, \overline{s}]$ of ρ. After learning their signals, firms simultaneously decide whether or not to apply for leniency. A strategy for a firm is then of the form:

$$\phi : [\underline{s}, \overline{s}] \to \{\text{Apply, Do not apply}\}.$$

As a firm's signal is presumably informative as to the true ρ, firms' signals will tend to be positively correlated. Though firm i does not get to observe firm j's signal, it will have some information as to s_j by virtue of s_i. Let $H(s_j|s_i)$ be firm i's cumulative distribution function (cdf) on firm j's signal conditional on its own signal, $i, j = 1, 2$ and $i \neq j$. To capture the positive correlation between firms' signals, assume A1.

A1 $H(s_j|s_i)$ $(j \neq i)$ is continuously differentiable in s_i and s_j. If $s'' > s'$ then $H(\cdot |s_i = s'')$ weakly first-order stochastically dominates (FOSD) $H(\cdot |s_i = s')$.

A higher signal for a firm results in it attaching more probability to high signals for its rival.

If only one firm applied for leniency then it pays a penalty of θF and the other firm pays F (hence, it is assumed conviction occurs for sure because of a cooperating cartel member). If both firms apply for leniency then each has an equal chance of being the one to receive leniency, so each has an expected fine of $(\frac{1 + \theta}{2})F$. If no one applied for leniency then firms are convicted with probability ρ and each pays F in that event, which means firm i's expectation on its penalty is $E[\rho|s_i]F$ where $E[\rho|s_i]$ is its expectation on ρ conditional on its signal. It is assumed that:

A2 $E[\rho|s_i]: [\underline{s}, \bar{s}] \rightarrow (0, 1)$ is continuously differentiable and increasing in s_i.

In light of preceding research focusing on the case of public signals, I will begin Section 2.4 by comparing the incentives between when signals are private and when they are public in order to identify the unique features introduced by allowing firms to have private information. To do so, a game when firms' signals (s_1, s_2) are common knowledge is explored so that, when they simultaneously decide whether or not to apply for leniency, they have a common expectation $E[\rho|s_1, s_2]$ on ρ. A firm's strategy is then of the form $\psi: [\underline{s}, \bar{s}]^2 \rightarrow \{\text{Apply, Do not apply}\}$. Assume A3.

A3 $E[\rho|s_1, s_2]: [\underline{s}, \bar{s}] \rightarrow (0, 1)$ is continuously differentiable, responds symmetrically to s_1 and s_2, and is increasing in s_1 and s_2.

2.3 LITERATURE REVIEW

Since the main modeling innovation of this chapter is in terms of information, the literature review will focus on the informational assumptions of previous work and their implications. For a more complete review of research on leniency programs, see Spagnolo (2008).

The initial class of models examining the effect of a leniency program on cartel stability modified the standard infinitely repeated oligopoly game (usually, the Prisoners' Dilemma) by assuming that, in each period that firms are colluding, there is a fixed probability ρ that firms are caught by the CA – in which case they pay a fixed penalty – and firms have the option to apply for leniency to receive reduced penalties. Firms make the leniency decision simultaneously and models differ in terms of whether it occurs after the current period's prices are revealed (for example, Motta and Polo, 2003) or a firm makes its price and leniency decisions simultaneously, in which case it can undercut the collusive price and apply for leniency at the same time (for example, Harrington and Chang, 2009).[3] With ρ being fixed and known over time, the stationarity of the environment implies that if equilibrium involves firms colluding then firms never apply for leniency. For if leniency is used as part of an equilibrium then, given stationarity, it occurs in the first period, but if conviction prevents reformation of the cartel (for a sufficiently long time) then firms would cheat in the initial period (as they anticipate collusion ending because a firm applied for leniency), which then makes collusion unstable. For reasonable parameter values, a fixed and known value for ρ implies that leniency is not used in equilibrium.[4]

In practice, firms do form a cartel and then may, at some point in time, apply for leniency. This will occur if the environment changes so that it was initially optimal for firms to collude and not apply for leniency, but at some later time it becomes optimal to apply. This possibility is explored in Harrington (2008) where it is assumed ρ is not fixed – it is *iid* over time – but the assumption that ρ is public information among firms is maintained. A Pareto-efficient equilibrium is now characterized by a cut-off value for ρ such that if ρ exceeds that cut-off then firms stop colluding and all apply for leniency – because the prospects of being caught by the CA are sufficiently great so as to cause the cartel to collapse – and otherwise firms collude and do not apply.[5]

While allowing ρ to change over time is able to generate an equilibrium outcome in which firms collude for some length of time and then use the leniency program – consistent with observed cartel behavior – it has the unappealing property that either all firms apply or none do. This is due to firms' information being common, for if one firm applies for leniency then the optimal action for a rival firm is to apply as well. To generate what we actually do observe – a single firm applying for leniency – it is essential to allow for private information.

It is worth noting that there have been some analyses to allow for private information in a limited way. Silbye (2010b) assumes ρ is common knowledge but each firm possesses evidence that it could submit to convict the other firm if it applied for leniency. $\varepsilon_i \in [0, 1 - \rho]$ is the evidence possessed by firm i to assist in convicting firm j and is private information to firm i. If firm i receives leniency then firm j's expected penalty is $(\rho + \varepsilon_i)F$. If no one applies then each has an expected fine of ρF, which, as noted, is common knowledge. Sauvagnat (2010) allows the CA to have private information about the strength of its case and it is a strategic decision whether to open an investigation. (Previous work implicitly allowed for such private information but assumed the start of an investigation was exogenous.) Of particular relevance is that the CA may open an investigation even when its case is weak, as doing so may induce firms to apply for leniency. Finally, Pinna (2010) considers a strategic setting in which firms know whether or not they are colluding but the CA does not.

2.4 CHARACTERIZATION OF EQUILIBRIUM

2.4.1 Public Signals

To appreciate the new forces introduced with private information, let us begin by characterizing equilibrium when firms' signals (s_1, s_2) are public information. First note that there are only symmetric equilibria since applying for leniency is optimal when the other firm applies. Hence, either both apply or neither apply. The set of Bayes-Nash equilibria is:

$$\psi(s_1, s_2) = \begin{cases} \text{Apply} & \text{if } (s_1, s_2) \notin \Omega \\ \\ \text{Do not apply} & \text{if } (s_1, s_2) \in \Omega, \end{cases} \tag{2.1}$$

where

$$E[\rho|s_1, s_2] \leq \theta \; \forall (s_1, s_2) \in \Omega. \tag{2.2}$$

If $(s_1, s_2) \notin \Omega$, so that a firm's rival is going to apply for leniency, it is optimal for a firm to apply as well, as an expected penalty of $(\frac{1+\theta}{2})F$ is preferred to a sure penalty of F. Now consider $(s_1, s_2) \in \Omega$ so that a firm's rival is not expected to apply for leniency. If a firm does not apply then its expected penalty is $E[\rho|s_1, s_2]F$, while it is θF from applying. Hence, not applying is optimal if and only if (iff) $E[\rho|s_1, s_2] \leq \theta$. As long as

$$\theta > E[\rho|s_1 = \underline{s}, s_2 = \underline{s}],$$

so there are some signals for which it is equilibrium behavior for both not to apply, there are an infinite number of equilibria as there are an infinite number of sets Ω satisfying Equation (2.2).

Notice that if $(s_1, s_2) \notin \Omega$ and $E[\rho|s_1, s_2] < \theta$ then firms are incurring higher penalties by both applying for leniency than if both did not, as

$$E[\rho|s_1, s_2]F < \theta F < \left(\frac{1 + \theta}{2}\right)F,$$

where the term to the left of the first inequality is the expected penalty from both not applying and the term to the right of the second inequality is from both applying. This makes it useful to define the Pareto-efficient equilibrium,

$$\Omega^* \equiv \{(s_1, s_2) : E[\rho|s_1, s_2] \leq \theta\},$$

which has firms not apply whenever it is an equilibrium. This equilibrium minimizes expected penalties. Note that if

$$\theta < E[\rho|s_1, s_2] < \frac{1 + \theta}{2},$$

expected penalties are higher with both applying compared to both not applying but it is not an equilibrium for both not to apply given those signals. In Harrington (2008), this is referred to as the 'Race to the Courthouse' effect, and it serves to deter cartel formation by increasing expected penalties.

2.4.2   Private Signals

Now suppose firms' signals are private information, and consider a symmetric strategy profile which is a cut-off strategy:

$$\phi(s_i) = \begin{cases} \text{Do not apply} & \text{if } s_i \in [\underline{s}, x] \\ \\ \text{Apply} & \text{if } s_i \in (x, \bar{s}]. \end{cases} \tag{2.3}$$

A firm applies for leniency iff its signal exceeds x. The set of symmetric cut-off Bayes-Nash equilibrium can then be characterized by the set of values for x such that ϕ is a Bayes-Nash equilibrium. Given firm 2 uses this strategy, the expected penalty to firm 1 from not applying is

$$\int_{\underline{s}}^x E[\rho|s_1, s_2] FH'(s_2|s_1) ds_2 + [1 - H(x|s_1)]F$$

or

$$H(x|s_1) E[\rho|s_1, s_2 \le x]F + [1 - H(x|s_1)]F. \tag{2.4}$$

If $s_2 \le x$ then firm 2's signal is sufficiently low that it does not apply, in which case firm 1's expected penalty from not applying is its expectation on ρ multiplied by F. This expectation, $E[\rho|s_1, s_2 \le x]$, is conditional on firm 1's signal *and* firm 2 not applying for leniency. If $s_2 > x$ then firm 2 applies for leniency, in which case, by not applying, firm 1 is convicted and pays F. If instead firm 1 applies for leniency then its expected penalty is

$$H(x|s_1)\theta F + [1 - H(x|s_1)]\left(\frac{1 + \theta}{2}\right)F. \tag{2.5}$$

If $s_2 \leq x$ then it is the only firm to apply for leniency so its penalty is θF, while if $s_2 > x$ then both firms have applied, in which case firm 1's expected penalty is $\left(\frac{1+\theta}{2}\right) F$.

Firm 1 strictly prefers to apply for leniency iff Equation (2.4) exceeds Equation (2.5):

$$H(x|s_1)E[\rho|s_1, s_2 \leq x]F + [1 - H(x|s_1)]F > H(x|s_1)\theta F$$

$$+ [1 - H(x|s_1)]\left(\frac{1+\theta}{2}\right)F, \qquad (2.6)$$

where recall that each firm is making a choice to minimize expected penalties. This expression can be rearranged to

$$E[\rho|s_1, s_2 \leq x] > \theta - \left(\frac{1-\theta}{2}\right)\left[\frac{1 - H(x|s_1)}{H(x|s_1)}\right]. \qquad (2.7)$$

It is optimal to apply for leniency when the expected probability of being caught by the CA – given no firm is a cooperating witness through the leniency program – is sufficiently large relative to the leniency parameter θ. The relevant expectation on being caught by the CA is for when no one applies for leniency, which is the expectation on ρ conditional on a firm's own signal *and* its rival's signal is sufficiently low that it does not apply for leniency.

Using Equation (2.7), define

$$\Delta(s_1, x) \equiv E[\rho|s_1, s_2 \leq x] - \theta + \left(\frac{1-\theta}{2}\right)\left[\frac{1 - H(x|s_1)}{H(x|s_1)}\right].$$

Given signal s_1 and threshold x, applying is optimal for firm 1 iff $\Delta(s_1, x) > 0$. Next note that leniency becomes relatively more attractive when a firm's own signal is higher since a higher signal makes it more likely it will be caught by the CA:

$$\frac{\partial \Delta(s_1, x)}{\partial s_1} = \frac{\partial E[\rho|s_1, s_2 \leq x]}{\partial s_1} - \left(\frac{1-\theta}{2}\right)\left[\frac{\partial H(x|s_1)/\partial s_1}{H(x|s_1)^2}\right] > 0 \quad (2.8)$$

as

$$\frac{\partial E[\rho|s_1, s_2 \leq x]}{\partial s_1} > 0$$

by A2 and

$$\frac{\partial H(x|s_1)}{\partial s_1} \leq 0$$

by A1. Hence, applying for leniency is optimal when $s_1 > x$ iff $\Delta(x, x) \geq 0$, as then $\Delta(s_1, x) > 0, \forall s_1 > x$. Not applying is optimal when $s_1 < x$ iff $\Delta(x, x) \leq 0$, as then $\Delta(s_1, x) < 0, \forall s_1 < x$. Therefore, if $x \in (\underline{s}, \bar{s})$ then ϕ is a Bayes-Nash equilibrium iff $\Delta(x, x) = 0$.

Define

$$\Phi(x) \equiv \Gamma(x)\Delta(x, x)$$

$$= \Gamma(x)\{E[\rho|s_1 = x, s_2 \leq x] - \theta\} + \left(\frac{1 - \theta}{2}\right)[1 - \Gamma(x)],$$

where $\Gamma(x) \equiv H(x|x)$ and is the probability that $s_2 \leq x$ conditional on $s_1 = x$. It will be easier to work with $\Phi(x)$ because it is bounded as $x \to \underline{s}$. Here are some sufficient conditions for equilibrium, with the first condition summarizing the preceding analysis.

- If $\Phi(s') = 0$ then $x = s'$ is an equilibrium cut-off.
- $x = \underline{s}$ is an equilibrium cut-off. Note that

$$\Phi(\underline{s}) = H(\underline{s}|s_1 = \underline{s})\{E[\rho|s_1 = \underline{s}, s_2 \leq \underline{s}] - \theta\}$$

$$+ \left(\frac{1 - \theta}{2}\right)[1 - H(\underline{s}|s_1 = \underline{s})] = \frac{1 - \theta}{2} > 0,$$

which, by Equation (2.8), means $\Delta(s_1, \underline{s}) > 0 \ \forall \ s_1$, and, therefore, applying is strictly preferred to not applying for all signals. In other words, if a rival is going to apply for leniency for sure (that is, for every signal) then it is optimal to do so as well.
- If $\Phi(\bar{s}) \leq 0$ then $x = \bar{s}$ is an equilibrium cut-off. Again by Equation (2.8), $\Delta(s_1, \bar{s}) \leq 0 \ \forall \ s_1 < \bar{s}$, which implies it is never optimal to apply. Thus, not applying for all signals is an equilibrium if, conditional on the other firm never applying, a firm prefers not to apply even when it receives the strongest signal $\bar{s}$.

2.5   INCENTIVES TO APPLY: PRIVATE VERSUS PUBLIC SIGNALS

With public signals and assuming the other firm does not apply for leniency, a firm prefers to apply iff

$$E[\rho|s_1, s_2] - \theta > 0. \tag{2.9}$$

Focusing on the Pareto-efficient equilibrium, leniency is used only when the likelihood attached to the CA prosecuting and convicting them exceeds the leniency parameter. Behavior is entirely driven by beliefs as to CA behavior.

By comparison, consider the situation when firms' signals are private. Firm 1 prefers to apply for leniency iff

$$\underbrace{E[\rho|s_1, s_2 \leq x] - \theta}_{\text{Prosecution effect}} > \underbrace{-\left(\frac{1-\theta}{2}\right)\left[\frac{1-H(x|s_1)}{H(x|s_1)}\right]}_{\text{Pre-emption effect}} \tag{2.10}$$

In contrasting Equation (2.9) and Equation (2.10), first note that the left hand side is different, which encompasses what is referred to as the 'prosecution effect' for it is the differential between beliefs as to the CA's probability of successful prosecution (without use of the leniency program) and the leniency parameter. With public signals, the likelihood attached to the CA levying penalties is based on firms' common signals. With private signals, a firm doesn't know its rival's signal and so its expectation is based on its own signal and its rival's signal being sufficiently low so it chooses not to apply. The relationship between these two expectations – $E[\rho|s_1, s_2]$ and $E[\rho|s_1, s_2 \leq x]$ – is ambiguous. What is not ambiguous is the relationship between the right hand side of these two conditions. With private signals, a firm is not assured as to what the other firm will do. Even if firm 1's signal is very low – suggesting that being caught by the CA is unlikely and thus firms should not apply for leniency (that is, the prosecution effect is weak) – it realizes that firm 2's signal could be high, in which case firm 2 would apply. Note that $1 - H(x|s_1)$ is the probability that a rival applies for leniency conditional on a firm's signal, in which case the right hand side of Equation (2.10) is lower and the more likely it is that the other firm will apply for leniency. This provides a second reason for firm 1 to go for amnesty, which is quite independent of whether it thinks the CA will catch them. I refer to it as the pre-emption effect because it captures a firm's concern with its rival applying for leniency prior to the firm having information that would make it preferable for it to apply.

In sum, it is not immediately clear whether information being private makes firms more or less inclined to apply for leniency. While the pre-emption effect is present only with private signals and clearly serves to enhance the attractiveness of applying for leniency – whether the prosecution effect is stronger or weaker with private signals is not clear at this point.

2.6   AN EXAMPLE

To gain some initial insight into how private information influences behavior, here I consider a specific structure to the signals and derive equilibria under both public and private signals. Assume $\rho = s_1 + s_2$ where s_1 and s_2 are independent with a uniform distribution on $[0, 1/2]$. One might interpret each firm as learning about a particular body of mutually exclusive evidence and, furthermore, the probability the CA convicts is linear in the sum of the evidence. This signal structure satisfies A1–A3 though A1 only weakly since firms' signals are independent.

2.6.1   Public Signals

With public signals, the Pareto-efficient equilibrium is

$$\phi(s_1, s_2) = \begin{cases} \text{Apply} & \text{if } s_1 + s_2 > \theta \\ \text{Do not apply} & \text{if } s_1 + s_2 \leq \theta \end{cases}$$

so the probability of leniency being used is[6]

$$\Pr(s_1 + s_2 > \theta) = \begin{cases} 1 - 2\theta^2 & \text{if } \theta < 1/2 \\ 2(1 - \theta)^2 & \text{if } \theta \geq 1/2. \end{cases} \quad (2.11)$$

The probability of conviction – which is the probability of at least one firm applying for leniency plus the probability of conviction conditional on no firm applying – equals

$$\begin{cases} (\tfrac{4}{3})\theta^3 - 2\theta^2 + 1 & \text{if } 0 \leq \theta \leq 1/2 \\ \\ -(\tfrac{4}{3})\theta^3 + 4\theta^2 - 4\theta + \tfrac{11}{6} & \text{if } 1/2 \leq \theta \leq 1. \end{cases} \quad (2.12)$$

The relationship between the probability of conviction and the leniency parameter is depicted in Figure 2.1. More leniency (lower θ) results in a greater chance of conviction.

2.6.2   Private Signals

For when signals are private, the difference between expected penalties from not applying and from applying, given a firm's signal is at the cut-off value, is shown in the Appendix to be:

$$\Phi(x) = 3x^2 - (1 + \theta)x + \frac{1 - \theta}{2}.$$

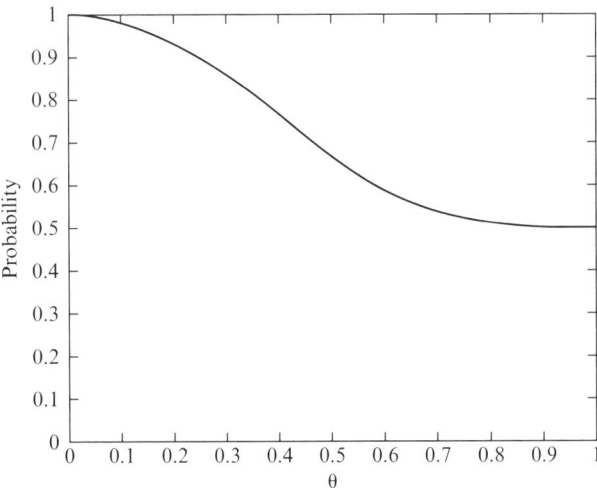

Figure 2.1   Probability of conviction (public signals)

Since $\underline{s} = 0$ and $\bar{s} = 1/2$, recall that: (i) $x = 0$ is an equilibrium cut-off; (ii) if $x \in (0, 1/2)$ and $\Phi(x) = 0$ then x is an equilibrium cut-off; and (iii) if $\Phi(1/2) \leq 0$ then $x = 1/2$ is an equilibrium cut-off. If $\theta < \frac{\sqrt{21} - 4}{6}$ then $\Phi(x) > 0 \;\forall x$ which implies a unique equilibrium of $x = 0$; an example of which is shown in Figure 2.2 as the dotted curve. If $\theta = \sqrt{21} - 4$ then $\Phi(\frac{\sqrt{21} - 3}{6}) = 0$ and $\Phi(x) > 0 \;\forall x \neq \frac{\sqrt{21} - 3}{6} \approx .26$, in which case equilibria are $x \in \{0, \frac{\sqrt{21} - 3}{36}\}$. If $\theta > \sqrt{21} - 4$ then $\Phi(x) = 0$ has two roots,

$$\frac{1 + \theta - \sqrt{\theta^2 + 8\theta - 5}}{6}, \frac{1 + \theta + \sqrt{\theta^2 + 8\theta - 5}}{6}.$$

The lower root always lies in $(0, 1/2)$, while the upper root does iff $\theta < 3/4$. Hence, if $\theta \in (\sqrt{21} - 4, \frac{3}{4})$ then equilibrium cut-offs are $\{0, \frac{1 + \theta - \sqrt{\theta^2 + 8\theta - 5}}{6}, \frac{1 + \theta + \sqrt{\theta^2 + 8\theta - 5}}{6}\}$. This case is depicted as the dashed curve in Figure 2.2. Finally, if $\theta \in [\frac{3}{4}, 1)$ then equilibrium cut-offs are $\{0, \frac{1 + \theta - \sqrt{\theta^2 + 8\theta - 5}}{6}, \frac{1}{2}\}$; see the solid curve in Figure 2.2. With Figure 2.2, note that $\Phi(x)$ is decreasing in θ so $\Phi(x)$ shifts down as θ increases.

Summing up the preceding analysis, the set of cut-off equilibria with private signals is

If $\theta \in [0, \sqrt{21} - 4)$ then $x \in \{0\}$.
If $\theta = \sqrt{21} - 4$ then $x \in \{0, \frac{\sqrt{21} - 3}{36}\}$.
If $\theta \in (\sqrt{21} - 4, \frac{3}{4})$ then $x \in \{0, \frac{1 + \theta - \sqrt{\theta^2 + 8\theta - 5}}{6}, \frac{1 + \theta + \sqrt{\theta^2 + 8\theta - 5}}{6}\}$.
If $\theta \in [\frac{3}{4}, 1)$ then $x \in \{0, \frac{1 + \theta - \sqrt{\theta^2 + 8\theta - 5}}{6}, \frac{1}{2}\}$.

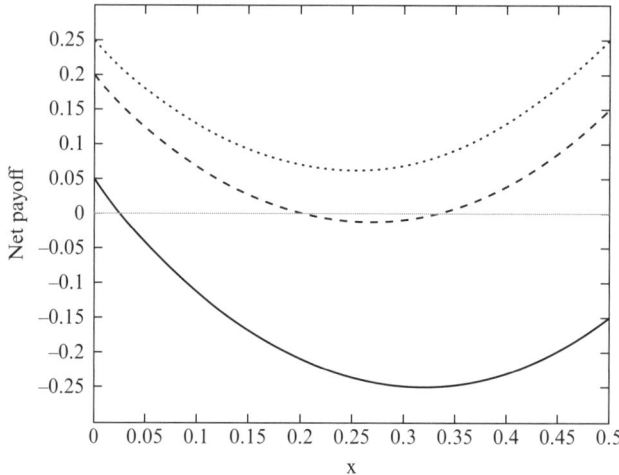

Note: Solid: $\theta = 0.9$; dash: $\theta = 0.6$; dot: $\theta = 0.5$.

Figure 2.2   *Impact of θ on Φ (x)*

2.6.3   Comparative Analysis of Public and Private Signals

In Figure 2.3, the equilibrium correspondence with private signals is plotted in terms of the minimum signal required for a firm to apply for leniency (solid line). The Pareto-efficient equilibrium is the maximum equilibrium threshold, which is zero up to around $\theta = \sqrt{21} - 4 \approx .583$, and is the upper branch of the correspondence for $\theta > \sqrt{21} - 4$. For the case of public signals, the Pareto-efficient equilibrium is plotted in terms of the minimum average signal – that is, $(s_1 + s_2)/2$ – required for them to apply for leniency (dashed line). All threshold values below the dashed line are also equilibria though are not Pareto-efficient. The interior intersection of the Pareto-efficient equilibrium for the private and public signals occurs at $\theta = 2 - \sqrt{2} \approx .586$.

If leniency is sufficiently strong – such as $\theta < \sqrt{21} - 4$ – then it is used more with private signals than with public signals. When both firms' signals are low then leniency is not used when signals are public. However, with private signals, even when a firm's signal is low, the probability that the other firm's signal is not low – so that it would apply – is high; and if one's rival is very likely to apply for leniency then it is optimal for a firm to do so as well, regardless of its own signal. Hence, with private signals, leniency is always used when leniency is sufficiently great. Intuitively, when leniency means having a high fraction of penalties waived, a firm is

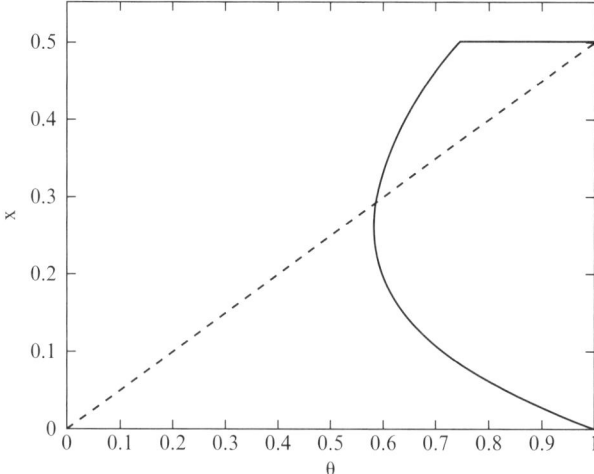

Note: Private signals: solid; public signals: dashed.

Figure 2.3   Equilibrium correspondence

going to use leniency unless it believes the CA is unlikely to catch them *and* it is confident the other firm will not apply. The latter can only be satisfied when signals are public so a firm knows what its rival believes. Note that the probability of being found guilty – which is the sum of the probability of using leniency plus the probability of conviction conditional on not using leniency – is higher as well with private signals.

Suppose leniency is sufficiently weak: $\theta > 2 - \sqrt{2}$. Now we find that a firm is more likely to apply for leniency when signals are public rather than private. With a weak leniency program, the inclination is not to apply for leniency unless a firm is confident that the CA will catch them. Such confidence is more likely when firms' signals are public as then there is more information to substantiate the hypothesis that the CA is likely to convict them. With private signals, even if a firm gets a strong signal, it knows that its rival's signal is likely not to be strong and thus there is not sufficient information to warrant applying for leniency. But when signals are public and both of them are consistent with the CA having a strong case, firms will then apply out of fear of being prosecuted. Intuitively, with a weak leniency program, the default is not to apply unless one is confident that the CA will catch them or the other firm will apply, and such confidence cannot be achieved when firms' signals are private. Though each firm may be more inclined to apply for leniency when signals are public, it doesn't follow that the probability of being found guilty is higher with public signals for all it takes is one firm to apply for leniency for guilt to be established. However, when $\theta \geq 3/4$, firms never use leniency with private signals so the probability of being found guilty must be lower.

Next let us compare the probability of conviction between public and private signals, and we will do so for the Pareto-efficient equilibrium (which means leniency usage is minimized). The probability of conviction for the case of public signals is Equation (2.12). For when signals are private, the probability of conviction, given cut-off x, is

$$\int_0^x \left[\int_0^x (s_1 + s_2) 2ds_2 + 1 \times \int_x^1 2ds_2 \right] 2ds_1 + \int_x^{1/2} 1 \times 2ds_1 = 4x^3 - 4x^2 + 1. \tag{2.13}$$

The Pareto-efficient equilibrium value for x is

$$\begin{cases} 0 & \text{if} & 0 \leq \theta < \sqrt{21} - 4 \\ \frac{1 + \theta + \sqrt{\theta^2 + 8\theta - 5}}{6} & \text{if} & \sqrt{21} - 4 \leq \theta \leq 0.75 \\ 0.5 & \text{if} & 0.75 \leq \theta \leq 1. \end{cases} \tag{2.14}$$

Inserting Equation (2.14) into Equation (2.13), the probability of conviction is

$$\begin{cases} 1 & \text{if} & 0 \leq \theta < \sqrt{21} - 4 \\ 4(\frac{1 + \theta + \sqrt{\theta^2 + 8\theta - 5}}{6})^3 - 4(\frac{1 + \theta + \sqrt{\theta^2 + 8\theta - 5}}{6})^2 + 1 & \text{if} & \sqrt{21} - 4 \leq \theta \leq 0.75 \\ 0.5 & \text{if} & 0.75 \leq \theta \leq 1 \end{cases}$$

and is depicted in Figure 2.4.

The difference between the probability of conviction under public signals and under private signals is plotted in Figure 2.5. Generally, conviction is much more likely under private signals when leniency is sufficiently low ($\theta < 0.715$), and is (slightly) more likely under public signals when leniency is sufficiently high ($\theta > 0.715$).

2.7   CONCLUDING REMARKS

Though a special example, some of its key properties are shown to generalize in Harrington (2011). First, and fully consistent with the example, it is proven that if a leniency program is sufficiently generous then the probability of conviction is higher when firms' signals are private rather than public. Second, and partially consistent with the example, sufficient conditions are provided for a leniency program to be more effective when signals are public, and it tends to occur when the program is relatively mild

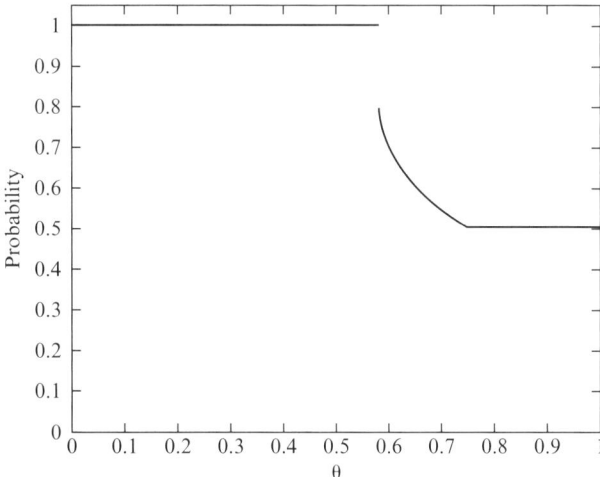

Figure 2.4   Probability of conviction (private signals)

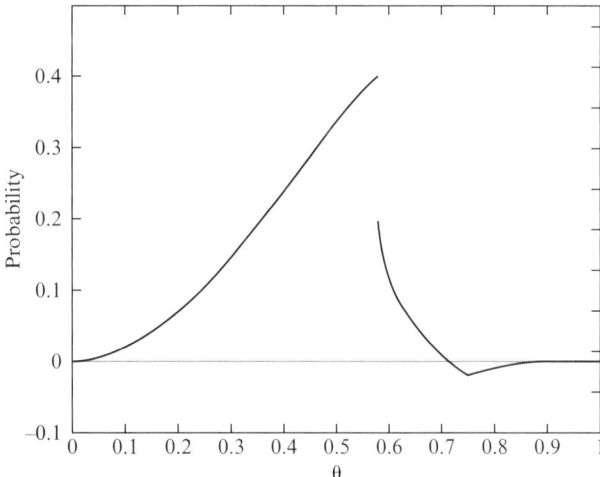

Figure 2.5   Probability of conviction under private signals minus probability of conviction under public signals

in the amnesty it awards. An important issue not pursued here is how a CA, through its behavior, can exacerbate the tendency to pre-empt when there is private information and thus induce greater usage of the leniency program. A preliminary analysis of that issue is provided in Harrington (2011).

NOTES

1. I very much appreciate the comments of Martin Peitz, seminar participants at the University of Copenhagen, and the participants of CRESSE 2011.
2. It is also shown that subjects apply for leniency even when $p = 0$, which is inconsistent with the theory articulated here. Here it is assumed that firms achieve a Pareto-efficient equilibrium which implies that no firm applies for leniency when there is no chance of being caught by the competition authority. As a result, there must be a prosecution effect (that is, $p > 0$) in order for there to be a pre-emption effect.
3. Bigoni et al. (2010) conduct experiments and allow subjects both to apply for leniency when setting its price or, in the event that no firm has applied for leniency, to apply after prices are revealed and firms learn whether or not there was a deviation.
4. There is also an equilibrium – referred to as 'collude and report' – in Motta and Polo (2003) for which firms collude and apply for leniency in every period. This occurs when the cartel can immediately reform and leniency is sufficiently generous. Though it can be an equilibrium, I do not believe it is an empirically relevant solution.
5. Harrington (2008) also considers a policy space that provides leniency if and only if ρ is sufficiently low (that is, the CA's case is not too strong). Silbye (2010a) enriches the policy space to when the amount of leniency can depend continuously on ρ.
6. This and all ensuing derivations are in the Appendix.

REFERENCES

Bigoni, M., S.-O. Fridolfsson, C. Le Coq and G. Spagnolo (2010), 'Trust, salience, and deterrence: evidence from an antitrust experiment', SSE/EFI Working Paper Series in Economics and Finance No. 696, January.

Harrington, J.E. Jr (2008), 'Optimal corporate leniency programs', *Journal of Industrial Economics*, **56**, 215–46.

Harrington, J.E. Jr (2011), 'Corporate leniency programs when firms have private information: the push of prosecution and the pull of pre-emption', Working Paper, Johns Hopkins University, Baltimore, November (*Journal of Industrial Economics*, forthcoming).

Harrington, J.E. Jr and M.-H. Chang (2009), 'Modelling the birth and death of cartels with an application to evaluating antitrust policy', *Journal of the European Economic Association*, **7**, 1400–1435.

Motta, M. and M. Polo (2003), 'Leniency programs and cartel prosecution', *International Journal of Industrial Organization*, **21**, 347–79.

Pinna, A. (2010), 'Optimal leniency programs in antitrust', Università di Cagliari and Università di Sassari, CRENoS Working Paper 2010/18.

Sauvagnat, J. (2010), 'Prosecution and leniency programs: a fool's game', Toulouse School of Economics Working Paper Series 10–188, September.

Silbye, F. (2010a), 'Optimal leniency programs with case-dependent fine discounts', in *Topics in Competition Policy: Cartels, Leniency, and Price Discrimination*, PhD Thesis, University of Copenhagen, August.

Silbye, F. (2010b), 'Asymmetric evidence and optimal leniency programs', in *Topics in Competition Policy: Cartels, Leniency, and Price Discrimination*, PhD Thesis, University of Copenhagen, August.

Spagnolo, G. (2008), 'Leniency and whistleblowers in antitrust', in P. Buccirossi (ed.), *Handbook of Antitrust Economics*, Cambridge, MA: MIT Press, pp. 259–303.

APPENDIX

Assume $\rho = s_1 + s_2$ where $s_i \sim U[0, 1/2]$ and s_1 and s_2 are independent with a uniform distribution on $[0, 1/2]$. If signals are public, the probability of using leniency is $\Pr(s_1 + s_2 > \theta)$. If $t \leq 1/2$ then

$$\Pr(s_1 + s_2 = t) = \int_0^t \Pr(s_2 = t - s_1)\Pr(s_1)ds_1 = \int_0^t (2 * 2)ds_1 = 4t,$$

while if $t > 1/2$ then

$$\Pr(s_1 + s_2 = t) = \int_0^t \Pr(s_2 = t - s_1)\Pr(s_1)ds_1$$

$$= \int_0^{t-1/2} \Pr(s_2 = t - s_1)\Pr(s_1)ds_1 + \int_{t-1/2}^{1/2} \Pr(s_2 = t - s_1)\Pr(s_1)ds_1$$

$$= \int_0^{t-1/2} 0 * 2ds_1 + \int_{t-1/2}^{1/2} (2 * 2)ds_1$$

$$= \int_{t-1/2}^{1/2} (2 * 2)ds_1 = 4s_1]_{t-1/2}^{1/2} = 2 - 4t + 2 = 4(1 - t).$$

Therefore,

$$\Pr(s_1 + s_2 = t) = \begin{cases} 4t & \text{if } t < 1/2 \\ 4(1 - t) & \text{if } t \geq 1/2. \end{cases}$$

If $\theta \geq 1/2$ then

$$\Pr(s_1 + s_2 \leq \theta) = \int_0^{1/2} 4t dt + \int_{1/2}^{\theta} 4(1 - t)dt$$

$$= 2t^2]_0^{1/2} + \int_{1/2}^{\theta} 4(1 - t)dt$$

$$= 1/2 + 4t - 2t^2]_{1/2}^{\theta} = 1/2 + 4\theta - 2\theta^2 - 2 + 1/2$$

$$= -2\theta^2 + 4\theta - 1 = 2\theta^2 - 4\theta^2 + 4\theta - 1 = 2\theta^2 - (2\theta - 1)^2$$

$$\Pr(s_1 + s_2 \leq \theta) = \begin{cases} 2\theta^2 & \text{if } \theta < 1/2 \\ 2\theta^2 - (2\theta - 1)^2 & \text{if } \theta \geq 1/2. \end{cases}$$

Thus, the probability of using leniency is

$$\Pr(s_1 + s_2 > \theta) = \begin{cases} 1 - 2\theta^2 & \text{if } \theta < 1/2 \\ 2(1 - \theta)^2 & \text{if } \theta \geq 1/2. \end{cases}$$

If $0 \le \theta \le 1/2$ then the probability of conviction is

$$\int_0^\theta \left[\int_0^{\theta - s_1} (s_1 + s_2) 2ds_2 + \int_{\theta - s_1}^{1/2} 1 \times 2ds_2 \right] 2ds_1 + \int_\theta^{1/2} 1 \times 2ds_1$$

$$= \left(\frac{4}{3} \right) \theta^3 - 2\theta^2 + 1$$

and, if $1/2 < \theta \le 1$, it takes the value

$$\int_0^{\theta - 1/2} \int_0^{1/2} (s_1 + s_2) 2ds_2 2ds_1 + \int_{\theta - 1/2}^{1/2} \left[\int_0^{\theta - s_1} (s_1 + s_2) 2ds_2 + \int_{\theta - s_1}^{1/2} 1 \times 2ds_2 \right] 2ds_1$$

$$= -\left(\frac{4}{3} \right) \theta^3 + 4\theta^2 - 4\theta + \frac{11}{6}.$$

Hence, the probability of conviction is

$$\begin{cases} (\tfrac{4}{3})\theta^3 - 2\theta^2 + 1 & \text{if} \quad 0 \le \theta \le 0.5 \\ -(\tfrac{4}{3})\theta^3 + 4\theta^2 - 4\theta + \tfrac{11}{6} & \text{if} \quad 0.5 \le \theta \le 1. \end{cases}$$

For when signals are private, the difference between expected penalties from not applying and from applying, given a firm's signal is at the cut-off value, is

$$\Phi(x) = \Gamma(x) (E[\rho|s_1 = x, s_2 \le x] - \theta) + \left(\frac{1-\theta}{2} \right) [1 - \Gamma(x)]$$

$$= \Gamma(x) (x + E[s_2|s_2 \le x] - \theta) + \left(\frac{1-\theta}{2} \right) [1 - \Gamma(x)]$$

$$= 2x \left(x + \frac{x}{2} - \theta \right) + \left(\frac{1-\theta}{2} \right) (1 - 2x) = 3x^2 - 2x\theta + \frac{1-\theta}{2} - (1-\theta)x$$

$$= 3x^2 - 2x\theta + \frac{1-\theta}{2} - (1-\theta)x = 3x^2 - (1+\theta)x + \frac{1-\theta}{2}.$$

Since $\underline{s} = 0$ and $\bar{s} = 1/2$, recall that: (i) $x = 0$ is an equilibrium; (ii) if $x \in (0, 1/2)$ and $\Phi(x) = 0$ then x is an equilibrium cut-off; and (iii) if $\Phi(1/2) \le 0$ then $x = 1/2$ is an equilibrium cut-off.

To derive the set of equilibria, begin by deriving some properties of $\Phi(x)$. It is convex in x and reaches its minimum at $x = \frac{1+\theta}{6}$,

$$\Phi'(x) = 6x - 1 - \theta \gtreqless 0 \text{ as } x \gtreqless \frac{1+\theta}{6}.$$

Hence, if

$$\Phi\left(\frac{1+\theta}{6}\right) > 0$$

then Φ is always positive, in which case the unique equilibrium is $x = 0$. If

$$\Phi\left(\frac{1+\theta}{6}\right) < 0$$

then there exists at least one interior equilibrium and $x > 0$ for the Pareto-efficient equilibrium. To evaluate which of these cases holds, consider:

$$\Phi\left(\frac{1+\theta}{6}\right) = 3\left(\frac{1+\theta}{6}\right)^2 - (1+\theta)\left(\frac{1+\theta}{6}\right) + \frac{1-\theta}{2}$$

$$= \frac{(1+\theta)^2}{12} - \frac{(1+\theta)^2}{6} + \frac{1-\theta}{2} = -\frac{(1+\theta)^2}{12} + \frac{1-\theta}{2}$$

$$= (1/12)[-(1+\theta)^2 + 6(1-\theta)] = 12[-1 - 2\theta - \theta^2 + 6 - 6\theta]$$

$$= (1/12)(-\theta^2 - 8\theta + 5).$$

Solving this quadratic,

$$\Phi\left(\frac{1+\theta}{6}\right) \gtreqless 0 \text{ as } \theta \lesseqgtr \sqrt{21} - 4, \text{ for } \theta \in [0, 1].$$

From the preceding analysis, if $\theta < \frac{\sqrt{21}-4}{6}$ then $\Phi(x)$ is positive at its minimum value; hence, $\Phi(x) > 0 \,\forall x$, which implies a unique equilibrium of $x = 0$. If $\theta = \sqrt{21} - 4$ then $\Phi(\frac{\sqrt{21}-3}{6}) = 0$ and $\Phi(x) > 0 \,\forall x \neq \frac{\sqrt{21}-3}{6}$, in which case equilibria are $x \in \{0, \frac{\sqrt{21}-3}{36}\}$. If $\theta > \sqrt{21} - 4$ then $\Phi(x) = 0$ has two roots,

$$\frac{1+\theta - \sqrt{\theta^2 + 8\theta - 5}}{6}, \frac{1+\theta + \sqrt{\theta^2 + 8\theta - 5}}{6}.$$

Note that the lower root is decreasing in θ and the upper root is increasing in θ:

$$\frac{\partial \frac{1+\theta - \sqrt{\theta^2 + 8\theta - 5}}{6}}{\partial \theta} = \left(\frac{1}{6}\right)\left[1 - \frac{1}{2}(\theta^2 + 8\theta - 5)^{-\frac{1}{2}}(2\theta + 8)\right]$$

$$= \left(\frac{1}{6}\right)\left[1 - \frac{\theta + 4}{(\theta^2 + 8\theta - 5)^{\frac{1}{2}}}\right] < 0 \Leftrightarrow$$

$$\theta + 4 > (\theta^2 + 8\theta - 5)^{\frac{1}{2}} \Leftrightarrow \theta^2 + 8\theta + 16 > \theta^2 + 8\theta - 5 \Leftrightarrow 11 > -5.$$

$$\frac{\partial \frac{1 + \theta + \sqrt{\theta^2 + 8\theta - 5}}{6}}{\partial \theta} = \left(\frac{1}{6}\right)\left[1 + \frac{1}{2}(\theta^2 + 8\theta - 5)^{-\frac{1}{2}}(2\theta + 8)\right] > 0.$$

The lower root always lies in $(0, 1/2)$ as long as

$$\frac{1 + \theta - \sqrt{\theta^2 + 8\theta - 5}}{6} > 0$$

$$\Leftrightarrow 1 + \theta > \sqrt{\theta^2 + 8\theta - 5} \Leftrightarrow 1 + 2\theta + \theta^2 > \theta^2 + 8\theta - 5$$

$$\Leftrightarrow 6 > 6\theta \Leftrightarrow 1 > \theta$$

and

$$\frac{1}{2} > \frac{1 + \theta - \sqrt{\theta^2 + 8\theta - 5}}{6} \Leftrightarrow 2 > \theta - \sqrt{\theta^2 + 8\theta - 5},$$

which are indeed true. One immediate implication is that the upper root is positive:

$$\frac{1 + \theta + \sqrt{\theta^2 + 8\theta - 5}}{6} > 0.$$

To determine whether the upper root is less than $1/2$, consider

$$\frac{1}{2} > \frac{1 + \theta + \sqrt{\theta^2 + 8\theta - 5}}{6}$$

$$\Leftrightarrow 3 > 1 + \theta + \sqrt{\theta^2 + 8\theta - 5} \Leftrightarrow 2 - \theta > \sqrt{\theta^2 + 8\theta - 5}$$

$$\Leftrightarrow 4 - 4\theta + \theta^2 > \theta^2 + 8\theta - 5 \Leftrightarrow 9 > 12\theta \Leftrightarrow 3/4 > \theta.$$

Hence, if $\theta \in (\sqrt{21} - 4, \frac{3}{4})$ then equilibrium cut-offs are $x \in \{0, \frac{1 + \theta - \sqrt{\theta^2 + 8\theta - 5}}{6}, \frac{1 + \theta + \sqrt{\theta^2 + 8\theta - 5}}{6}\}$, where

$$0 < \frac{1 + \theta - \sqrt{\theta^2 + 8\theta - 5}}{6} < \frac{1 + \theta + \sqrt{\theta^2 + 8\theta - 5}}{6} < \frac{1}{2}.$$

If $\theta \in [\frac{3}{4}, 1)$ then $x \in \{0, \frac{1 + \theta - \sqrt{\theta^2 + 8\theta - 5}}{6}, \frac{1}{2}\}$.

3. The economics of pending patents

Johannes Koenen and Martin Peitz[1]

3.1 INTRODUCTION

Imagine yourself playing chess with an acquaintance, with whom you are not necessarily friendly, so that the outcome of the game matters to you. Your acquaintance bought the board and pieces, and as a compensation for his investment, you agree that you are not allowed to use your left bishop for the first 20 moves – if you do, your opponent may appeal to a referee who will dole out an expensive punishment to you. The rules are clear: you are at a disadvantage which your opponent has earned through his prior investment. In the course of the first 20 moves of the game, your immobilized figure may become redundant, as the focus of the game has shifted elsewhere, or it may even be removed from the board by a move of your adversary. It will almost definitely burden the progress of your other figures that you are trying to develop. Now picture the same situation with just a slight twist: for the first couple of moves, you do not know which figure it is that you are not allowed to touch. Which situation would a strategic player prefer to be in?

The former setting resembles the way the patent system is generally understood by lawmakers, the press and many academics up until now: patents encourage innovation by awarding a clearly defined (by the claims in the patent document), temporary (20 years from the date of application) strategic advantage over competitors. The latter, as we argue in this chapter, is – at least along one dimension – perhaps closer to the kind of strategic situation that firms in industries with patents actually face. In addition to the clearly defined, observable patents that have been granted (and whose infraction firms are mostly able to avoid, if this is determined prudent) there are different types of pending patents in the market: some of which are completely invisible (at least up until 18 months from application), all of which are generally unchallengeable – yet they still exert influence from their inception, which becomes even stronger if a patent is later awarded.

In this chapter, we provide a treatment of a number of questions pertaining to pending patents – a subject that has so far mainly been discussed *en passant* in the existing literature. We proceed as follows: first, we briefly present the underlying institutional and legal framework that governs pending patents and introduce the necessary terminology for our pursuits. As a next step, we focus on the strategic considerations of firms in the earliest stage of the patenting process and the interplay with the patent office. We also explicitly focus on the perspective of the patent and trademark offices (PTOs): we consider different mechanisms of how to allocate available resources, while keeping track of the aims that the PTO must bear in mind. Finally we ask the provocative question, why we do not observe (even) more abuse of patent applications aimed at obtaining pending patents and point to potential answers.

In the spirit of a survey article, for each of the topics we indicate the relevant literature that we rely on, though we do not aim to be complete and the selection, therefore, is idiosyncratic.[2] Further, we attempt to point out subjects and questions that in our eyes are deserving of a closer look, empirically or theoretically.

3.2   INSTITUTIONAL FRAMEWORK

The rules governing the patent system have been subject to significant changes in the last decades, whether with regard to patentable subject matter – consider the controversies regarding (and finally introduction of) the patentability of software code[3] or business methods[4] – the disclosure of patent applications, which we will discuss in some detail below, or, most recently, the switch from a first-to-invent to a first-to-file system in the USA.[5] The latter constitutes a further step towards harmonizing the major patent regimes, the so-called 'Triad' of Europe, Japan and the USA.[6]

In this section, we discuss some relevant features of the existing institutional frameworks that are particularly pertinent to pending patents: patent grant delays (and patent protection), patent grant rates, the disclosure duties regarding the information included in the patent application and the expected gains during the pending phase.

3.2.1   How Long are Patents Pending?

Internationally, patents generally grant 20 years of protection for the included claims. The 'clock' starts at the priority date, that is, the initial date of application,[7] while protection – with important exceptions[8] – sets in at the time that the patent is granted. This clearly makes grant delays, the time between an application and the decision by the PTO, a potentially important issue: a five-year grant delay, for example, reduces the duration of full patent protection to 15 years. Add to this the fact that patent applications must be made public 18 months after the priority date (if the application is upheld by the applicant),[9] which, in addition, creates time-windows during which ideas are in the public realm without much protection. The first issue we address as a basis for our further discussion is the duration of grant lags within different patent regimes.

Much happens between the original filing of an application for a patent and the decision of the PTO whether or not to grant the individual claims outlined therein. A naive first approach to quantify this would be to look at the average time that elapses (though we will see that considering averages is not that helpful). A number of studies have computed this kind of figure: Hall and Harhoff (2004) found that the average time of pendency for patents at the US PTO was around 24 months in 2002 (up from 18 months in 1990), which can be related to a yearly increase of the number of patent applications of about 5 per cent since the 1970s. As the capacities of the PTO have not increased analogously, they estimate that the average workload of each examiner, measured by cases per year, increased by more than 20 per cent in the five years until 2002. In their sample, Popp et al. (2004) find an average lag of around 27 months for US patents, analysing data on all applications for utility patents in the USA between 1976 and 1996. King (2003) reports an increase in the average pending duration between 1988 to 1999 from 20 months to around 25 months. Note that therefore the 1995 reform replacing the 17-year term from granting to a 20-year term from application would on average increase the duration of patent protection in the USA.[10] As discussed below, it is more complicated (and potentially more valuable) patents which require longer inspection and whose protection may therefore be shorter after the reform. For Europe, Harhoff and Wagner (2009) find a substantially longer average decision lag of 52 months at the European Patent Office (EPO), for applications filed between 1978 until 1998.

What happens during this interval at the PTOs? We outline the processes very briefly below.[11] In the USA, the following steps take place:

1. Upon reception, the completeness of the application is ascertained (if the application is deemed incomplete, it is returned to the applicant who has a chance to resolve remaining issues) and the priority date is determined. Then the application is assigned a classification. Based on this classification, the file passes through two filters, the Technology Center[12] and subsequently the Specialized Art Unit,[13] which further differentiate its classification.

2. As a result, the file is assigned to an individual examiner by the director of the Art Unit and enters the examiner's queue. This point of the

process is where the backlog at the patent office accumulates and has accumulated.

3. Once the examiner arrives at the application, she must determine the contents of each claim made, and then commences the prior art search, based on existing local and foreign patents as well as scientific and trade literature, aided by specialized electronic databases. A report, including any problems and conflicts that were discovered, is then issued and presented to the applicant.

4. Upon receiving the report on the prior art search, the applicant has six months to respond regarding the issues that have been raised. Note that this process can be repeated: the examiner must reply within two months, which grants the applicant a further six-month window to respond in turn. For this exchange, the examiner must determine whether the amendments are still within the realm of the original application, or whether the process must be started anew.

5. After these correspondences the examiner must decide whether to grant or reject the patent. In the latter case, the applicant can decide to appeal the decision or file a so-called continuation: the latter can be interpreted as a request for a renewed (complete) examination of the (potentially amended) patent application, which keeps the original filing date. For details on this, see Quillen and Webster (2001) and Quillen et al. (2002). Further reasons for continuation is a separation of the original application into multiple patents, or improvements to the original design which require the application to be updated.

Note that both researchers and the US PTO itself have suggested introducing tweaks to the current procedure in order to deal with the problems created by backlogs more efficiently by inducing self-selection of applicants. The US PTO has suggested introducing a two-track application process, in which applicants can request a faster treatment over the current procedure. Also, applicants would be able to delay patent examination by up to 30 months, a practice that is used in, for example, Germany, Korea and Japan.[14] In a similar vein, instead of faster examination, Bar and Atal (2011) suggest introducing 'gold-plated' patent applications, in which applicants with a higher prior patent quality would be more likely to request a more intense and critical examination through the PTO.

How should one interpret the puzzling observation that a patent examination at the EPO takes, on average, about twice as long as the US PTO examination? Can this be attributed to the institutional framework of the examination process? The workload for each examiner is rather similar by the numbers, at about 110 cases per examiner and year in the USA[15] and about 120 cases per examiner and year at the EPO[16] at the end of the periods examined in the studies mentioned above. At both institutions, despite efforts at hiring, examiner workloads have substantially increased over time; but these processes have run almost parallel at both institutions, so that the ratio of examiners to applications has remained very similar and cannot explain the observed difference.[17] If anything, practitioners communicate the impression that the circumstances at the US PTO are substantially less comfortable than at the EPO.

There is no fundamental institutional difference, such as additional inspection steps, between the European and the US system.[18] The process at the EPO is separated into two stages: a prior art search after the application has been filed, followed by the substantive examination of claims if requested by the applicant after she has received the search report. As opposed to the USA, the application does not have to include a list of references submitted by the applicant. It appears unlikely though that this is responsible for the observed differences. Popp et al. (2004) include a brief discussion with US PTO examiners resulting in the observation that depending on their quality and length, reference lists provided by applicants can both slightly decrease but also substantially increase the required examination efforts. During the substantive examination, communication between the EPO and the applicant may take place – for each correspondence, the examiner is able to determine how quickly the applicant must answer within the range of 2–6 months. When requesting the substantive examination, the applicant may request accelerated examination, which significantly and substantially reduces the grant lag, as Harhoff and Wagner (2009) find as a result of their survival analysis of more than 200,000 EPO applications. Despite – or perhaps because of – the feasible opportunity to speed things up, an accelerated examination was only requested in about 2 per cent of cases in their huge sample. Strategic factors (and moral hazard) may be at play here: one observes an actual acceleration through the request only for those patent applications that result in a patent being granted. If, on the other hand, the application is withdrawn or rejected, a request for accelerated examination is actually associated with an increased duration of pendency. Assuming that it is more important inventions for which the request is submitted, this could indicate a stronger willingness of applicants to drag out the application process for these valuable applications if they realize that it will not come to a successful conclusion.

Various papers study the determinants of patent grant lags: applications with more claims, from more sophisticated technology fields, and higher 'importance' (measured by family size or number of citations) take significantly longer to be examined, effects that generally hold for both jurisdictions – see, for example, van Zeebroeck (2007), Harhoff and

Wagner (2009) for Europe and Popp et al. (2004) and Johnson and Popp (2003) for the USA. Regibeau and Rockett (2010) provide evidence to the contrary – they hypothesize, based on a theoretical model, that applicants significantly contribute to the delay at the patent office. More valuable patents, in the probability of patenting and the flow profits generated, should pass through the examination process more quickly. Their empirical results bear this prediction out – Regibeau and Rockett (2010) argue that this contrast to the existing literature might be explained by the fact that other papers did not take the so-called innovation cycles into account: whenever a ground-breaking new technology is developed, the patent office requires some time to learn how to deal with it adequately, therefore there will be a tendency for new (and important) technologies to be examined for longer periods of time. Controlling for this, they find that more valuable applications have shorter grant lags.

But what explains the differential – why do EPO applications take so much longer? One possible and rather straightforward explanation is that the examination process is stricter and more rigorous in Europe, which simply takes more time. Strongly differing grant rates that appear to be systematically higher for the USA than for Europe, as discussed in the following section, serve as some evidence for this line of argumentation. As we point out in Section 3.3, this may also provide quite different incentives to applicants to delay the process through strategic use of communication.

One important difference between the US and the European patent regimes that may further explain this difference is related to the incentive structures of the patent examiners. First note that it is non-trivial to determine the quality of the work of patent examiners: If a patent is (falsely) rejected, then there are a number of paths for the applicant (appeal, in some cases continuations) to resolve this issue – most of these are not observable from available data. What is observable, though, is post-grant litigation of patents, in which courts deem granted patents invalid *ex post*. This subject has been analysed by Cockburn et al. (2003) and King (2003). But this process takes a substantial amount of time (multiple years, especially in the case of appeals of the initial judgment), therefore, as Friebel et al. (2006) and Schuett (2011) note, it must be seen in connection with the career paths of patent examiners. In its September 2007 report, the US Government Accountability Office (GAO)[19] found that of the 4818 examiners that were employed at the time, more than 20 per cent were in their first year of tenure, which indicates substantial hiring efforts. But the US PTO employee base is subject to substantial attrition: between 2002 and 2006, one (experienced) examiner departed for every two new hirings. Schuett (2011) points to fundamentally different tenure structures of the European and the US patent offices: while more than a quarter of examiners at the EPO have been at the institution for more than 15 years, the equivalent figure for the US PTO is at only around 10 per cent. According to the GAO report, only about 50 per cent of examiners in the USA could look back at a tenure of longer than five years. In most cases, therefore, incentives attached to the quality of decisions in the sense of court re-evaluations of patents will not be feasible for the USA and individual examiners will be little inclined to overly consider their reputations. One might hope to address this issue by retaining examiners and thereby extending their average tenure (initiatives to achieve this are underway), but certain institutional details are difficult (if at all possible) to overcome: Patent examiners are highly specialized within their areas of expertise and obtain a valuable inside view into the processes within the PTO. Moreover, as Popp et al. (2004) elicited from PTO insiders, at least the first year of tenure must be considered a kind of training period, in which substantial investments into the human capital of new examiners are made. These kinds of expertise are highly prized in the market and industry poaching plays an important role.

There is a second, perhaps more obvious, difference between the incentives at the US PTO and the EPO: while the incentive structure at the EPO is flat – at any given pay level, there is a fixed salary – examiners in the USA receive bonuses based on the number of applications that they process each year.[20] By most estimates, see in particular Friebel et al. (2006), it takes an examiner about twice as long to reject a patent as it does to grant it.[21] Far more effort must be exerted in drafting the reports and the examiner must expect a substantial increase in correspondence with the applicant as well as the potential for appeals and litigation. This structure, together with the lack of a corrective via a reputation mechanism, as discussed above, makes it doubly attractive for US examiners to quickly issue grants for patents in their queue to accumulate more processed applications – which on average could speed up the process substantially, at the cost of inspection quality.[22]

To summarize the discussion of patent grant lags: due to a substantial increase in applications over the last two decades, significant grant lags are observed at all major patent offices. As a result, patents spend on average more than 10 per cent (in the USA), or even up to 25 per cent (in Europe) of their lifetime in pendency. Different prerogatives and incentive structures probably account for much of the difference in pendency between Europe and the USA – with the USA focusing on relatively timely processing and the European office stressing the (more time-consuming) detection of undeserving applications – but this issue is worth additional empirical analysis. One issue that we have so far not addressed is that applicants may contribute to the pendency durations through action of their own

– we discuss different motives and methods for this below in Section 3.3, but first turn to other framework issues.

3.2.2 Disclosure of Applications, Protection and Grant Rates

Let us briefly recount the normal timeline of the patenting process: after the initial application is submitted, the applicant has a 18-month window of time during which she may withdraw the application and thereby keep it secret. Generally, if she wants to uphold the application at this point of time, she has to agree to it being disclosed to the public, that is, secrets contained within enter the public domain. While this has been common practice in most jurisdictions internationally, it has only become the rule in the USA relatively recently with the American Inventors Protection Act of 1999.[23] And there is an exception to this rule: according to 35 U.S.C. 122(b), when filing an application to the US PTO, inventors can request non-publication (until the patent is granted), given that the applicant certifies in her request that the invention in question 'has not been and will not be the subject of an application filed in another country'. Though this exception has been criticized frequently in the past,[24] it was not repealed during the recent reform, according to our reading of the new legislation.

Disclosure of patent applications involves conflicts of interest: for the inventor, disclosure prior to receiving a patent grant constitutes a serious gamble – it takes away other possible venues of protecting her intellectual property, for example, as a trade secret, that are no longer feasible once the application is on record and in the public realm.[25] Depending on the expectations of the inventor regarding the quality of protection – in this case this also includes the likelihood that the PTO will grant claims to the extent necessary for the inventor's business, in addition to the later enforceability in court – these other options may become even more appealing. As Anton and Yao (2004) demonstrate in a theoretical model, it may in particular be important inventions for which inventors then opt for secrecy, which reduces the dissemination of knowledge. Focusing specifically on pre-grant patent publication in the context of a cumulative innovation model, Aoki and Spiegel (2009) show that a pre-grant publication can reduce the incentives to patent basic technologies and might also lead to less research as a result, especially if patent protection is imperfect. From a social perspective, this can be desirable in their model, nevertheless, as the increased probability of spillovers given a patent application can lead to more products reaching the market, which increases consumer welfare.

Other controversial issues may have to be taken into account as well. In particular, allowing patent applications to be kept secret for indefinite time increases the likelihood of hold-up situations arising due to so-called 'submarine' patents. Consider that firm A has made some technological process and applied for a patent in an area, in which firm B is commercially active. As long as A's application is pending and secret, B has no possibility to infer that its activities may lead to infringement of A's intellectual property. It may even apply for a patent for technology that it has independently developed later on, since A's application will not appear in a prior art search – not even for the patent examiner in charge of B's later application. Note that with the mounting patent backlogs in mind, these kinds of potential redundancies in the activities of patent examiners pose a significant problem in themselves. But the situation for firm B can become extremely expensive, once it has sunk the investments for a new product line that potentially infringes A's prospective patent. Because at this point, A may choose to let its patent 'surface', that is, pursue its application more seriously and let it enter the public realm, from which a typical hold-up problem for B arises.

Two features of the patent systems render the problem of submarine patents somewhat mute: patent lifetime starting at application introduces an additional tradeoff which makes the 'submarine' strategy less attractive and, more importantly, publication, which limits the potential term under water to 18 months. This is what makes the exception according to which applications can remain secret potentially problematic. Aoki and Spiegel (2009) quote PTO figures stating that the exception was only invoked in about 10 per cent of cases. As more data becomes available and the lifetime of these patents accumulates, it will be important to better understand in which cases this exception is applied. There is a first selection bias due to the fact that no international protection is being sought, which one would expect to make this option interesting in particular for (smaller) entities whose operations are centred in the USA. As a further issue, it will be impossible for the econometrician to observe those (secret) applications that are rejected or withdrawn because they never enter the public realm. But there is one important question that can and should be studied: in the medium run, it will be interesting to observe whether and how often secret applications that later are granted as patents are involved in litigation. Two potential forces could be at play that lead to more litigation: on the one hand, secrecy makes it substantially harder to design around the patent, as also proposed, for example, in Bessen and Meurer (2006). On the other hand, if there are strategic considerations at play in keeping a patent secret, that is, if the applicant is trying to pursue the submarine strategy, this should further increase the probability of litigation. This kind of investigation would both let us better understand the true significance of the publication exception in US law, as well as the different motivations for patenting in general.

Sometimes advocates raise the spectre of the time-window between publication and the granting of the patent, arguing that the idea is completely unprotected during this period. This may at first seem intuitive, but considering that any competitor would have to invest in technological capabilities, production methods and infrastructure as well as human capital, it appears rather unlikely that he would expose himself to hold-up, if and when the patent is granted later on. Whether or not the idea is therefore de facto protected between publication and patent grant depends on the likelihood, both objective and subjective, that a patent will be granted for the application. We very briefly therefore turn to this subject next.

Official figures typically put grant rates at around 50 per cent for the EPO and the Japanese Patent Office (JPO) and substantially higher at around 60 per cent for the US PTO.[26] As van Pottelsberghe de la Potterie (2010) points out, official statistics typically relate the total number of actions of examiners in a given final year to the number of grants and, therefore, do not paint a completely reliable picture.[27] For this, one would have to take a given generation of patents and study their respective outcomes – just one factor that complicates this that we have discussed in the previous section is that apparent refusals of patents may still be overturned in the process of continuations. As a result, we would expect the official figures to underestimate the true situation; which is precisely the result that, for example, Lazaridis and van Pottelsberghe de la Potterie (2007) arrive at using a cohort approach as discussed: they find that in the 1990s, despite the extraordinary increase in the number of applications, grant rates at the EPO were and remained above 60 per cent.[28] As a result, for any given application that competitors observe, without any further knowledge they should expect it to become a patent in about two-thirds of cases.

A further highly interesting factor is the relative propensity of patent offices to grant patents. We would like to point out the results of one study in particular, with further added relevance due to the introduction of fast post-grant patent reviews through the recent reform in the USA. Hall and Harhoff (2004) use the following intuitive approach. They take cohorts of patents already granted in the USA and try to match them to applications to the EPO with identical claims. Then they compare this to EPO applications following a granted priority application to another foreign office apart from the USA. By comparing the outcomes in a kind of difference-in-difference approach, this is a straightforward way to analyse the development of the strictness of the US PTO. The results are striking. While in 1979 the EPO was as likely to grant an application based on a granted US versus a granted international patent, the quality of US patents has decreased significantly since then – in 1995, a US patent was about 15 per cent less likely to be awarded a European patent than an application based on a non-US patent. This strongly indicates a stricter standard being applied at the European than at the US patent office, which corroborates our considerations in the previous section. Hall and Harhoff (2004) link this disparity to the existence of a post-grant review system in Europe, which did not exist for the USA at the time, a point also argued by Mossinghoff and Kuo (2002). Immediately after a patent being granted, third parties can initiate a comparatively cheap and fast process to oppose granted patents without invoking an expensive patent trial. A similar method has now been established in the USA, and therefore it will be interesting to observe the effects on US patent quality.

After discussing the duration of pendency as well as disclosure obligations and grant rates, we next turn our attention to a further important dimension with regard to the strategic calculus: the economic value during the pendency of patents.

3.2.3   The Value of Pending Patents

We have discussed in the previous section how any pending patent application exposes competitors to a certain kind of risk: if they develop products or otherwise engage in activities that infringe upon claims in the application, and a patent is granted later on, the value of the associated investment is destined to take a substantial hit. For a manufacturing firm, the declaration 'patent pending' on a product can, thus, grant competitive advantages in the spirit of the chess-match analogy in the introduction. It signals to a competitor that he must tread carefully, and for 18 months (at least, as discussed) he does not even have the opportunity to find out the exact circumstances. Abuse of the terms 'patent pending' and 'patent applied for' are sanctioned with fines by law, in the USA according to 35 U.S.C. 292 – fines are incurred in the case that no patent application was submitted (or the application is no longer pending), but without any regard to the patentability of the subject matter, that is, the likelihood of patentability. As a placative example: a firm stamping a bread box with 'patent pending' is perfectly within its rights, as long as there is a patent application related to the bread (or packaging, or baking method) currently pending at the PTO. On the flip side, no rights are conveyed to the applicant through this stamp: any gains derive from inducing competitors (or potential licensees) to behave in a desirable fashion when faced with the pending patent. As we will show below, these gains are substantial.

Let us first consider a licensing situation between the inventing firm I, whose patent application is pending, and a potential licensee L. L faces the following problem: it can either enter into a licensing agreement and commence the necessary investments for production immediately, or it can let its behaviour depend on the outcome of the examination process. If I's application is rejected, then no licence is required, and the corresponding fees are avoided – at the disadvantage of either postponing the investments and thereby production start or of investing under additional uncertainty with the possibility of having to bargain with I later on in a classical hold-up situation. It is not surprising therefore that one observes substantial licensing activity regarding pending patents, with one important group of players in this field being university technology licensing offices, as discussed by Henderson et al. (1998). To quantify: Gans et al. (2008) generate a dataset in which patent and licensing information for technology licensing agreements in the 1990s is combined to study this question. They find that in more than a quarter of cases, the licensing agreements are concluded prior to the corresponding patent being granted. From the perspective of hazard rates though, there is a substantial and significant spike at the date of the patent grant (about a fivefold increase), but considering the complexity of this kind of sophisticated contract, this can be taken as an indication that the parties generally come to an agreement previously, even if formalization takes place only when the patent is granted.

Beside this licensing story, Henkel and Jell (2010) and Harhoff and Wagner (2009) each speculate about further channels by which pending patents can create value for firms, potentially even more so than if they have already been granted: a first, direct effect is that the payment of search and renewal fees can be postponed.[29] In the spirit of our motivating analogy, the firm can also use the time during pendency to evaluate the market situation and better judge the value of the idea – the possibility of adapting the application in the course of the process (within boundaries) further enhances this. And finally, the uncertainty created for the competitor creates strategic opportunities, such as extending first-mover advantages and making it harder to design around the patent.

The overall effect also appears in the data, especially in the context of young firms in technology-intensive settings. Using data from 269 Israeli technology start-ups, Greenberg (2009) analyses the impact of pending and granted patents on firm values. The study separates the sample into software and non-software firms; for non-software firms, pending patents on average raise the valuation by between 3.8 and 4.7 million USD, with granted patents leading to a significantly higher raise. The fact that this does not hold for software firms may, on the other hand, indicate the dubious value of software patents. An important factor for the success of young technology firms is the availability of external financing through venture capital companies. Both Häussler et al. (2009) and Cockburn and MacGarvie (2009) analyse this question, and both find that pending patents are associated with a significantly higher probability to obtain venture capital financing. According to Cockburn and MacGarvie (2009), this effect is even stronger for pending than for already granted patents. This probably reflects a taste for growth potential, which pending applications satisfy even better than granted patents already in the stock of the company.

3.3 STRATEGIC INTERACTION BETWEEN APPLICANT AND PTO

After outlining the general framework that applies to pending patents, which one could consider the macro-level, we now turn to the micro-level: the actual interactions between the applicant and the examiners. If one were to study the patent application process in detail as a strategic game, it would be surprisingly complex – as we will outline below, the applicant has substantial discretion both with regard to designing the application and the claims included within and with regard to accelerating or dragging out the examination process. This is not our goal. Instead, we wish to briefly outline some of the tradeoffs involved, while pointing both to work that has already been done and to subjects that merit further study in our opinion. We first discuss the most important options available to the applicant, before we briefly turn our focus to the PTO perspective.

3.3.1 The Applicants' Toolbox

In the course of this section, we will focus on two (interrelated) dimensions of discretion that the applicant has: first, discretion regarding the formulation of the application, that is, the specification and claims; then, we turn our attention towards the different procedural possibilities and choices available to applicants. In both steps, the aim is to try to understand how observable data can be structured and then approached to learn more about the state of the patent system and the quality of applications.

The formulation of patent applications can almost be considered a two-part art form, consisting of the specification and the claims.[30] What makes the subject so interesting is that the incentives of the inventor and society in general, represented through the PTO, are misaligned. The specification is the clear description of the idea, which is supposed to enable a competent person to understand (and reproduce) the invention. It is (mainly) the specification that catapults the inventor's know-how into the public realm. Therefore, it is in the interest of the public that the specification be phrased as clearly, precisely and completely as possible. On the other hand, the claims encompass the basic rights of the inventor after a patent has been granted: whom she can exclude from which kind of activity in which situation. *Ex post*, after investments for innovation have been sunk, it appears to be in the interest of society to limit the scope of these claims, while – at least at first glance – the inventor wants them to be as broad as possible; 'possible' being defined by whatever can be enforced through the courts. The claims and specifications are interrelated, in that the former must derive from the latter.[31] One can easily envision a bargaining process that takes place between the examiner and the applicant as the original application is adjusted and tweaked reacting to the examiner's criticism throughout the process.

Since both sides need to invest effort into the process, one can translate this situation into a problem of moral hazard in teams. In Prady (2009), an inventor can invest into the clarity of his application, which reduces the effort required by the examiner to inspect the application. This may give low-quality inventors an incentive to try to induce shirking of the examiner by sending 'scrambled' signals that require more effort to parse. But our previous discussion implies that an opaquely phrased application does not necessarily indicate a bad patent: anticipating the examiner's reaction and demands to redact, it can also be a way to extend the period of pending while giving the applicant additional strategic flexibility. Harhoff and Wagner (2009) point out that in the process of redacting, the applicant is also granted the valuable opportunity to adjust her claims to new developments in the competitive setting. It would be a fascinating (though rather involved) exercise to systematically compare the original specifications with those in the finally granted patent, taking the duration of the examination (and correspondence) into account. Among other things due to the costs involved, for example, for legal counselling, one might expect different effects for individuals or small versus large firms. Further, one might be able to relate a measure of 'similarity' of the initial application and the final version to the quality or value of the granted patent.[32]

Apart from the formulation of the application, there are a number of formal instruments available to the applicant to influence the duration of pendency, whose details differ by jurisdiction. In the following, we present a selection of these as well as interesting questions related to observable data for each.

- Requests for accelerated examination. Data for the application of this option is currently available for the EPO. As noted above, Harhoff and Wagner (2009) find that it is only used in around 2 per cent of cases, despite the fact that it substantially reduces grant lag. Similar to the discussion concerning the secrecy exception above, it would be highly interesting to better understand who makes use of this instrument, for example, by the research intensity or level of competition within the industry, as well as the likelihood that these patents will later be involved in litigation.

- Delayed examination. The option to delay examination is available to applicants in a number of jurisdictions either directly or indirectly, among them Germany, Korea and Canada. Henkel and Jell (2010) analyse this issue using data from the German PTO, where applicants can defer the process by up to seven years by postponing the filing of the request for examination. They find that in their sample of patent applications filed between 1986 and 2000, around 50 per cent of applications were delayed by the applicants and for around 20 per cent, the delay even lasted for the maximum possible seven years. In a subsequent survey sent out to inventors, they establish that strategic considerations do play a central role in extending the pending process: in particular, patents with the aim of inducing uncertainty for competitors were likely to be delayed, with different effects by industry.[33]

- Patent Cooperation Treaty (PCT) application. A PCT filing provides the applicant a 30-month time-window during which she can apply in each PCT country, that is, it extends the cut-off regarding the novelty criterion in these countries. If the applicant wishes to seek patent protection in any of these countries, it also tends to substantially expedite the process, as the original examination also includes an international search report.[34] The PCT filing has a second important effect: it tends to delay the examination in the original country, by about a year in Germany according to regression results in Henkel and Jell (2010); significant delays are also found by van Zeebroeck (2007) for Europe. If firms are interested in international patent protection, a PCT filing offers easier access to foreign patents, but a delayed grant in the priority country, which may be problematic for important innovations. In the context of delays it would be interesting to investigate whether there are PCT filings that lead to grants in the priority country, without any international filings taking place afterwards. This would be a further potential way to identify delaying tactics.

- Filing of provisional patent applications. Since June 1995, 35 U.S.C. 111(b) gives applicants in the USA the option to file a 'provisional application for patent'. This method allows an inventor to (relatively cheaply) establish priority, for example, the requirement to file a prior art statement is waived. There is a 12-month pendency period for the provisional application, during which the applicant is allowed to use the term 'patent pending'. The application can be converted to a standard application, by filing a corresponding patent application, which has the important advantage that its patent term begins only at the filing date of the subsequent 'full' application. In other words, filing a provisional application is a way to delay the patenting process by one year, while also extending the duration of patent protection.

As shown in this section, firms and inventors both have the tools to extend the pending period of applications substantially and they also make use of them for different reasons, at least some of which are related to the strategic interaction with competitors – factors that for so long were not considered part of the 'mission statement' of the patent system. A further unsettling trend seems to materialize in the data: van Zeebroeck (2007) finds that the longer the inspection process for a patent, the more likely it is that the inventor will let it lapse, even if it is granted by the EPO. Together with the findings on the extension of pendency, this raises the spectre of firms actually protecting their interests more effectively through pending than through granted patents: with the former being much more difficult to oppose by third parties. This issue should be studied in more detail, as such a development would seriously undermine the efficacy of examination in deterring abuses of the patent system. In the extreme, this might be considered a de facto shift from an inspection (granted patents) towards a registration (pending patents) regime.

3.3.2   The PTO Perspective

Longer grant delays affect the aims of the PTO as well. First, turn your attention towards the quality of the match between the application and an examiner. Cockburn et al. (2003) study the effects of the observable characteristics of patent examiners on the outcomes of litigation that arise after patents have been granted, a measure for inspection quality that we have briefly discussed above. They do not find significant effects of examiner experience on the likelihood of a court finding a patent invalid and also the examiner workload does not have a significant effect. What does significantly influence the probability of a patent being invalidated by the courts is the technology field that it originated in. This may indicate matching difficulties in especially faddish fields or in fields in which it is systematically difficult to have adequate examiners. More generally, it suggests that the quality of the match is affected by the flexibility a PTO has when allocating patent applications to examiners. This flexibility is affected by the length of the patent pending phase.

To illustrate the importance of the length of the patent pending phase, as a brief thought experiment, consider the case of a patent office as a 'closed system', in which for each time period as many applications are received as decisions can be made by examiners: the PTO has the capacity to exactly deal with the incoming applications. By extending the inspection period, that is, the average time each application spends in the queue waiting to be examined, the patent office might then be able to achieve a better match between examiners and applications. The following example illustrates this line of thought. A PTO covers two technological fields, termed A and B, and employs two specialized examiners, a and b. In each period, two applications are submitted to the patent office. Each examiner can consider exactly one submission per period. Suppose that each application falls within either field with equal probability and that all draws are independent. Thus, in a given period, with probability 1/4 both applications belong to field A, with probability 1/4 both applications belong to field B, and with probability 1/2 one application belongs to field A and the other to field B. First, consider an inspection period of one period, that is, in each period, incoming and outgoing applications must be the same. In this case, whenever two applications from the same field arise, one of them must be treated by a non-specialist. Hence, with probability 1/2 there is a mismatch. On the other hand, if we extend an inspection period to two periods, a mismatch only happens if the two applications that were not investigated in the previous period and the two applications that are submitted in the current period belong to the same field. Thus, if the two applications from the previous period that remain on the desk of the two examiners belong to field A, with probability 1/4 there will be a mismatch. Similarly, for remaining applications that belong to field B. In order to derive the overall probability of a mismatch, we determine the stationary distribution of the Markov chain with state space (A, A), (A, B) and (B, B), which keeps track of the applications that remain on the desk of the examiners, that is, we determine the probability that these three states occur in the long run. Concerning the transition probabilities, we write the process such that examiners avoid a mismatch whenever possible. In this simple example, the stationary distribution is easily calculated as (1/3, 1/3, 1/3). Hence, with a two-period inspection period, a mismatch occurs with probability (1/4)(1/3) + (1/4)(1/3) = 1/6. Hence, by increasing the inspection period from one to two periods the probability of a mismatch is reduced by 2/3.

This simple thought experiment points towards some very interesting tradeoffs within a PTO. While longer queues may contribute to improving the matching quality (one could easily extend the example to also cover increasing workloads), they could also lead to (or indicate, which has the equivalent effect) an overload problem as proposed by Jaffe and Lerner

(2004). Caillaud and Duchene (2009) theoretically study such a situation in which a PTO can implement either a strict policy, in which it diligently examines each application and sifts out low-quality patents that should not be granted, or a lax policy, in which the large number of applications force the PTO to spend less time with each and therefore low-quality ideas are patented with higher probability. Each of these policies can be an equilibrium, depending on the beliefs of prospective applicants. If they expect the inspection to be lax, many applications are submitted, which forces the inspection to be lax; if they expect the inspection to be strict, then fewer applications are submitted, which grants the PTO the opportunity to diligently examine each application. This demonstrates why a PTO should attempt to not even appear to be suffering from overload. Note that there are different ways of achieving this: both implementing a stricter inspection policy with the given capacities and increasing the inspection capacity, or, of course, a combination of these measures would be beneficial. Both of these steps are currently being implemented, with the EPO arguably focusing more on the quality/strictness of inspection and the US PTO on inspection capacities and hiring/retaining of qualified examiners. Allowing variability in queues may serve as an information gathering device in this context, as shifts help detect fields in which hiring or qualification measures should be focused (or can be relaxed).

Apart from the situation within PTOs, there is also an interesting dynamic between the PTOs of different countries. Some efforts have been undertaken to determine how identical (or at least originally identical)[35] patent applications fare at patent offices in different countries. Similar to the study by Hall and Harhoff (2004) discussed in the context of relative grant rates in Section 3.2.2, Webster et al. (2007) construct a sample starting with patents that were granted in the USA with priority dates between 1990 and 1995 that could be matched with applications both to the EPO and JPO with identical priority applications, without them being PCT applications. This leaves a sample of about 70,000 US patents. Similar to Hall and Harhoff (2004), they find that a substantial share of patents that were granted in the USA are declined by the overseas patent offices. They further show that the treatment by the European and Japanese offices appear to differ systematically depending on the technological field and location of the priority application.

There is a very interesting facet of the data that lies somewhat outside the scope of Webster et al. (2007). The inspection outcomes at the two non-US agencies are not independent, which can easily be derived from the descriptives displayed in their study (with the caveat in place that we do not know the sequence of events). Overall, the frequency of withdrawals at the JPO was 29.6 per cent and at the EPO was 18.5 per cent.

Considering only those patents that turned out to be rejected by the other agency, the equivalent withdrawal frequencies are substantially higher, at 52.5 per cent and 23.1 per cent, respectively.[36] Compared to the withdrawal rates of the patents granted by the other institution (22 per cent and 9 per cent, respectively), the jumps are even more prominent, which also allows to control for the effect of time on the probability of withdrawals. Examination outcomes at the EPO, if they were faster, therefore affect the workload of the JPO and vice versa, and this effect holds via the channel of withdrawals, whether or not one institution is informed about the outcome of the other's examination process. If this information is transmitted, take the case of rejections, then the incentive to dither and acquire this information may further increase. Add this effect to the additional information accruing to the applicant over time discussed above, such as marketability, which may lead to withdrawals as well, and it becomes clear why, for example, the US PTO might consider introducing deferred patent applications but also why the introduction of provisional patent applications, which are substantially cheaper and can be interpreted as a kind of deferral as discussed above, has been so successful.[37]

3.4   ABUSE OF PENDING PATENTS

As we have documented above, pending patents are seen as valuable. For this reason, a firm may excessively apply with ideas that are not sufficiently novel. In particular, a pending patent may lead competitors not to enter the market or to sign licensing agreements already in the patent pending phase. At first glance this suggests that a long patent pending phase may even contribute towards excessive patenting; but a more careful look at this issue reveals that a firm may not go unpunished if it misuses the patent system and applies with ideas of no or little value, at least if this firm frequently generates new ideas.

The disciplining force is the reputation of (or trust in) firms that comes into play for companies that repeatedly invest in innovative ideas. Koenen and Peitz (2011) provide a theoretical framework to address this issue. They propose an infinite horizon setting in the spirit of Klein and Leffler (1981) and Choi (1998): each period, with a certain probability strictly smaller than 1, a firm generates an objectively patentable idea. Even when it does not, though, it can submit a patent application to the PTO. After some periods of inspection, the PTO grants patents to good ideas with certainty, while due to first-order mistakes it also grants patents to bad applications with a positive probability. If a patent has been granted, the firm holds it for the remainder of the patent lifetime (possibly qualified by competitors' challenges). During the pending phase, a firm generates income from each pending patent, depending on the publicly held belief regarding the patent quality. These beliefs are based on the observable history of the game. To focus on PTO inspection, it is postulated that publicly available information is limited mainly to the results of the PTO's examinations of patent applications. In particular, beliefs are not conditioned on potential post-grant lawsuits. For each granted patent in the firm's portfolio, the firm receives a (belief-dependent) income for each period of the patent lifetime.

An equilibrium that supports reputation or trust consists in the firms applying for patents only if an objectively patentable idea has been generated and to resist from doing so if the idea is of questionable value. This equilibrium is supported by a belief system with which competitors punish observed deviations from such a strategy, by becoming more sceptical about the quality of patent applications. Given such belief formation, reputation can be sustained in equilibrium if future profits play an important role. This basic result holds independent of a firm's existing patent portfolio. Note that since pending patent are valuable and applications take time to evaluate, there would be short-term gains from deviating even if the PTO perfectly distinguished between patent applications which merit protection and those which do not.

An additional important insight is that a large patent portfolio makes it easier to support reputation in equilibrium. The reason is that not only expected profits from future ideas are endangered by deviating but that even existing ideas that are patent pending or protected by a patent lose value if a deviation is detected. The reason is that these patents (or pending patents) are more likely to be challenged and defending them is costly. Such behaviour by competitors can be expected on the grounds that the public does not exactly know when the innovating firm has started to deviate from the reputation strategy. Thus, after an observed detection, competitors question the validity of other granted or pending patents within the portfolio of that firm. Thus, not only current and future behaviour of the firm is thrown into doubt, but past behaviour as well. This results in enhanced negative effects on the profitability of a firm whose deviation is uncovered. This suggests that the change of market value of a deviating firm should not only include changes in discounted profits due to a particular rejected application but should include a multiplier accounting for earlier ideas that are still under protection as well as its reliance on generating profits from innovation in the future (for example, the frequency of submitting patent applications). The theory predicts that more post-grant lawsuits should be observed for patents within the firm's patent portfolio (consisting of pending patents and those granted patents that have not yet expired) after an application has been rejected.

A policy lesson that emerges from this insight is that a firm with a strong patent portfolio (including pending patents) is less likely to put its reputation at risk and, optimally using scarce resources, should therefore be investigated with less scrutiny by the PTO than a firm with a weaker portfolio. The second policy lesson concerns the question of whether the 'US' policy of fast inspection with a relatively high rate of first-order mistakes or the 'European' method of more careful scrutiny at the cost of relatively slow inspection is superior. Based on the reputation argument, it may be well worth the 'price' to pay for the PTO to take more time to investigate if the associated benefit of fewer first-order mistakes is sufficiently large. This holds in particular in the case of firms with a strong patent portfolio since a deviation puts the value of the existing portfolio at risk and, thus, delaying the action by the PTO may not make a deviation much more attractive. However, the general tradeoff between more rapid action and more precision also applies to a reputation model.

3.5   CONCLUSION

Various factors, such as the overload at the patent offices, the deterioration of patent quality[38] and the substantial increase of patent litigation,[39] paint the picture of a crisis in patenting. The USA has recently reacted by carrying out a substantial legislative reform. Despite this picture, or rather contributing to it, there is an unbroken trend of increased patenting activity at all major PTOs. As a result, applications will continue to spend a significant share of the patent life-span in the 'purgatory' of pendency. This fundamentally affects the economics of patenting. To paint a particularly threatening future: as the incentive to uphold patents once they are granted deteriorates due to their dwindling remaining lifetime, for some industries pending patents may become the new standard, with the more expensive actual patents turning into an afterthought. Due to the limited possibilities to oppose pending patents, this would subvert the traditional system of patent inspection into a pure registration system. These worries highlight how important it is to further improve our understanding of pending patents. In this chapter, we addressed several issues within this subject and raise questions that we find important. Owing to both the breadth and the relevance of this topic, our endeavour is necessarily incomplete. Therefore we are hoping for and looking forward to relevant new research on the economics of pending patents.

NOTES

1. We would like to thank Georg Licht, Centre for European Economic Research (ZEW), Mannheim, for helpful comments.
2. For a comprehensive survey on recent research in the area of patenting in general, see, for example, Hall and Harhoff (2012).
3. Following the 1981 *Diamond* decision, the US PTO has let this subsequently become more common practice.
4. According to the United States Court of Appeals for the Federal Circuit *State Street* decision in 1998, business methods can be protected by a patent if (a) practical applications are involved and (b) it produces a useful, tangible result. This decision revoked the previous notion that business methods were specifically to be excluded from patentable subject matter.
5. The so-called America Invents Act was approved by the Senate on 8 September 2011. This is not to be confused with the American Inventors Protection Act of 1999.
6. For more details on this process, see Straus and Klunker (2007); for a discussion on the controversy regarding the switch to the first-to-file system in the USA, see Edward Wyatt 'Fighting backlog in patents, Senate approves overhaul', *New York Times*, 9 September 2011, p. B4. For a discussion of the results of patent reforms prior to 2000 in the USA, see Gallini (2002).
7. In the USA, this has replaced a rule of 17 years of protection from the year of the patent grant in the course of the Uruguay round Word Trade Organization (WTO) negotiations in 1995, see, for example, Johnson and Popp (2003) and Maskus (2006).
8. Once the application is filed, this precludes other parties from successfully applying for a patent on the same subject matter. In some jurisdictions, such as Europe (EPO applications) and Germany (§§30,140 German Patent Law), once the application is published it grants protection contingent on the patent being granted later on. For more details on the USA, see Section 3.2.2.
9. We further discuss this rule – and its exceptions – in Section 3.2.2.
10. For further recent numbers on the net effect of the introduction of 20-year from application rule, see Dennis Crouch's analysis at http://www.patentlyo.com/patent/2010/12/one-of-the-most-important-attributes-of-a-patent-is-its-term-or-duration-of-enforceability-in-1995-the-us-patent-system-beg.html (accessed 8 February 2012).
11. For a detailed description of the US process, we refer to the excellent Popp et al. (2004) and King (2003). For a description of the process in the form of a flow chart, see http://www.inventorbasics.com/Patent%20Process.htm (accessed 8 February 2012).
12. Currently there are nine Patent Technology Centers at the US PTO, a list of which can be found at http://www.uspto.gov/about/contacts/phone_directory/pat_tech (accessed 8 February 2012).
13. For a current list of the patent classes arranged by Art Units, see http://www.uspto.gov/patents/resources/classification/art/index.jsp (accessed 8 February 2012). Art unit 3783, for example, covers matters related to 'Internal-Combustion-Engines', while 2785 is responsible for 'Error Detection/Correction and Fault Detection/Recovery'.
14. See the 2010 press release for details, at http://www.uspto.gov/news/pr/2010/1024.jsp. Currently, the US PTO has an optional deferred examination rule in place, which is, in fact, basically not being applied according to practitioners – see both the post and discussion at http://www.patentlyo.com/patent/2009/01/deferred-examination-pto-to-hold-roundtable-discussion.html (accessed 8 February 2012).
15. See footnote 19 in Hall and Harhoff (2004), referring to 2002.
16. See Harhoff and Wagner (2009) for 1998.
17. For details, see EPO (2009) and US PTO (2009).
18. For a stylized overview of the European patent inspection process, see the figure in Harhoff and Wagner (2009). For detailed descriptions of the examination process, see the EPO guide for applicants at http://www.epo.org/applying/european/

Guide-for-applicants/ and, even more detailed, for examiners at http://www.epo.org/law-practice/legal-texts/guidelines.html (accessed 8 February 2012).

19. See http://www.gao.gov/new.items/d071102.pdf (accessed 8 February 2012).
20. For details, see Popp et al. (2004).
21. At the EPO, examiners qualify for promotions and raises through a point system – twice as many points are awarded for rejections as for grants, which takes the relative efforts that are required into account.
22. Schuett (2011) points out that the PTO may face a tradeoff between inspection quality and examiners' willingness to truthfully reveal their findings. Incentives that push examiners towards granting patents can be socially desirable in his model.
23. See, for example, Popp et al. (2004).
24. See, for example, Mossinghoff and Kunin (2008) who – apparently falsely – cite removal of this exception as one of the reform steps that should be completely uncontroversial.
25. While trade secrets are typically seen as substitutes for patents, in the case of complex innovations they may actually be complements; see the discussion in Denicolò and Franzoni (2008).
26. See, for example, US PTO (2009).
27. Hall and Harhoff (2012) point out a further issue that may systematically skew reported grant rates: if one regime allows patent deferrals, while the other does not, then the longer time-window to let a patent lapse will tend to lead to more withdrawals of patents and therefore lower grant rates.
28. Note that depending on the methodology, the grant rates that researchers arrive at differ substantially. Straus and Klunker (2007), for example, report that about 40 per cent of 2005 patent applications were granted in the USA, while the figure for Europe was below 30 per cent. But due to the timing of the study, this conflates grant lags and rejections.
29. The fee for an application at the EPO currently is between 105 and 203 euros. The search fee (prior art search) and the inspection fee are significantly higher at between 800 and 1785 euros and between 1480 and 1645 euros, respectively. The grant fee, which covers the first two years of patent protection, is 830 euros. After this, renewal fees increase from 420 euros per year to 1420 euros starting from the tenth year; see http://www.epo.org/applying/forms-fees/fees.html. The fee structure in the USA is very similar, though fees tend to be somewhat lower overall. For details, see http://www.uspto.gov/web/offices/ac/qs/ope/fee092611.htm (accessed 8 February 2012).
30. For a recent guide to composition, we refer to Slusky (2007).
31. In fact, it may be in the interest of the inventor to formulate a relatively broad specification, as it can function as a fallback position if claims are drawn into doubt in the course of court proceedings.
32. Measuring the quality and value of patents in general, and individual patents in particular, is a rather thorny issue; see, for example, Schankerman (1998), Cornelli and Schankerman (1999) or Hall et al. (2005) for different approaches to valuation and discussions of the potential problems.
33. For further, more detailed examinations of the effects of the opportunity to defer applications, see Hall and Harhoff (2012) as well as Thomas (2010).
34. For additional details, we refer to the description in Harhoff and Wagner (2009).
35. Excluding amendments during the application process.
36. The sample includes 2672 patents that were rejected by the EPO and 10,230 patents rejected by the JPO.
37. About a quarter of all patent filings in the USA are provisional applications; see US PTO (2009) for a brief discussion on the development and on who files provisional applications; see also http://www.patentlyo.com/patent/2008/06/a-first-look-at.html.
38. For comprehensive discussions, see Jaffe and Lerner (2004) and Bessen and Meurer (2008).

39. For a recent empirical study on some of the determinants, see Cook (2007). For an empirical assessment of the relationship of firms' strategies and litigation, see Lanjouw and Schankerman (2001).

REFERENCES

Anton, J.J. and D.A. Yao (2004), 'Little patents and big secrets: managing intellectual property', *RAND Journal of Economics*, **35**, 1–22.

Aoki, R. and Y. Spiegel (2009), 'Pre-grant patent publication and cumulative innovation', *International Journal of Industrial Organization*, **27**, 333–45.

Bar, T. and V. Atal (2011), 'Patent quality and a two-tiered patent system', mimeo, Cornell University.

Bessen, J.E. and M.J. Meurer (2006), 'Patent litigation with endogenous disputes', *American Economic Review – Papers and Proceedings*, **96**, 77–81.

Bessen, J.E. and M.J. Meurer (2008), *Patent Failure*, Princeton, NJ: Princeton University Press.

Caillaud, B. and A. Duchene (2009), 'Patent office in innovation policy: nobody's perfect', Paris School of Economics Working Paper No. 2009-39.

Choi, J.P. (1998), 'Brand extension as informational leverage', *Review of Economic Studies*, **65**, 655–69.

Cockburn, I.M. and M.J. MacGarvie (2009), 'Patents, thickets and the financing of early-stage firms: evidence from the software industry', *Journal of Economics and Management Strategy*, **18**, 729–73.

Cockburn, I.M., S. Kortum and S. Stern (2003), 'Are all patent examiners equal? Examiners, patent characteristics, and litigation outcomes', in W.M. Cohen and S.A. Merrill (eds), *Patents in the Knowledge-based Economy*, Washington, DC: National Academy Press, pp. 19–53.

Cook, J.P. (2007), 'On understanding the increase in U.S. patent litigation', *American Law and Economics Review*, **9**(1), 48–71.

Cornelli, F. and M. Schankerman (1999), 'Patent renewals and R&D incentives', *RAND Journal of Economics*, **30**, 197–213.

Denicolò, V. and L.A. Franzoni (2008), 'Innovation, duplication, and the contract theory of patents', in R. Cellini and L. Lambertini (eds), *The Economics of Innovation*, Bingley, UK: Emerald Group, pp. 15–32.

EPO (2009), *European Patent Office – Annual Report 2009*, Brussels: European Patent Office.

Friebel, G., A.K. Koch, D. Prady and P. Seabright (2006), 'Objectives and incentives at the European Patent Office', IDEI Report, Toulouse.

Gallini, N.T. (2002), 'The economics of patents: lessons from recent U.S. patent reform', *Journal of Economic Perspectives*, **16**, 131–54.

Gans, J., D. Hsu and S. Stern (2008), 'The impact of uncertain intellectual property rights on the market for ideas: evidence for patent grant delays', *Management Science*, **54**, 982–97.

Greenberg, G. (2009), 'Small firms, big patents? Estimating patent value using data on start-ups' financing rounds', mimeo, Bocconi University.

Hall, B.H. and D. Harhoff (2004), 'Post-grant reviews in the U.S. patent system – design choices and expected impact', *Berkeley Technology Law Journal*, **19**(3), 989–1015.

Hall, B.H. and D. Harhoff (2012), 'Recent research on the economics of patents', NBER Working Paper No. 17773, January.

Hall, B.H., A. Jaffe and M. Trajtenberg (2005), 'Market value and patent citations', *RAND Journal of Economics*, **36**, 16–38.

Harhoff, D. and S. Wagner (2009), 'The duration of patent examination at the European patent office', *Management Science*, **55**, 1969–84.

Häussler, C., D. Harhoff and E. Müller (2009), 'To be financed or not . . . – the role of patents for venture capital financing', ZEW – Centre for European Economic Research Discussion Paper, No. 09-003(7115).

Henderson, R., A.B. Jaffe and M. Trajtenberg (1998), 'Universities as a source of commercial technology: a detailed analysis of university patenting, 1965–1988', *Review of Economics and Statistics*, **80**(1), 119–27.

Henkel, J. and F. Jell (2010), 'Patent pending – why faster isn't always better', mimeo, Technical University Munich.

Jaffe, A.B. and J. Lerner (2004), *Innovation and Its Discontents: How Our Broken Patent System is Endangering Innovation and Progress, and What to Do About It*, Princeton, NJ: Princeton University Press.

Johnson, D.K.N. and D. Popp (2003), 'Forced out of the closet: the impact of the American Inventors Protection Act on the timing of patent disclosure', *RAND Journal of Economics*, **34**(1), 96–112.

King, J.L. (2003), 'Patent examination procedures and patent quality', in W.M. Cohen and S.A. Merrill (eds), *Patents in the Knowledge-based Economy*, Washington, DC: National Academy Press, pp. 54–73.

Klein, B. and K.B. Leffler (1981), 'The role of market forces in assuring contractual performance', *Journal of Political Economy*, **89**, 615–41.

Koenen, J. and M. Peitz (2011), 'Firm reputation and the incentives to milk pending patents', mimeo, University of Mannheim.

Lanjouw, J. and M. Schankerman (2001), 'Characteristics of patent litigation: a window on competition', *RAND Journal of Economics*, **32**(1), 129–51.

Lazaridis, G. and B. van Pottelsberghe de la Potterie (2007), 'The rigour of EPO's patentability criteria: an insight into the "induced withdrawals"', *World Patent Information*, **29**(4), 317–36.

Maskus, K.E. (2006), *Reforming U.S. Patent Policy – Getting the Incentives Right*, CSR, Council on Foreign Relations, **19**.

Mossinghoff, G.J. and S.G. Kunin (2008), 'The need for consensus on patent reform', *The Bureau of National Affairs Patent, Law and Trademark Daily*, 1 February, 20, available at http://www.oblon/com/files/news/389.pdf via OBLON SPivat, 9 (accessed 8 February 2012).

Mossinghoff, G. and V. Kuo (2002), 'Post-grant review of patents: enhancing the quality of the fuel of interest', *IDEA, Journal of Law and Technology*, **43**(1), 83–110.

Popp, D., T. Juhl and D.K. Johnson (2004), 'Time in purgatory: examining the grant lag for U.S. patent applications', *Topics in Economic Analysis and Policy*, **4**, 1–43, Article 29.

Prady, D. (2009), '"Is that a gun in your pocket . . .?" Advertising and evaluation', mimeo, Toulouse School of Economics.

Quillen, C.D.J. and O.H. Webster (2001), 'Continuing patent applications and performance of the U.S. Patent Office', *Federal Circuit Bar Journal*, **11**(1), 1–21.

Quillen, C.D.J., O.H. Webster and R. Eichmann (2002), 'Continuing patent applications and performance of the U.S. Patent and Trademark Office – extended', *Federal Circuit Bar Journal*, **12**(1), 35–55.

Regibeau, P. and K. Rockett (2010), 'Innovation cycles and learning at the patent office: does the early patent get the delay?', *Journal of Industrial Economics*, **58**(2), 222–46.

Schankerman, M. (1998), 'How valuable is patent protection? Estimates by technology field', *RAND Journal of Economics*, **29**, 77–107.

Schuett, F. (2011), 'Patent quality and the incentives at the patent office', mimeo, University of Tilburg.

Slusky, R.D. (2007), *Invention Analysis and Claiming: A Patent Lawyer's Guide*, Chicago, IL: American Bar Association.

Straus, J. and N.-S. Klunker (2007), 'Harmonisation of international patent law', *International Review of Intellectual Property and Competition Law*, **8**, 907–36.

Thomas, J.R. (2010), 'Deferred examination of patent applications: implications for innovation policy', *Congressional Research Service Report*, 7-5700.

US PTO (2009), *United States Patent and Trademark Office Performance and Accountability Report Fiscal Year 2009*, Alexandria, VA: United States Patent and Trademark Office.

van Pottelsberghe de la Potterie, B. (2010), 'The quality factor in patent systems', CEPR Discussion Paper No. 7921.

van Zeebroeck, N. (2007), 'Patents live only twice: a patent survival analysis of the determinants of examination lags, grant decisions and renewals', CEB Working Paper 07/028.

Webster, E., A. Palangkaraya and P.H. Jensen (2007), 'Characteristics of international patent application outcomes', *Economics Letters*, **95**, 362–8.

4. Testing for the presence of a maverick in the French audit industry

Marc Ivaldi, Sébastien Mitraille and Catherine Muller[1]

4.1 INTRODUCTION

Competition authorities in Europe and France are paying considerable attention to the risks of collective dominance when assessing the economic effects of a merger. A particular focus is on the operations that change the nature of competition or reinforce anti-competitive practices: indeed, the post-merger structure of an industry may offer new opportunities of coordinated behaviour amongst rival companies that were absent in the ante-merger situation;[2] the post-merger structure may also increase the incentives or facilitate tacit collusion of companies that already coordinated.[3] To assess the risks of collective dominance, competition authorities in Europe refer to the case law of the European Court of Justice: in the decision *Airtours v. Commission* of 6 June 2002,[4] the Court of First Instance of the European Communities (CFI) defined three cumulative conditions that are required to establish that a merger can potentially lead to collective dominance. First, the market must be transparent enough so that dominant companies can monitor the aggressiveness of their rivals. Second, dominant companies must be able to retaliate and punish the aggressiveness of a rival, if this firm decides to cheat on a tacit agreement by being more aggressive on the market. Finally, no competitor, no entrant or no client should be able to win market share over competitors engaged in a tacit agreement by undercutting them. This last condition requires the absence of a 'maverick' on the market, which, as defined by M. Ivaldi, B. Jullien, P. Rey, P. Seabright and J. Tirole in 'The economics of tacit collusion',[5] 'can be interpreted as a firm with a drastically different cost structure, which is unwilling to participate to a collusive action'. The definition of Ivaldi et al. emphasizes the asymmetry in terms of costs of production between the 'maverick' and the other companies which may tacitly collude. A maverick has a cost structure that allows him to impose his supply to consumers, when other rivals are colluding tacitly to maintain some stability in market shares together with high price cost margins. The approach adopted by the CFI in *Airtours v. Commission* has been confirmed by the European Court of Justice (ECJ) in its *Bertelsmann v. Impala* decision dated 13 July 2006,[6] adding the requirement that a general economic mechanism of potential tacit coordination must be proposed to the Court.[7]

A large wave of mergers has recently occurred in the audit industry in Europe and France. The first occurred between Price Waterhouse Coopers and Lybrand in 1998 and reduced the Big Six to the Big Five. This merger, accepted by the European Commission,[8] raised some questions on its impact on competition. Following the Enron case, Ernst & Young acquired Andersen France in 2002, with the clearance of the European Commission in application of the 'failing firm defence' theory. Nonetheless the high concentration of market shares in the audit industry in terms of volume, value and market capitalization,[9] as well as the resulting risk of little competition on this market, clearly appeared. Various studies available on the European Commission website show that concentration increased further.[10] In France, KPMG and Salustro Reydel[11] merged in 2004, then Deloitte/BDO Marque et Gendrot[12] in 2006, and finally Deloitte/Constantin in 2008. The market share of dominant firms increased as a result of these mergers. With the approval of competition authorities and of courts that reviewed their decisions,[13] the audit industry in France and Europe transformed into an oligopoly composed of four major players (the Big Four, Ernst & Young, PriceWaterhouse Coopers Deloitte and KPMG) competing with a residual fringe of smaller or larger firms, depending on the country.

During the examination of these mergers, the evaluation of the risks of coordinated conduct has been a key concern. Indeed a coordinated behaviour may ultimately affect the transparency and the independence of auditors, thereby damaging the quality of service this industry provides to the economy: an increase in oligopolists' margins can be obtained through a rise in prices and/or a decline in the quality of service, when quality is a valuable characteristic costly to produce. Hence a coordinated conduct could lead auditors to reduce the quality of the audit service, for example, by reducing the amount of controls and being more indulgent in the audit of financial statements, in order to gain customer loyalty and stabilize their market share, or to prevent other rival firms from growing on the market. This is obviously detrimental to society as a whole, which expects and earns a positive surplus from the quality of financial information. A coordinated conduct may therefore create a divergence between the level of quality of the audit service provided by the industry and the optimal level that society as a whole, and in particular investors, would like.

In this chapter, we contribute to the assessment of the risks of collective dominance by proposing a test for the presence of a maverick on the market. We perform this test on the French audit sector, whose specificity is to ask companies to hire an audit committee of two firms. We estimate alternative specifications of the supply of competitors, and compare the results against each other. To perform these comparisons, we collected an original dataset over the period 2004 to 2006 that contains all the fees paid to audit committees by companies listed on the French marketplace in Paris that are part of the SBF120 index which contains the 120 largest market capitalizations on the market.

The rest of the chapter is organized as follows: in Section 4.2, we describe the legal and institutional background of the French audit sector: Section 4.3 details the institutional reasons for which the three cumulative *Airtours* criteria may be met. In Section 4.4, we explain how we collected our data. Section 4.5 presents the structure and performance of the audit industry in France. Section 4.6 presents the econometric test we ran on our dataset. Finally, section 4.7 concludes.

4.2 THE LEGAL AND INSTITUTIONAL BACKGROUND OF THE FRENCH AUDIT SECTOR

Following some international financial scandals such as the Enron affair, the main text governing the relations between auditors and audited companies is Title III of the Law on Financial Security ('Loi de Sécurité Financière', Loi 2003-706 dated 1 August 2003, LSF hereafter), on the modernization of the statutory audit of financial statements and transparency. Within the legal framework defined by LSF, auditors may realize different types of mission for their customers.[14]

The first type of mission is a 'legal mission': companies must establish financial statements and provide them to the official registration services, and may have to appoint a statutory auditor depending on the legal form of the company. Two statutory auditors are required for all joint stock companies legally bound to publish consolidated financial statements.[15] This obligation of appointing an audit committee applies to all but one firm of our database.

The second type of mission is called a 'contractual mission', which is performed independently or complementary to the legal mission. As a contractual mission may involve certain consulting services,[16] a legal auditor may sometimes be prohibited from realizing these missions due to the 'principle of independence', which imposes the separation of audit and non-audit activities.[17] As this prohibition applies to national and international networks (a member of a network cannot certify the financial statements of a company whose chartered accountant is another member of the same network), audit firms have been restructured to adapt to this new legal environment: a division hosts the teams responsible for chartered accounting services, with consulting services potentially under a separate structure; another hosts the teams responsible for statutory audits. The principle of independence is also strengthened by the obligation of respecting a mandatory waiting period (*délai de carence* or *délai de viduité*) of two years between the conduct a consulting mission and a legal audit for the same company.[18]

Finally, if auditors must advertise their offer in a 'discreet manner' so as to not 'prejudice the independence, dignity and honour of the profession' (our translation), each statutory auditor must submit *a posteriori* an annual business statement to the regional branch of their professional body (*Compagnie Régionale des Commissaires aux Comptes*). To our knowledge, this detailed information is not public but must be accessible to some players, increasing the market transparency. The profession's internal controls also give third parties access to most commercial data. Finally, the dates of renewal of the legal auditors and the fees they charge to customers must be published in the official financial statements of any listed company. Since 1 January 2005 the preparation of financial statements must comply with the International Financial Reporting Standards (IFRS),[19] established by the International Accounting Standard Committee (IASC). The IASC includes representatives from the major chartered accountant and audit firms (in particular, the Big Four). Standards are adopted through vote, but operational expertise is considered greater within the major audit firms. Hence, the certification of these auditors is more valuable than that of their smaller rivals.

4.3   INVESTIGATING THE APPLICABILITY OF THE THREE CUMULATIVE *AIRTOURS* CRITERIA

We now investigate whether the three cumulative *Airtours* criteria are satisfied; we focus on the institutional factors that indicate the level of transparency and the possibility of retaliation. The current legal framework implies that the *Airtours* criteria are most probably met.

For collective dominance to be effective, the market must be transparent enough, as it allows competitors to reach a common understanding of how to behave on the market as well as the monitoring of rivals. The more complex the functioning of a market, the more difficult it is to collude without forbidding it, as horizontal mergers guidelines in Europe and France reaffirm.[20]

The mergers that occurred in the audit sector led to diverging conclusions: the European Commission considered in 1998 that the audit market had a high level of price and cost transparency;[21] the French Minister for the Economy and the Conseil d'Etat considered that the audit market was characterized by a low degree of transparency.[22] This assessment changed in the evaluation of the Deloitte/BDO Marque et Gendrot merger: the French Minister for the Economy indicated that a number of elements tended to show that 'major audit firms can easily forecast the behaviour of players in the statutory audit segment' (our translation). Nevertheless, he concluded that 'the degree of transparency cannot be established with certainty'[23] (our translation).

There are three main reasons for transparency to be high on the audit market: (1) the obligation of legal publication to which listed companies (clients of the auditors) are subject; (2) the obligation of appointment of an audit committee of two members, which allows any auditor to find out the amount of fees charged by a rival on the audit they jointly realize; and (3) the internal control of the profession.

Indeed listed companies are obliged according to French laws to publish the names, fees and renewal dates of their auditors.[24] A study of the annual financial information submitted by SBF120 companies rapidly reveals the fees charged since 2004. Second, transparency is reinforced by the obligation of appointing an audit committee of two members. This factor has also been identified by competition authorities when investigating mergers in the audit sector:[25] each member of the committee has access to the fees paid to the other, as this information must also be audited. Third and finally, transparency is increased by the quality control conducted by professional bodies (such as the *Haut Conseil du Commissariat aux Comptes*, H3C). Competition authorities who have investigated this sector share this opinion.[26]

This price transparency is reinforced by cost transparency: it seems relatively simple for a player to estimate the costs incurred to audit a specific company as information on its numbers of subsidiaries, employees and countries in which the company operates is publicly available. Added to the fact that the renewal date of an auditor is known, these factors ensure that an external auditor can make an offer that directly competes with the bids submitted by the acting statutory auditors. As customers' and suppliers' characteristics are known at the time of the call for tenders by the various rivals, statutory auditors who lose a bid are quite able to identify the level of rivals' aggressiveness based on their own offer or deducted from potential client feedback; they can ascertain whether the successful bidder has followed a collusive conduct or not.

Tacit collusion is only possible when companies can observe their rivals' strategy and, if applicable, identify a deviation from the coordinated conduct to which they can retaliate. In the present case, if the Big Four interact on a sufficiently frequent basis, or if they interact on multiple markets (for example, when being awarded a related mission for which there is no incompatibility), they may sustain abnormally high prices non-cooperatively over time. While no quantitative public information is available on the markets other than statutory audits, the obligation of hiring at least two auditors in France multiplies the opportunities to compete compared with a single auditor system, due to the different dates of their renewal, increasing the retaliation power.

The market share for contractual audit services must be studied as it is a potential source of revenue for audit firms and may be of great importance when examining the capacity of audit firms to retaliate. Although they cannot substitute the statutory audit missions from a client's perspective, contractual audit missions are a source of revenue for which firms potentially involved in collective dominance compete, increasing the retaliation opportunities. In this regard, it has been held by the French Ministry for the Economy that the diversity of players on contractual audit markets and the absence of an individual dominant position of the Big Four were sufficient to rule out any potential punishment on the contractual audit markets.[27] However, it appears to us that these markets may have been considered more fragmented than they really are. The effect of this hypothesis is not only to artificially reduce the breadth of the risks of coordination but also, more generally, to lead to an underestimation of the concomitant risk of an increase in prices for missions other than statutory audits, which require the skills of audit and chartered accountancy firms.

The pricing behaviour can indeed be affected by the possibility that auditors offer statutory and contractual or legal audit missions. First, reducing a price to gain a statutory (or contractual) audit mission is an investment that allows identification of other profitable audit missions for the same customer if the auditor can accept both missions. The premium given to 'insiders' reinforces the importance of this strategy on the audit market. The principle of independence prevents statutory auditors from bidding for contractual audit missions and the waiting period prevents 'contractual' auditors from bidding for statutory audit missions. These rules reduce the incentives of auditors to price aggressively, as there is no point in increasing competition on a mission that cannot legally be realized: losing a bid (for a statutory or contractual audit) almost always ensures winning another (a contractual or statutory audit), discouraging aggressive pricing. But current rules do not prevent the statutory auditor of a listed company from aggressive bidding for a contractual audit mission (if the missions are not incompatible with each other), for example, to punish a competitor for past aggressive bidding (retaliation remains possible). Since the identity of the legal auditors is public, any player can punish this particular auditor for its past aggressive bidding. The regulations regarding incompatibility could therefore result in an increase in prices for all complementary missions, favouring, in turn, coordination.

Mergers have also increased the Big Four labour force. They allowed these companies to enjoy a larger retaliation power and increased their ability to trigger price wars in response to aggressive pricing. The low price elasticity of demand acknowledged by competition authorities and the arguments developed above lead us to consider whether members of the dominant oligopoly would see any incentive to price aggressively. The Minister for the Economy admitted in this regard, at least implicitly, that dominant firms would not benefit from aggressive competition if there was no hope of significantly increasing their market share.[28]

Finally, for coordination to be effective, it must not be disrupted by other market players, either potential current rivals (maverick firms) or clients with a strong buyer power.[29] None of these forces seems to be strong enough on the audit market.

There are strong reasons to doubt there is a maverick on this market that can significantly reduce the profit of the dominant firms by being aggressive due to a drastically different cost structure:[30] first, audit missions are awarded by companies further to bidding processes to which most major audit firms participate. According to economic theory, if the cost structure of alternative firms like Mazars or Grant Thornton were making them more efficient than the Big Four, these firms would own a larger market share. It is not the case as our data show. Second, the size of the international network of Mazars or Grant Thornton is smaller than that of the Big Four (Table 4.1). Third, market shares neither expressed in volume nor in value prove that Mazars or Grant Thornton have proprietary technical capacity that would give them a leading position. We investigate this question further in Section 4.5 econometrically.

Finally, on the audit market the number of capable suppliers is significantly smaller than the number of customers, and the European

Table 4.1   Statistics on the evolution of the number of missions for each possible audit committee

Auditor Name	No.	2006											2005		
		(1)	(2)	(3)	(4)	(5)	(6)	(7)	(8)	(0)	Total	(1)	(2)	(3)
Deloitte	(1)	0	13	9	4	5	1	2	1	4	39	0	13	8
Ernst & Young	(2)	13	1	12	7	10	2	0	0	12	57	13	2	12
PWC	(3)	9	12	2	7	5	1	0	0	5	41	8	12	2
KPMG	(4)	4	7	7	2	5	0	0	1	5	31	3	8	7
Mazars	(5)	5	10	5	5	0	0	0	0	0	25	3	13	4
BDO	(6)	1	2	1	0	0	0	0	0	0	4	1	2	1
Constantin	(7)	2	0	0	0	0	0	0	0	0	2	1	0	0
Grant Thornton	(8)	1	0	0	1	0	0	0	0	2	4	1	0	0
Other	(0)	4	12	5	5	0	0	0	2	2	32	5	12	5
Total		39	57	41	31	25	4	2	4	32	235	35	62	39

Commission has held that significant barriers to entry exist, so that the number of suppliers is not likely to change. To evolve in this industry one needs to employ workers with the same qualifications and in the same conditions as the Big Four, or audit a significant number of major listed companies or, more likely, both. The audit sector has indeed many characteristics of a two-sided platform which brings large companies in contact with experts in accounting, auditing and certification of financial statements, and on which cumulative reputational effects create a barrier to entry.

The fixed (and known) date of bidding contributes to greater transparency of market operations and may ease potential retaliation, should a rival become excessively aggressive. It may also give players the opportunity to get involved in 'bid-rigging'. In practice, with four major audit firms working in a paired statutory auditor scheme, this would mean they would 'win' one call for tenders out of four, or belong to an audit committee out of every two. The amount of fees at stake is well known for future years, and the details on the terms of office of each auditor are known as well, so that the dates of calls for tenders are known. The strategic uncertainty that would be constantly present if mandates could be renewed any time therefore completely disappears, reducing the opportunities for rivals to deviate from the joint practice, simplifying the control of oligopolists' conduct.

	2005							2004								
(4)	(5)	(6)	(7)	(8)	(0)	Total	(1)	(2)	(3)	(4)	(5)	(6)	(7)	(8)	(0)	Total
3	3	1	1	1	5	35	0	17	4	3	2	0	1	1	8	36
8	13	2	0	0	12	62	17	2	9	7	13	1	0	0	15	64
7	4	1	0	0	5	39	4	9	2	4	3	1	0	0	4	27
2	5	0	0	0	6	31	3	7	4	2	5	0	1	0	8	30
5	0	0	0	0	0	25	2	13	3	5	0	0	0	0	2	25
0	0	0	0	0	0	4	0	1	1	0	0	0	0	0	0	2
0	0	0	0	0	0	1	1	0	0	1	0	0	0	0	0	2
0	0	0	0	0	2	3	1	0	0	0	0	0	0	0	2	3
6	0	0	0	2	2	34	8	15	4	8	2	0	0	2	3	45
31	25	4	1	3	34	234	0	64	27	30	25	2	2	3	45	234

4.4 THE DATA

To investigate econometrically the question of the presence of a maverick, we collected data on the various audit firms involved in the legal audit of companies listed in the SBF120. When available, we collected information on the audit firms' organization for France and for the world: the total workforce, the number of managers (partners and auditors; non-executive employees have been deducted from the difference between the number of workers and the number of managers), the number of offices and the number of countries in which the audit firm is present. We used alternative websites of the Big Four, Mazars and Grant Thornton. Data for BDO Marque et Gendrot were obtained from a presentation brochure of the company from 2004. The data for Constantin were obtained from *Le Guide des Cabinets d'Audit et d'Expertise-Copmptable* (3rd edition), by Caura Barszcz (Editions du Management, Paris, 2004; hereinafter 'Guide'). Finally, the data concerning small firms were obtained from the Guide and the entry of the chartered accountants in the databases of Kompass, Diane and Astrée.

We then gathered information on the legal audit missions from the official documents of the SBF120 companies The sample we used includes the SBF120 companies for the accounting years ending in 2004, 2005 and 2006. These data were collected manually using the different sources of information. The names of the auditors of listed companies, the fees, the dates of first appointment, the dates of renewal and the ending date of each appointment were obtained by consulting the general financial statements of these companies for the years 2006 and 2005 (*document de référence*). The statement for 2005 contains in most cases the amount of fees paid to auditors for 2004. These statements for listed companies are available either on the website of the Autorité des marchés financiers (AMF) (http://www.amf-france.org) or on the website of each company, usually under the heading entitled 'Investors'. Only two companies in our database are not forced to appoint two auditors, and audit fees were missing for two companies only in 2004 or 2005.[31] Overall the market for audit services generated by the SBF120 contains 238 mandates.[32]

4.5   THE STRUCTURE AND PERFORMANCE OF THE AUDIT INDUSTRY IN FRANCE

In the *Ernst & Young/Andersen France* case, the European Commission detailed the criteria considered by companies that raise equity on financial markets when appointing statutory auditors: first, auditors must have recognized skills and an international reputation; second, their technical expertise must be of sufficient quality and comply with the recent IFRS standards; last, their network must allow the audit of multiple international subsidiaries. The SBF120 companies is a specific market where these requirements are met. The market for chartered accountancy services is more fragmented, and as evoked in Section 4.2, French laws pay particular attention to conflicts of interest and to the impartiality of legal auditors. Therefore the same audit firm cannot provide both chartered accountancy and statutory audit services, and audit firms may be reluctant to offer consulting services before the renewal of a legal mission for which they would like to bid. We therefore neglect the market for accounting and consulting services, even if economically it would make sense to account for the possibilities of multi-market contact offered by these markets.

The degree of vertical differentiation on the audit market has been acknowledged by competition authorities to be important. When assessing certain mergers, the French competition authority[33] presented a classification that we used to distinguish across companies: on the SBF120, which was retained as the relevant market to assess the merger, Big Four firms were distinguished from the fringe of medium-size auditors (namely Mazars, BDO Marque et Gendrot, Constantin, RSM Salustro and Grant Thornton), and from the smaller companies (such as Corevise or Dauge in Table 4.2). Table 4.1 confirms that the Big Four and their few large rivals operate on most committees of the statutory audit market. Let us describe its content.

Table 4.2   Statistics on the evolution of concentration in market shares (volume and value)

Name	2006				2005				2004			
	No.	C(i) in No. (%)	Fee (m €)	C(i) in Fee (%)	No.	C(i) in No. (%)	Fee (m €)	C(i) in Fee (%)	No.	C(i) in No. (%)	Fee (m €)	C(i) in Fee (%)
Ernst & Young	57	24.3	298.86	29.8	62	26.5	295.13	32.8	64	27.4	297.07	35.1
Deloitte	39	40.9	215.34	51.2	35	41.5	203.72	55.4	36	42.7	177.60	56.1
KPMG	41	58.3	222.13	73.4	38	57.7	183.67	75.8	27	54.3	176.43	76.9
PWC	31	71.5	172.71	90.6	31	70.9	139.56	91.3	30	67.1	110.61	90.0
Mazars	25	82.1	73.40	97.9	26	82.1	60.83	98.1	25	77.8	45.72	95.4
Grant Thornton	4	83.8	4.16	98.3	3	83.3	3.77	98	3	79.1	4.43	95.9
BDO	4	85.5	1.38	98.5	4	85.0	1.14	98.6	2	79.9	0.53	96.0
Constantin	2	86.4	3.18	98.8	1	85.5	0.97	98.7	2	80.8	1.54	96.2
Others	32	100	12.14	100	34	100	11.45	100	45	100	32.45	100
Total	235		1003.32	100	234		900.23	100	234		846.38	100

For each year in our database (2004, 2005 and 2006), Table 4.1 presents the number of missions each audit committee of two members has obtained with a number given to each auditor, from Deloitte (1) to Grant Thornton (8). The first four numbers are given to the Big Four, and the number (0) summarizes all other small audit companies. For example, for 2006, Ernst & Young (2) and PWC (3) jointly audited 12 SBF120 companies. The table is symmetric along the diagonal, and the column 'Total' indicates the number of SBF120 companies each firm audits that year, that is, the marginal distribution of the number of missions across the different auditors. As mentioned, some of the SBF120 companies had either a single auditor, or the information was missing: hence the diagonal of the table is not empty. This does not apply to the cell at the intersection of line and column (0): two companies have had their accounts constantly audited by two different pairs of small audit firms.[34]

A couple of observations can be made. First, the individual market shares of the Big Four are much larger than all others. This huge difference does not change over the years studied: the medium-size auditors keep the same number of missions, while smaller auditors have lost a significant number of missions, suffering a reduction from 45 in 2004 to 32 audit missions in 2006. The area in grey in Table 4.1 also emphasizes the fact that the Big Four mostly work together, and not with smaller auditors, apart Ernst & Young which works with Mazars and smaller auditors regularly over the three years. Smaller firms can sometimes audit the financial statements of listed companies, but this very unusual situation occurs only when smaller firms act together with a bigger auditor, and only for a very small fee suggesting that a small number of tasks are performed.

Concentration in market shares is very high on this market, as Table 4.2 shows, in terms of volume but also in terms of value, measured by the amount of audit fees controlled by each of the companies. This concentration is also stable over the period. To examine the supply abilities of audit companies, we analysed the information on the number of workers when available. Substantial differences in sizes between the Big Four and medium-size auditors appear in Table 4.3: the ability of medium-size auditors to operate in France is much lower than that of the Big Four. The technology to conduct an audit or chartered accountancy mission is essentially intensive in highly qualified labour; the capacity of a firm to lead a large number of missions depends on the number of qualified employees it has and the speed at which they can adapt to the specific mission. Highly qualified and flexible labour is therefore required. The main markets in which audit firms are active are therefore service markets (audit and chartered accountancy missions) as a supplier, but also the highly skilled labour market as a buyer: audit firms, especially the Big Four, hire junior

Table 4.3 Statistics on auditors

Auditor	Category	Averages 2004–2005–2006		Data (compiled from multiple sources)						
		Average number of missions	Average audit fees	Number of executives (France)	Number of workers (France)	Total (executives + workers) (France)	Number of offices (France)	Number of workers + executives (World)	Number of offices (World)	Number of countries
Ernst & Young	Big	61	10,045.79	355	4,723	5,078	15	114,000	640	140
PriceWaterhouse Coopers	Big	33	12,653.85	290	3,210	3,500	25	142,000	770	129
Deloitte	Big	50	98,38.05	171	3,829	4,000	100	135,000	670	150
KPMG	Big	23	9,874.96	350	6,650	7,000	195	113,000	731	148
Mazars	Medium	21	3,715.81	130	1,870	2,000	19	13,000	ua*	55
Grant Thornton	Medium	3	1,258.59	70	806	876	25	22,066	484	100
BDO Marque et Gendrot	Medium	3	164.33	76	724	800	15	22,000	560	100
Constantin	Medium	1	1,200	72	428	500	26	14,856	448	n.a.
RSM Salustro	Medium	6	70,83.33	100	1,300	1,400	195	20,500	600	75
Corevise	Small	3	356.67	5	45	50	1	n.a.	n.a.	n.a.
Dauge	Small	3	284.67	4	19	23	1	n.a.	n.a.	n.a.

auditors from French engineering and business schools who are attracted by career prospects based both on potential partnership and the chance to meet top management of major listed groups.

4.6   AN ECONOMETRIC TEST FOR THE PRESENCE OF A MAVERICK

We now present a test of the presence of a maverick on the audit market in France for the SBF120 companies. As described in the introduction, the definition of a maverick given in Ivaldi et al. emphasizes the asymmetry in terms of cost of supply of the 'maverick' and those of other companies that may tacitly collude. As our data show, the auditors of the medium-size group have a much smaller market share than the Big Four, indicating that their infrastructure does not allow them to bid more aggressively than any of the Big Four in a call for tender. Nonetheless, amongst them Mazars is sufficiently close to KPMG in terms of market share to test whether it is a maverick or not.

In terms of international network, Mazars has offices in 55 countries, while the Big Four operate in 140 countries on average, as Table 4.1 shows. Similarly, Mazars employs 13,000 people internationally, while on average the Big Four employ 126,000 people abroad. If Mazars decided to sharply reduce its prices for obtain new missions, how would it handle this workload, given its limited production capacity (that is, the number of employees) well below that of the Big Four? Actually a too fast reading of Tables 4.2 and 4.3 would suggest that Mazars, which owns a similar number of audit missions as KPMG (before its takeover of Salustro), is in a better position than KPMG: indeed it is offering its services at an average price over the period three times lower than that of KPMG. The same simplistic analysis would suggest that this price differential could be the consequence of a cost differential: Mazars employs an overall number of workers two times smaller than KPMG. But these observations do not take into account either the international dimension of the auditing services delivered by the Big Four, or their technical ability in terms of geographical coverage. It suffices to compare the number of workers employed worldwide to understand this difference. This phenomenon is amplified by audit fees differentials: if Mazars and KPMG have market shares that are close enough in volume before the takeover of Salustro, the market value of the firms Mazars audits is much smaller than that of KPMG. Only an econometric analysis allows us to solve this contradiction. The same applies to the other medium-size group auditors. Moreover, if any of them owned the technical capabilities or had a drastically different cost structure allowing then to win tenders against the Big Four, the market share of this firm would be much higher than that of the Big Four. The market share of auditors of the medium-size group is at best similar and generally lower than that of the Big Four: in practice, therefore, there is no evidence that any firm of the medium-size group can compete directly with the Big Four. Hence we limit the test to verify whether Mazars plays this role or not.

We can now detail the econometric strategy we followed. As most SBF120 companies must have a committee composed of at least two auditors whose identities are public, we propose to model the supply of audit missions: the dependent variable we seek to explain is the sum of the market capitalizations of the companies audited by a couple of auditors in the market, that is, we added up for each pair of auditors the market capitalizations of all companies of the SBF120 they are auditing. This is a direct measure of the effective supply of audit services. Indeed, as the market capitalization of a company measures its profitability, past, present and future, it measures implicitly the complexity as well as the amount of audit works it requires. It is expected to increase with output prices (namely audit services prices) and to decrease with input prices. As a couple of auditors provides their services at the minimum cost for a given quality, the explanatory variables are related to observable cost, such as the number of employees abroad that the pair of auditors employs, to observable quality measured by specific effects and to unobservable quality.

The estimated model is of the form:

$$\ln y_i = \delta_i + \alpha p_i + \zeta_i,$$

where i is the index representing a pair of auditors, y_i is the proposed measure of supply by i, δ_i is a combination of observable cost and quality variables of the chosen pair of auditors, ζ_i is a non-observable effect and, finally, p_i is the fee for this pair of auditors, measured as the sum of the average fees charged by each of the two auditors on all of their mandates in the SBF120. In other words, this price is a representative price of this pair of auditors. We estimate this model for the year 2006, and we test various specifications of the variables describing the quality of the auditors, with different estimation techniques. Table 4.4 provides the ordinary least squares (OLS) estimates.[35]

In the estimations reported in Table 4.4a, the observable quality δ_i of the pair of auditors includes the sum and the product of the number of foreign employees of the two auditors of the committee, and two dummies, one that is worth 1 if the two auditors belong to the Big Four group and 0 otherwise, and the other that is equal to 1 if one of the auditors belongs

Table 4.4a   OLS estimation of the model of choice of an audit committee: Mazars considered as a medium-size auditor

Variable	Estimated parameter	Student value
Constant	7.12239	9.8
Price	0.00047	2.8
Number of workers abroad: sum	−0.02193	−2.0
Number of workers abroad: product	−0.00033	−1.6
Pair of auditors contains 2 'Big'	9.12148	3.0
Pair of auditors contains 1 'Big' and 1 'Medium'	2.24342	3.8
R-square	0.77	

Table 4.4b   OLS estimation of the model of choice of an audit committee: Mazars considered as a big-size auditor

Variable	Estimated parameter	Student value
Constant	7.15209	10.1
Price	0.00003	0.1
Number of workers abroad: sum	0.00246	0.2
Number of workers abroad: product	0.00004	0.5
Pair of auditors contains 2 'Big'	3.26505	4.1
Pair of auditors contains 1 'Big' and 1 'Medium'	0.61200	1.2
R-square	0.78	

to the Big Four and the other belongs to the group of medium-size firms. All variables are statistically significant. The price index has a positive estimated coefficient, indicating that supply increases with the audit fees. As expected, the audit committees composed of two auditors amongst the Big Four have a larger supply than the committees composed of one Big Four and a medium-size auditor, or composed of no Big Four at all. This indicates that the quality of the Big Four is perceived as larger than the quality of other auditors, once price and auditors' characteristics (as the number of employees) have been controlled for. In this first estimation, Mazars has been considered as a 'medium' firm.

To test for the presence of a maverick according to the definitions retained by competition authorities, we estimated this model again, but moving Mazars from the medium to the Big Four category. The estimation results are presented in Table 4.4b. All the results have been turned

Table 4.4c *OLS estimation of the second model of choice of an audit committee: Mazars considered as a medium-size auditor*

Variable	Estimated parameter	Student value
Constant	6.35317	7.0
Price	0.00062	7.3
At least one of the 2 auditors is 'Big'	−2.64721	−2.4
At least one of the 2 auditors is 'Medium'	0.74177	1.7
R-square	0.65	

upside down: only the dummy indicating that both auditors of the committee are Big Four firms remains statistically significant outside of the constant. Neither the price nor the dummy which indicates that the committee is composed of a Big Four and a medium-size auditor are significant anymore. In other words, considering Mazars as a Big Four is not accepted by the data generating process, and hence it cannot be considered as a competitor endowed with the same abilities as the Big Four. It is interesting to note that the estimated price effect is drastically changed by the new specification of the model: the effect of an increasing fee is divided by 2, and not significant anymore.

To analyse the observable quality and further isolate the effects of the classification of the auditors, we keep only the dummy variables that relate to the auditors' classification, and we remove the variables relating to the number of employees. In the estimation reported in Table 4.4c, the dummy variables that characterize the quality include a dummy that takes the value 1 when at least one of two auditors for a pair of auditors is a Big Four and zero otherwise, and a dummy equal to 1 when at least one of two auditors for a couple of auditors is a 'medium' firm and zero otherwise. To put it differently, the estimated constant term is the constant of the equation estimated for an audit committee composed of two small firms. In the first estimation, Mazars is again considered a 'medium'. The estimated parameters are all significant. Supply is an increasing function of the price paid. The increase in supply caused by the quality of the audit committee is reduced compared to the first model estimated: the dummy 'at least one Big Four in the committee' includes all SBF120 committees except four. It is noticeable that when an auditor is 'big' then the quality is higher than when an auditor is 'medium'. Table 4.4d shows the results of the same model when Mazars is considered as a Big Four. The results in this last specification do not change too much, apart from the statistical significance of the dummy indicating the presence of a medium-size firm.

Table 4.4d   OLS estimation of the second model of choice of an audit committee: Mazars considered as a big-size auditor

Variable	Estimated parameter	Student value
Constant	6.63413	−6.9
Price	0.00062	7.0
At least one of the 2 auditors is 'Big'	−2.78557	−2.5
At least one of the 2 auditors is 'Medium'	0.17160	0.3
R-square	0.62	

Again this test suggests that Mazars is not ranked well when considered as a Big Four.[36]

4.7 CONCLUSION

This chapter contributes to the assessment of the risks of collective dominance in the audit industry in France by following the *Airtours* criteria and proposing a test for the presence of a maverick on the market. We estimate alternative specifications of the supply of competitors on the market, and compare the results of these various estimations against each other. To perform these comparisons, we collected an original dataset over the period 2004 to 2006 that contains all the fees paid to audit committees by companies listed on the French marketplace in Paris that are part of the SBF120 index. The specificity of the French audit sector on which we perform this test is to ask companies to hire an audit committee composed of two firms; this obligation increases transparency and reduces the number of firms competing to obtain a mission. This industry is characterized by a huge concentration of market shares, both in volume (number of missions) and in value (audit fees), and by a high degree of vertical differentiation: the Big Four and the medium-size audit firms do not seem to be competing on the same market. The consequences of the French legislation in force in the audit sector are to increase market transparency and ensure that retaliation is possible as we discussed. The third criterion, that is, the absence of a competitive force that can break collective dominance, is supported by an econometric test: the supply of medium-size companies is not considered as a substitute for the supply of the Big Four. Hence our work tends to prove that the three cumulative *Airtours* criteria are met. From a policy perspective, our study calls for a clarification of regulatory rules to create a level playing field facilitating competition in the audit market and to ensure that the audit industry as a whole provides the optimal level of financial information required by our economy.

NOTES

1. The authors participated in certain mergers referred to in the chapter in their professional capacity. The opinions expressed herein are purely personal and in no way bind the firms and/or institutions in which the authors practice, nor their clients.
2. Guidelines on the assessment of horizontal mergers under the Council Regulation on the control of concentrations between undertakings, point 22 b), OJEU C 31/5, 5 February 2004; Guidelines of the Competition Authority, 'Autorité de la Concurrence', on merger control, point 453, at http://www.autoritedelaconcurrence.fr/doc/ld_mergers_dec09.pdf.
3. Ibid.
4. CFI, 6 June 2002, case T-342/99, *Airtours v. Commission of the European Communities*.
5. See http://ec.europa.eu/competition/mergers/studies_reports/the_economics_of_tacit_collusion_en.pdf.
6. ECJ, 13 July 2006, case C-413/06, *Bertelsmann v. Impala*.
7. ECJ, 13 July 2006, case C-413/06, *Bertelsmann v. Impala*, supra, points 123 to 125.
8. Decision of the European Commission dated 20 May 1998 in case No. IV/M.1016 – *PriceWaterhouse Coopers & Lybrand*.
9. Decision of the European Commission dated 5 September 2002 in case No. COM/M.2816 – *Ernst & Young/Andersen France*.
10. See http://ec.europa.eu/internal_market/auditing/index_en.htm.
11. C 2004-157 – Letter of the Minister of State, Minister for the Economy, Finance and Industry dated 19 November 2004 to Counsel for KPMG SA related to a merger in the audit and chartered accountancy sector.
12. C 2006-91 – Letter of the Minister for the Economy, Finance and Industry dated 15 December 2006 to Counsel for Deloitte related to a merger in the audit, chartered accountancy and consulting sectors.
13. Decisions of the European Commission in cases No. IV/M.1016 and No. COMP/M.2816, supra; decisions of the Minister for the Economy and Finance in cases C 2004-157 and C 2006-91, supra, Conseil d'Etat ('CE'), 30 June 2006, No. 283479, Fiducial Audit and Fiducial Expertise; CE, 31 July 2009, No. 305903, Fiducial Audit and Fiducial Expertise.
14. Discussion is based on O. Billard, M. Ivaldi and S. Mitraille (2011), 'Evaluation of the risks of collective dominance in the audit industry in France', *European Competition Journal*, 7(2), August.
15. Article L. 823-2 of the Commercial Code.
16. This may include management consulting, financial assistance and taxation, advisory services for failing firms, or audit and chartered accountancy services for small- and medium-sized companies.
17. See Article L.822-11-II of the French 'Code de Commerce' (commercial code hereafter).
18. Moreover since 1 August 2006, article L.822-14 of the commercial code prohibits individual statutory auditors from certifying the financial statements of a listed company for more than six consecutive fiscal years. This is of no concern for our database that covers 2004 to 2006.
19. Directive 2003/71/EC of the European Parliament and of the Council of 4 November 2003 on the prospectus to be published when securities are offered to the public or admitted to trading and amending Directive 2001/34/EC.
20. Guidelines on the assessment of horizontal mergers under the Council Regulation on the control of concentrations between undertakings, point 47, OJEU C 31/5, 5

February 2004; Guidelines of the Competition Authority on merger control, point 461, at http://www.autoritedelaconcurrence.fr/doc/ld_mergers_dec09.pdf.

21. Decision of the European Commission dated 20 May 1998 in case No. IV/M.1016 – PriceWaterhouse Coopers & Lybrand, point 100.

22. C 2004-157 – Letter of the Minister of State, Minister for the Economy, Finance and Industry dated 19 November 2004 to Counsel for KPMG SA related to a merger in the audit and chartered accountancy sector; CE, 31 July 2009, No. 305903, Fiducial Audit and Fiducial Expertise.

23. C 2006-91 – Letter of the Minister for the Economy, Finance and Industry dated 15 December 2006 to Counsel for Deloitte related to a merger in the audit, chartered accountancy and consulting sectors.

24. Article 22-3 of the Autorité des Marchés Financiers regulations.

25. C 2006-91 – Letter from the Minister for the Economy, Finance and Industry dated 15 December 2006 to Counsel for Deloitte, related to a merger in the audit, chartered accountancy and consulting sectors. Decision of the European Commission dated 5 September 2002 in case No. COMP/M.2816 – *Ernst & Young France/Andersen France*.

26. Letter from the Minister for the Economy, 15 December 2006, C 2006-91, *Deloitte/ BDO Marque et Gendrot*.

27. C 2006-91 – Letter of the Minister for the Economy, Finance and Industry dated 15 December 2006 to Counsel for Deloitte related to a merger in the audit, chartered accountancy and consulting sectors.

28. C 2006-91 – Letter of the Minister for the Economy, Finance and Industry dated 15 December 2006 to Counsel for Deloitte related to a merger in the audit, chartered accountancy and consulting sectors, p. 22.

29. Guidelines on the assessment of horizontal mergers under the Council Regulation on the control of concentrations between undertakings, points 56 and 57, OJEU C 31/5, 5 February 2004; Guidelines of the Competition Authority merger control, point 467, at http://www.autoritedelaconcurrence.fr/doc/ld_mergers_dec09.pdf.

30. Guidelines of the Competition Authority on merger control, point 467.

31. Details are available upon request.

32. However, in theory, public corporations may not be obliged to publish consolidated financial statements and are therefore not bound to appoint two statutory auditors.

33. The French Ministry of Economy through the DGCCRF was in charge of assessing the economic effect of the Deloitte/BDO merger.

34. These companies of the SBF120 are Rodriguez group and Guyenne Gascogne.

35. The results of the IV estimation with the average price for 2004 and 2005 as an instrument are available upon request. Computer programs for estimation and preparation of databases are also available from the authors upon request.

36. The IV estimation we performed gives the same results.

5. Optimal decisions in two-stage bundling

Xeni Dassiou and Dionysius Glycopantis

5.1 INTRODUCTION

Bundling has been discussed as an instrument of second degree price discrimination with distinct original contributions by a number of authors. Among them are Adams and Yellen (1976), McAfee et al. (1989) and Schmalensee (1984). There is also an original contribution by Stigler (1968). Typically a uniform distribution was used to describe the valuation of consumers for two goods. On the other hand, Schmalensee used the bivariate normal distribution.

In Dassiou and Glycopantis (2006, 2008), using the uniform distribution we show that mixed bundling (where the consumers self-select among buying neither good, only one good or both goods bundled together) leads to an increase in profits and if practised by a monopsonist to an increase in trade for its trading partners.

The discussions in the literature have produced concrete results. We refer to these and where appropriate we explain the contribution in the present chapter. We assume that the buyers' valuations of the two goods are distributed according to a bivariate normal distribution. The monopolist firm uses a pure bundling approach through the construction of a composite good. We will explain this approach in detail below.

Bundling increases the proportion of valuations around the mean by reducing the dispersion among the buyers. While this is good news in the case of low marginal costs, in the opposite case the seller will want to increase rather than decrease the dispersion of valuations. This is because if the marginal costs are greater than the mean valuation, bundling will decrease profits – by reducing the size of the lucrative fraction of buyers whose mean valuation exceeds the marginal cost of the bundle.

This suggests that the manipulation of the mean valuation is as important. Yet this is largely neglected in the bundling literature; instead the focus has been on the fact that bundling reduces dispersion and this allows the monopolistic firm to extract more of the consumers' surplus. In our chapter we study a form of pure bundling that is not mean preserving. We return to this point below.

A second point regards the manipulation of dispersion. The standard deviations of the valuations for the goods in a bundle are sub-additive unless the goods are perfectly correlated. In other words, bundling reduces the effective dispersion of the reservation prices. However, bundling is based on the conventional approach of assigning equal weights for the two goods in a bundle. Schmalensee notes that if symmetry (that is, $\sigma_1 \simeq \sigma_2$) does not hold, pure bundling is less likely to be profit or welfare enhancing. He therefore argues that in this case the mixed bundling approach is preferable.

However, if the weights of pure bundling can be optimized by the firm this may no longer be the case. The ability to set weights may effectively resolve the problem of a lack of symmetry in standard deviations without having to resort to a mixed bundling approach. Weight manipulation may ameliorate the desire to reduce dispersion. Moreover, it might also lead to an increase in the weight of a good that despite its relatively higher dispersion has a substantially higher mean valuation.

There are also a number of results in the literature that highlight the importance of the correlation in tastes. Crawford (2008) notes that the heterogeneity reduction in tastes achieved by bundling networks is greater the more negatively correlated the tastes for the goods included are. Using bundle-sized pricing, Chu et al. (2011) show that if consumers can themselves select which goods (theatrical plays in their example) to include in a bundle of predetermined size and price, they will include goods for which tastes are positively correlated. While this is still profit enhancing, it is less so than that of combining goods whose valuations are negatively correlated as in the Crawford example.

Issues connected explicitly with risk aversion have been considered by De Graba (2005) who introduces the idea of price discrimination without bundling. He finds that the firm will be willing to sacrifice some profit in order to increase the probability of making a sale to a large purchaser. Dana (1998, 1999a, 1999b) argues that price dispersion occurs because of stochasticity, and that firms set different prices, including discounts, to smooth out demand and reduce uncertainty. The work of Dana is discussed in Gaggero and Piga (2009) within the context of pricing strategies pursued by airlines.

Dana and De Graba show that the existence of price differentials is a 'defensive mechanism' for responding to uncertainty, rather than an 'aggressive mechanism' for extracting surplus through price discrimination as it is typically stressed in the bundling literature. In our model risk aversion intensifies the desire to reduce dispersion. The reduction in dispersion may enable the firm to better capture consumer surplus and this will lead to an increase in profits. The desire to reduce dispersion may be either tempered or strengthened by the desire to increase the average (mean) demand for the bundle.

In the literature the weights of the two goods in the bundle are taken as fixed. For example, Schmalensee assumes that the two goods participate in the bundle with a ratio of 1:1. The firm determines the optimal bundle price through the maximization of its profit function. Our chapter breaks from this tradition. We first formulate a utility function of the firm based on the composition of the bundle means, variances, correlation in tastes and the firm's degree of risk aversion. The weights of the two goods are chosen by the firm using a portfolio maximization approach. It is then that the monopolist proceeds to determine through profit maximization the bundle price. Comparing our optimal pure bundling to Schmalensee's, we show that in our framework the optimal relative weights are equal only when the difference in the net (of costs) means of the valuations for the two goods is equal to the degree of absolute risk aversion times the difference in the variances.

Our analysis has important policy implications. The first important point is that while portfolio optimization attempts by a company to reduce dispersion through bundling may be detrimental to consumer surplus, this may be counteracted by the fact that at the same time an increase in the bundle mean may be achieved, which is both profit as well as consumer surplus enhancing. The second, more striking point is that the desire to increase the bundle mean may ultimately lead to a choice of weights such that the result is an increase rather than a decrease in dispersion. In this case, bundling will lead to a further increase in consumer surplus and hence to it being an unambiguously welfare enhancing practice.

Section 5.2 provides a preliminary background to the main investigation. It considers the case of unbundled sales and derives comparative static results for profits, consumer surplus and social welfare with respect to the mean and dispersion of the normal distribution that describes the consumers' valuations for a single good. The results are of relevance for the next section, as the bundle is in effect a composite good. Section 5.3 discusses in detail our approach to pure bundling where the consumer valuations of the two goods are given by a bivariate normal distribution. It analyses how the optimal weights and then the bundle price are obtained. It derives comparative static results and makes comparisons with the conventional fixed weights approach. Section 5.4 concludes the discussion.

5.2   RESULTS BASED ON SEPARATE SALES OF GOODS

Our model is based on Schmalensee's specification. We examine briefly the case of one good and derive comparative static results that we will use in our analysis of pure bundling. We are interested in the effect of changes in the mean and dispersion on profits, the consumer surplus and total welfare.

Assuming a density function of buyers for a single good sold separately $g(x)$, the demand for this good can be written as:

$$Q(P) = \int_P^\infty g(x)\,dx. \tag{5.1}$$

$g(x)$ is the underlying distribution of the buyers' valuations for the good and $Q(P)$ is the cumulative distribution. Each consumer who has a valuation for the good greater than its price buys one unit of the good. This valuation is described by $g(x)$ that is assumed to follow the normal distribution with mean and standard deviation μ and σ.

Let $f(t)$ be the standard normal density function, and define:

$$1 - F(x) = 1 - \int_{-\infty}^x f(t)\,dt. \tag{5.2}$$

$F(x)$, the cumulative distribution function, is everywhere strictly increasing and it is straightforward to show that:

$$F'(x) = f(x),\ F''(x) = \tfrac{df(x)}{dx} = -xf(x),\ \int_x^\infty tf(t) = f(x),\ \tfrac{f(x)}{1 - F(x)} > x.$$

The demand for a single good is thus given by $Q(P) = 1 - F(\frac{P - \mu}{\sigma})$. Below we will examine the impact on profits and consumer surplus of changes in the mean and the dispersion.

Calculating the derivatives $Q'(P)$ and $Q''(P)$ we see that the demand function is decreasing and strictly convex for $P > \mu > 0$, and strictly concave for $P < \mu$. We can think of the curvature of the demand function as being measured by $A = -\frac{Q''(P)}{Q'(P)} = \frac{P - \mu}{\sigma^2}$. A has the same sign as $Q''(P)$, which is negative for $P < \mu$; $A < 0$ is similar to the absolute risk aversion parameter applied to a utility function. For a concave function of utility of demand, its absolute risk aversion measure α ($\alpha > 0$) is enhanced by A in this case (for example, $\alpha > |A|$). We will return to this discussion in the next section.

The profit function of the supplying firm also follows the normal distribution as it is linear in demand:

$$\Pi = (P - C)\left(1 - F\left(\frac{P - \mu}{\sigma}\right)\right). \tag{5.3}$$

Profit maximization results to the following first order conditions (FOC) and second order conditions (SOC) respectively:

$$\left(1 - F\left(\frac{P* - \mu}{\sigma}\right)\right) = \frac{P* - C}{\sigma} f\left(\frac{P* - \mu}{\sigma}\right), \tag{5.4}$$

$$(P* - C)(P* - \mu) < 2\sigma^2. \tag{5.5}$$

Combining the price cost margin condition $\frac{P* - C}{P*} = \frac{1}{\eta}$, where η is the absolute value of the elasticity of demand, with $\frac{f(x)}{1 - F(x)} > x$ we obtain:

$$(P* - C)(P* - \mu) < \sigma^2. \tag{5.6}$$

The above means that the SOC is always satisfied. It can be rewritten as:

$$\frac{\mu + C - \sqrt{(\mu - C)^2 + 4\sigma^2}}{2} < P* < \frac{\mu + C + \sqrt{(\mu - C)^2 + 4\sigma^2}}{2}. \tag{5.7}$$

The inclusion of $P* = \mu$ in the above interval means that the demand, and through it the profit function, are not globally concave.

We need to obtain the effect of a change in the parameters of the demand on the profit maximizing optimal price. From implicit differentiation of the FOC with respect to μ and invoking relation (5.6) is easy to show that:

$$0 < \frac{dP*}{d\mu} < 1. \tag{5.8}$$

Similarly,

$$\frac{dP*}{d\sigma} = \frac{(P* - C)(P* - \mu)^2 - [2P* - (\mu + C)]\sigma^2}{(P* - C)(P* - \mu) - 2\sigma^2} \frac{1}{\sigma}. \tag{5.9}$$

It is important to establish conditions for the sign of the change in optimum price with respect to the dispersion. The above two results are used repeatedly below in calculating the various comparative static results. Using straightforward calculations we establish the theorem below.

Theorem 1   For $P* > \mu$ we have $\frac{dP*}{d\sigma} > 0$. For $P* < \mu$ we have $\frac{dP*}{d\sigma} < 0$ unless $\frac{\mu + C + \sqrt{(\mu - C)^2 + 4\sigma^2}}{2} > P* > \frac{\mu + C}{2}$.

This means that a higher dispersion raises the price when the latter is above the mean. A higher dispersion will continue to do so even if the price is a little below the mean (that is, if $P*$ is larger than $\frac{\mu + C}{2}$ without violating the SOC upper boundary for $P*$). Once the price is significantly below the mean a higher dispersion reduces the price.

Next, we wish to consider the impact mean and dispersion changes on the maximum profit. Taking $\frac{d\Pi*}{d\mu}$ and using the envelope theorem we obtain:

$$\frac{d\Pi*}{d\mu} = (P* - C)\left(f\left(\frac{P* - \mu}{\sigma}\right)\right)\frac{1}{\sigma} = \left(1 - F\left(\frac{P* - \mu}{\sigma}\right)\right). \quad (5.10)$$

Invoking the properties of the cumulative distribution function we obtain $0 < \frac{d\Pi*}{d\mu} < 1$. Moreover we have $\frac{d^2\Pi*}{d\mu^2} > 0$. Hence $\Pi*$ is an increasing, convex function of μ.

We also obtain:

$$\frac{d\Pi*}{d\sigma} =$$

$$\left(\frac{P* - C}{\sigma}\right)\left(\frac{P* - \mu}{\sigma}\right)f\left(\frac{P* - \mu}{\sigma}\right) = \left(\frac{P* - \mu}{\sigma}\right)\left(1 - F\left(\frac{P* - \mu}{\sigma}\right)\right). \quad (5.11)$$

It therefore follows that $\Pi*$ is increasing in σ for $P* > \mu$ and decreasing for $P* < \mu$.

We next examine the consumer surplus, CS, given by the sum of the valuations which exceed the price:[1]

$$CS = \int_P^\infty (x - P)f(x)\,dx = CS = \sigma f(\tfrac{P - \mu}{\sigma}) - (P - \mu)(1 - F(\tfrac{P - \mu}{\sigma})).$$

This implies that $CS|_{P=P*} = \sigma f(\frac{P* - \mu}{\sigma})(1 - \frac{(P* - \mu)(P* - C)}{\sigma^2})$. This means that the consumer surplus is strictly positive unless $\sigma = 0$. Hence, the existence of dispersion in demand gives the consumers the opportunity to capture some of the welfare in society, while in the case where $\sigma = 0$ all consumers' valuations are the same and nobody extracts a surplus. Below we examine under what circumstances $CS|_{P=P*}$ is an increasing function of dispersion.

Note that $\frac{\partial CS}{\partial P} = -(1 - F(\frac{P - \mu}{\sigma}))$. Therefore the consumer surplus is a strictly decreasing function of price. It is instructive to split the direct and indirect effect:

$$\frac{dCS}{d\sigma}\Big|_{P=P*} = f\left(\frac{P* - \mu}{\sigma}\right) + \frac{\partial P*}{\partial\sigma}\frac{\partial CS}{\partial P*}\Big|_{P=P*}, \tag{5.12}$$

which means that the direct effect of dispersion on consumer surplus is always positive.

For $P* < \mu$, the consumer surplus is an increasing function of σ always, as both effects are positive unless $P* > \frac{\mu + C}{2}$. This implies that the share of the consumer surplus in the total surplus is larger the smaller dispersion is. As we show in the next section, one of the reasons (albeit not the only one) that may drive the firm into using pure bundling with flexible weights is to manipulate dispersion.

On the other hand, if $P* > \mu$, then the indirect effect is now negative and hence the overall impact depends on whether the direct or indirect effect dominates.

Finally, by adding together the producer and consumer surplus we have:

$$W = \sigma f\left(\frac{P - \mu}{\sigma}\right) + (\mu - C)\left(1 - F\left(\frac{P - \mu}{\sigma}\right)\right). \tag{5.13}$$

Straightforward calculations show that:

$$\frac{\partial W}{\partial P}\Big|_{P=P*} = -\frac{P* - C}{\sigma}f\left(\frac{P - \mu}{\sigma}\right) < 0, \tag{5.14}$$

$$\frac{dW}{d\mu}\Big|_{P=P*} = \left[1 - F\left(\frac{P* - \mu}{\sigma}\right)\right]\left(2 - \frac{\partial P*}{\partial\mu}\right). \tag{5.15}$$

As $\frac{dW}{d\mu}\Big|_{P=P*} = \frac{dCS*}{d\mu} + \frac{d\Pi*}{d\mu}$ and $\frac{d\Pi*}{d\mu} = \frac{(P* - C)}{\sigma}f(\frac{P* - \mu}{\sigma})$ we also have:

$$\frac{dCS*}{d\mu} = \left[1 - F\left(\frac{P* - \mu}{\sigma}\right)\right]\left(1 - \frac{\partial P*}{\partial\mu}\right). \tag{5.16}$$

Given (5.8), the above two relations imply that both $W*$ and $CS*$ are increasing functions of the mean valuation.

Furthermore we can obtain:

$$\frac{dW}{d\sigma}\Big|_{P=P*} = f\left(\frac{P* - \mu}{\sigma}\right)\left(\frac{(P* - C)^2 - 2\sigma^2}{(P* - C)(P* - \mu) - 2\sigma^2}\right). \tag{5.17}$$

The above means that if the profit maximizing price is within $(C - \sqrt{2}\sigma, C + \sqrt{2}\sigma)$, welfare is an increasing function of dispersion. Using the normal distribution frequency tables we can conclude that for $P^* \in (\mu - 0.147\sigma, \mu + 0.147\sigma)$ welfare is a decreasing function of dispersion. We focus on the range of values for which $P^* < \mu$.

For P^* which is less than μ and greater than the critical value $\mu - 0.147\sigma$, we have $\frac{d\Pi^*}{d\sigma} < 0$ and $\frac{dW^*}{d\sigma} < 0$. As both profits and welfare are decreasing functions of dispersion, its reduction is beneficial to society as a whole as it also increases welfare. This means that a reduction in dispersion will, in this case, be beneficial to society as a whole. However this range of values for P^* corresponds to just 7 per cent of the total range of values that the optimal price can take.

If P^* falls below this critical value then $\frac{d\Pi^*}{d\sigma} < 0$ while $\frac{dCS^*}{d\sigma}, \frac{dW^*}{d\sigma} > 0$. In other words, the desire of a profit maximizing firm to decrease dispersion can damage both consumer surplus as well as overall welfare.[2]

The above comparative static results are important for the bundling analysis and conclusions below.

5.3   TWO-STAGE PURE BUNDLING AND COMPARISONS WITH PREVIOUS FORMULATIONS

5.3.1   The Framework of the Analysis

The setting of optimal weights by a risk averse firm in constructing a pure bundle, and the willingness to sacrifice profits in the process of reducing risk can be better understood in the context of two articles that have inspired our approach.

Eckel and Smith (1992) focus their analysis on the cost side of things. The firm manipulates the dispersion of a convex cost function using a portfolio optimization approach. By setting prices for the different demand groups that determine their contribution in total demand, expected outputs are affected and through them expected costs.

Anam and Chiang (2006) look at a risk averse monopolist. The firm faces two different markets with stochastic and correlated demands. They note that the ability to price discriminate if combined with risk aversion may lead to unconventional results. In its drive to reduce dispersion the firm may decide to price the good with the more elastic demand but also risk a higher price. Hence the conventional direction of third price discrimination may be reversed if the sacrifice in expected profit is more than compensated for by the corresponding decrease in profit risk exposure.

We employ a portfolio optimization approach; however unlike Eckel and Smith, this is not mean preserving. We show that the existence of risk aversion may mean that the bundle weights chosen by the monopolist may not only lead to a change in the bundle mean, but also an increase in the bundle dispersion. In this case, the conventional result of an equal weights bundling firm where pure bundling is used as an instrument of reduction in the dispersion of valuations is reversed. This is analogous to the Anam and Chiang's possibility of a reversion of the conventional result in third degree price discrimination.

As we discuss below, the motives of altering the mean and the dispersion can be both in the same direction or in opposite directions. The consumer and welfare implications in the latter case will depend on which of the two effects dominates over the other. The existence of risk aversion from the side of the firm may ameliorate or even reverse competition policy concerns that bundling may be damaging to the interests of consumers; in fact, in some instances the bundle dispersion in the valuations of the consumers may end up to be super-additive (that is, larger than that of the separate sales, $\sigma_1 + \sigma_2$) rather than sub-additive.

We analyse briefly below how the firm determines its portfolio of goods in the bundle. We derive comparative static results for the optimal composition of goods in the bundle. On the basis of this choice the firm then chooses the optimal bundle price. The comparative statics results derived in Section 5.2 are used in comparing the consumer and welfare implications of our results to those of the fixed weights approach by Schmalensee.

5.3.2   Step One: Optimal Weights in Fixed Bundling

We start our analysis with a packaged good, a unit of which is defined. In a way analogous to the previous section, each consumer if she purchases the package has a one unit demand for it. A unit of the composite good consists of a given total number of individual units of Good 1 and Good 2. These goods are measured in similar units, for example, their weights. Although throughout we are concerned with one unit of the packaged good, its composition may vary. Costs, means and standard deviations are all perfectly divisible into fractions of less than one.

For example, imagine a package in mobile phone services that both offers text messages and phone calls (all measured in minutes) for a given monthly fee (bundle price). If the bundle consists of, say, 300 phone calls and 600 text messages, this means that one-third of the bundle is phone calls and the other two-thirds is text messages. Hence one package has 900 minutes.

The decision that the monopolist has to make is first to optimally divide this package into texts and phone calls, and second to price it. We set as λ

the relative weight of Good 1 (phone calls, $\lambda = \frac{1}{3}$) and as $1 - \lambda$ the relative weight of Good 2 (texts) in the package. Normalizing to an overall sum of 2 we obtain $k = 2\lambda = 0.67$ and $2 - k = 2(1 - \lambda) = 1.33$ respectively.[3] The decision that each consumer then has to make is whether to buy this package, that is, the 900 minutes with the weights and price offered by the monopolist.

A number of examples one can think of that this type of bundling belongs to is the family of goods that can be digitized, that is, information goods, where marginal costs are low and constant. We draw our inspiration from the paper by Crampes and Hollander (2005) and that by Crawford, which explain that TV bundles may be composed by combining movies and sport channels.

Optimization is a two-stage approach. In the first step when determining the optimal composition in the bundle we assume risk aversion from the point of view of the monopolist. Once the optimal bundle composition has been set we then proceed to the second step of the calculation of optimal profits. Hence risk aversion is incorporated in the construction of the optimal bundle, which is an internal calculation; the firm is then risk neutral in the calculation of the bundle price that will maximize profits.

The firm's objective before it sets the bundle price, P_B, is to maximize its expected utility, given the bivariate normal distribution $f(x, y)$[4] of the buyers' reservation prices (valuations). The firm decides whether it is worthwhile to bundle and if so at what relative weights. In the second stage the firm calculates the bundle price.[5] As we have mentioned, by manipulating the weights we can affect dispersion and the level of demand.

The marginal densities are given by

$$f_X(x) = \frac{1}{\sqrt{2\pi}\sigma_x} \exp\left(-\frac{(x - \mu_x)^2}{2\sigma_x^2}\right),$$

$$f_Y(y) = \frac{1}{\sqrt{2\pi}\sigma_y} \exp\left(-\frac{(y - \mu_y)^2}{2\sigma_y^2}\right).$$

The valuations x and y for Goods 1 and 2 can be in money form, and so will be the valuation of the bundle $xk + y(2 - k)$. We assume that $\mu_x, \mu_y > 0$. The firm will first set weights to the two goods to maximize its utility function. The utility function is determined by the valuations' distribution characteristics (mean, variance and correlation) as well as the degree of risk aversion by the firm. We will use the term α to express risk aversion; this will reflect the firm's sensitivity to dispersion and other risk aversion factors. We assume that α is constant and positive, as in the usual case of constant absolute risk aversion. Hence we want to:

$$maxJ = \int_{-\infty}^{\infty}\int_{-\infty}^{\infty} -\exp[-\alpha(xk + y(2 - k))]f(x, y)dxdy^{6,7}$$

and it is clear that the risk aversion coefficient α is associated with the normalization $k = 2\lambda$. The above means that we wish to maximize J, the utility function of the firm through a choice of the weights in the bundle. Using the moment generating function, $M_{X,Y}(t_1, t_2) = \exp[(\mu_x t_1 + \mu_y(2 - t_2)) + \frac{\sigma_1^2 t_1^2 + 2\rho\sigma_1\sigma_y t_1 t_2 + \sigma_2^2 t_2^2}{2}]$, with $t_1 = -\alpha k$ and $t_2 = -\alpha(2 - k)$ we can rewrite the optimization function as:

$$maxJ =$$

$$-\exp[-ak\mu_1 - \alpha(2 - k)\mu_2 + (-\alpha)^2\frac{\sigma_1^2 k^2 + 2\rho\sigma_1\sigma_2 k(2 - k) + \sigma_2^2(2 - k)^2}{2}].$$

Applying a monotonic transformation to the above the problem simplifies into:

$$maxK = \mu_1 k + \mu_2(2 - k) - \alpha\frac{\sigma_1^2 k^2 + 2\rho\sigma_1\sigma_2 k(2 - k) + \sigma_2^2(2 - k)^2}{2}.$$

$K > 0$. In other words, the firm wishes to create an optimal bundle, where the weights of the two participating goods are such that the expected utility from the bundle is maximized given the valuations by the consumers and the production costs. In determining the bundle the firm will also take into account the costs of producing the good. We therefore adjust the means so that they are set as net from their corresponding costs. The firm maximizes with respect to λ the following revenue certainty equivalent function which accounts for the loss of utility that the firm experiences given its risk aversion:

$$(\mu_1 - C_1)\lambda + (\mu_2 - C_2)(1 - \lambda) - \alpha\lambda^2\sigma_1^2 - 2\alpha\rho\sigma_1\sigma_2\lambda(1 - \lambda)$$

$$- \alpha(1 - \lambda)^2\sigma_2^2. \tag{5.18}$$

Theorem 2   For $\mu_i - C_i > \mu_j - C_j$, a positive weight for good j requires that $\mu_i - \mu_j - (C_i - C_j) < 2\alpha\sigma_i(\sigma_i - \rho\sigma_j)$. Hence the decision of whether to pure bundle or not, as well as how to balance the goods within the bundle, are both endogenous decisions.

Proof   By first order and second order differentiation of the above expression with respect to λ, we derive the FOC and the SOC. The SOC is satisfied for $\alpha > 0$.[8] From the FOC we obtain the optimal split of the two-unit bundle between the two goods as set out below:

$$k^* = 2\lambda = \frac{(\mu_2 - \mu_1) - (C_2 - C_1) - 2\alpha\sigma_2(\sigma_2 - \rho\sigma_1)}{-\alpha(\sigma_1^2 + \sigma_2^2 - 2\rho\sigma_1\sigma_2)}$$

and

$$2 - k^* = 2(1 - \lambda) = \frac{(\mu_1 - \mu_2) - (C_1 - C_2) - 2\alpha\sigma_1(\sigma_1 - \rho\sigma_2)}{-\alpha(\sigma_1^2 + \sigma_2^2 - 2\rho\sigma_1\sigma_2)}. \quad (5.19)$$

The denominator in the above ratios is the SOC, and hence negative. Note 6 derived previously explains why corner solutions will apply in the case where $\alpha = 0$. It follows that unless $(\mu_i - \mu_j) - (C_i - C_j) < 2\alpha\sigma_i (\sigma_i - \rho\sigma_j)$, good j will receive a zero weight within the bundle. This implies either the deletion of an entire product line from the bundle or, less drastically, that the firm needs to consider the use of mixed bundling.

Obviously for $\rho > 0$, a necessary (though not sufficient) requirement for a strictly positive share of the good with the lower mean net of cost, say j, is that the dispersion of tastes in good j multiplied by the correlation coefficient is smaller that the dispersion for the other good, that is, $\sigma_i > \rho\sigma_j$. This is obviously increasingly binding as ρ increases. On the other hand, if $\rho < 0$ this is no longer a requirement.

From inspection of the equalities in (5.19) and assuming that the weights are strictly positive it follows that:

1. For $\mu_i - C_i > \mu_j - C_j$, if $\alpha(\sigma_i^2 - \sigma_j^2) < \mu_i - \mu_j - (C_i - C_j)$, good i has a greater share in the bundle than good $j(k^* > 1)$.
2. The Schmalensee format of one unit of each good pure bundling becomes optimal when $(\mu_i - \mu_j) - (C_i - C_j) = \alpha(\sigma_i^2 - \sigma_j^2)$.
3. For $\mu_i - C_i > \mu_j - C_j$, if $\alpha(\sigma_i^2 - \sigma_j^2) > \mu_i - \mu_j - (C_i - C_j)$, good j has a greater share in the bundle than good i ($k^* < 1$).

(1) and (3) set that the good with the higher net mean in consumer valuations will have a higher (lower) weight if the difference in the net means is more (less) than the difference in the variances multiplied by the risk aversion parameter.

In case (2) the good with the higher net mean valuation also has a higher dispersion and the difference in the net means is exactly offset by the differences in the variances multiplied by the risk aversion parameter. As a result each good will receive an equal weight. This means that equal relative weights is a special case of our approach.

Clearly case (1) will always be satisfied if $\sigma_i < \sigma_j$, as then the left hand side of the inequality is negative. In this case good i is superior to good j both in terms of the net of cost mean, as well as in terms of the variance criterion.

However good i may still be given a greater weight than j in the bundle even when $\sigma_i > \sigma_j$. Hence pure bundling in our model is not always dispersion reducing, as the latter is not always optimal. As shown in (1) if the difference in the net means is sufficiently large, then good i will have a greater weight in the bundle than j despite the fact that $\sigma_i > \sigma_j$. This may cause the dispersion of the bundle to exceed the sum of the dispersion of the two stand-alone goods. We shall return to this point later.

Combining Theorem 2 and (1) we obtain the following result. For an optimal bundling decision such that the good with the higher net mean is given the higher, but strictly less than one relative weight, the condition is:

$$2\alpha\sigma_i(\sigma_i - \rho\sigma_j) > \mu_i - \mu_j - (C_i - C_j) > \alpha(\sigma_i^2 - \sigma_j^2).$$

Going back to the case where $\sigma_i < \sigma_j$, it is still possible for good j to feature in the bundle as long as $\sigma_i > \rho\sigma_j$, which will be more easily (always) satisfied in the case of a low (negative) value of ρ. Hence low correlation between the two goods makes bundling more desirable. While this is a result shared with the Schmalensee paper, given that pure bundling lowers profits the closer ρ is to 1, the weight of each good here is determined, among other things, by the correlation coefficient. We show this more formally below, by first differentiating k^* with respect to ρ.

From the expression for k^* we calculate the derivatives with respect to these various parameters and we obtain the following comparative static results.

As $\frac{dk^*}{d\alpha} = \frac{(\mu_2 - \mu_1) - (C_2 - C_1)}{\alpha^2(\sigma_1^2 + \sigma_2^2 - 2\rho\sigma_1\sigma_2)}$, the weight of the good with the higher net mean (for example, $k^* > 1$) is a decreasing function of α, the degree of absolute risk aversion. As implied by the derivative, the higher the degree of risk aversion, the lower will be the absolute value of its impact on that weight. In other words, risk aversion encourages bundling by enhancing the contribution of the weaker good (the one with the lower net mean) into the bundle, all other things being equal.

Moreover, it is straightforward to show that if $k^* > 1$, $\frac{dk^*}{d\rho} > 0$, while if $k^* < 1$, $\frac{dk^*}{d\rho} < 0$. In other words, the share of the good with a relative weight λ larger than a quarter in the bundle is an increasing function of the correlation coefficient, ρ, while the share of the other good is a decreasing function. A lower ρ boosts the share of the latter good in the bundle and improves its odds of having a non-zero participation in the bundle. Therefore low positive correlation values promote bundling, and even more so negative values of ρ.

If $\frac{dk^*}{d(\sigma_1)} = \frac{2k^*(\rho\sigma_2 - \sigma_1) - 2\rho\sigma_2}{(\sigma_1^2 + \sigma_2^2 - 2\rho\sigma_1\sigma_2)} < 0$ then consequently $\frac{d(2 - k^*)}{d(\sigma_1)} > 0$, the weight of each good is inversely (directly) related to its own (the other good's dispersion).

Finally, as $\frac{dk^*}{d(\mu_i)} = \frac{1}{\alpha(\sigma_1^2 + \sigma_2^2 - 2\rho\sigma_1\sigma_2)} > 0$, the optimal weight of each good in the bundle is directly related to its mean and, as can be easily shown, inversely related to the mean of the other good in the bundle. Also $\frac{dk^*}{d(C_i)} = \frac{1}{-\alpha(\sigma_1^2 + \sigma_2^2 - 2\rho\sigma_1\sigma_2)} < 0$, that is, the optimal weight of each good in the bundle is inversely related to its cost, and, as can easily be shown, directly related to the cost of the other good in the bundle.

5.3.3 Step Two: Optimal Bundle Price

Having derived the optimal weights for the two goods, we now proceed to derive the profit maximizing bundle price. The firm will offer the bundle good at the specific price as a take it or leave it option (pure bundling). As this composite good consists of Goods 1 and 2, its valuation will be the weighted sum of the valuations x and y and it will itself be normally distributed.

We define the profit function of the composite good, using our profit function as defined in relation (5.3) of Section 5.2. As Π^*_{B,k^*} is the optimal profit when the weights are set as $k = k^*$ and $2 - k = 2 - k^*$, that is,

$$\Pi^*_{B,k^*} = (P^*_{B,k^*} - C_{B,k^*})\left[1 - F\left(\frac{P^*_{B,k^*} - \mu_{B,k^*}}{\sigma_{B,k^*}}\right)\right].$$

Equivalently $\Pi^*_{B,k=2-k}$ is optimal profit when weights are set as $k = 2 - k = 1$, for example, in the Schmalensee model. Π^*_{B,k^*} is different to $\Pi^*_{B,k=2-k}$ unless $\mu_i - \mu_j - (C_i - C_j) = \alpha(\sigma_1^2 - \sigma_2^2)$.

The mean, cost and dispersion of the composite good are defined as:

$$\mu_{B,k^*} = k^*\mu_1 + (2 - k^*)\mu_2,$$

$$C_{B,k^*} = k^*C_1 + (2 - k^*)C_2,$$

$$\sigma_{B,k^*} = \sqrt{(k^*)^2\sigma_1^2 + (2 - k^*)^2\sigma_2^2 + 2k^*(2 - k^*)\theta_{k^*}(1 - \theta_{k^*})} \Leftrightarrow$$

$$\sigma_{B,k^*} = (k^*\sigma_1 + (2 - k^*)\sigma_2)\sqrt{1 - 2(1 - \rho)\theta_{k^*}(1 - \theta_{k^*})},$$

where ρ is the correlation coefficient of the joint reservation distribution and $\theta_{k^*} = \frac{k^*\sigma_1}{k^*\sigma_1 + (2 - k^*)\sigma_2}$.

We note the case where the good i whose net mean and dispersion are both relatively larger also receives a higher weight in the bundle if $(\sigma_i^2 - \sigma_j^2) < \mu_i - \mu_j - (C_i - C_j)$. Setting as $\delta_{k^*} = \sqrt{1 - 2(1 - \rho)\theta_{k^*}(1 - \theta_{k^*})} (0 \leq \delta_{k^*} \leq 1)$, this means that in this case $k^*\sigma_1 + (2 - k^*)\sigma_2 > \sigma_1 + \sigma_2$ and $\delta_{k^*} \geq \delta_{k=2-k}$. Consequently,

$\sigma_{B,k^*} > \sigma_{k=2-k}$. This case is further discussed as Case 3 in Section 3.4 and is of particular interest as it is possible that σ_{B,k^*} may even be larger than $\sigma_1 + \sigma_2$, if $k^*\sigma_1 + (2 - k^*)\sigma_2$ and δ_{k^*} are sufficiently larger than $\sigma_1 + \sigma_2$ and $\delta_{k=2-k}$ respectively.

More generally, the above results imply that optimization alters the bundle dispersion in two ways: by affecting δ_{k^*} as well as by affecting the weighted sum of the two dispersions. θ_{k^*} is in our model a function of ρ; by differentiating with respect to ρ we find that θ_{k^*} is an increasing (decreasing) function of ρ when $\sigma_2 > \sigma_1 (\sigma_2 < \sigma_1)$. If the net means of the two goods are equal, then we have $\theta_{k^*} = \frac{\sigma_2 - \rho\sigma_1}{(1 - \rho)(\sigma_1 + \sigma_2)}$, which for as long as $\sigma_2 > \rho\sigma_1$ guarantees a positive weight for Good 1.

Using relation (5.10) in Section 5.2, it is easy to calculate in an analogous manner that $\frac{\partial\Pi_B^*}{\partial(\mu_{B,k^*} - C_{B,k^*})} = 2[1 - F(\frac{P_{B,k^*}^* - \mu_{B,k^*}}{\sigma_{B,k^*}})]$, which means that:

$$0 < \frac{\partial\Pi_{B,k^*}^*}{\partial(\mu_{B,k^*} - C_{B,k^*})} < 2. \tag{5.20}$$

The derivative of the optimal profit with respect to the variance of the bundle is:

$$\frac{\partial\Pi_{B,k^*}^*}{\partial\sigma_{B,k^*}^2} = \frac{1}{2\sigma_{B,k^*}}\frac{\partial\Pi_{B,k^*}^*}{\partial\sigma_{B,k^*}} = \left(\frac{P_{B,k^*}^* - \mu_{B,k^*}}{2(\sigma_{B,k^*})^2}\right)\left[1 - F\left(\frac{P_{B,k^*}^* - \mu_{B,k^*}}{\sigma_{B,k^*}}\right)\right]. \tag{5.21}$$

Corresponding range of values and expressions can be derived for the welfare function $\frac{\partial W_{B,k^*}^*}{\partial(\mu_{B,k^*} - C_{B,k^*})}(0 < \frac{\partial W_{B,k^*}^*}{\partial(\mu_{B,k^*} - C_{B,k^*})} < 3)$ and $\frac{\partial W_{B,k^*}^*}{\partial\sigma_{B,k^*}^2}$ respectively.[9] These will be of relevance in the discussion below.

5.3.4 Welfare and Policy Implications of Two-stage Bundling in Relation to Conventional Pure Bundling

In order to analyse the consumer and welfare implications of our pure bundling and make comparisons with the conventional equal weights bundling found in Schmalensee's model we consider three cases.

Using the small increments formula we can define an approximate equality for the difference between the welfare in our model minus the welfare in the conventional equal weights bundling as $\Delta W_{B,k^*}^*$:

$$\Delta W_{B,k^*}^* \cong \frac{\partial W_{B,k^*}^*}{\partial(\mu_{B,k^*} - C_{B,k^*})}\Delta_{nm} + \frac{\partial W_{B,k^*}^*}{\partial\sigma_{B,k^*}^2}\Delta_{var}. \tag{5.22}$$

We set as $\Delta_{nm} = \mu_{B,k^*} - C_{B,k^*} - (\mu_{B,k=2-k} - C_{B,k=2-k})$ the difference in the net bundle means of our model minus that of Schmalensee's pure bundling. We also define $\Delta_{var} = \sigma_{B,k^*}^2 - \sigma_{B,k=2-k}^2$, which is the difference in the variance of the bundle in our model minus the bundle variance in the 1:1 bundling model.

Case 1 $\mu_i - C_i > \mu_j - C_j$ and $\sigma_i < \sigma_j$.

Then $k^* > (2 - k^*)$, $\Delta_{nm} > 0$ and $\Delta_{var} < 0$. Since profit is an increasing function of the net mean and a decreasing function of the dispersion, we have $\Pi_{B,k^*}^* \geq \Pi_{B,k=2-k}^*$. The impact of using optimal bundling on consumer surplus is ambiguous. According to the findings from Section 5.2, consumer surplus is an increasing function of both the net mean as well as dispersion (as $P_{B,k^*}^* < \mu_{B,k^*}$).

Inspecting the impact on welfare, if $(P_{B,k^*}^* - C_{B,k^*})^2 - 2\sigma_{B,k^*}^2 > 0$, then $\frac{\partial W_{B,k^*}^*}{\partial \sigma_{B,k^*}^2} < 0$ as derived from relation (5.17) in Section 5.2. A smaller bundle dispersion increases welfare, and this is further reinforced by a larger bundle mean. Hence in this case our bundling is superior to Schmalensee's both in terms of the profits as well as the total welfare.

On the other hand, if $(P_{B,k^*}^* - C_{B,k^*})^2 - 2\sigma_{B,k^*}^2 < 0$,[10] then $\frac{\partial W_{B,k^*}^*}{\partial \sigma_{B,k^*}^2} > 0$. A larger net mean would still increase welfare, but this will have to be compared to the reduction in welfare from a smaller bundle dispersion. Hence, in this case it is unclear whether the reduction in welfare is smaller or larger than the decrease in welfare induced in the pure bundling of Schmalensee. In other words, while dispersion is further reduced by our brand of pure bundling, the bundle net mean is increased. The latter can more than or less than offset the negative impact on welfare of a larger reduction in the former. We attempt to bring some clarity to this ambiguity below.

It can be shown that:

$$\Delta_{var} = \frac{\Delta_{nm}}{\alpha} + \Delta_{nm} \frac{\sigma_2^2 - \sigma_1^2}{(\mu_2 - \mu_1) - (C_2 - C_1)} \frac{\sigma_2^2 + \sigma_1^2 + 2\rho\sigma_1\sigma_2(1 - 2\alpha)}{\sigma_1^2 + \sigma_2^2 - 2\rho\sigma_1\sigma_2}. \quad (5.23)$$

As in Case 1 $\Delta_{var} < 0$ and $\Delta_{nm} > 0$, we have $\Delta_{nm} < |\Delta_{var}|$ if and only if

$$\frac{(\sigma_2^2 - \sigma_1^2)}{(\mu_1 - \mu_2) - (C_1 - C_2)} \frac{\sigma_2^2 + \sigma_1^2 + 2\rho\sigma_1\sigma_2(1 - 2a)}{\sigma_1^2 + \sigma_2^2 - 2\rho\sigma_1\sigma_2} > 1 + \frac{1}{\alpha}. \quad (5.24)$$

Comparing the size of the rate of change of welfare with respect to the variance to that of the rate of change with respect to the net mean we establish (see Dassiou and Glycopantis, 2011) that the absolute size of the former is smaller than the size of the latter, that is, $\left|\frac{\partial W_{B,k^*}^*}{\partial \sigma_{B,k^*}^2}\right| < \frac{\partial W_{B,k^*}^*}{\partial(\mu_{B,k^*} - C_{B,k^*})}$. Hence, $\Delta W_{B,k^*}^* \geq 0$ if $\frac{\partial W_{B,k^*}^*}{\partial \sigma_{B,k^*}^2} \leq 0$, or if $\frac{\partial W_{B,k^*}^*}{\partial \sigma_{B,k^*}^2} > 0$ and $\Delta_{nm} \geq |\Delta_{var}|$. The change in welfare $\Delta W^*_{B,k*}$ will still be non-negative even if $\frac{\partial W^*_{B,k*}}{\partial \sigma^2_{B,k*}} > 0$, and $\Delta_{nm} < |\Delta_{var}|$, unless the following proposition (proved in Dassiou and Glycopantis, 2011) holds:

Proposition 1 $\Delta W^*_{B,k*} < 0$ *if and only if* $\frac{\partial W^*_{B,k*}}{\partial \sigma^2_{B,k*}} > 0$, $\Delta_{nm} < |\Delta_{var}|$ *and* $\frac{|\Delta_{var}|}{\Delta_{nm}} =$

$$\frac{\sigma^2_{B,k=2-k} - \sigma^2_{B,k*}}{\mu_{B,k*} - C_{B,k*} - (\mu_{B,k=2-k} - C_{B,k=2-k})} > \frac{\frac{\partial W^*_{B,k*}}{\partial (\mu_{B,k*} - C_{B,k*})}}{\frac{\partial W^*_{B,k*}}{\partial \sigma^2_{B,k*}}}.$$

In other words, the case where our type of bundling is welfare inferior to that of the conventional approach is relatively rare. It occurs only when the ratio of the absolute value of the change in the bundle variance to the change in the bundle net mean exceeds the fraction of the marginal rate of change of welfare with respect to the net mean divided by the marginal rate of change with respect to the variance, provided that the latter is positive.

Below we discuss Cases 2 and 3 in which there is a trade off as far as the firm is concerned. It faces a dilemma as the good with the larger net mean also has a larger dispersion. Therefore it has to choose between its desire to increase the former and decrease the latter in order to enhance its profits.

Case 2 $\mu_i - C_i > \mu_j - C_j$, $\sigma_i > \sigma_j$ and $\mu_i - \mu_j - (C_i - C_j) < \alpha(\sigma^2_i - \sigma^2_j)$.

Then $k* < (2 - k*)$, $\Delta_{nm} < 0$ and $\Delta_{var} < 0$. Hence both the mean as well as the dispersion are smaller than that in conventional pure bundling. The inequality $\mu_i - \mu_j - (C_i - C_j) < \alpha(\sigma^2_i - \sigma^2_j)$ means that in this case the overriding criterion for the company in setting the bundle weights is a decrease in dispersion rather than an increase in the bundle net mean. Hence, the optimal weights chosen by the firm will not only produce a smaller dispersion relative to that of conventional bundling, but also a smaller bundle mean. As a result, consumer surplus will be smaller than that in the equal weights bundling as it is an increasing function of both the mean as well as the dispersion. This means that Case 2 is a case where a competition authority is justified to intervene if its primary objective is the protection of consumer surplus.

We now turn our attention to the overall welfare implications. Given that both Δ_{var} and Δ_{nm} are negative, if $\frac{\partial W^*_{B,k*}}{\partial \sigma^2_{B,k*}} > 0$, then both terms in the small increments formula will be negative and welfare will unambiguously decrease. Only in the case where $\frac{\partial W^*_{B,k*}}{\partial \sigma^2_{B,k*}} < 0$ and $|\Delta_{nm}| < |\Delta_{var}|$ we will have to weight the overall positive impact of the change in the variance against the overall negative impact of the change in the net mean in the small increments formula. Then it follows that (Dassiou and Glycopantis, 2011):

Proposition 2 $\Delta W^*_{B,k*} > 0$ *if and only if* $\frac{\partial W^*_{B,k*}}{\partial \sigma^2_{B,k*}} < 0$, $|\Delta_{nm}| < |\Delta_{var}|$ *and* $\frac{|\Delta_{var}|}{|\Delta_{nm}|} =$

$$\frac{\sigma^2_{B,k=2-k} - \sigma^2_{B,k*}}{(\mu_{B,k=2-k} - C_{B,k=2-k}) - (\mu_{B,k*} - C_{B,k*})} > \frac{\frac{\partial W^*_{B,k*}}{\partial(\mu_{B,k*} - C_{B,k*})}}{\left|\frac{\partial W^*_{B,k*}}{\partial \sigma^2_{B,k*}}\right|}.$$

Case 3 $\mu_i - C_i > \mu_j - C_j, \sigma_i > \sigma_j$ and $\mu_i - \mu_j - (C_i - C_j) > \alpha(\sigma_i^2 - \sigma_j^2)$.

Then $k* > (2 - k*)$, $\Delta_{nm} > 0$ and $\Delta_{var} > 0$. Here the overriding criterion for the company in setting the bundle weights is an increase in the bundle mean rather than a decrease in dispersion. Clearly, the assignment of a larger relative weight to the good with the larger dispersion in valuations will mean that consumer surplus will definitely be larger than that of the conventional case of equal relative weights pure bundling as the company constructs a composite good whose mean and dispersion are both larger. This will lead to a larger consumer surplus on both counts. This is one case where the policy makers should view bundling in variable proportions favourably as such a strategy followed by the company is very likely to increase consumer and welfare surplus as compared to the case where pure bundling is restricted to fixed proportions.[11] This stance is further strengthened if the weight assigned to the good with the relatively larger mean and variance is such that $\sigma_{B,k*}$ is even larger than $\sigma_1 + \sigma_2$.

5.4   CONCLUDING REMARKS

In this chapter we have analysed a pure bundling model that reflects economic reality and decisions better that the conventional assumption made in the literature. In our discussion we break from the usual approach that assumes that the two goods form a bundle of a fixed 1:1 ratio. Instead we obtain the optimal participation of the goods in the bundle through the maximization of the utility function. This captures through an absolute risk aversion parameter the attitude of the firm as regards demand valuation dispersion.

While the corresponding bundle price is obtained through maximizing profits, our model has the distinct characteristic that the firm is not simply interested in profit, but also in taking only an acceptable level of risk as defined through the optimal bundle composition.

We proceed to consider the consumer surplus and welfare implication of our bundling approach. We distinguish between three different cases characterized by the relation between the net means and dispersions of the implied marginal distributions for the two goods.

In Case 1, the inequalities in the differences in the net means and dispersions are in opposite directions and the company will end up with a smaller bundle dispersion than the one obtained in conventional bundling, while achieving a large profit through a larger bundle mean. If welfare depends positively on dispersion, it is possible that optimal bundling will have an adverse effect on welfare, which is however tempered by the fact of the impact of a larger bundle mean. Unless the dispersion of our bundling method is so substantially smaller than that of the conventional bundling that the impact on the net means is not sufficient to offset the damage this will do, our flexible weights bundling will cause less welfare damage than conventional bundling.

Case 2 is characterized by the fact that (1) the differences in the net means and dispersions are in the same direction and (2) the difference in the net means is smaller than that in the variances multiplied by the parameter of risk aversion. The firm will have bundle net mean and variance smaller than the ones derived in conventional bundling as it will attach a lower weight to the good with the higher dispersion and larger net mean. This affects adversely both the consumer surplus and welfare to a larger extent than conventional fixed weights bundling.

Case 3 is characterized by the fact that (1) the differences in the net means and dispersions are in the same direction and (2) the difference in the net means is larger than that in the variances multiplied by the parameter of risk aversion. The firm will construct a package with a larger variance in tastes by attaching a larger weight to the good with the relatively larger dispersion. The composite good with also have a larger net mean. This will have a beneficial effect in both consumer surplus and welfare relative to that of fixed equal weights.

Finally, we note that the existence of risk aversion makes it possible to have cases of optimal pure bundling where there is no conflict between the bundling decisions of the firm and its effects on society. If the optimal weights are such that the reduction in bundle dispersion is substantial, we may end up with $\sigma_{B,k^*} > \sigma_1 + \sigma_2$. This means that optimal pure bundling will in this case lead to an increase rather than a decrease in the dispersion not only relative to conventional bundling, but also in relation to the case of separate selling of the two goods.

NOTES

1. For a detailed analysis, see Dassiou and Glycopantis (2011) where derivation of formulae and proofs are obtained in the text and in a mathematical appendix.
2. Of course when demand is strictly convex ($P^* > \mu$), the dispersion increasing behaviour of a profit maximizing firm will be beneficial to society as well for as long as $P^* > \mu + 0.147\sigma$.

3. It must be stressed that the use of k is only for computational convenience in the calculations that follow below, and in no way implies two units of the composite good.
4. The underlying distribution for the buyers' valuations for the two goods x (Good 1 valuation) and y (Good 2 valuation) is

$$f(x, y) = \frac{1}{2\pi\sigma_x\sigma_y\sqrt{1 - \rho^2}} \exp\left(-\frac{z}{2(1 - \rho^2)}\right),$$

where $z = \frac{(x - \mu_x)^2}{\sigma_x^2} - \frac{2\rho(x - \mu_x)(y - \mu_y)}{\sigma_x\sigma_y} + \frac{(y - \mu_y)^2}{\sigma_y^2}$ and ρ is the correlation coefficient of the reservation valuations.

5. If P_B is the bundle price then the demand function can be written as: *see notes with corrections*

$$\int_{-\infty}^{\infty}\int_{P_{B-y}}^{\infty} f(x, y)\,dx\,dy.$$

$P_B - y$ P. 13

+p. 104

6. The firm's utility function has a constant absolute risk aversion functional form $-\exp[-\alpha(xk + y(2 - k))]$. If $\alpha = 0$ then the utility function is of the linear form $xk + y(2 - k)$ (Kreps, 1990, p. 85). Hence, expected value maximization will be of the form

$$maxJ = \max\int_{-\infty}^{\infty}\int_{-\infty}^{\infty} [(xk + y(2 - k))]f(x, y)\,dx\,dy = \max[k\mu_1 + (2 - k)\mu_2].$$

The above expression indicates that in this case the firm has zero dispersion sensitivity, corresponding to the case of a risk neutral firm. So for maximizing the firm will need to assign all the weight to either Good 1 or Good 2 depending on which of the two goods has the highest mean (or net mean). Hence, the weights will be either $(0, 2)$ or $(2, 0)$.

7. We show in Dassiou and Glycopantis (2011) that if the utility function is multiplicative and the correlation coefficient between the valuations of the two goods is equal to zero, the combination $k^* = 2 - k^* = 1$ is optimal. This corresponds to Schmalensee's type of conventional bundling.

8. This translates into $P < \mu$. If $A > 0$ ($\alpha < 0$, and positive utility) then there can only be corner solutions where goods are offered separately. This optimality of no bundling when the demand function is convex is also confirmed by Schmalensee who concludes that pure bundling is less profitable than unbundled sales for $P > \mu$.

9. The derivations of these can be found in the mathematical appendix of the Dassiou and Glycopantis (2011) paper as relations (50) and (51) respectively.

10. As $\frac{P_{B,k^*}^* - C_{B,k^*}}{\sigma_{B,k^*}} < \sqrt{2}$ implies that P_{B,k^*}^* is below the critical value $\mu_{B,k^*} - 0.147\sigma_{B,k^*}$.

11. The case of $\Delta W_{B,k^*}^* < 0$ is quite remote: first, we need P_{B,k^*}^* to exceed the critical value $\mu_{B,k^*} - 0.147\sigma_{B,k^*}$ for

$$\frac{\partial W_{B,k^*}^*}{\partial \sigma_{B,k^*}^2} < 0.$$

By inspection of the normal distribution tables there is only a 7 per cent probability of this happening. Additionally, we need $\Delta_{nm} < \Delta_{var}$ and

$$\frac{\Delta_{var}}{\Delta_{nm}} = \frac{\sigma_{B,k^*}^2 - \sigma_{B,k=2-k}^2}{\mu_{B,k^*} - C_{B,k^*} - (\mu_{B,k=2-k} - C_{B,k=2-k})} > \frac{\frac{\partial W_{B,k^*}^*}{\partial(\mu_{B,k^*} - C_{B,k^*})}}{\left|\frac{\partial W_{B,k^*}^*}{\partial \sigma_{B,k^*}^2}\right|} \text{ for } \Delta W_{B,k^*}^* < 0.$$

REFERENCES

Adams, W.J. and J.L. Yellen (1976), 'What makes advertising profitable?', *Economic Journal*, **87**, 427–49.

Anam, M. and S.-H. Chiang (2006), 'Price discrimination and social welfare with correlated demand', *Journal of Economic Behavior and Organization*, **61**, 110–22.

Chu, S., P. Leslie and A. Sorensen (2011), 'Bundle-size pricing as an approximation to mixed bundling', *American Economic Review*, **101**(1), 263–303.

Crampes, C. and A. Hollander (2005), 'Product specification, multi-product screening and bundling: the case of pay TV', *Information Economics and Policy*, **17**(1), 35–59.

Crawford, G.S. (2008), 'The discriminatory incentives to bundle in the cable television industry', *Quantitative Marketing and Economics*, **6**(1), 41–78.

Dana, J.D. (1998), 'Advance-purchase discounts and price discrimination in competitive markets', *Journal of Political Economy*, **106**(2), 395–422.

Dana, J.D. (1999a), 'Equilibrium price dispersion under demand uncertainty', *RAND Journal of Economics*, **30**(4), 632–60.

Dana, J.D. (1999b), 'Using yield management to shift demand when the peak time is unknown', *RAND Journal of Economics*, **30**(3), 456–74.

Dassiou, X. and D. Glycopantis (2006), 'The economic theory of price discrimination via transactions bundling: an assessment of the policy implications', *Review of Law and Economics*, Berkeley Electronic Press, **2**(2), 323–48.

Dassiou, X. and D. Glycopantis (2008), 'Price discrimination through transactions bundling: the case of monopsony', *Journal of Mathematical Economics*, **44**(7–8), 672–81.

Dassiou, X. and D. Glycopantis (2011), 'Optimal pure bundling under Gaussian demand', mimeo, City University.

De Graba, P. (2005), 'Quantity discounts from risk averse sellers', Federal Trade Commission Bureau of Economics, Working Paper 276.

Eckel, C.E. and W.T. Smith (1992), 'Price discrimination with correlated demands', *Southern Economic Journal*, **59**(1), 58–65.

Gaggero, A.A. and C.A. Piga (2009), 'Airline market power and intertemporal price discrimination', Discussion Paper Series, Department of Economics, Loughborough University.

Kreps, D.M. (1990), *A Course in Microeconomic Theory*, Hemel Hempstead, Hertfordshire: Harvester-Wheatsheaf, UK.

McAfee, R.P., J. McMillan and M. Whinston (1989), 'Multiproduct monopoly, commodity bundling and correlation of values', *Quarterly Journal of Economics*, **103**, 371–83.

Schmalensee, R. (1984), 'Gaussian demand and commodity bundling', *Journal of Business*, **57**(1), part 2, S211–S30.

Stigler, G.A. (1968), 'Note on block booking', in G. Stigler (ed.), *The Organisation of Industry*, Homewood, IL: Richard D. Irwin, pp. 165–70.

6. Competition policy and firm's damages

Panagiotis N. Fotis[1,2]

6.1 INTRODUCTION

Antitrust policy aims at preventing companies from abusing market power, restraining free trade and/or forming anti-competitive agreements. Its objective is to foster competition in the interest of consumer welfare. Therefore, effective antitrust laws imposed by competition authorities are fundamental in competition policy as they prevent firms from distorting effective competition.

Regulators can impose legal and regulatory penalties on firms that are caught infringing the competition law so as to dishearten them from engaging in cartels and other anti-competitive behaviour. Optimal antitrust policy demands the costs that firms incur when found guilty of antitrust infringement are high enough to make the infringement unprofitable. The financial sanction should exceed the expected profits from the anti-competitive activity in order to compensate for ineffective detection. Sanctions also may offer an incentive to cartel participants to deviate from the cartel and provide critical information to competition authorities to benefit from leniency.

In this chapter, I carry out an econometric analysis to explore the effect of antitrust and abuse of dominant position investigations on the share value of firms that have infringed Greek competition law. I analyse a sample of major Greek antitrust and abuse of dominant position cases during the period from 2000 to 2010 and I evaluate the private damages imposed to the infringed firms. For this purpose I define the 'Investigation period', which begins from the outset of the investigation and ends when the competition authority issues its final decision to the infringed firms and the 'Deterrence period', which follows the 'Investigation period' and ends with the final judgment of the court of appeal.

I use aggregated data analysis (regression-based approach) to explore the average effect of antitrust and abuse of dominant position cases on the share value of involved firms. The econometric estimations suggest that during the release of the final decisions of the Hellenic Competition

Commission (HCC) and the Supreme Court, the Cumulative Average Residuals (CAR) of the infringed firms drop by –6.04 per cent and –5.07 per cent respectively. Therefore, the release of both decisions negatively affects the share value of the infringed firms.

However, the empirical results also indicate that the down raids, the Statement of Objections (SoO) by the General Directorate of Competition (GDC) of the HCC and the decision of the court of appeal do not significantly affect the share value of the involved firms in the anti-competitive practices.

The remainder of the chapter is organized as follows. Section 6.2 provides the institutional framework and Section 6.3 provides the major steps of an antitrust and abuse of dominant position case during the 'Investigation period' and the 'Deterrence period'. Section 6.4 reviews the literature and Section 6.5 presents the sample and the econometric models. Section 6.6 gives the empirical results and Section 6.7 concludes and provides criteria for further research.

6.2 THE INSTITUTIONAL FRAMEWORK

6.2.1 Calculation of Fines

The HCC is the only competition authority for the enforcement of Greek Competition Law, whose main provision against antitrust and abuse of dominant position infringements are Articles 1[3] and 2 of Law No. 3959/2011[4] (Greek Competition Law).

Fines are imposed on firms that have infringed competition law according to the May 2006 guidelines for setting the amount of fines, in relation to Articles 101 and 102 of the Treaty on the Functioning of the European Union (TFEU).[5] Article 8 of the guidelines states that the base fines may be up to 30 per cent of the company's annual sales in the market to which the antitrust and abuse of dominant position infringement relates. The amount of fine is cumulatively calculated on the annual sales for each year of the offence.

From 2000 to 2009 the HCC imposed a total amount of fines of 290,500,000 euros with respect to Articles 1 and 2 of Greek Competition Law and Article 25(2)[6] of former Competition Law No. 703/77 (Table 6.1).

6.3 MAJOR STEPS OF AN INVESTIGATION BY GDC OF HCC

The GDC of the HCC starts its investigation either at its own initiative (a publication in the media, a non-paper, an unofficial complaint and so on) or

Table 6.1   Total amount of fines for infringements of Articles 1, 2 and 25 of Greek Competition Law from 2000 to 2009 (in thousand euros)

	Years									
	2000	2001	2002	2003	2004	2005	2006	2007	2008	2009
Amount of fines per year	4.4	–	3.3	1.1	0.6	19.2	0.02	103.6	55.5	102.8
Total amount of fines					290,500					

Note: See note 5.

Source: http://www.epant.gr/img/x2/categories/ctg324_1_1275909535.pdf (in Greek).

on the basis of an official complaint[7] by a third party. Generally speaking, there is no public announcement for the outset of an official investigation.

An antitrust and abuse of dominant position investigation contains two crucial sub-periods: the 'Investigation period', which begins from the beginning of the investigation and ends when the competition authority issues its final decision to the infringed firms, and the 'Deterrence period', which follows immediately after the Investigation period and ends with the final judgment of the court of appeal.

The crucial steps of procedure during the Investigation period are the dawn raids, the SoO and the final decision of the HCC. If the GDC has suspicions that there has been an infringement which violates Articles 1 and 2 of Greek Competition Law, it carries out a surprise inspection at the premise(s) of the firm(s) under investigation so as to gather critical documentary evidences for the infringement.

After a period of investigation the GDC issues the SoO and sends it to the firms under investigation. At the same date it publishes a press release with the main points of the SoO, subject to the final decision of the HCC.

Following the period of the trial procedure, which may last from one to three months, and the submission of statements from the involved firms in the case, the HCC issues its final decision, which may or may not accept the SoO by the GDC. At the same date, the HCC publishes a press release with the main points of its decision (Figure 6.1).

The Deterrence period[8] begins immediately after the issue of the final decision of the HCC. Firms that have been fined can appeal to the courts of appeal and the Supreme Court. The courts' judgments may annul, reduce, uphold or even increase[9] the fine as well as annul or uphold the overall HCC's decision.

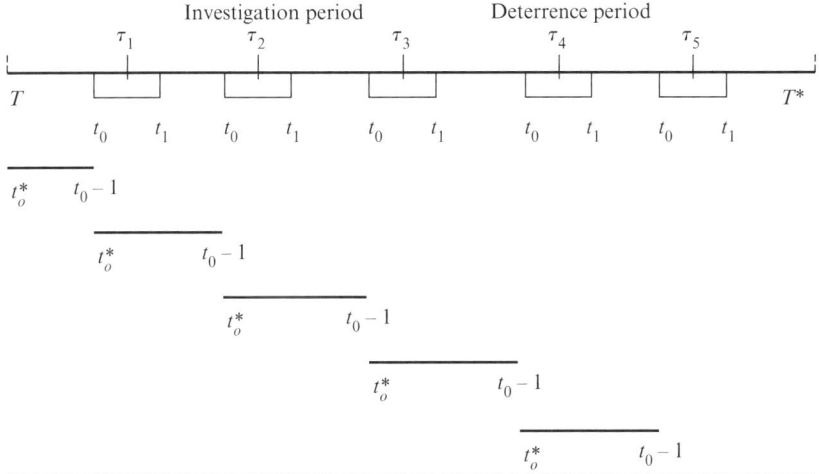

Figure 6.1 Non-overlapping steps of an antitrust and abuse of dominant position case

In this chapter I assume the following public information, which may affect the share price of the infringed firms: (a) the dawn raids; (b) the issue of the SoO; and (c) the final decision of the HCC, which constitute the Investigation period, and the court of appeal decisions, which constitute the Deterrence period.

I denote $t = 0$ the date of release of public information. In Figure 6.1 there are five specific dates which correspond to the five major steps of the case under scrutiny (τ_1 = dawn raids, τ_2 = Statement of Objections, τ_3 = Final Decision of HCC, τ_4 = Pre-final Court of Appeal Decision,[10] τ_5 = Final Court of Appeal Decision). Around τs there are $t = 1 \ldots n$ days that may be affected from the release of the public information. I symbolize the beginning of such a period as t_0 and its end as t_1. Prior to t_0 there are $n - 1$ days that are not affected from the above-mentioned release. I denote t_o^* the beginning of the unaffected period and $t_0 - 1$ its end. The whole period under investigation (T, T^*) includes five sets of $t = 1 \ldots n$ days and five sets of $n - 1$ days that correspond to different periods of time (non-overlapping steps of an antitrust and abuse of dominant position case).

6.4   REVIEW OF THE LITERATURE

Major studies in the last two decades that have attempted to measure the effect of an anti-competitive action on an involved firm's share value are those of Bosch and Eckard (1991), Thompson and Kaserman (2001), Feinberg and Round (2005), Detre et al. (2005), Lübbers (2009), Langus and Motta (2006) and Günster and Mathijs (2010). These studies[11] follow a disaggregate regression event approach in order to evaluate the impact of the antitrust actions on the cumulative residual of the infringed firms.[12]

Bosch and Eckard (1991) analyse a sample of 127 firms involved in 57 US federal price-fixing infringements from 1962 to 1980 and find a statistically significant –1.08 per cent drop of cumulative residual across the infringed firms around the release of the public information. They point out that the critical part of the estimated residual is expected loss of conspiracy-generated profits, rather than reputation damage. Also, they state that price fixing infringement is a profitable deal since its profits exceed expected fines, implying that the deterrence effect of antitrust enforcement actions is small.

Thompson and Kaserman (2001) examine a sample of publicly traded firms in the USA from 1981 to 2000.[13] They outline significant short-term effects on share value of price-fixing firms. They also indicate that virtually all infringed firms' share value losses are regained within one year – suggesting little expectation by investors of long-term changes in an infringed company's behaviour.

Feinberg and Round (2005) examine 13 price-fixing cases brought by the competition authority in Australia for the decade 1992–2001. They found little share value response to price-fixing investigations during the period of investigation. They conclude that relatively small fines have led investors to underestimate the significance of antitrust policy in Australia.

Detre et al. (2005) examine 24 US price-fixing cases involving 31 firms from 1981 to 2001 and find a –3.41 per cent drop of stock return around the release of the public information. The authors do not further evaluate possible causes of the negative effect of public information on firm's share value.

Lübbers (2009) examines the effects of a coal cartel (Rhenish-Westphalian Coal Syndicate or RWKS) that operated in Germany in the late nineteenth and early twentieth centuries on the share value of its members. He concludes that 'contemporary investors believed that the profitability of cartel members would be almost unaffected by the foundation of the RWKS'. The author also evaluates 'accounting, financial, and output figures "which" show neither a positive nor a negative effect of cartelisation on company performance, measured by the Return on Assets (RoA) or Tobin's q'.[14]

Langus and Motta (2006) examine the stock market reaction of 88 firms to 55 European Commission Decisions from 1969 to 2005. They find a statistical drop of the residual of the involved firms in the infringement by

2 per cent around the dawn raid (τ_1) and by 3 per cent around the issuing of the Final Decision (τ_3) of the European Commission (EC). They suggest that the negative impact of the Investigation period on infringed firm's share value results predominantly from lost monopoly profits.

Günster and Mathijs (2010) analyse the stock market response to anti-trust investigation announcements, infringement decisions and appeals. The sample of involved firms includes 253 firms involved in 118 European antitrust cases over the period 1974–2004. They found significantly nega-tive stock price responses of almost –5 per cent around the dawn raid and 2 per cent around the Final Decision (τ_3). They also highlight a signifi-cantly positive response of up to 4 per cent around a successful appeal, which corresponds to a total market value loss of €24 billion euros around events.

There are also several US studies that investigate various aspects of antitrust policy. Among them are those of Burns (1977), Garbade et al. (1982), Gilligan (1986), Bizjak and Coles (1995), Bittlingmayer and Hazlett (2000) and De Vany and McMillan (2004).[15]

This chapter differs from the above-mentioned articles in the follow-ing way: firstly, it estimates an aggregate regression-based approach with which it presents the average and cumulative average effect of the release of non-overlapping steps of an antitrust and abuse of dominant position case by the GDC of the HCC on an infringed firm's share value; secondly, it evaluates a sample of antitrust and abuse of dominant position cases from the HCC during the period from 2000 to 2010; and thirdly, it uses adjusted trade to trade stock returns in order to get serially independent residuals.

6.5 SAMPLE SELECTION AND EMPIRICAL METHODOLOGY

6.5.1 Sample Selection

The sample includes ten completed cases of Articles 1 and 2 of Greek Competition Law during the period 2000–10 and five cases that are still under investigation. I define a completed case when the court of appeal has issued a decision and a case under investigation when only the HCC has issued its final decision. I include the completed cases in both periods under scrutiny, whereas I include the uncompleted cases only in the Investigation period.[16]

The sample of completed cases includes three cases of Article 2 and seven cases of Article 1 of Law No. 3959/2011. The sample of uncompleted cases includes five cases of Article 1 of the same law. In the former sample, the court of appeal has reduced the fine. The reduction ranges from 19 per cent to 80 per cent of the imposed fine by the HCC, while in one case the court of appeal annuls the HCC's final decision. For each case I explicitly determine five τs (see Figure 6.1) and the period around the release of public information from t_0 to t_1. The latter includes five trading days prior and after each τ. I also define the unaffected period t_o^* to $t_0 - 1$ from the release of the public information, which includes 300 trading days prior to t_0.

6.5.2   Empirical Methodology

Calculation of share returns
Daily continuously compound share return for firm j at date t is calculated as follows:

$$R_{j,t} = \ln(P_{j,t}) - \ln(P_{j,t-1}) \tag{6.1}$$

Following Maynes and Rumsey (1993), Bartholdy et al. (2007) and Fotis and Polemis (2012),[17] I incorporate in the calculation of infringed firms' share returns the infrequent trading phenomenon. The latter appears when some stocks do not trade daily in the stock exchange. In such a case, the estimated variance and co-variance of the stock perform-ance will positively correlate with their trade frequency.

I use adjusted trade to trade return with the time interval of non-trading dates. That is, assuming a stationary one day return generating process, the multi-period return for firm j ending on date t is[18]

$$R_t = \ln\left[\frac{P_{j,t}\hat{P}_{j,t-1}\cdot \cdots \cdot\hat{P}_{j,t\ldots\ldots\ldots n_t+1}}{\hat{P}_{j,t-1}\hat{P}_{j,t-2}\cdot \cdots \cdot\hat{P}_{j,t\ldots\ldots\ldots n_t}}\right], \tag{6.2}$$

where n_t is the length of the interval of non-trading dates[19] ending at date t and $\hat{P}_{j,t-u}$ is the unobserved stock price of firm j for date $t - u$ ($u = 1 \ldots \ldots n_t - 1$). Therefore, the trade to trade return is the sum of n_t unobserved one day returns. By dividing Equation (6.2) by n_t I derive the adjusted trade to trade return, which adjusts the variability in the interval length. Following Equation (6.1), the adjusted trade to trade return is as follows:[20]

$$R_{j,t} = \frac{\ln(P_{j,t}) - \ln(P_{j,t-u})}{n_t} \tag{6.3}$$

The trade to trade approach uses all available information about total stock and market returns over time and no bias is introduced by attempting to estimate unobserved daily stock returns as occurs with the lumped or uniform techniques.[21] However, since trade to trade returns ignore information about daily market returns over non-trading periods, it is not clear that it is theoretically superior to the lumped method (see below).[22]

Also, even when returns are calculated on a trade to trade basis, there is a possibility that a high prevalence of zero returns may occur. Those zero returns are likely to lead to positive serial correlation in the return series. In that case, the trade to trade approach will only reduce, but not eliminate, the bias on findings towards the rejection of serial independence. In this chapter the percentage of zero returns is low (less than 10 per cent of the total number of observations).

In the literature there have been proposed alternative methodologies to deal with the infrequent trading phenomenon.[23] The most frequently used method is the lumped returns method that calculates daily returns from the stock price series and produces zero returns for non-trading days and relatively large positive or negative returns on days when the stock trades. This method underestimates the variance of returns and therefore biases the t-statistics used to test abnormal performance.

The simple returns method[24] calculates daily returns only for days for which stock prices are available. The daily abnormal return is obtained by subtracting the market return on these days. This method produces unbiased estimates of abnormal returns on the days calculated, but gives no information of returns on days with any trade. It may produce inconclusive outcomes regarding the event study if the number of days of no trade is quite long.

The uniform returns method calculates the daily returns between trading days and allocates the average daily return to each day for which trade does not occur. Therefore, the same share return is allocated for all of the non-trading days. This method performs about the same as the lumped returns method.

6.5.3   The Empirical Model

I estimate the average effect of five releases of public information (τ_1 = dawn raids, τ_2 – Statement of Objections, τ_3 = Final Decision of HCC, τ_4 = Pre-final Court of Appeal Decision, τ_5 = Final Court of Appeal Decision) on the infringed firm's share value. For this scope, I elaborate the following econometric model for each τ over the combined period (T, T^*).

$$\overline{R}_{j,\tau} = a + \beta\overline{R}_{j,\tau}^m + \sum_{\tau=t_0}^{t_1}\gamma\Delta_{\tau,t} + AR(p) + \varepsilon_\tau, \tag{6.4}$$

where

$$\overline{R}_{j,\tau} = \frac{\sum_{i=1}^{\kappa}R_{j,\tau}}{k}, j = 1\ldots\ldots\kappa: \kappa*j\text{'s trade to trade stock returns of infri-}$$

nged firms at $\tau = 1\ldots5$;

$$\overline{R}_{j,\tau}^m = \frac{\sum_{i=1}^{\kappa}R_{j,\tau}^m}{\kappa}: \text{ the average return of market index of each } j \text{ in the } \tau;$$

Δs: dummy variables assuming value one on date $\tau = t_0\ldots\ldots t_1$ and zero on $n - 1$ dates prior to t_0;
$AR(p)$: the autoregressive component of order p.

Each dummy variable coefficient corresponds to the average effect (residual) of τ on the infringed firm's share value.

Despite the fact that the averaging is not over the same time points (that is, different infringed firms from different antitrust and abuse of dominant position cases), the regression works quite well since the values of Greek letters α and β in Equation (6.4) are the same as the estimated values of Equation (6.4) under the assumption of equally weighted porto-folios (that is, different infringed firms from the same antitrust and abuse of dominant position case).[25] The null hypothesis of estimated Equation (6.4) is

$$H_{0,\tau}: \gamma's = 0. \tag{6.5}[26]$$

I use Ljung-Box Q-statistics to evaluate the null hypothesis that there is no autocorrelation in the residuals up to order p. In case of serially cor-related residuals I estimate an AR(p) model.[27] If the autoregressive model does not ameliorate the volatility in residuals I estimate a GARCH(1,1) model, which been found to adequately capture the stock return volatility clustering. That is, a GARCH(1,1) model can be written as follows:

$$\sigma_t^2 = \omega + \alpha\varepsilon_{t-1}^2 + \beta\sigma_{t-1}^2, \tag{6.6}$$

where σ_t^2 is the one period ahead forecast variance based on past infor-mation (conditional variance), ε are the residuals from Equation (6.4), ω the constant term of Equation (6.6), ε_{t-1}^2 the ARCH term and σ_{t-1}^2 the GARCH term.[28]

6.6   EMPIRICAL RESULTS

6.6.1   Descriptive Statistics

Tables 6.2 and 6.3 summarize the descriptive statistics of infringed firms' share returns in both t_0 to t_1 and t_o^* to $t_0 - 1$ periods. From Table 6.2 we see that the mean of the average share returns is higher in the t_0 to t_1 period than in the t_o^* to $t_0 - 1$ period, but its difference is not statistically significant in terms of p-values of Table 6.3.

Table 6.2   Descriptive statistics

Sample Statistics: τ_1^{**}					
	Mean	Std.	Skew.	Kurt.	Obs.
t_0 to t_1 Period***	−0.01	0.6	1.5	4.44	11
t_o^* to $t_0 - 1$ Period****	0.11	0.47	−0.12	−3.43	300
Total	0.11	0.47	−0.12	3.44	311
Sample Statistics: τ_2^{**}					
	Mean	Std.	Skew.	Kurt.	Obs.
t_0 to t_1 Period***	−0.2	0.84	−1.31	4.02	11
t_o^* to $t_0 - 1$ Period****	0.02	0.8	0.06	3.45	300
Total	0.02	0.8	0.01	3.52	311
Sample Statistics: τ_3^{**}					
	Mean	Std.	Skew.	Kurt.	Obs.
t_0 to t_1 Period***	−0.2	0.87	−0.5	2.63	11
t_o^* to $t_0 - 1$ Period****	0.05	0.67	0.16	3.08	300
Total	0.04	0.67	0.1	3.15	311
Sample Statistics: τ_4^{***}					
	Mean	Std.	Skew.	Kurt.	Obs.
t_0 to t_1 Period***	−0.36	0.6	−1.68	5.6	11
t_o^* to $t_0 - 1$ Period****	−0.01	0.64	−0.1	2.98	300
Total	−0.01	0.64	−0.13	3.12	311
Sample Statistics: τ_5^{**}					
	Mean	Std.	Skew.	Kurt.	Obs.
t_0 to t_1 Period***	−0.47	0.62	0.002	2	11'
t_o^* to $t_0 - 1$ Period****	−0.01	0.58	0.07	3.38	300
Total	−0.03	0.59	0.04	3.34	311

Note: **τ_1: Dawn raids, τ_2: Statement of Objections, τ_3: HCC Decision, τ_4: Pre-final Court of Appeal Decision, τ_5: Final Court of Appeal Decision. ***$t = 1 \ldots n$ days around the release of τs, ****$n - 1$ days prior to t_0.

Source: Author's elaboration of the data.

*Table 6.3   Equality tests of means and variances in t_0 to t_1, t_o^* to $t_0 - 1$ periods****

Returns: τ_1**		
	Mean[+]	Variance[++]
t-test	2.18	4.42
p-value	0.17	0.1
Returns: τ_2**		
	Mean[+]	Variance[++]
t-test	0.83	80.19
p-value	0.58	0.00
Returns: τ_3**		
	Mean[+]	Variance[++]
t-test	1.93	1.57
p-value	0.21	0.27
Returns: τ_4**		
	Mean[+]	Variance[++]
t-test	1.47	3.22
p-value	0.32	0.09
Returns: τ_5**		
	Mean[+]	Variance[++]
t-test	2.92	3.45
p-value	0.21	0.08

Note: a = 0.10 (p-value < 0.10), a = 0.05 (p-value < 0.5), a = 0.01 (p-value < 0.01).
[+]F-Anova test, [++]Welch F-test. *** t_o^*: the beginning of the unaffected period, $t_0 - 1$: the end of the unaffected period, $t_0 - t_1$: $t = 1 \ldots n$ days around the release of τs.

Source: Author's elaboration of the data.

Additionally, the difference of the estimated standard deviation of the average returns of involved firms in almost all events ranges from 5 to 20 per cent (except from average returns in τ_4). However, the specified difference in their variance is not statistically significant in four out of five τs (except τ_2), indicating that the stock returns of infringed firms in τ_2 may exhibit a volatility effect due to the release of public information at date $t = 0$. In order to deal with the volatility effect I use the GARCH(1,1) model (see Equation 6.7 below).

Table 6.4 reports the Jarque-Bera normality test of residuals of estimated equations (Table 6.5). It is evident from the reported p-values of all tests that the normality assumption cannot be rejected even at a $= 0.10$ level of significance. The p-values of the normality test

Table 6.4   Normality tests (residuals) regression-based approach

Residuals: Dawn raids	
	AR(4)
Jarque-Bera test	0.74 (0.69)
Residuals: Statement of Objections	
	GARCH(1,1)
Jarque-Bera test	1.84 (0.40)
Residuals: HCC Decision	
	AR(8)
Jarque-Bera test	2.65 (0.27)
Residuals: Pre-final Court of Appeal Decision	
	OLS
Jarque-Bera test	1.06 (0.59)
Residuals: Final Court of Appeal Decision	
	AR(2)
Jarque-Bera test	1.19 (0.55)

Note: a = 0.10 (p-value < 0.10), a = 0.05 (p-value < 0.5), a = 0.01 (p-value < 0.01). p-values in parentheses.

Source: Author's elaboration of the data.

concerning the estimated equations around the release of the final and pre-final court of appeal decisions as well as down raids indicate that the probability of making a mistake about the normality assumption is quite low.

6.6.2   Econometric Results

Table 6.A1 in the Appendix reports the econometric results from the estimated Equations (6.4) and (6.6). Table 6.5 summarizes their main findings.

On the one hand, during the Investigation period, the Cumulative Average Effect (CAE) of the issuing of the final decision by the HCC (τ_3) on the infringed firm's share value is negative and highly statistical significant. At $t = 0$ the issuing of the final decision causes a -4.3 per cent[29] cumulative average drop, while the overall average effect ($t = +5$) negatively affects the infringed firm's share value (-6.04 per cent).[30]

Moreover, prior the issuing of the final decision of the HCC,[31] the Average Residual (AR) of involved firms in the infringement is negative and statistically significant at a $= 0.01$ level of significance. This may

Table 6.5   Econometric estimations from regression-based approach:
summary of results

Cumulative Average Residual	Non-overlapping steps of an antitrust and abuse of dominant position case*				
	(τ_1)*	(τ_2)*	(τ_3)*	(τ_4)*	(τ_5)*
$t = 0$	−0.09 (> 0.10)	3.98 (> 0.10)	−2.94 (≤ 0.01)	−0.67 (> 0.10)	−2.16 (≤ 0.05)
$t = +5$	0.53 (> 0.10)	4.18 (> 0.10)	−2.85 (≤ 0.01)	−1.56 (> 0.10)	−2.78 (≤ 0.05)

Note: * See Table 6.2. p-values in parentheses.

Source: Table 6.A1 in the Appendix and Equation (6.7).

indicate that the negative decision of the HCC was expected by the financial investors.

On the other hand, during the Deterrence period the final decision of the court of appeal (τ_4) causes a statistically significant −5.07 per cent drop in the share value of the infringed firms.[32] The same picture holds at the date of the release of the public information ($t = 0$). The AR of the share value of the involved firms statistically declines by −1.26 per cent (coefficient D 0 in Table 6.A1 in the Appendix). Following Langus and Motta (2006), 'This implies a very quick rely of the news to the investors.'

The release of τ_1, τ_2 and τ_4 events does not cause a statistically significant effect (either negative or positive) in the infringed firm's share value during the period under examination. The CAR on the day of the surprise inspection (τ_1) is negative but not statistically significant,[33] suggesting a −0.09 per cent drop in the firm's share value at the date $t = 0$. The overall CAE is positive (0.72 per cent), but not statistically significant (coefficient D +5 in Table 6.A1 in the Appendix).

However, prior to the surprise inspection,[34] the AR is negative and statistically significant at a = 0.10 level of significance, while after the completion of the dawn raid,[35] the value of AR alternates signs, but continues to be statistically significant at the a = 0.10 level of significance.

Additionally, the temporal recall of the final decision of the HCC (τ_4) negatively affects the share value of involved firms, either at date $t = 0$ or at date $t = +5$. However, the AR of infringed firms five and two dates prior to the issuing of τ_4 is positive and statistically significant at the a = 0.01 level of significance, whereas it drops at date $t = +4$, indicating that the release of public information causes a statistically significant (a = 0.01) negative effect of −2.91 per cent in the share value of infringed firms.

As it concerns τ_2, I make use of a GARC(1,1) model in order to estimate its volatility effect of the issuing of the SoO on infringed firms' share value.

It is evident from the estimated results of Equation (6.7) that during the period under scrutiny,[36] the AR of infringed firms' share value at date $t = 0$ is positive and statistically significant at the a $= 0.01$ level of significance.[37] The same holds one day after the release of public information.

$$\bar{P}_{j,2} = 0.04 + 0.59\bar{P}_{j,2}^{m} + 1.68\Delta_{(-5),2} - 0.55\Delta_{(-4),2} + 0.10\Delta_{(-3),2} + 2.62\Delta_{(-2),2} - 0.35\Delta_{(-1),2}$$

$$\quad (0.86) \quad (8.34) \qquad (4.43) \qquad\quad (-0.15) \qquad\quad (0.28) \qquad\quad (6.35) \qquad\quad (-0.06)$$

$$\quad (0.39) \quad (0.00) \qquad (0.00) \qquad\quad (0.88) \qquad\quad (0.80) \qquad\quad (0.00) \qquad\quad (0.99)$$

$$\quad + 0.48\Delta_{0,2} + 0.79\Delta_{+1,2} + 0.95\Delta_{+2,2} - 0.34\Delta_{+3,2} - 0.03\Delta_{+4,2} - 1.17\Delta_{+5,2} \; 0.15\,AP(4)$$

$$\quad\quad (0.15) \qquad (1.34) \qquad (0.18) \qquad\;\; (-0.27) \qquad (-0.00) \qquad (-0.73) \qquad\quad (2.83)$$

$$\quad\quad (0.88) \qquad (0.18) \qquad (0.85) \qquad\;\; (0.79) \qquad\quad (0.99) \qquad\;\; (0.47) \qquad\quad (0.00)$$

$$\sigma_{\tau}^{2} = 0.20 + 0.12\varepsilon_{\tau-1}^{2} + 0.45\sigma_{\tau-1}^{2}$$

$$(1.45) \; (1.74) \qquad (1.42)$$

$$(0.15) \; (0.08) \qquad (0.15),$$

$$(6.7)$$

where

$$\sum_{i=-5}^{+5} \Delta_{j,\tau}\text{: Average Residuals of } \tau = 2 \text{ in } t_0 \text{ to } t_1 \text{ period.}$$

Estimated results: first row; z-statistic: second row; p-values: third row.

Table 6.A1 in the Appendix also reports diagnostic tests (Ljung-Box Q-statistic) and equality tests (Brown-Forsythe statistic) of the variance of residuals. The results of diagnostic tests imply that the above-mentioned methods of estimation equally capture the volatility effect of anti-competitive actions on infringed firms' share value in the residuals. The p-value of the equality tests of residual's variance between the t_0 to t_1 and t_o^* to $t_0 - 1$ periods in all cases rejects the null hypothesis of statistically significant difference between the aforementioned residual's variance.

6.7   CONCLUDING REMARKS AND FURTHER RESEARCH

In this chapter I assume the following public information that may affect the share price of the infringed firms: (a) the dawn raids; (b) the issue of the SoO; and (c) the final decision of the HCC, which constitute the Investigation period, and the court decisions, which constitute the Deterrence period. I use an aggregate regression-based approach to evaluate the effect of the release of the above-mentioned public information in the share price of the firms that infringe Articles 1 and 2 of Greek Competition Law. I estimate a dummy variable model with autoregressive components of order p and a GARCH(1,1) model in the case where a volatility effect persists in the residuals for each release of public information.

The econometric estimations suggest that during the Investigation and Deterrence periods, the CARs of the infringed firms drop by –6.04 per cent and –5.07 per cent respectively. The release of the final decisions of the HCC and the Supreme Court negatively affect the share value of the infringed firms.

On the contrary, the empirical results also indicate that the dawn raids, the SoO by the GDC of the HCC and the decision of the court of appeal do not significantly affect the share value of the involved firms in the anti-competitive practices.

The results of diagnostic tests imply that the above-mentioned methods of estimation equally capture the volatility effect of anti-competitive actions on infringed firms' share value in the residuals.

Firm level analysis may also be desirable to capture the effect of the public information on the infringed firm's share value. For this purpose, Equation (6.4) in conjunction with Boehmer et al. (1991) t-test may be used for single firm analysis. Weighted least squares (WLS) with robust standard errors and maximum likelihood estimation (MLE) with non-proportional heteroscedasticity may be useful supplements to OLS with robust standard errors.[38] Lastly, quantitative event study may be a useful extension of this chapter.[39]

NOTES

1. The views expressed in this chapter are solely those of the author and do not reflect by any means the General Directorate of Competition, Hellenic Competition Commission and any individual Commissioner.
2. This research is part of an announcement in the Sixth International Conference on Competition and Regulation, CRESSE, 1–3 July 2011, Rhodes, Greece. I am grateful to the Conference Advisory Committee and the panelists of the special policy session on enforcement for a constructive debate on competition issues. The usual disclaimer applies.
3. See Fotis (2012) for an analysis of competition policy in periods of economic downturn.
4. Article 1 of Greek Competition Law deals with cartels, while Article 2 of the same law deals with anti-competitive practices concerning abuse of dominance position.
5. See http://www.epant.gr/img/x2/categories/ctg253_3_1193315361.pdf (in Greek).
6. Article 25(2) of the former Competition Law No. 703/77 (see also Article 38(3) of Greek Competition Law, as applicable) stated that in case of refusal, recalcitrance or delay in providing the requested information by the GDC of the HCC or inaccurate and incomplete information, the HCC may (a) impose a fine of 15,000 million euros or at least 1 per cent of turnover in each of the involved firms in the violation and for any

offence, as calculated in accordance with Article 4f of the law and (b) officially initiate disciplinary proceedings for the above violations that constitute a disciplinary offence.

7. See Article 36 of Greek Competition Law.

8. I call it 'Deterrence period' since after the issuing of the final decision the imposed penalties may dishearten firms from engaging in cartels and other anti-competitive behaviour.

9. To the best of my knowledge, the Supreme Courts' judgments have never increased fines that have been imposed by the HCC. Due to data limitations, in this chapter Courts' judgments refer to Court of appeals' decisions.

10. The court of appeal temporarily recalls the final decision of the HCC until the issuing of its final decision.

11. Lübbers (2009) also elaborates different performance measures calculated from accounting and financial data in a dynamic panel data framework to evaluate the impact of antitrust actions on firms' share value.

12. See also Fotis et al. (2011) for a study which examines the possible effect of the derogation from suspension of concentrations by the HCC on the stock performance of the requested firms.

13. See Thompson and Kaserman (2001), p. 329.

14. See Lübbers (2009), p. 3.

15. Garbade et al. (1982) investigate 34 companies that infringed the Sherman and Clayton Acts from 1934 to 1974, Gilligan (1986) analyses 43 firms convicted for resale price maintenance from 1962 to 1985, Bizjak and Coles (1995) evaluate 481 antitrust cases in the USA in the period 1973–83, Bittlingmayer and Hazlett (2000) analyse the US federal antitrust action against Microsoft in the 1990s and De Vany and McMillan (2004) report the effect of infringed actions by vertically integrated movie studios during the period 1939–49.

16. Due to data limitations I have not included five cases in the sample of Deterrence period.

17. See also Fotis and Polemis (2010, 2011) and Fotis (2011b).

18. See also Equation (3) in Mayens and Rumsey (1993).

19. The period of trading dates between the trade at period t and the previously successful traded date.

20. See Fotis and Polemis (2011), p. 330.

21. Ibid.

22. See Fotis (2011a), p. 9. The lumped returns method is analysed in the subsequent paragraphs.

23. See Bartholdy et al. (2007), pp. 5–6 and Maynes and Rumsey (1993), pp. 147–9.

24. See Fotis and Polemis (2010a), pp. 5, 9.

25. The underlying assumption behind that is that the βs estimates of each firm are not related to a specific date return. So, following Pynnönen (2005), 'the covariation between them can be assumed to be approximately zero'.

26. See also the results of the Jarque-Bera normality test of estimated equations' residuals in Table 6.4.

27. Except for τ_4 I use ordinary least squares (OLS) regression. See Table 6.A1 in the Appendix.

28. Since the period around the release of public information from t_0 to t_1 does not include several days, Equation (6.6) captures different volatility levels for different $t_0 \leq t's \leq t_1$ without requiring a large number of observations.

29. See CAR of coefficient D 0 and its associated p-value in Table 6.A1 in the Appendix.

30. See CAR of coefficient D + 5 and its associated p-value in Table 6.A1 in the Appendix.

31. Specifically, five, three and two days prior $t = 0$ of τ_3. See also ARs of coefficients D − 5, D − 3 and D − 2 and their associated p-values in Table 6.A1 in the Appendix.

32. See CAR of coefficient D + 5 and its associated p-value in Table 6.A1 in the Appendix.

33. See CAR of coefficient D 0 and its associated p-value in Table 6.A1 in the Appendix.

34. Especially four and one days prior to $t = 0$ of τ_1.

35. Especially two and three days prior to $t = 0$ of τ_1.
36. Especially five and two days prior to $t = 0$ of τ_2.
37. See p-values of coefficients $\Delta_{(-5),2}$ and $\Delta_{(-2),2}$ in Equation (6.7).
38. See Pynnönen (2005), p. 339 and the references therein.
39. See Schwert (1991) for this kind of method.

REFERENCES

Bartholdy, J., D. Olson and P. Peare (2007), 'Conducting event studies on a small stock exchange', *European Journal of Finance*, **13**(3), 227–52.
Bittlingmayer, G. and W.T. Hazlett (2000), 'DOS Kapital: has antitrust action against Microsoft created value in the computer industry?', *Journal of Financial Economics*, **55**(3), 329–59.
Bizjak, J. and J.L. Coles (1995), 'The effect of private antitrust litigation on the stock-market valuation of the firm', *American Economic Review*, **85**(3), 436–61.
Bosch, J.C. and E.W. Eckard (1991), 'The profitability of price fixing: evidence from stock market reaction to federal indictments', *Review of Economics and Statistics*, **73**(2), 309–17.
Burns, R.M. (1977), 'The competitive effect of trust-busting: a portfolio analysis', *Journal of Political Economy*, **85**(4), 717–39.
De Vany, A. and H. McMillan (2004), 'Was the antitrust action that broke up the movie studios good for movies? Evidence from the stock market', *American Law and Economics Review*, **6**(1), 135–53.
Detre, J.D., A. Golub and J.M. Connor (2005), 'The profitability of price fixing: have stronger antitrust sanctions deterred?', Paper Presented at the International Organization Conference 3, Atlanta, Georgia, 8–9 April.
Feinberg, M.R. and K.D. Round (2005), 'Share-price responses to antitrust enforcement in Australia: do investors care about price-fixing cases?', *Competition and Consumer Law Journal*, **13**(1), 23–39.
Fotis, P. (2011a), 'Antitrust investigations and firm's damages: evidences from normal returns', Paper presented at the Sixth Annual Competition and Regulation European Summer School and Conference, Advances in the Analysis of Competition Policy and Regulation (CRESSE 2011), Rhodes, Greece, 1–3 July.
Fotis, P. (2011b), 'Firm's damages from antitrust & abuse of dominant position investigations', MPRA Working Paper, 32788.
Fotis, P. (2012), 'Competition policy in periods of economic downturn', *International Journal of Economics and Business Research*, **4**(5), 570–76.
Fotis, P. and M. Polemis (2010), 'Are mergers and acquisitions competitive in specific Greek relevant markets? Evidence from small stock exchange', Paper presented at the Fifth Annual Competition and Regulation European Summer School and Conference, Advances in the Analysis of Competition Policy and Regulation (CRESSE 2010), Chania, Greece, 2–4 July.
Fotis, P. and M. Polemis (2011), 'The use of economic tools in merger assessment', *European Competition Journal*, **7**(2), 323–47.
Fotis, P. and M. Polemis (2012), 'The short-run competitive effects of merger enforcement', *European Competition Journal*, **8**(1), 183–210.

Fotis, P., M. Polemis and N. Zevgolis (2011), 'Robust event studies for deroga-tion from suspension of concentrations in Greece during the period 1995–2008', *Journal of Industry Competition and Trade*, **11**(1), 67–89.

Garbade, K.D., W.J. Silber and L.J. White (1982), 'Market reaction to the filing of antitrust suits: an aggregate and cross-sectional analysis', *Review of Economics and Statistics*, **64**(4), 686–91.

Gilligan, T.W. (1986), 'The competitive effects of resale price maintenance', *RAND Journal of Economics*, **17**(4), 544–56.

Günster, A. and A.D. Mathijs (2010), 'The impact of European antitrust policy: evidence from the stock market', available at Dijkhttp://papers.ssrn.com/sol3/papers.cfm?abstract_id=1598387 (accessed 15 May 2011).

Langus, G. and M. Motta (2006), 'On the effect of EU antitrust investigations and fines on infringing firms' market value', in C.-D. Ehlermann and I. Atanasiu (eds), European Competition Law Annual 2006, *Enforcement of Prohibition of Cartels*, Oxford: Hart Publishing, pp. 363–76.

Lübbers, T. (2009), 'Is Cartelisation Profitable? A case study of the Rhenish Westphalian Coal Syndicate, 1893–1913', available at http://www.coll.mpg.de/pdf_dat/2009_09online-.pdf (accessed 14 April 2011).

Maynes, E. and J. Rumsey (1993), 'Conducting event studies with thinly traded stocks', *Journal of Banking and Finance*, **17**(1), 145–57.

Pynnönen, S. (2005), 'On regression based event study', available at http://lipas.uwasa.fi/~sjp/-articles/sp_acta_wasaensia_143_327-354.pdf (accessed 25 April 2011).

Schwert, G.W. (1981), 'Using financial data to measure the effect of regulation', *Journal of Law and Economics*, **24**(1), 121–57.

Thompson, S.J. and L.D. Kaserman (2001), 'After the fall: stock price move-ments and the deterrent effect of antitrust enforcement', *Review of Industrial Organization*, **19**(3), 329–34.

APPENDIX

Table 6.A1 Coefficient estimates: regression-based approach

$-\tau_1 - AR(4)$

Coefficients	AR[‡]	Std (AR)	t-AR	p-value	CAR[‡‡]	Std(CAR)	t-CAR	p-value[‡‡‡]
a	0.07	0.03	2.61	**0.01**				
$\overline{R^\tau_{j,m}}$	0.72	0.08	9.50	**23**				
D-5	−0.48	0.41	−1.17	0.24	−0.48	0.41	−1.17	
D-4	0.68	0.41	−1.66	**0.09**	0.20	0.58	0.34	
D-3	0.13	0.41	0.32	0.75	0.33	0.71	0.46	
D-2	−0.27	0.41	−0.65	0.51	0.06	0.82	0.07	
D-1	−0.70	0.41	−1.68	**0.09**	−0.64	0.92	−0.70	
D0	0.55	0.42	1.30	0.19	−0.09	1.03	−0.09	> 0.10
D+1	0.54	0.41	1.31	0.19	0.45	1.08	0.41	
D+2	−1.09	0.42	−2.62	**0.01**	−0.64	1.19	−0.54	
D+3	0.97	0.42	2.34	**0.02**	0.33	1.26	0.26	
D+4	0.36	0.41	0.88	0.38	0.69	1.30	0.53	
D+5	0.03	0.41	0.07	0.94	0.72	1.36	0.53	
AR(4)	0.13	0.06	2.29	**0.02**				

Diagnostic Statistics (Ljung-Box Q-statistic)

	Stat.	p-value
Q (4) residual	2.99	0.4
Q (4) residual^2	0.86	0.84

p-value for F-test for equality of event and non-event residual variances (Brown-Forsythe statistic)

p-value 0.42

$-\tau_3 - AR(8)$

Coefficients	AR[‡]	Std (AR)	t-AR	p-value	CAR[‡‡]	Std(CAR)	t-CAR	p-value[‡‡‡]
a	0.06	0.03	1.87	**0.06**				
$\overline{R}^{\tau}_{j,m}$	0.37	0.07	5.05	**0.00**				
D-5	-2.17	0.63	-3.43	**0.00**	-2.17	0.63	-3.44	≤ 0.01
D-4	-0.12	0.64	-0.20	0.84	-2.29	0.91	-2.53	
D-3	-0.67	0.63	-3.43	**0.00**	-2.96	1.09	-2.71	
D-2	-1.11	0.63	-1.76	**0.08**	-4.07	1.26	-3.23	
D-1	-0.07	0.63	-0.10	0.92	-4.14	1.41	-2.94	
D 0	-0.39	0.63	-0.61	0.54	-4.53	1.54	-2.94	
D+1	-0.51	0.63	-0.80	0.42	-5.04	1.67	-3.02	
D+2	-0.42	0.63	0.67	0.50	-5.46	1.78	-3.06	
D+3	-0.74	0.64	-1.16	0.25	-6.20	1.92	-3.23	
D+4	0.69	0.64	1.08	0.28	-5.51	2.02	-2.72	
D+5	-0.53	0.64	-0.83	0.41	-6.04	2.12	-2.85	
AR(8)	-0.15	0.06	-2.59	**0.01**				

Diagnostic Statistics (Ljung-Box Q-statistic)

	Stat.	p-value
Q (4) residual	8.68	0.28
Q (4) residual[2]	5.40	0.61

p-value of F-test for equality of event and non-event residual variances (Brown-Forsythe statistic)

	p-value	
	0.41	

135

Table 6.A1   (continued)

− τ₄ – OLS

Coefficients	AR[‡]	Std (AR)	t-AR	p-value	CAR[‡‡]	Std(CAR)	t-CAR	p-value[‡‡‡]
a	0.02	0.04	0.48	0.63				
R_m	0.42	0.09	4.89	**0.00**				
D-5	−0.41	0.62	−0.66	0.51	−0.41	0.62	−0.66	
D-4	0.37	0.62	0.60	0.55	−0.04	0.88	−0.05	
D-3	−0.49	−0.62	−0.80	0.42	−0.53	−1.07	0.49	
D-2	0.29	0.62	0.47	0.64	−0.24	1.24	−0.19	
D-1	−0.38	0.62	−0.62	0.53	−0.62	1.39	−0.45	
D 0	−0.40	0.62	−0.65	0.51	−1.02	1.52	−0.67	> 0.10
D+1	0.00	0.62	0.00	0.99	−1.02	1.64	−0.62	
D+2	0.03	0.62	−0.05	0.96	−0.99	1.75	−0.56	
D+3	−0.19	0.62	−0.31	0.75	−1.18	1.86	−0.63	
D+4	−1.79	0.62	−2.91	**0.00**	−2.97	1.96	−1.51	
D+5	−0.19	0.61	−0.32	0.75	−3.16	2.02	−1.56	

Diagnostic Statistics (Ljung-Box Q-statistic)

	Stat.	p-value
Q (until 12 lags) residual	>0.10	
Q (until 36 lags) residual²	>0.30	

p-value of F-test for equality of event and non-event residual variances (Brown-Forsythe statistic)

	p-value
	0.71

$- \tau_5 - AR(2)$

Coefficients	AR[+]	Std (AR)	t-AR	p-value	CAR[++]	Std(CAR)	t-CAR	p-value[+++]
a	0.02	0.04	0.64	0.52				
R_m	0.41	0.06	7.17	**0.00**				
D-5	0.11	0.54	0.20	0.84	0.11	0.54	0.20	≥ 0.10
D-4	-1.08	0.54	-2.00	**0.05**	-0.97	0.76	-1.27	
D-3	-0.37	0.55	-0.67	0.50	-1.34	0.95	-1.41	
D-2	-0.86	0.55	-1.57	0.11	-2.20	1.10	-2.00	≤ 0.05
D-1	0.55	0.55	1.00	0.32	-1.65	1.23	-1.34	≥ 0.10
D0	-1.26	0.55	-2.30	**0.02**	-2.91	1.35	-2.16	
D+1	0.12	0.55	0.23	0.82	-2.79	1.46	-1.92	
D+2	-0.32	0.55	-0.56	0.57	-3.11	1.56	-2.00	
D+3	-0.31	0.55	-0.56	0.58	-3.42	1.65	-2.07	≤ 0.05
D+4	-1.45	0.55	-2.65	**0.01**	-4.87	1.74	-2.80	
D+5	-0.20	0.55	-0.36	0.72	-5.07	1.82	-2.78	
AR(2)	0.18	0.06	3.09	**0.00**				

Diagnostic Statistics (Ljung-Box Q-statistic)

	Stat.	p-value
Q (2) residual	1.04	0.31
Q (2) residualF	0.72	0.40

p-value of F-test for equality of event and non-event residual variances (Brown-Forsythe statistic)

p-value
0.10

Table 6.A1 (continued)

−τ_2 − GARCH(1,1)

Coefficients	AR[‡]	Std (AR)	t-AR	p-value	CAR[‡‡]	Std(CAR)	t-CAR	p-value[‡‡‡]
a	0.04	0.07	0.86	0.39				
R_m	0.59	0.07	8.34	**0.00**				
D-5	1.68	0.40	4.43	**0.00**	1.68	0.40	4.20	**0.00**
D-4	−0.55	3.79	−0.15	0.88	1.13	5.36	0.21	> 0.10
D-3	0.10	0.42	0.25	0.80	1.23	0.73	1.69	**0.09**
D-2	2.62	0.41	6.35	**0.00**	3.85	0.82	4.70	**0.00**
D-1	−0.35	5.68	−0.06	0.95	3.50	12.70	0.28	> 0.10
D0	0.48	3.29	0.15	0.88	3.98	8.06	0.49	> 0.10
D+1	0.79	0.59	1.34	0.18	4.77	1.56	3.06	**0.00**
D+2	0.95	5.14	0.18	0.85	5.72	14.54	0.39	> 0.10
D+3	−0.34	1.27	−0.27	0.79	5.38	3.81	1.41	> 0.10
D+4	−0.03	72.14	0.00	0.99	5.35	228.13	0.02	> 0.10
D+5	−1.17	1.60	−0.70	0.47	4.18	5.31	0.79	> 0.10
AR(4)	0.15	0.05	2.83	**0.00**				

Variance Equation

	Coef.	Std (AR)	t-value	p-value
Constant	0.20	0.14	1.45	0.15
ARCH	0.13	0.07	1.74	0.08
GARCH	1.45	0.32	1.42	0.15

Diagnostic Statistics (Ljung-Box Q-statistic)

	Stat.	p-value
Q (4) residual	2.00	0.57
Q (4) residual^2	3.00	0.40

p-value of F-test for equality of event and non-event residual variances (Brown-Forsythe statistic)

	p-value
	0.83

Note: a = 0.10 (p-value < 0.10), a = 0.05 (p-value < 0.5), a = 0.01 (p-value < 0.01). ^{a}Average Residual, ^{aa}Cumulative Average Residual, ††(two-tailed). Degrees of Freedom: 298. τ_1: Dawn raids, τ_2: Statement of Objections, τ_3: HCC Decision, τ_4: Pre-final Court of Appeal Decision, τ_5: Final Court of Appeal Decision.

Source: Author's elaboration of the data.

7. Social-welfare-enhancing collusion and trade

George Deltas, Alberto Salvo and Helder Vasconcelos[1]

7.1 INTRODUCTION

This chapter offers additional results and extensions derived from the model in Deltas, Salvo and Vasconcelos (2012). That paper, which at the request of an editor focused on the consumer welfare effect of collusion, developed a model of geographically separated markets in which two horizontally differentiated goods are sold by cost asymmetric suppliers. The source of the cost asymmetry is spatial, in that in a given market a 'home firm,' with production facilities located in the market, competes with a 'foreign firm' that, to bring its differentiated product to market, needs to incur an additional cost of trade from its offshore plant. Our motivation, then as well as now, is: (1) the observation that several real world cartels have adopted a 'home-market principle,' whereby cartelized firms enjoy large shares in their home markets (Motta 2004; Harrington 2006),[2] combined with (2) off-the-record speculation by executives in the Brazilian cement industry that spatial cartels, by curbing competitive cross-hauling, can raise social welfare.

In Deltas et al. (2012), we show that consumer surplus and social welfare can increase on shifting from oligopolistic competition to full collusion (monopoly). Section 7.2 of this chapter briefly lays out the basic model of that paper. We then add an analysis of first-best social outcomes (Section 7.3) to the existing derivation of equilibrium outcomes under a Nash equilibrium in prices (imperfect competition) and the joint-profit maximizing cartel (full collusion). We show that a social planner would go further than the perfect cartel in reducing the share of the foreign variety. From the social viewpoint, competition leads to excessive cross-hauling, a failure that collusion only partially addresses: trade is still too high in the collusive outcome relative to society's first-best outcome.

It is instructive to highlight the intuition behind the welfare comparison. From a welfare point of view, prices cancel out because they are a transfer. Only market allocations matter, and what is important for these are relative prices. Since markets and all equilibria are symmetric, we can consider welfare effects in a single market. Consider first the Nash equilibrium. In this equilibrium, the foreign firm chooses a lower margin than the home firm, since being the high-cost seller it has a smaller market share and thus more aggressive pricing results in smaller revenue losses from the sales to inframarginal consumers. Therefore, the price difference between the imported and home varieties is lower than the cost difference (the trade cost). As a result, the number of consumers who purchase from the importing firm is too high relative to the social optimum. The cartel, while shifting the market allocation away from the imported variety, does not eliminate this distortion entirely because some price discrimination against each producer's home-market buyers – who in equilibrium constitute the majority of its buyers – increases the cartel's surplus. In contrast, a social planner would set the price difference between the two firms equal to the trade cost.

Section 7.4 then extends the model to a setting where consumers exhibit home bias. No longer is it the case that at equal prices the two firms would have an equal market share: we generalize the earlier set-up by specifying, for each consumer, an additional willingness to pay for the home variety relative to the imported variety. This preference for the domestic product could be due to 'patriotism,' concerns about the local economy, or simply because the homefirm has superior knowledge about local tastes and can better appeal to them. We then show that our analysis is robust to, and in fact somewhat strengthened by, the introduction of home bias. For example, home bias reduces cross-hauling, but by less under competition than it does under collusion.

Deltas et al. (2012) considered conditions under which banning trade entirely resulted in higher consumer surplus. Section 7.5 of this chapter completes this result by considering conditions under which the autarkic regime enhances social welfare – the sum of consumer surplus and producer surplus – over trade regimes. In the trade literature, Brander and Krugman (1983) show that exogenously moving from autarky (no cross-hauling) to trade competition in a homogeneous-good Cournot oligopoly, with free entry, is welfare-enhancing: '(t)he pro-competitive effect of having more firms and a larger overall market dominates the loss due to transport costs in this second best imperfectly competitive world' (p. 314). With entry barriers, however, two-way trade in the identical good when the trade cost is high enough is 'wasteful,' lowering total welfare relative to autarky. We obtain a similar result that autarky welfare-dominates trade regimes (both competitive and collusive) except when the trade cost is low.[3] Finally, Section 7.6 examines how the first-best social outcome can be implemented. We consider tax and subsidy policies, as well as price regulation.

This chapter shows that in a workhorse industrial-organization model with only standard ingredients, spatial cartels can enhance social welfare by restricting costly trade and yet still trade more than the social optimum.[4] It, therefore, complements the consumer-surplus results in Deltas et al. (2012).

7.2   THE BASIC MODEL (DELTAS, SALVO, AND VASCONCELOS, 2012)

In this section, we briefly repeat for convenience the model set-up in Deltas et al. (2012), before we proceed to the derivation of novel results in subsequent sections. We consider a geographically segmented industry that operates in two markets (1 and 2) and where goods are horizontally differentiated. Shipping product from one market to another – cross-hauling – incurs a unit trade cost $t > 0$. Each local market consists of a continuum of consumers distributed uniformly over the interval [0, 1]. The disutility from consuming a variety other than one's ideal variety is linear in the distance along this Hotelling interval, with slope $\theta > 0$. There are two firms, A and B, each firm producing one variety. In geographic space, firm A's plant is located in market 1 while firm B's plant is located in market 2. In product space, firm A's product is located at the left endpoint of the unit interval while firm B's product is located at the right endpoint. The marginal cost of production is $c \geq 0$ for both firms. Consumers purchase one unit or none. Let $x \in [0, 1]$ – the consumer's type – denote the distance from the left endpoint of the unit interval. A firm's price can vary across the two markets though not within a market. Consider either one of the local markets, and denote the vector of prices by $p = (p_A, p_B)$; for simplicity, we momentarily omit market subscripts. Finally, let V denote the reservation price for a consumer's ideal product. Then, a consumer located at x has utility of $U_A \equiv V - \theta x - p_A$ from purchasing product A, and $U_B \equiv V - \theta(1 - x) - p_B$ from purchasing product B. We impose the two technical assumptions,

$$A1: t < 2\theta, \text{ and}$$

$$A2: 2(V - c) > t + 3\theta,$$

which ensure cross-hauling and full market coverage in equilibrium under both competition and collusion.[5] Thus, consumers to the left of $\tilde{x} \equiv 1/2 + (p_B - p_A)/(2\theta)$ will purchase product A, while those to the right will purchase product B.

In the competitive regime, the strategic interaction of the firms is separable across the two markets, given that marginal cost is constant in output. For market 1, the two firms choose prices to maximize $\Pi_{1A} = (p_A - c)\tilde{x}$ and $\Pi_{1B} = (p_B - c - t)(1 - \tilde{x})$, respectively (and similarly for market 2, which we will henceforth ignore). Equilibrium prices are given by $p_{1A}^C = c + \frac{1}{3}t + \theta$ and $p_{1B}^C = c + \frac{2}{3}t + \theta$, where the superscript C denotes the competitive equilibrium. These prices correspond to the market division given by $\tilde{x}_1^C = \frac{1}{2} + \frac{1}{6}\frac{t}{\theta}$, and yield profits of $\Pi_{1A}^C = \frac{1}{18\theta}(3\theta + t)^2$ and $\Pi_{1B}^C = \frac{1}{18\theta}(3\theta - t)^2$.

For the collusive regime, we derive the fully collusive outcome, taking as given that the firms can sustain it.[6] Even though we refer to joint-profit maximization as arising from collusion, we note that it is equivalent to a merger to monopoly. In a joint-profit maximizing outcome (denoted by the superscript JM), prices set by the firms leave the marginal consumer in each market with zero surplus (if not, both prices could be increased symmetrically to yield higher profit). Thus, fully collusive prices satisfy $U_A(p_A; \tilde{x}(p)) = 0$ (or equivalently $U_B(p_B; \tilde{x}(p)) = 0$), which can be rewritten as $2V - \theta - p_A - p_B = 0$. Then, the perfect cartel's problem

$$\max_{p_A, p_B}(p_A - c)\frac{\theta - p_A + p_B}{2\theta} + (p_B - c - t)\left(1 - \frac{\theta - p_A + p_B}{2\theta}\right)$$

$$\text{s.t.} \, U_A(p_A; \tilde{x}(p)) \geq 0$$

collapses to the univariate problem

$$\max_{p_A}(p_A - c)\frac{V - p_A}{\theta} + (2V - \theta - p_A - c - t)\left(1 - \frac{V - p_A}{\theta}\right),$$

yielding prices $p_{1A}^{JM} = V - \frac{1}{4}t - \frac{1}{2}\theta$ and $p_{1B}^{JM} = 2V - \theta - p_{1A}^{JM} = V + \frac{1}{4}t - \frac{1}{2}\theta$. The corresponding location of the marginal consumer is $\tilde{x}_1^{JM} = \frac{1}{2} + \frac{1}{4}\frac{t}{\theta}$, where $\tilde{x}_1^{JM} > \tilde{x}_1^C$.

Equilibrium profits are $\Pi_{1A}^{JM} = \frac{1}{16\theta}(2\theta + t)(4V - 4c - t - 2\theta)$ and $\Pi_{1B}^{JM} = \frac{1}{16\theta}(2\theta - t)(4V - 4c - 3t - 2\theta)$. A1 ensures that the home firm's share under collusion is less than 1.[7]

We compare social welfare across the competitive and collusive regimes. Given that all consumers purchase one unit of the good in both regimes, we need only consider (1) the different total cost of cross-hauling product between geographic markets, and (2) the different total disutility from consuming a variety other than one's ideal. The total cost of cross-hauling under price competition exceeds the cost from cross-hauling under full collusion, as there is more trade in the competitive regime. The total consumer taste disutility under price competition is $\int_0^{\tilde{x}_1^C} \theta x dx + \int_{\tilde{x}_1^C}^1 \theta(1-x)dx = \frac{1}{2}\theta(2(\tilde{x}_1^C)^2 - 2\tilde{x}_1^C + 1)$, while that under full collusion is obtained similarly. The former is lower than the latter, as the marginal consumer in the competitive regime lies closer to the midpoint of the Hotelling interval than the marginal consumer in the collusive regime. Combining terms and taking the difference, we obtain $W^{JM} - W^C = \frac{7}{144}\frac{t^2}{\theta} > 0$. Thus, the first of the effects described above dominates the second, and welfare is higher under collusion. From the social point of view, the oligopolistically competitive equilibrium is characterized by 'excessive trade.' Collusion serves as a mechanism to correct this failure, but only partially, as we show in the subsequent section.

7.3   FIRST-BEST SOCIAL OUTCOMES IN THE BASIC MODEL

The immediate question then is how distortionary are the market-based behavioral regimes derived above? We now compute the set of first-best outcomes, where social welfare is maximal, and compare them to the competitive and collusive outcomes. As we explain, what characterizes a first-best social outcome is the price difference between the home good and the imported good, which is equal to the trade cost. We then provide price levels for two alternative (and extreme) first-best outcomes, where the division of surplus between producers and consumers is reversed: prices set by a 'business-friendly' social planner, and prices set by a 'consumer-friendly' social planner. To be clear, our planner's bias between pro-business and pro-consumer does not affect the price of the imported good relative to the home good, which determines the welfare trade-off between meeting consumers' love of variety and saving on trade costs.

Denote this first-best outcome by the superscript *FB* and consider market 1 (again market 2 is analogous). Express the location of consumer $\tilde{x}_1^{FB}$, who is indifferent between the two inside goods, as lying at a distance d to the right of the midpoint of the unit interval of product characteristics, that is, $\tilde{x}_1^{FB} = \frac{1}{2} + d$. For this marginal consumer to be indifferent to buying the home good or the imported good, the fact that she finds the home good less appealing must be offset by a price difference in its favor. The relative taste disutility of the home good is that of traveling a distance $2d$ (a distance d to the midpoint $(1/2)$, and then another d), costing the marginal consumer $2d\theta$. Now, the social planner equates this relative disutility $2d\theta$ with the cost of cross-hauling t, that is, $2d\theta = t$, from which $d = t/(2\theta)$ and the location of the marginal consumer follows:

$$\tilde{x}_1^{FB} = \begin{cases} \dfrac{1}{2} + \dfrac{1}{2}\dfrac{t}{\theta} & \text{if } t < \theta \\ 1 & \text{otherwise.} \end{cases}$$

Relative to the competitive and collusive regimes, the social planner reduces wasteful cross-hauling, opting for less trade – and none at all when $\theta \leq t < 2\theta$ – and a greater share for the home good (for $t \geq \theta$ there is a corner solution). There is no price discrimination against a firm's home-market buyers, as the price difference is equated to the trade cost t, in contrast to the market-based regimes where price discrimination was substantial (that is, the price difference was as low as $(1/2)t$ under collusion and $(1/3)t$ under competition).

The market share of the imported good is plotted, as a function of t, in Figure 7.1, which summarizes the quantity cross-hauled (and the welfare) in each regime. The figure also covers values of t that extend beyond the restricted space of parameters. Consider for a moment raising the trade cost beyond the upper bound set by A1, $t < 2\theta$. For $t \geq 2\theta$ both the fully collusive cartel and the social planner would choose to not cross-haul at all, that is, in this region, $\tilde{x}_1^{JM} = \tilde{x}_1^{FB} = 1$. Social welfare under full collusion would then be maximal. Moreover, for $2\theta \leq t < 3\theta$, while collusion would eliminate cross-hauling, this would still not be the case under price competition. There would thus still be welfare gains from collusion relative to competition. Further raising t, for $t \geq 3\theta$, cross-hauling would now cease also in the competitive regime, $\tilde{x}_1^C = \tilde{x}_1^{JM} = \tilde{x}_1^{FB} = 1$, with competition now also yielding optimal social welfare. Notice the concavity of welfare differences across regimes with respect to trade costs. At the low end, as t goes to 0, all three regimes coincide in terms of the degree of cross-hauling and welfare – the consumer taste disutility is minimal, as each consumer acquires the good that is closest to her ideal. At the high end, as t reaches 3θ, all three regimes again coincide: there is no cross-hauling and both competition and collusion are first-best.

For the left-most region in Figure 7.1, where the parameter values satisfy both A1 and A2 and where cross-hauling is positive for all regimes, the welfare result is summarized in the following proposition.

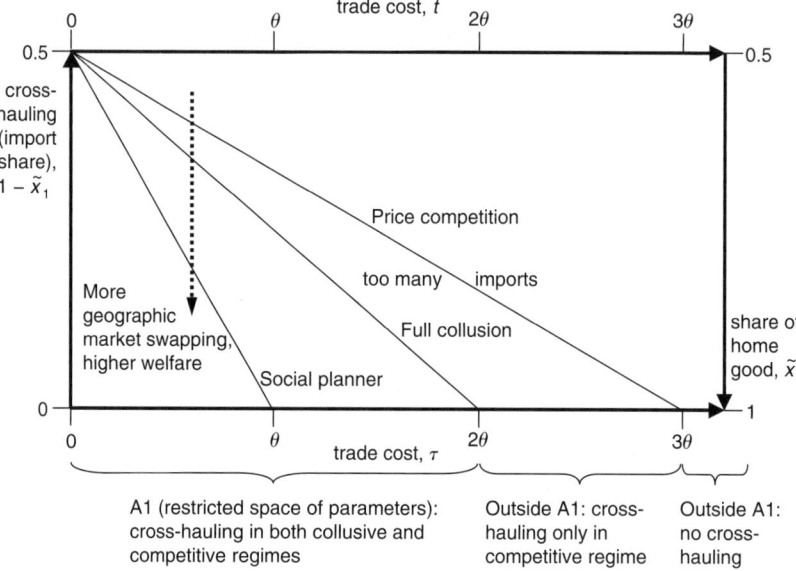

Figure 7.1   Import market shares and trade costs: market outcomes and the social optimum

Proposition 1   Social welfare under full collusion, though higher than under price competition, is suboptimal. Relative to the fully collusive outcome, a social planner would raise the price of the imported good relative to the price of the home good, further restricting the penetration of imports, that is, the social planner would further enhance geographic market-swapping at the expense of consumers' taste for variety.

Proof   When $0 < t < \theta$, the (per market) increase in social welfare in a first-best outcome relative to full collusion is

$$
\begin{aligned}
W^{FB} - W^{JM} &= t(1 - \tilde{x}_1^{JM}) + \frac{1}{2}\theta(2(\tilde{x}_1^{JM})^2 - 2\tilde{x}_1^{JM} + 1) \\
&\quad - t(1 - \tilde{x}_1^{FB}) - \frac{1}{2}\theta(2(\tilde{x}_1^{FB})^2 - 2\tilde{x}_1^{FB} + 1) \\
&= \frac{1}{16}\frac{t^2}{\theta} > 0.
\end{aligned}
$$

This is increasing in t and decreasing in θ. When $\theta \leq t < 2\theta$,

$$
W^{FB} - W^{JM} = \frac{1}{16\theta}(3t - 2\theta)(2\theta - t) > 0.
$$

Notice that $\partial(W^{FB} - W^{JM})/\partial t = (4\theta - 3t)/(8\theta)$, which is positive for low t and negative for high t. Also, $\partial(W^{FB} - W^{JM})/\partial\theta = (3t^2 - 4\theta^2)/(16\theta^2)$, which is negative for low t and positive for high t.

Though an improvement over competition, the perfect cartel still imports too much. Seen from the socially optimal outcome, the cartel disproportionately raises the price of the home good, which has a large market share, leading to large revenue gains from the sales to the many inframarginal consumers. Now, to illustrate, consider alternative price levels within the set of first-best social outcomes. A pro-business ('pro-b') social planner, wishing to maximize producer surplus conditional on total welfare being optimal, would set prices such that the marginal consumer's surplus is fully extracted, $U_A(p_A; \tilde{x}_1^{FB}) = 0$, that is,

$$p_{1A}^{FB,pro-b} = V - \theta\tilde{x}_1^{FB} = V - \frac{1}{2}\min(t + \theta, 2\theta),$$

$$p_{1B}^{FB,pro-b} = p_{1A}^{FB,pro-b} + t = V + t - \frac{1}{2}\min(t + \theta, 2\theta).$$

Profits are then given by

$$\Pi_{1A}^{FB,pro-b} = \begin{cases} \dfrac{1}{4\theta}(\theta + t)(2V - 2c - t - \theta) & \text{if } t < \theta \\ V - c - \theta & \text{otherwise} \end{cases}$$

$$\Pi_{1B}^{FB,pro-b} = \begin{cases} \dfrac{1}{4\theta}(\theta - t)(2V - 2c - t - \theta) & \text{if } t < \theta \\ 0 & \text{otherwise.} \end{cases}$$

A firm's total profit in this business-friendly first-best solution $\Pi_{1A}^{FB,pro-b} + \Pi_{2A}^{FB,pro-b}$ falls short relative to the fully collusive outcome:[8]

$$\Pi_{1A}^{FB,pro-b} + \Pi_{2A}^{FB,pro-b} - \left(\Pi_{1A}^{JM} + \Pi_{2A}^{JM}\right) =$$

$$= \begin{cases} -\dfrac{1}{8}\dfrac{t^2}{\theta} < 0 & \text{if } t < \theta \\ -\dfrac{1}{8\theta}(2\theta - t)^2 < 0 & \text{otherwise.} \end{cases}$$

One might at first be surprised that, in an environment with no aggregate demand effects, the collusive allocation and the pro-business social planner's outcome differ. To understand why this is the case, recall that the marginal consumer earns zero surplus in both outcomes. However, on switching from pro-business first-best prices to the cartel's prices, the typical (that is, non-marginal) home good consumer is made worse off, while the typical imported good consumer is made better off (and by the same amount). Since there are more consumers who purchase the home good, the collusive regime leads to more surplus extraction than the pro-business social optimum. This additional surplus outweighs the increase in cross-hauling costs. This essentially follows from the envelope theorem: marginally shifting the marginal consumer to the left has a small effect on total welfare but a first-order effect on surplus extraction, and thus it is profitable for the cartel. Progressively larger shifts to the left yield incrementally smaller increases in surplus extraction (as the market shares become more equal) but they increase hauling costs linearly; at the cartel outcome, these effects cancel each other out at the margin.

Alternatively, a pro-consumer ('pro-c') social planner, wishing to maximize consumer surplus conditional on total welfare being optimal, would adopt marginal cost pricing:

$$p_{1A}^{FB,pro-c} = c, p_{1B}^{FB,pro-c} = p_{1A}^{FB,pro-c} + t = c + t$$

The inefficiency of oligopoly outcomes in markets with asymmetric firms has been noted previously in the literature. In our model, the source of inefficiency is the price discrimination against buyers whom a firm has an advantage in serving from the standpoint of lower trade costs.[9]

As one may expect, the inefficiency would disappear were firms able to price discriminate within markets. For every consumer x, a monopolist would compare $V - \theta x$ (the price it would charge for the home good and extract all the consumer's surplus) against $V - \theta(1 - x) - t$ (the price on the imported good that extracts all the consumer's surplus, minus the trade cost it incurs); equating the two expressions yields the first-best allocation $\tilde{x}_1^{FB}$. As for a competitive duopoly, were firms to dispute every consumer separately (that is, there are no inframarginal consumers), the home firm would win consumers $x < \tilde{x}_1^{FB}$ while the importer would win consumers $x > \tilde{x}_1^{FB}$; to see this, note that both firms would be equally placed to win the consumer at $\tilde{x}_1^{FB}$ since the relative taste disutility from consuming the home good, $2(\frac{1}{2}\frac{t}{\theta})\theta$, equals the relative price discount offered by the home firm, t (there would be marginal cost pricing at $\tilde{x}_1^{FB}$ as the effects of product differentiation and cost asymmetry offset one another).

7.4 EXTENSION: THE EFFECTS OF HOME BIAS

Very often, consumers in a market favor locally sourced products over competing imports. Part of the reason may be national sentiment and concern over local jobs (witness the prominent 'Made in the USA' label on goods produced and sold in the American market), or environmental considerations (for example, the green movement promotes consumption of local produce in an attempt to curb greenhouse gas emissions generated from transportation). Similarly, local market knowledge may enable home brands to better appeal, on average, to national tastes.

We now ask what the effect of 'home bias' in consumer preferences would be in each of the three regimes. It is clear that if consumers favor the local brand, less cross-hauling will occur in all regimes. Less clear is which regime, if any, will be most affected. To fix ideas, we generalize the earlier set-up by specifying, for each consumer, an additional willingness to pay $h > 0$ for the home variety relative to the imported variety, that is, $V_{1A} = V_{2B} = V + h$ while maintaining $V_{1B} = V_{2A} = V$. The consumer who is indifferent between goods A and B is now located at

$$\tilde{x}_1^{hb}(p) = \frac{\theta - p_A + p_B + h}{2\theta}, \tag{7.1}$$

where superscript *hb* denotes the presence of home bias. (Restate restrictions A1' and A2', which define the space of interest, as $t + h < 2\theta$ and $2(V - c) > t + 3\theta - h$, respectively.) Repeating the derivations of the preceding sections (and again considering market 1), the competitive equilibrium is now characterized by prices

$$p_{1A}^{C,hb} = p_{1A}^C + \frac{1}{3}h, \, p_{1B}^{C,hb} = p_{1B}^C - \frac{1}{3}h$$

and home-good quantity share

$$\tilde{x}_1^{C,hb} = \tilde{x}_1^C + \frac{1}{6}\frac{h}{\theta}, \tag{7.2}$$

where the absence of *hb* in the superscript denotes the particular case where there is no home bias, $h=0$, seen earlier. As expected, increasing home bias (from zero) raises the share of the home good. The relative change in shares results, in equilibrium, in a reduction in the relative price of the imported good, $p_{1B}^{C,hb} - p_{1A}^{C,hb} = \frac{1}{3}(t - 2h)$. Similarly, prices and the quantity share of the home good in the fully collusive regime are now

$$p_{1A}^{JM,hb} = p_{1A}^{JM} + \frac{3}{4}h, \, p_{1B}^{JM,hb} = p_{1B}^{JM} + \frac{1}{4}h$$

$$\tilde{x}_1^{JM,hb} = \tilde{x}_1^{JM} + \frac{1}{4}\frac{h}{\theta}. \tag{7.3}$$

Comparing Equations (7.3) and (7.2), an increase in the home bias raises the share of the home good by more in the collusive regime than in the competitive regime. In other words, the presence of home bias results in more cross-hauling in the non-cooperative equilibrium relative to collusion, reinforcing our prior results. It is also easy to verify that, though home bias again raises price discrimination in favor of buyers of the imported good, it does so by less under collusion than under competition, reinforcing our finding of collusion as a (partial) correction mechanism. Finally, consider the socially first-best market allocation. As in Section 7.3, write the location of the marginal consumer as $\tilde{x}_1^{FB,hb} = \frac{1}{2} + d$. The relative taste disutility of the home good for this consumer is now $2d\theta - h$, which the social planner equates with the cross-hauling cost t, and thus $\tilde{x}_1^{FB,hb} = \frac{1}{2} + \frac{1}{2}(t + h)/\theta$, or

$$\tilde{x}_1^{FB,hb} = \begin{cases} \tilde{x}_1^{FB} + \dfrac{1}{2}\dfrac{h}{\theta} \text{ if } t + h < \theta \\ 1 \text{ otherwise.} \end{cases}$$

The equilibrium outcomes in market 1 (the home market of firm A) under all three regimes and in the presence of home bias are shown in Figure 7.2. Relative to the competitive and collusive outcomes, the effect of home bias – expanding the home-good share – is most pronounced under first-best $(+h/(2\theta))$, reinforcing our earlier result. To understand why, notice that $p_{1B}^{FB,hb} - p_{1A}^{FB,hb} = t$: as in the earlier set-up without home bias ($h = 0$), the planner equalizes each variety's price-cost margins across the two markets. In contrast, dumping is maximal – and increasing in h – in the competitive regime. The effect of h on the collusive market division is intermediate to the socially optimal and competitive regimes, as was the case for $h = 0$. For notational simplicity, we return to the case of no home bias for the remainder of this chapter.

7.5   CAN AUTARKY IMPROVE WELFARE OVER MARKET-BASED TRADE REGIMES?

Deltas et al. (2012) compare the consumer surplus under competition with that obtained in the absence of any cross-hauling, that is, under autarky. In this section, we compare the two regimes with respect to aggregate

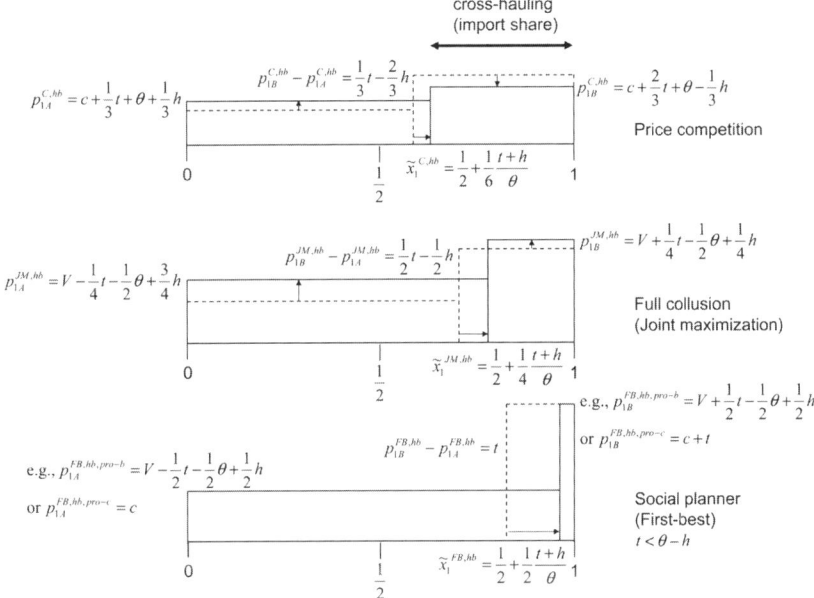

Figure 7.2   Competitive, collusive, and socially optimal prices and market shares in the presence of home bias

welfare. These comparisons are typical in the trade literature. We pose here the following question. Is it possible that certain (competitive or even collusive) markets lead to so much wasteful trade that society is better off in autarky? Instinctively, one would think not. Imagine the two markets initially shut off from each other. Why would a government forestall the entry in each market of a high-cost (importing) firm that better meets the tastes of some consumers and (recalling that a perfect cartel engages in trade) is privately profitable? We show, however, that the government can improve welfare over market-based trade regimes by directly imposing autarky. The reason is that once entry is allowed, the government cannot dictate the scale of entry. Though autarky can only be worse than allowing limited trade, under first-best, it can be better than allowing unrestricted trade. In other words, it is ideal if the government can somewhat limit trade, but if that is not possible (say because, in an international setting, only the blunt instrument of blocking entry through health/safety regulations is available, rather than the finer instrument of tariffs), then it may make sense to ban trade outright.

This paragraph, which follows Deltas et al. (2012), briefly derives the equilibrium under autarky. In the autarkic regime (denoted by the superscript $AUTK$) there are two kinds of monopoly outcomes. The first corresponds to V high enough that the autarkic monopolist fully covers the market. As can be verified below, this occurs for $V - c \geq 2\theta$. In this full coverage case, the monopolist sets price such that the consumer at $x = 1$ has zero surplus, that is, $V - \theta - p^{AUTK} = 0$, so $p^{AUTK} = V - \theta$ and thus $\Pi^{AUTK} = V - c - \theta$. In the second (complementary) case, where $V - c < 2\theta$, full coverage is not optimal for the monopolist. At the monopoly price, the consumer at $\check{x}^{AUTK} < 1$ is indifferent between the inside good and the outside good, that is, $V - \theta\check{x}^{AUTK} - p^{AUTK} = 0$, or $\check{x}^{AUTK} = (V - p^{AUTK})/\theta < 1$.[10] The monopolist's problem in this case is then:

$$\max_{p}(p - c)\frac{V - p}{\theta},$$

yielding $p^{AUTK} = \frac{1}{2}(V + c)$ and $\Pi^{AUTK} = (V - c)^2/4\theta$, and where the share of the inside good is $\check{x}^{AUTK} = (V - c)/2\theta < 1$. In summary, the autarkic price and per-market profit are given by

$$p^{AUTK} = \begin{cases} \dfrac{1}{2}(V + c) \text{ if } V - c < 2\theta \text{ (incomplete coverage)} \\ V - \theta \text{ otherwise (full coverage)} \end{cases}$$

and

$$\Pi^{AUTK} = \begin{cases} \dfrac{1}{4\theta}(V - c)^2 \text{ if } V - c < 2\theta \text{ (incomplete coverage)} \\ V - \theta - c \text{ otherwise (full coverage).} \end{cases}$$

The following proposition states regions in parameter space for which society would be better off under autarky relative to market-based trade regimes. Put simply, autarky welfare-dominates market-based trade regimes except when the trade cost t is low; for these low t cases, the welfare shortfall under autarky narrows as t is raised.

Proposition 2 For a sufficiently high unit trade cost, social welfare under autarky exceeds social welfare under full collusion (and, thus, exceeds social welfare under price competition). In particular, $W^{AUTK} > W^{JM}(>W^C)$ holds (i) for $\theta \leq t(<2\theta)$ (here there is full market coverage under autarky); and (ii) for $\frac{2}{3}\theta < t < \theta$ and $V - c \geq 2\theta$ (that is, whenever there is full market coverage under autarky). Further, (iii) for $\frac{3}{5}\theta < t \leq \frac{2}{3}\theta$ and $V - c \geq 2\theta$, social welfare under autarky exceeds social welfare under price competition but is lower than social welfare under full collusion, that is, $W^{JM} \geq W^{AUTK} > W^C$. Outside these regions, any welfare shortfall under autarky relative to price competition (and thus relative to full collusion) narrows as the trade cost increases. In particular, (iv) for $t \leq \frac{3}{5}\theta$ and $V - c \geq 2\theta$, increasing t raises both $W^{AUTK} - W^C \leq 0$ and $W^{AUTK} - W^{JM} < 0$ toward zero; and (v) for $V - c < 2\theta$ (market coverage is incomplete under autarky, occurring for $t \leq 2(V - c) - 3\theta < \theta$, increasing t raises both $W^{AUTK} - W^C$ and $W^{AUTK} - W^{JM}$ toward zero (and possibly beyond).

Proof Within the space of parameters defined by A1 and A2, we begin by examining the subspace where full market coverage obtains in autarky (this occurs if $V - c \geq 2\theta$), followed by the subspace where coverage in autarky is incomplete (that is, $V - c < 2\theta$). Consider A1: $t < 2\theta$. Notice that a sufficient condition for full coverage in autarky is $t \geq \theta$, since $V - c > \frac{1}{2}(t + 3\theta) \geq 2\theta$. For $t < \theta$, full coverage in autarky may or may not obtain, as $\frac{1}{2}(t + 3\theta) < 2\theta$ and thus $V - c$ can be either larger or smaller than 2θ. To emphasize, incomplete coverage ($V - c < 2\theta$) implies that $t < 2(V - c) - 3\theta < \theta$.

Now compute (per-market) social welfare under autarky. Consider the case of full coverage. Consumer surplus is $\frac{1}{2}\theta$ (the area of a triangle with height $V - p^{AUTK} = \theta$ and unit width) and producer surplus is $\Pi^{AUTK} = V - c - \theta$, the sum of which yields social welfare: $W^{AUTK} = V - c - \frac{1}{2}\theta$. Next, consider the case of incomplete coverage. Consumer surplus is $(V - c)^2/(8\theta)$ (the area of a triangle with height $V - p^{AUTK} = \frac{1}{2}(V - c)$ and width $\check{x}^{AUTK} = (V - c)/2\theta)$ and producer surplus is $\Pi^{AUTK} = (V - c)^2/(4\theta)$, with welfare totaling $W^{AUTK} = 3(V - c)^2/(8\theta)$.

Next compute social welfare in each of the two trade regimes (for these regimes and range of parameters, the market is fully covered and cross-hauling occurs). Consumer surplus is calculated as explained in Section 7.2. Producer surplus is given by the sum of a firm's profit on home sales and its profit on foreign sales, as stated in Section 7.2. For brevity, we simply state the sum of consumer surplus and producer surplus in each regime:

$$W^C = (36V\theta - 36c\theta - 18t\theta + 5t^2 - 9\theta^2)/(36\theta) \text{ and}$$

$$W^{JM} = (16V\theta - 16c\theta - 8t\theta + 3t^2 - 4\theta^2)/(16\theta).$$

We now calculate welfare differences across regimes, first considering parameter values for which there is full coverage under autarky. We compute $16\theta(W^{AUTK} - W^{JM}) = -3t^2 + 8t\theta - 4\theta^2$, which, being concave in t and having roots $t = \frac{2}{3}\theta, 2\theta$, is strictly positive over the interval $\frac{2}{3}\theta < t < 2\theta$: hence (recalling prior results) we have $W^{AUTK} > W^{JM} > W^C$. This proves statements (i) and (ii). Further, proof of the second part of statement

(iv) follows from noting that $-3t^2 + 8t\theta - 4\theta^2$ is negative for $t < \frac{2}{3}\theta$, but increasing in t. Similarly, we compute $36\theta(W^{AUTK} - W^C) = -5t^2 + 18t\theta - 9\theta^2$, which is strictly positive over the interval $\frac{3}{5}\theta < t < 3\theta$. So for $\frac{3}{5}\theta < t \leq \frac{2}{3}\theta$ we have $W^{JM} \geq W^{AUTK} > W^C$, proving statement (iii). Proof of the first part of statement (iv) follows, similarly, from noting that, for $t \leq \frac{3}{5}\theta$, $-5t^2 + 18t\theta - 9\theta^2$ is non-positive and increasing in t.

We now prove statement (v), pertaining to incomplete market coverage in autarky. We compute $16\theta(W^{AUTK} - W^{JM}) = 2(V - c)(3V - 3c - 8\theta) + (-3t^2 + 8t\theta + 4\theta^2)$. Since $V - c > 0$ and $V - c - 2\theta < 0 \Leftrightarrow 3V - 3c - 6\theta < 0 \Rightarrow 3V - 3c - 8\theta < 0$, the first bunch of terms is negative and invariant in t. Noting that, over the interval $0 < t \leq 2V - 2c - 3\theta < \theta$, the parabola defined by $-3t^2 + 8t\theta + 4\theta^2$ is positive and increasing in t, it follows that $W^{AUTK} - W^{JM}$ can be either positive or negative and that $W^{AUTK} - W^{JM}$ increases in t. Similarly, we compute $16\theta(W^{AUTK} - W^C) = 2(V - c)(3V - 3c - 8\theta) + \frac{4}{9}(-5t^2 + 18t\theta + 9\theta^2)$ where the same first bunch of terms is negative and, over the interval $0 < t \leq 2V - 2c - 3\theta < \theta$, the parabola $\frac{4}{9}(-5t^2 + 18t\theta + 9\theta^2)$ is positive and increasing in t. It follows that $W^{AUTK} - W^C$ can be either positive or negative and increases in t. This proves (v). With incomplete coverage under autarky, we further show that as $t \to 0^+$, $(W^{AUTK} - W^{JM} <) W^{AUTK} - W^C < 0$. The left inequality follows from prior results. The right inequality follows from noting that as $t \to 0^+$, $8\theta(W^{AUTK} - W^C) \to (V - c)(3V - 3c - 8\theta) + 2\theta^2 < 0$. To see this, notice that $(V - c)(3V - 3c - 8\theta) + 2\theta^2 < 0 \Leftrightarrow -(3V - 3c - 8\theta)(V - c) > 2\theta^2$, and that $V - c < 2\theta \Leftrightarrow -(3V - 3c - 8\theta) > 2\theta > 0$ and $V - c > \frac{1}{2}t + \frac{3}{2}\theta > \theta > 0$. Also, with incomplete coverage under autarky, we show (by example) that as $t \to 2V - 2c - 3\theta < \theta$, $W^{AUTK} - W^C$ remains negative (for example, $V = 3$, $c = 1.2$, $\theta = 1$) or can be positive (for example, $V = 3$, $c = 1.05$, $\theta = 1$). Similarly, as $t \to 2V - 2c - 3\theta < \theta$, $W^{AUTK} - W^{JM} (< W^{AUTK} - W^C)$ remains negative or can be positive (see the same examples).

Notice that statement (i) of the proposition is quite intuitive. Recall that in the interval $\theta \leq t(<2\theta)$ the first-best social outcome involves no cross-hauling – unlike the collusive regime, let alone the competitive regime, where cross-hauling obtains. Since in this region the autarkic monopolist would fully cover the market, autarky is thus first-best. Statements (ii) through (iv) pertain also to regions where there is full market coverage in autarky: conditional on full coverage, autarky is preferred to price competition (if not to full collusion) for t no less than $\frac{3}{5}\theta$. Statement (v) says that in the region where there is incomplete market coverage in autarky (this is a strict subspace of $t < \theta$), it may be that either $(W^{JM} >) W^C > W^{AUTK}$, $W^{JM} > W^{AUTK} \geq W^C$, or $W^{AUTK} \geq W^{JM} (> W^C)$; importantly, however, as t increases in this region (holding other parameters fixed) the undesirability of autarky relative to market-based regimes diminishes and may be reversed.

7.6 GOVERNMENT INTERVENTIONS: TAX AND SUBSIDY POLICIES, AND PRICE REGULATION

We now examine how the first-best can be implemented. We show that a social planner, rather than setting prices directly (as suggested in Proposition 1), can replicate the socially optimal market allocation through a system of taxes and subsidies. Say that a government, with oversight responsibility over the two local markets, can (in each market) impose a unit tax (tariff) $\tau \geq 0$ on sales of the imported good and a unit subsidy $\omega \geq 0$ on sales of the home good. The tax and subsidy policy is set prior to the firms setting prices. (Alternatively, in an international context, one can envision two countries coordinating to reciprocally tax imports and subsidize the domestically produced variety. Clearly, a government acting unilaterally and taking into consideration only domestic welfare, that is, attaching no value to foreign firms or consumers, would not choose the first-best tariff level.) For a market-based regime with either price competition or full collusion, Proposition 3 describes the symmetric tax and subsidy policy that yields the welfare-optimal market allocation.

Proposition 3 An appropriate tax and subsidy policy can be used to induce the market-based regime – either price competition or full collusion – to limit trade across geographic markets to the socially optimal level. In particular, an optimal unit tax on imports and unit subsidy on home-good sales pair (τ, ω) satisfies (i) $\tau + \omega = 2t$ in the competitive regime, and (ii) $\tau + \omega = t$ in the collusive regime.

Proof We start by considering the collusive regime. With the tax and subsidy (and assuming an interior solution), the perfect cartel's univariate problem of Section 7.2 changes to

$$\max_{p_A}(p_A - c + \omega)\frac{V - p_A}{\theta} + (2V - \theta - p_A - c - t - \tau)\left(1 - \frac{V - p_A}{\theta}\right).$$

This yields prices and profits

$$p_{1A}^{JM}(\tau, \omega) = V - \frac{1}{4}(t + \tau + \omega) - \frac{1}{2}\theta,$$

$$p_{1B}^{JM}(\tau, \omega) = 2V - \theta - p_{1A}^{JM}(\tau, \omega) = V + \frac{1}{4}(t + \tau + \omega) - \frac{1}{2}\theta$$

$$\prod_{1A}^{JM}(\tau, \omega) = \frac{1}{16\theta}(2\theta + t + \tau + \omega)(4V - 4c - t - \tau + 3\omega - 2\theta)$$

$$\prod_{1B}^{JM}(\tau, \omega) = \frac{1}{16\theta}(2\theta - t - \tau - \omega)(4V - 4c - 3t - 3\tau + \omega - 2\theta).$$

The marginal consumer, who has zero surplus, is now located at:

$$\tilde{x}_1^{JM}(\tau, \omega) = \frac{1}{2} + \frac{1}{4}\frac{t + \tau + \omega}{\theta}.$$

For the first-best market allocation to attain, that is, in order for $\tilde{x}_1^{JM}(\tau, \omega)$ $= \tilde{x}_1^{FB}$, it is clear from Section 7.6 that $(t + \tau + \omega)/(4\theta) = t/(2\theta)$ and thus a necessary condition for $\tilde{x}_1^{JM}(\tau, \omega) \to \tilde{x}_1^{FB}$ is $\tau + \omega = t$. As expected, $p_{1B}^{JM}(\tau, \omega) - p_{1A}^{JM}(\tau, \omega) = t$. To verify the example provided in the text, $(\tau, \omega) = (t, 0)$, notice that by construction of the cartel's univariate problem, the marginal consumer's utility is zero, while profits on both the home good and the imported good are non-negative.

For the equilibrium of the competitive regime with a tax and a subsidy, prices solve the system of first order conditions of profit maximization of both firms, yielding prices and profits

$$p_{1A}^C(\tau, \omega) = c + \frac{1}{3}(t + \tau - 2\omega) + \theta,$$

$$p_{1B}^C(\tau, \omega) = c + \frac{1}{3}(2t + 2\tau - \omega) + \theta$$

$$\prod_{1A}^C(\tau, \omega) = \frac{1}{18\theta}(3\theta + t + \tau + \omega)^2,$$

$$\prod_{1B}^C(\tau, \omega) = \frac{1}{18\theta}(3\theta - t - \tau - \omega)^2.$$

The equilibrium location of the marginal consumer is given by

$$\tilde{x}_1^C(\tau, \omega) = \frac{1}{2} + \frac{1}{6}\frac{t + \tau + \omega}{\theta}.$$

Similar to the above, for the first-best market allocation to attain, that is, in order for $\tilde{x}_1^C(\tau, \omega) = \tilde{x}_1^{FB}$, it follows that $(t + \tau + \omega)/(6\theta) = t/(2\theta)$ and thus a necessary condition for $\tilde{x}_1^C(\tau, \omega) \to \tilde{x}_1^{FB}$ is $\tau + \omega = 2t$.

Note that $p_{1B}^C(\tau, \omega) - p_{1A}^C(\tau, \omega) = t$. It is now straightforward to verify that the marginal consumer's utility is positive, as are the profits on both goods, for the example provided in the text $(\tau, \omega) = (2t/3, 4t/3)$.

Still considering the competitive regime, for the cartel market allocation to attain, that is, for $\tilde{x}_1^C(\tau, \omega) = \tilde{x}_1^{JM}$, a necessary condition is $(t + \tau + \omega)/(6\theta) = t/(4\theta)$ or $\tau + \omega = t/2$ for $\tilde{x}_1^C(\tau, \omega) \to \tilde{x}_1^{JM}$, where, as expected, $p_{1B}^C(\tau, \omega) - p_{1A}^C(\tau, \omega) = p_{1B}^{JM} - p_{1A}^{JM} = (1/2)t$. Verifying the example provided, $(\tau, \omega) = (t/4, t/4)$, profits on both home and imported goods are similarly positive, and the marginal consumer's utility is $U_A(p_{1A}^C(\frac{1}{4}t, \frac{1}{4}t)$; $\tilde{x}_1^{JM}) = \frac{1}{2}(2V - 2c - t - 3\theta) > 0$. Thus individual rationality constraints are met. For this example, both consumer surplus and firm profits turn out to be higher relative to the tax-and-subsidy-free competitive outcome. Calculating $CS^C(\frac{1}{4}t, \frac{1}{4}t) = \int_0^{\tilde{x}_1^{JM}}(V - \theta x - p_{1A}^C(\frac{1}{4}t, \frac{1}{4}t))dx + \int_{\tilde{x}_1^{JM}}^1(V - \theta(1 - x) - p_{1B}^C(\frac{1}{4}t, \frac{1}{4}t))dx$ and subtracting CS^C, it follows that $CS^C(\frac{1}{4}t, \frac{1}{4}t) - CS^C = \frac{5}{144}t^2/\theta > 0$. Also, each firm's profit increases by $\Pi_{1A}^C(\frac{1}{4}t, \frac{1}{4}t) + \Pi_{1B}^C(\frac{1}{4}t, \frac{1}{4}t) - \Pi_{1A}^C - \Pi_{1B}^C = \frac{5}{36}t^2/\theta > 0$.

The proposition states the necessary conditions for the first-best market allocation, $\tilde{x}_1^{FB}(>\tilde{x}_1^{JM} > \tilde{x}_1^C)$, to be replicated in both competitive and collusive regimes. The reason why these conditions are not sufficient is that individual rationality constraints, for both firms and consumers, need to be satisfied as well. Consider an example, for each regime, of a policy that attains first-best. In the competitive regime, the social planner could optimally tax the imported good at $\tau = 2t/3$ and subsidize the home good at $\omega = 4t/3$. In the collusive regime, the social planner could optimally tax the imported good at $\tau = t$ and not subsidize the home good. Intuitively, an optimal tax and subsidy induces competitive or cartelized firms to set prices such that the price of the imported good exceeds the price of the home good exactly by t, which eliminates price discrimination and excessive cross-hauling.

A natural question concerns how government, facing the wasteful competitive regime, can implement a tax and subsidy policy to replicate the market allocation observed in the 'less wasteful' collusive regime $\tilde{x}_1^{JM}(>\tilde{x}_1^C)$ (that is, as calculated in Section 7.2, free of tax and subsidy). As we show in the proof of the preceding proposition, a necessary (though again insufficient) condition for government to replicate the cartel's market allocation is that the (τ, ω) pair satisfies $\tau + \omega = t/2$. For example, the competitive duopoly would be induced to cross-haul the same amount of product as the cartel would (or, equivalently, price discriminate just as the cartel would, $p_{1B}^C(\tau, \omega) - p_{1A}^C(\tau, \omega) = p_{1B}^{JM} - p_{1A}^{JM} = \frac{1}{2}t)$ were, say, $(\tau, \omega) = (t/4, t/4)$. In this particular example, as we show, both consumer surplus and firm profits turn out to be higher relative to the tax-and-subsidy-free competitive outcome. In sum, tax and subsidy policies can be used in any regime to replicate another regime's market allocation scheme.

Finally, notice that as a potentially simpler alternative to the optimal tax and subsidy policy above, the government can induce the first-best market allocation by mandating mill pricing, that is, enacting 'anti-dumping' regulation. On prohibiting price discrimination for the same product across both markets – and it is likely that this form of price regulation would be more politically palatable than direct command-and-control pricing measures – a socially optimal outcome ensues. Intuitively, recalling that aggregate volume effects are assumed away, inefficiency arises solely from the fact that, absent intervention, a (competitive or cartelized) importer chooses to absorb a portion of the freight costs. Firms would now be required to either fully pass through transport costs to consumers or outsource shipping to a competitive third-party industry (which would, in equilibrium, charge a price equal to the transport cost).

7.7   CONCLUDING REMARKS

In the context of trade where aggregate demand effects are small, we have provided a model – that is robust to the introduction of home bias – where the following unconventional results obtain: (i) collusion reduces, though does not eliminate, trade relative to competition, leading to a cartel allocation consistent with the 'home-market principle'; (ii) this collusive reduction in trade enhances total welfare; (iii) the welfare gain from collusion occurs even when the trade cost is low; (iv) even collusion involves some degree of excessive trade relative to the welfare optimum; and (v) for a sufficiently high trade cost, even the prohibition of trade – that is, imposing autarky – improves welfare over the (tax-and-subsidy-free) competitive and collusive trade regimes. We believe these results may be useful in assessing international cartels which, as evidence suggests (for example, Levenstein and Suslow, 2004, selectively count 42 international cartels that were successfully prosecuted during the 1990s), are an important phenomenon in the contemporary global economy.

NOTES

1.   We would like to thank Marco Castaneda, Judy Chevalier, Juan Delgado, Joe Harrington, Johannes Horner, Jun Ishii, SajalLahiri, Qihong Liu, Massimo Motta, Marco Ottaviani, Jason Pearcy, Rob Porter, Alexander Rasch, Fiona Scott Morton, Yossi Spiegel, Jonathan Vogel, Alison Watts, Michael Whinston, Eleftherios Zacharias, and seminar participants at the Advances in Industrial Organization Workshop (Vienna), CRESSE, EARIE, the International Industrial Organization Conference, Jornadas de Economía Industrial, Southern Illinois University, Tulane University, and the Yale Applied Microeconomics Summer Lunch Workshop for helpful comments. Financial support from the Spanish Ministry of Science (ECO2008-01300) and from the Portuguese Ministry of Science and Technology (PTDC/EGE-ECO/099784/2008) is gratefully acknowledged.
2.   According to Harrington (2006), an implication of a market-sharing scheme such as this is that while '(i)n a competitive market, one would expect a rise in a firm's price . . ., to result in more imports . . ., an allocation scheme based on the home-market principle

3. would result in the combination of a higher price and *fewer* imports' (p. 36, original emphasis). Providing a vivid example, Röller and Steen (2006) examine an official Norwegian cement cartel, documenting the role of a common sales office whose task was to prevent cross-transportation and unprofitable competition (p. 324).

3. Friberg and Ganslandt (2008) extend Brander and Krugman's (1983) welfare analysis of autarky (the no-entry case) to a linear-demand differentiated-goods Bertrand oligopoly. When market structure is sufficiently concentrated, they find that trade competition is welfare-enhancing relative to autarky. It should be noted, however, that neither Brander and Krugman (1983) nor Friberg and Ganslandt (2008) are concerned with the welfare effect of collusion, the central motivation of this chapter.

4. We note that the argument that higher welfare can be attained through some form of coordination has been made previously. In Foros et al. (2002), firms internalize investment spillovers by colluding in an investment stage prior to competing in a product market stage. In Banal-Estanol (2007), merging parties share information.

5. We subsequently discuss the case $2\theta \leq t < 3\theta$, where cross-hauling occurs in the competitive regime but not in the collusive one.

6. Collusion that yields the joint-profit maximum can be supported as a subgame perfect equilibrium outcome of an infinitely repeated game with perfect monitoring if the discount factor is sufficiently high.

7. Outside A1, the perfect cartel does not cross-haul at all.

8. Since the price of the imported good rises relative to that in the fully collusive equilibrium, the price-cost margin remains positive. As there is no price discrimination, price-cost margins on the home and imported goods are now equal (unlike in the collusive and competitive regimes where the home good has a higher margin).

9. For example, in Bester and Petrakis's (1996) spatial model, price discrimination under imperfect competition reduces both efficiency and firm profits (for a generalization, see Liu and Serfes, 2004). Our chapter goes beyond this literature by examining the effects of collusion relative to both competition and first-best.

10. We use $\bar{x}$ rather than $\tilde{x}$ since all along $\tilde{x}$ has denoted the location of the consumer who – when trade is allowed – is indifferent between either inside good A or B.

REFERENCES

Banal-Estanol, A. (2007), 'Information-sharing implications of horizontal mergers', *International Journal of Industrial Organization*, **25**, 31–49.

Bester, H. and E. Petrakis (1996), 'Coupons and oligopolistic price discrimination', *International Journal of Industrial Organization*, **14**, 227–42.

Brander, J.A. and P.R. Krugman (1983), 'A reciprocal dumping model of international trade', *Journal of International Economics*, **15**, 313–21.

Deltas, G., A. Salvo and H. Vasconcelos (2012), 'Consumer-surplus-enhancing collusion and trade', *RAND Journal of Economics*, forthcoming.

Foros, Ø., B. Hansen and J.Y. Sand (2002), 'Demand-side spillovers and semi-collusion in the mobile communications market', *Journal of Industry, Competition and Trade*, **2**(3), 259–78.

Friberg, R. and M. Ganslandt (2008), 'Reciprocal dumping with product differentiation', *Review of International Economics*, **16**, 942–54.

Harrington, J. (2006), 'How do cartels operate?', *Foundations and Trends in Microeconomics*, **2**(1), 1–105.

Levenstein, M.C. and V.Y. Suslow (2004), 'Contemporary international cartels and developing countries: economic effects and implications for competition policy', *Antitrust Law Journal*, **71**, 801–52.

Liu, Q. and K. Serfes (2004), 'Quality of information and oligopolistic price discrimination', *Journal of Economics and Management Strategy*, **13**, 671–702.

Motta, M. (2004), *Competition Policy. Theory and Practice*, Cambridge: Cambridge University Press.

Röller, L.-H. and F. Steen (2006), 'On the workings of a cartel: evidence from the Norwegian cement industry from 1955–1968', *American Economic Review*, **96**, 321–38.

PART II

Online search, advertising and two-sided markets

8. A note on vertical search engines' foreclosure

Emanuele Tarantino[1]

8.1 INTRODUCTION

Vertical search engines are websites that address users' queries related to a particular subject matter. For example, Expedia is a vertical search engine that provides users with information on flights, Yahoo! Finance specializes in financial information and services, Weather.com on weather news and forecasts.

In *Ciao v. Google* and *Foundem v. Google*, the European Commission is investigating whether Google has acted to favor its own products and services by distorting search results. At the same time, the Federal Trade Commission (FTC) has recently announced its intention to investigate the impact of Google's dominance on the Web.[2] Allegedly, Google would manipulate its search algorithms to push integrated vertical websites to the top of Google search results, possibly at the expense of superior competing products. In this way, Google would limit competing websites' chances of being clicked by Internet users and threaten Internet plurality and 'neutrality.'

In Figure 8.1, I report the organic search results returned by Google after a query with keyword 'finance' conducted in June 2011. Google Finance links are at the first and at the second position, whilst Yahoo! Finance links rank third and fourth.[3] In a survey published in April 2010, comScore documents that Yahoo! Finance is the most popular finance vertical website and Google Finance ranked 60th. The question arises whether the one in Figure 8.1 is an instance of a vertical search engine's foreclosure: although users seem to prefer Yahoo! Finance, Google puts its own pages at the top of its organic search results. Were it a case of fore-closure, the intent might be to increase the number of visits received by the Google vertical platform. In a May 2010 report, Chitika Research shows that the first two spots in a standard search outcome on Google receive more than 50 percent of all clicks. More clicks imply more visits and more visits increase the value of a website to advertisers.

Figure 8.1   Google organic search results returned after a query with keyword 'finance', June 2011

Lately, the issue of vertical search engines foreclosure has been widely debated both in the media[4] and by scholars in the fields of law and economics. For example, Edelman and Lockwood (2011) review several examples of potentially deceptive practices carried out by general search engines (and in particular Google). Manne and Wright (2011) emphasize the difficulties that a competition authority would incur when investigating to determine whether a given search engine has engaged in competing verticals' foreclosure. Etro (2011) focuses on the role of dominance in the Internet search market and its impact on advertising.

In this chapter, I discuss the structure of the search intermediation market and then provide a review of the contributions in the economics literature to the understanding of the functioning of Internet search engines. Although a number of features in the industry are well understood, like the role of network effects in the formation of users' scale and the mechanisms that govern advertising auctions, there are still open issues, such as the relationship between online and offline advertising and the role of general search engines as information gatekeepers. Thus, I analyse general search engines' incentives to bias search results in order to favor integrated websites. I try to identify the trade-offs arising from search engines' manipulating practices, both in (1) the organic and (2) the sponsored search realm.

1. Organic search results are displayed in the main body of the web page in response to users' queries. The manipulation of organic search outcomes can be undertaken by shifting a vertically integrated website's link to the top of the results' list and it can raise a trade-off for the engine. On the one hand, the manipulating entity can increase the number of visits received by integrated websites. On the other hand, if the experience offered by the integrated site in terms of fitness with the query (and relative to its position in the list) is lower than expected, then users may realize that a manipulation has taken place and switch to competing platforms.

2. Sponsored search results are listings of advertisers' links displayed at the top and to the right-hand side of the results' page. The exact position of an ad is assigned via an auction in which each advertiser submits a bid relative to a specific keyword and the engine determines the ranking by discounting each bid by a measure of the advertiser's relevance to users. Sponsored search manipulation would be undertaken by biasing competing websites' measure of relevance, in order to favor integrated entities. The trade-off associated with this kind of practice is as follows: on the one hand, the manipulating entity expects to increase the number of visits received by integrated websites; on the other hand, users' and advertisers' participation in the search platform may be adversely affected. Manipulation can induce users to leave if the experience generated by the integrated page is lower than expected. In the case of advertisers, manipulation may impair their incentives to bid in the auction and therefore reduce the auctioneer's revenue.

Search engines can design experiments to alleviate the nuisances caused by manipulation. Engines regularly engage in experimentation, for example, to test users' appreciation of a new graphical layout or the efficiency of a new search algorithm.[5] Experiments' success depends on the accuracy of the design and in this respect, for experiments to be reliable it is crucial that the sample group is adequately representative.[6] The experimenter assesses the impact of the treatment by analysing the reaction of the individuals that experienced the change; therefore only an engine that has access to a large number of users is able to implement valid experiments. Throughout the section devoted to the search intermediation market, I discuss the importance of users' scale to engines and analyse the economic forces that may inflate it.

8.2   THE SEARCH INTERMEDIATION MARKET

8.2.1   Market Structure and Business Model

In Europe in 2009 the market shares of Google were above 90 percent in most countries, while the market shares of Microsoft (Bing) and Yahoo! were in the 5–10 percent range (data from the European Commission, Microsoft/Yahoo! decision[7]). In the United States, the picture was slightly different in 2009: Google market share was above 70 percent while, overall, Microsoft and Yahoo! accounted for 20 percent of the market.

Advertising is the major source of revenues for search engines: in its 2010 report to the Securities Exchange Commission (SEC), Google declared that search and display advertising accounted for 96 percent of its total revenues. In the United States, eMarketer documents that the 2011 market share of Google in the search advertising market is expected to be equal to 75.9 percent, with Microsoft and Yahoo! at 8 percent each.[8] In the Microsoft/Yahoo! decision, the European Commission reports that the European search advertising market exhibits a similar structure.

In principle, consumers can easily switch between search engines and several pieces of evidence confirm that this is indeed the case. Accuracast. com reports that over 2006–07[9] more than 60 percent of search engines' visitors used at least two different platforms. Moreover, the evidence (mostly anecdotal) reported by Evans (2008) documents that over the course of a month, more than a third of users visit multiple search platforms. However, Evans (2008) argues that whether a user does multi-homing seems to depend on the platform they primarily use: while only 40 percent of Google users employed one of the other platforms, 70 percent of Yahoo! users and 80 percent of MSN users visited one of the other two search platforms in a month.

On the advertisers' side of the market, Evans (2008) argues that major advertisers (like Amazon and WalMart) participate in all platforms. The reason is simple: the value of a click on a given search engine is independent from the value of a click on competing search platforms. In economic terms, the opportunity cost for an advertising firm of not placing an ad on a search engine amounts to the cost of establishing that search engine and running an ad campaign on it. Of course, things differ when small and medium advertisers are considered, as these tend to do single-homing and typically choose Google to place their ads. In the Microsoft/Yahoo! decision, the evidence provided by the European Commission supports the analysis in Evans (2008) and represents a market structure in which advertisers do multi-homing, even though Google is a must-have.

8.2.2 Vertical Search Engines

Vertical search engines can be defined as websites that provide content (information and services) tailored to address a specific subject matter. The term vertical is used to convey the idea that they are platforms on which users can search for topics within a specific industry, rather than across industries (as in the case of general search engines). A non-exhaustive list of areas covered by vertical engines includes financial services and inter-mediation, entertainment products (for example, music and videos), news (for example, weather), travel information, maps, patents, and so on.

Users click on vertical search engines to restrict the terms of their searches. From general engines it is possible to collect information at a relatively broad level, so they provide an ideal starting reference especially for uninformed users. However, whenever the same uninformed users need to further limit the scope of their queries or informed users need very specific information, vertical engines become valuable sources. This is because vertical platforms are able to process queries and return results that general platforms would provide by the use of complex combinations of keywords and longer searches. These features make vertical platforms particularly valuable also to advertisers: vertical search engines attract users with requirements that are very precise, so the ads posted on their pages exhibit larger click-through rates.[10]

Integration between general and vertical engines is a widespread phenomenon. Google's mission is 'to organize the world's information and make it universally accessible and useful';[11] inspired by such a corporate statement the company has undertaken a massive program of investment in vertical engines in multiple industries: from entertainment and news, to maps, patents, and financial services. Google is by no means an exception, as Microsoft and Yahoo! are also active on the vertical platforms' business. At the same time, there are vertical platforms that are stand-alone (for example, Expedia in the travel industry). Such heterogeneity of market players and business structures makes the analysis of the profitability of integration in this context a particularly interesting exercise.[12]

8.2.3 Intent Behind Foreclosure and the Role of Network Effects

Varian (2006) reports that, on average, a click on a given online ad converts into an actual purchase in nine per thousand of cases, which accounts for a conversion rate that is much higher than that characterizing TV or newspapers' advertising campaigns. Moreover, the May 2010 report published by Chitika Research[13] shows that the first two spots in a standard search outcome on Google receive more than 50 percent of all clicks.

These facts help to understand the intent behind (sponsored and organic) search manipulation. For general search engines, results' manipulation has one important objective: to increase the number of visitors on integrated specialized websites so that the value of placing an ad on the same sites increases.

At this stage, it is useful to briefly examine the main economic forces that contribute to inflate the number of users on a platform, beyond search engines' technical merits. In particular, the economics literature has deeply investigated the importance of network effects on agents' participation to a platform and the risk of market tipping in markets that exhibit network effects.[14]

In the case of search engines, network externalities may take two directions: from users to advertisers and between users in the same platform. Advertisers value the number of searchers on a platform for a simple reason: the higher the number of searchers, the larger the likelihood of a profitable match after an ad gets a click. On top of this, Evans (2008) claims that the presence of a larger number of searchers on a platform generates indirect network effects for other searchers on the same platform and the rationale is twofold. First, an increase in the number of platform's participants implies that advertisers have stronger incentives to join that search platform. Second, the presence of a larger number of searchers implies that more queries are processed, so that the search engine is able to extract more information from Internet users and improve the precision of its algorithm: this allows it to return more precise results even for less common combinations of keywords.

Argenton and Prüfer (2011) exploit the indirect network effects that would operate among searchers on the same platform to develop a model of search engines' competition. In the model, users disregard that by carrying out a query on an engine, the latter would store information and employ it to improve the precision of its algorithm. Information management contributes to inflate the engine's scale due to network externalities among users and the market tips over the engine that gains market leadership. The conclusion is that the search intermediation market exhibits an inherent tendency toward monopolization, with negative effects on welfare.

8.2.4   Online Advertising versus Offline Advertising

Advertising is the major source of revenues for general search engines and is therefore important to understand whether offline (for example, TV and newspapers) advertising belongs to the same market as online (search and non-search) advertising. Clearly, this would help shed light on the competitive forces that limit the profitability of manipulating practices.

The evidence on the relationship between offline and online advertising services is somewhat mixed. In the Google/DoubleClick[15] and Microsoft/ Yahoo! decisions, the European Commission found that online advertising is a relevant market per se. The French competition authority has recently reached the same conclusion in its 'Opinion No. 10-A-29 of 14 December 2010 on the competitive operation of online advertising.' Analogously, the FTC found that online and offline advertising belong to different markets in its review of the Google/DoubleClick merger.[16]

The investigation conducted by the European Commission in Microsoft/ Yahoo! documents that advertisers perceive that search ads are in a separate market, mainly for technological reasons: search ads (and to a growing extent also non-search ads) constitute an inherently different advertising channel because, unlike offline ads, they allow targeting of Internet users. However, assessing the degree of substitutability between two services by means of a comparison of their characteristics and/or uses can lead to misleading conclusions (Motta, 2004, chapter 3); it would certainly be more appropriate to conduct an analysis based on the competitive pressures that each service exerts on the other. Unfortunately, though, neither the European Commission nor the FTC base their decisions on the results of a hypothetical monopoly test.

There is anecdotal and empirical evidence documenting a certain degree of substitutability between online and offline advertising channels. Manne and Wright (2011) cite the example of Pepsi, which turned down its television advertising campaign for the 2010 Super Bowl to invest in an online campaign. At the same time, the results in Goldfarb and Tucker (2011) point to the existence of a relationship of substitutability between the two channels. Goldfarb and Tucker (2011) exploit the state level heterogeneity concerning lawyers' ability to solicit customers via traditional offline methods in cases related to personal injuries. They find that in the states where the ban is in place, personal injury keywords cost up to 7 percent more than other keywords related to legal services: this accounts for a significantly higher premium for personal injury keywords with respect to non-regulated states.

Although the analysis in Goldfarb and Tucker (2011) seems to suggest that advertisers substitute between offline and online campaigns, the thought experiment that characterizes their empirical strategy differs in a crucial aspect from the one of a small but significant non-transitory increase in prices (SSNIP) test:[17] the existence of a ban implies that the hypothetical price increase is infinite; instead in a SSNIP test the increase would be significant but small. Still, the results of the article threaten the reliability of the conclusions reached by the European Commission and the FTC, leaving open the issue of whether offline advertising and online advertising belong to the same market.

8.2.5   Search Engines as Information Gatekeepers

From several pieces of evidence, it emerges that the traffic to verticals is only partly originated by general search engines. For example, eBay reports that in the 30 days before February 2010 less than 10 percent of visits to its website came from a search engine. Moreover, comScore reports that in June 2011 only 4 percent of a user's time was spent on a search engine and Accuracast.com documents that during 2006–07,[18] searchers spent on average 27 minutes on a search engine per month (which accounted for about 3.4 percent of the time spent online).

At the same time, social networks occupy a growing share of Internet users' eyeball. According to a recent report by comScore, social networking represents one out of every six minutes spent online.[19] Moreover, the same comScore documents that as of June 2011 in the UK users spent more time on facebook than on any other site.[20]

These facts seem to contradict the prevalent approach in the policy debate that treats search engines as only information gatekeepers on the Internet.[21] In this respect, although the economic literature has investigated the role of Internet information gatekeepers on advertisers' pricing decisions (Baye and Morgan, 2001, 2002), a relatively unexplored question concerns how information gatekeepers endogenously arise on the Internet.

The rationale for a user that is unaware of a specific subject to click on a search engine is easily discerned: the query would return a list of links that provide them with a starting point for a deeper search on the Web. However, it is less clear whether informed users would employ a general search engine to conduct their searches on the Web. The question is whether users would rationally run a query on a search engine if already aware of the websites they want to reach. In a model with search costs, this is possible if users expect the engine to provide additional information to that they already have: for instance, if the engine suggests new websites or novel details on the specific subject of the query.

The next question is: in the case of informed users, would results' manipulation work? The answer is somewhat ambiguous. Users of this sort already have a certain knowledge of the subject they are searching on, so if an engine provides them with biased results, they could either realize it or believe that a 'new' ranking (in terms of results' relevance) is in place and update their priors accordingly. In other words, informed users' reaction to a manipulation seems to depend on the beliefs they have on the reliability of the engine relative to their command of the field of the query.

8.2.6 The Management of Advertising

Search engines can generate sponsored search results by running a position auction. To participate in the auction, an advertiser needs to submit a bid relative to a (combination of) keyword(s). For example, if a consulting firm would like to participate in an auction for the keywords 'business consultancy,' it needs to submit a monetary bid that captures its willingness to pay for each click it would receive by Internet users carrying out a query on those keywords.

The position of an advertiser in the list is determined by the value of its bid (b) and a measure of its relevance to users (m). Once the list is compiled by the auction system, advertisers pay a price for each click. The search engine needs to preserve advertisers' incentives to bid in the auction, so the position of each advertiser must depend on the monetary value of its bid. At the same time, the search engine wants to reward the websites that ensure a better experience to users; therefore the value of the bid is adjusted by an index of relevance. In the case of Google, the system that assesses websites' relevance is the Quality Score[22] and the weights attached to the bid and the index returned by the Quality Score to pin down advertisers' order in the list are not public information.

The per-click fee paid by advertiser i participating in a position auction is given by the bid of the next bidder, discounted by a relative measure of its relevance (m_i) with respect to the relevance of the next bidder. For example, if the value of b_i and m_i relative to advertiser i are such that i is ranked in position k by the system, then the per-click payment (p_i) due by firm i is given by a formula of the following sort:

$$p_i = b^{k+1} m^{k+1} (m_i)^{-1}.$$

This scheme implements a mechanism that shares important analogies with second-price auction models, because the advertiser in position k pays according to a function of the bid submitted by the advertiser in position $k+1$ (b^{k+1}). The Google advertising platform was the first to implement such a second-price system, followed by Overture (Yahoo!). Second-price auction mechanisms have two main merits. The first is that their functioning is intuitive and easy to explain to advertisers. The second, and more important, is that they are more stable than first-price mechanisms.

The first-position auction model to sell Internet advertising slots was introduced by Overture in 1997 and it was a first-price auction model. The system required advertisers to post their willingness to pay on a per-click basis for a particular keyword and the total price an advertiser would pay was equal to its bid per click multiplied by the number of clicks received by the ad link. The major problem of first-price systems was that advertisers had an incentive to revise their bids as often as possible in order to outbid their rivals, and this drawback could have eventually led them to invest in bidding robots, with harmful consequences for search engines' revenues (McAdams and Schwarts, 2007).

Edelman et al. (2007) discuss the evolution of the auctioning systems employed by search engines and present a generalized second-price auction mechanism to model the real system employed by Yahoo! and Google to sell respective slots. The article also studies the differences between the generalized second-price auction mechanism and the Vickrey-Clarke-Groves second-price mechanism, showing that they are not equivalent because the generalized second-price model does not always induce truth-telling by advertisers.

An important assumption in the model developed by Edelman et al. (2007) is that the weight m attached to a bid is determined by ad and position-specific factors (private value assumption). In other words, the value of being in a position is independent of the quality of the other advertisers in the list. Jeziorski and Segal (2010) find that the private value assumption is not confirmed in the data, insofar as the click-through rate on a given ad depends on which other ads are displayed in the list.

Athey and Ellison (2011) develop a position auction model that departs in several respects from the literature that followed Edelman et al. (2007) (for example, Varian, 2007; Edelman and Schwartz, 2010). In Athey and Ellison (2011), advertisers differ in terms of their ability to match consumers' needs, consumers bear a cost of clicking an ad, and they rationally choose the number and the sequence of links they click. As a consequence of these three assumptions, the value of being in a given position depends on all the other advertisers published in the list.

Athey and Ellison (2011) deliver several insightful results, which greatly contribute to the comprehension of the functioning of online advertising auctions models. First, the model shows that in a context with clicking costs, the imposition of a reserve price can, at the same time, increase consumers' welfare and raise an auctioneer's revenue.[23] The intuition is simple: the introduction of a reserve price can avoid inefficient searches and increase the number of links examined by Internet users.

Athey and Ellison (2011) also show that click-weighted auctions can reduce efficiency. In the model, the weight m attached to a given advertiser bid to determine its position in the list captures the probability that the same advertiser meets consumers' needs. Therefore, at equilibrium the engine can display the ads of generalists, although their quality is low. This would be inefficient for two reasons. First, if high-quality sites that serve narrower segments of individuals are displayed, then users could save in search costs. Second, the click-weighted auction mechanism may reduce the amount of information that consumers are able to grasp from ads' listings about the quality of advertisers.

8.3 MANIPULATION INCENTIVES

8.3.1 Organic Search Results' Manipulation

Organic search results are generated at no direct cost to websites they link and to Internet users. They are listings of links that the search engine ranks in order of importance, for given keyword(s) and (whenever possible) the user's profile. The algorithm generating the results assesses web page content relevance by looking at how many other relevant pages link to it and how many clicks it receives.

The Google algorithm is based on the PageRank system. PageRank was a major innovation introduced by Google to improve the fit of search engine's results to users' queries. As shown by Brin and Page (1998), the Google PageRank original model was designed to generate a probability distribution across web pages, so that the sum of all pages' PageRank is one. The early model has been developed to take into account users' language and query models (to handle spelling mistakes and control for people's use of language) and time models (to determine whether the best reply is a recent page or an old page).

Organic search manipulation can be undertaken by shifting a vertically integrated website's link on the top of the organic search results' page. A small perturbation of organic results is hardly perceived by users, although it can greatly raise a link's popularity. As Brin and Page (1998, p. 18) put it in the article that presented Google to the academic world:

> A search engine could add a small factor to search results from 'friendly' companies, and subtract a factor from results from competitors. This type of bias is very difficult to detect but could still have a significant effect on the market.

Of course, this quotation cannot prove that Google itself has effectively engaged in organic results' manipulating practices; still it reveals that, in principle, manipulations of this sort are technically feasible, difficult to detect, and (potentially) highly profitable for the manipulating entity.

The incentive to bias organic search results is augmented by a feedback effect that exploits an inherent feature of the search engines' algorithm. The pages that appear in prominent spots receive more clicks, are more popular, and are therefore likely to receive more links. The algorithm prizes web pages that receive more links and clicks (as in the Google PageRank system). Consequently, if, say, Google would bias its results in favor of a 'friendly' web page, the same 'friendly' page could climb not only Google, but also Bing and Yahoo! organic search results. In other words, this feed-back effect generates an externality on the queries processed by a search engine that competes against the manipulating platform: for the former it is difficult to disentangle the clicks and links received by a page due to its own relevance from the ones obtained because of search results' manipulation. Therefore, the bias can self-reinforce itself across time and search platforms.

The main threat behind organic results' manipulation is that after finding the 'friendly' page on top of the list (although an unbiased algorithm would not place it there) searchers may decide to leave the platform. After receiving a list of biased results, a user can update downward his/her valuation of an engine's quality and the platform's risk to their switching depends on the competition it faces from other search engines. If competition is one click away, that is, competitors' quality exerts a binding constraint to the manipulating entity, switching is relatively likely. Conversely, manipulations are profitable whenever the quality associated with the engine is so high that engaging in manipulating practices would not result in users' switching.

In this sense, a large scale is crucial to ensure an engine against switching. First of all, a large scale allows an engine to improve the quality of its services, attract more advertisers, and, in turn, new searchers. Moreover, a large scale makes experimentation easier. To limit the downside caused by manipulation, engines can design experiments of two sorts. They can (1) bias the response to the queries relative to the same keyword(s) across users and/or (2) manipulate the results returned to the queries performed by the same user across keywords. In either case, the outcome would be to render manipulation even more difficult to detect.

For example, in (1) an engine could test the reaction by a sample of users to biased organic search results and compare it with the reaction by a sample of users that did not receive biased listings. In this way, the engine can assess the attitude toward manipulated results across users and sort them according to respective type. In (2) the engine could design an experiment consisting of the submission of a biased search outcome to the same user but across a random set of keywords. This test would allow the platform to extract information at the user level regarding the response to manipulation per specific words/topics typed in a query.

Summarizing, the trade-off associated with shifting a 'friendly' website on top of organic search results is as follows. On the one hand, an engine profits from the number of clicks (and popularity) gained by the 'friendly' website. On the other hand, if the 'friendly' website is irrelevant users may realize that a manipulation has taken place and, consequently, they may decide to switch. The upside from results' manipulation is augmented by the feedback effect discussed above: if Google manipulates its results to make an integrated vertical search engine receive more clicks, then the same vertical is likely to climb Bing and Yahoo! search results. Finally, the cost of organic results' manipulation can be alleviated by experimentation, which is easier, the larger the scale of the search engine's users.

8.3.2 Sponsored Search Results' Manipulation

The manipulation of sponsored search results lowers competing advertisers' measure of relevance. The position auction system is designed in such a way that if two advertisers bid on the same combination of keywords, the page with a lower measure of relevance has to offer a higher bid to rank at the same position, *ceteris paribus*. Hence, to manipulate the auction system and favor an integrated site, an engine needs to manipulate the relevance measure of a competitor (for a given bid).

As for the case of organic search results' manipulation, by biasing position auctions' results a platform may impair users' participation. Assume a 'friendly' website is placed by the engine at the first spot of sponsored search results although, overall, its 'true' value would be such that it should have been placed second: users clicking on the first ad may realize that the corresponding website quality is not consistent with the first slot expected quality and, consequently, they may decide to leave the platform. Of course, leaving depends on the competitive pressure exerted by alternative search engines: if the manipulating entity provides users, on average, with a better experience than competing engines, then users may still decide to stay on the platform.

More importantly, sponsored results' manipulation may impair bidders' incentives. If advertisers perceive that the system is biased, then they have weaker incentives to bid consistently with their valuation of the ad per click. This could undermine the auction system's internal coherence, induce advertisers to leave the platform, and therefore lead to lower expected revenue for the auctioneer. To grasp the intuition of why this is the case, it is useful to refer to the result in Edelman et al. (2007) that the generalized second-price auction models employed by search engines do not necessarily induce advertisers to bid consistently with their valuation of the spot. It is therefore natural to conclude that if a search engine artificially distorts the results of the auction, advertisers have further incentives to misreport their true valuation.

The trade-off associated with manipulating a competing advertiser's measure of relevance to push a 'friendly' page on top of sponsored results is as follows. On the one hand, an engine gains from the increased number of clicks potentially leading to conversions in actual purchases on 'friendly' web pages. On the other hand, if advertisers and users perceive that the system is corrupt, their participation in the platform is adversely affected. Indeed, the manipulating practice may dilute advertisers' incentives to bid 'correctly.' Moreover, manipulation may imply that users are provided with a worse experience than expected in terms of sponsored search results' composition. Again, the cost of manipulating is alleviated by experimentation, which is easier, the larger the scale of advertisers participating in a platform.

8.4   CONCLUSIONS

Vertical search engines' foreclosure is the issue at the core of several antitrust cases on both sides of the Atlantic. In this chapter, I analyse the structure of the Internet search intermediation market and then survey the economics literature on some of the crucial features of this industry. Finally, I discuss the costs and the benefits associated with search manipulation. The main upside for the manipulating entity appears to be the likely increase in the number of visits received by integrated websites. However, this is not costs-free: as a consequence of manipulation, users' and advertisers' participation in the platform may be adversely affected.

NOTES

1. I thank Elena Argentesi, Susan Athey, Maria Bigoni, Federico Boffa, Giacomo Calzolari, Federico Etro, Bernhard Ganglmair, Massimo Motta, Chiara Valentini, and the participants at CRESSE 2011 (Rhodes) for useful comments and discussions. Usual disclaimers apply.
2. 'Feds to launch probe of Google', *Wall Street Journal*, 24 June 2011.
3. More examples of this sort can be found on Ben Edelman's web page (http://www.benedelman.org/).
4. For example, see 'Google's gatekeepers', *New York Times*, 30 November 2005 and 'Scrutinizing Google's reign', *New York Times*, 19 September 2011.
5. For example, for the launch of its new layout in June 2011 Google ran a number of experiments concerning the color of the new toolbar and the natural search results' text format, see http://www.ghacks.net/2011/05/07/google-search-new-layout-style/ (accessed February 2012).
6. A sample of Internet users and advertisers is representative if it reflects (as accurately as possible) the characteristics of the population of users and advertisers.
7. European Commission, case M. 5727, February 2010.
8. eMarketer, 'Google's share of search ad revenues rises, unaffected by Bing', 8 June, available at http://www.emarketer.com/PressRelease.aspxoR=1008451 (accessed February 2012).

9. AccuraCast, 'Search engine statistics for 2006–2007', February 2007.
10. For an empirical analysis of click-through rates received by vertical search engines in several industries, see the 'DoubleClick benchmarks report: 2009 year-in-review', at http://www.google.com/doubleclick/research/ (accessed February 2012).
11. http://www.google.com/about/corporate/company/ (accessed February 2012).
12. See Tarantino (2011) for a deeper investigation of the vertical search intermediation market and preliminary evidence on vertical engines' foreclosure.
13. Chitika Research, 'The value of Google result positioning', 25 May 2010, available at http://chitika.com/research/2010/the-value-of-google-result-positioning/ (accessed February 2012).
14. See Motta (2004), chapter 2 for a survey.
15. European Commission, case M. 4731, March 2008.
16. See Proposed Acquisition of Click Holding Company by Google Inc., File No. 0710170, available at http://ftc.gov/os/caselist/0710170/index.htm (accessed February 2012).
17. See Motta (2004), chapter 3 for a more exhaustive discussion on the SSNIP test and its implementation.
18. AccuraCast, 'Search engine statistics for 2006–2007', February 2007.
19. http://blog.comscore.com/2011/06/facebook_linkedin_twitter_tumblr.html (accessed February 2012).
20. http://www.comscoredatamine.com/2011/07/more-time-is-spent-on-facebook-than-any-other-uk-site/ (accessed February 2012).
21. As an example, see 'Google's gatekeepers', *New York Times*, 28 November 2008.
22. The exact factors that determine the Quality Score of a website are not public information. However, Google has acknowledged that the history of an advertiser's click-through rate, the landing page relevance, and load time are important components in the determination of the score.
23. This result stands in contrast to standard auction models, in which the introduction of a reserve price increases the seller's revenue at the cost of reducing consumers' surplus.

REFERENCES

Argenton, C. and J. Prüfer (2012), 'Search engine competition with network externalities', *Journal of Competition Law & Economics*, **8**(1), 73–105.

Athey, S. and G. Ellison (2011), 'Position auctions with consumers search', *Quarterly Journal of Economics*, **126**(3), 1213–70.

Baye, M. and J. Morgan (2001), 'Information gatekeepers and the competitiveness of homogeneous product markets', *American Economic Review*, **91**, 454–74.

Baye, M. and J. Morgan (2002), 'Information gatekeepers and price discrimination on the internet', *Economics Letters*, **76**(1), 47–51.

Brin, S. and L. Page (1998), 'The anatomy of a large-scale hypertextual web search engine', *Proceedings of the 7th International Conference on World Wide Web (WWW)*, Brisbane, Australia, pp. 107–17.

Edelman, B. and B. Lockwood (2011), 'Measuring bias in "organic" web search', available at http://www.benedelman.org (accessed February 2012).

Edelman, B. and M. Schwarz (2010), 'Optimal auction design and equilibrium selection in sponsored search auctions', *American Economic Review*, **100**(2), 597–602.

Edelman, B., M. Ostrovsky and M. Schwarz (2007), 'Internet advertising and the generalized second-price auction: selling billions of dollars worth of keywords', *American Economic Review*, **97**(1), 242–59.

Etro, F. (2011), 'Leadership in multi-sided markets and the dominance in online advertising', mimeo, University of Venice.

Evans, D.S. (2008), 'The economics of the online advertising industry', *Review of Network Economics*, **7**(3), 359–91.

Goldfarb, A. and C. Tucker (2011), 'Search engine advertising: channel substitution when pricing ads to context', *Management Science*, **57**(3), 458–70.

Jeziorski, P. and I. Segal (2010), 'What makes them click: empirical analysis of consumer demand for search advertising', mimeo, Johns Hopkins University.

Manne, G.A. and J.D. Wright (2011), 'Google and the limits of antitrust: the case against the antitrust case Against Google', *Harvard Journal of law and Public Policy*, **34**(1), 3–74.

McAdams, D. and M. Schwarts (2007), 'Who pays when auction rules are bent?', *International Journal of Industrial Organization*, **27**(5), 1144–57.

Motta, M. (ed.) (2004), *Competition Policy: Theory and Practice*, New York: Cambridge University Press.

Tarantino, E. (2011), 'A simple model of vertical search engines foreclosure', mimeo, University of Bologna.

Varian, H. (2006), 'The economics of internet search', *Rivista di Politica Economica*, **96**(6), 9–23.

Varian, H. (2007), 'Position auctions', *International Journal of Industrial Organization*, **25**(6), 1163–78.

9. Issues in online advertising and competition policy: a two-sided market perspective

Emilio Calvano and Bruno Jullien

9.1 INTRODUCTION

Online advertising accounted for $26.04 billion of the total US advertising pie in 2010, with annual growth rates in the double digits. In the past few years the Internet has continued to grow in significance when compared to other ad-supported media. In 2010, Internet advertising surpassed advertising revenues in newspapers. Advertising in general and online advertising in particular involves a large diversity of actors. The main actors on the supply side of the market are search engines and portals (for example, Google, Yahoo), online news outlets (for example, cnn.com, nyt.com), user generated content sites (YouTube, blogs), social networks (Facebook, Google+), and e-commerce outlets (eBay, Amazon).[1] What makes online advertising attractive is the wide range of new products and services offered. Sponsored search ads tie advertising messages to specific keyword searches. Sponsors can thus be matched to consumers who showed an interest in particular products/topics. Behavioral targeting and re-targeting techniques allow the use of information collected on an individual's browsing behavior, such as the pages he has visited or the searches he has made to select which advertisements to display to that individual. Performance-based pricing allows charging as a function of the outcome of the campaign. Cost per thousand impressions (CPM), cost per click-through (CPT), or cost per sale (CPS) are only some of the schemes employed by online outlets (often called 'platforms' in what follows) to attract advertisers.

Despite the wealth of innovation, the economics of online advertising is not fundamentally different than its offline counterpart. Online outlets (or platforms) create (or buy) content that is used to attract 'eyeballs.' The eyeballs are then used to attract advertisers. This is precisely what traditional media, such as newspapers or TV broadcasters, have been doing all along. For example, newspapers bundle news and advertising. Consumers pay (or not) for the content and typically choose their favorite outlet via price and quality considerations. Advertisers pay for the attention of consumers.

The advertising markets raise several issues for the conduct of competition policy that are related to the unconventional nature of the market and its functioning.

A first basic set of questions is about the optimal pricing choices and business models in these markets. TV networks such as ABC and NBC thrived until recently delivering free over-the-air content. This 'cross-subsidization' model has advertising as the sole source of revenues. At the other end of the spectrum, several cable channels have little or no advertising with subscribers paying for the service. Finally, newspapers, at least in their initial incarnations, frequently adopted a mixed model, revenue being generated on both sides of the market. Readers purchase copies while advertisers purchase space. It is not hard to find new instances of these 'old' business models on the Internet. For example, search engines and social networking sites are free to users and costly to advertisers. Other examples readily come to mind.

A first set of insights comes from a thriving research area in industrial organization on the general features of what have been called 'two-sided platforms' or 'two-sided markets.' Notable contributions include Caillaud and Jullien (2003), Rochet and Tirole (2003, 2006), Armstrong (2006), and Weyl (2010). These articles study the incentives of privately owned platforms, such as exchanges, that enable interactions between two (or more) different sets of users such as buyers and sellers. Search engines, news outlets, and social network websites are all instances of two-sided (or multi-sided) platforms. Their distinctive feature is the presence of externalities between different user types. That is, the value that users place on the platform depends on who else is using the platform. The success of these platforms depends crucially on their ability to account for these externalities when determining their pricing and investment strategies.

Although theories of platform competition are not specific to the Internet, they shed light on most of the basic trade-offs faced by Internet platforms and will be used here to set the stage. These theories contrast market outcomes with efficient (that is, welfare-maximizing) outcomes under various market configurations and governance structures. Accordingly in what follows we first discuss competition policy issues specific to two-sided intermediation that are relevant for advertising markets in general. We then turn to those aspects inherent to the online world that we believe can potentially lead to new intuitions or deserve specific treatment.

9.2 PART ONE: THE ECONOMICS OF MEDIA PLATFORMS

9.2.1 A Simple Framework

To fix ideas consider the simplest abstract model of a monopoly platform. This framework does not apply to the above examples where competition is the rule. However a theory of monopoly is essential to be able to talk about competition policy related issues such as market definition and the assessment of market power. Think about a news outlet with some predetermined content that deals with a large number of readers and advertisers. All advertisers' willingness to pay to access the platform (that is, to buy ad space) increases with circulation (that is, the number of readers). On the contrary, all readers' willingness to pay for the newspaper decreases with the number of advertisers. Because the emphasis here is on the quantity of agents on different sides of the market it is convenient to think of the platform as setting quantities rather than prices. Let $P_R(n_R, n_A)$ and $P_A(n_A, n_R)$ be the inverse demand function of readers and advertisers respectively. That is, the maximum price that the platform can ask readers and advertisers respectively if it wishes to sell n_R copies and n_A ads. Clearly P_R and P_A decrease with n_A, P_R decreases with n_R and P_A increases with n_R. The outlet then chooses its sales so as to maximize its profit as stated below (arguments omitted):

$$\max_{n_A, n_R \geq 0} P_A * n_A + P_R * n_R.$$

Alternatively one could think of the platform as setting prices and restate the problem as follows. Let $n_A(P_A, n_R)$ and $n_R(P_R, n_A)$ denote the number of advertisers and readers whose willingness to pay exceeds P_A and P_B respectively. n_A decreases with P_A and increases with n_R. n_R decreases with P_R and n_A. Once again the outlet chooses the prices that solve (arguments omitted):

$$\max_{P_A, P_R \geq 0} P_A * n_A + P_R * n_R.$$

This way of posing the problem highlights an important coordination issue in these markets. What each agent gets when using the platform depends on how many other agents are using the platform as well. So all agents need a conjecture of what the other agents will do in order to form a valuation of the platform's services. This means that for each pair of prices P_A and P_R there could be multiple levels of equilibrium participation. Coordination issues are important but will not be the focus of this chapter.

In what follows we sidestep this issue by assuming that the platform is always capable of coordinating users. Formally the assumption is that for each relevant pair of prices P_A and P_R there are unique levels of participation n_A and n_R consistent with those prices. The term consistent means that all users at these participation levels obtain more utility by participating than by not participating (see Caillaud and Jullien, 2003 for more details).

Starting from any set of prices, consider the impact of decreasing one price to one group of users, say readers. A first direct and familiar consequence is that demand on that side, that is, the number of readers, goes up. But a second effect is that attracting additional readers creates value for advertisers whose demand will also increase as a result. It follows that the amount of money that the platform is willing to give up to get an extra reader on board is lower than the physical marginal cost of serving a user, because of the two-sided externalities. The (robust) intuition that prices are equal to marginal cost plus a markup is still valid once we plug in the right notion of cost, that is, the 'opportunity cost.' Here:

Price = (physical cost − value created on the other side) + markup,

where the markup is a standard monopoly markup. Hence prices tend to be smaller than in a one-sided market.

Applying this logic to competition leads to new results. Indeed a key insight when accounting for two-sidedness is the different role played by competitive pressure in these markets. Typically competition will not affect the two sides of the market with the same intensity. For example, most of the competition for advertisers takes place through competition for the attention of consumers in the price and quality dimension. The reason being that the sole supplier of a given individual's attention allows extraction of a monopoly rent on the advertising side of the market.

A simple extension of the above model can be used to shed light on the issue of competition. Think about two platforms courting the same two sets of end-users. Platforms simultaneously post all their prices. End-users observe prices and choose one platform. (Later we consider the case in which end-users are allowed to choose more than one or none.) Suppose that all users have idiosyncratic tastes over the platforms. For given participation levels (that is, given their conjecture about what the other users will do at the posted prices) the differential value of choosing one platform over the other is heterogeneous within the population of users and continuously distributed on the real line. So some users will strictly prefer platform 1 to platform 2, others will prefer platform 2 to platform 1 and those with a differential value exactly equal to zero will be indifferent. Starting from any set of prices consider again the impact of decreasing one price to one group of users, say readers. The previous discussion is still valid but a new effect is at work. When competing by stealing readers the platform reduces the attractiveness of its competitor. As a result, a price reduction for readers attracts more advertisers than in the monopoly case. Taking this into account, a platform will choose prices according to:

$$\text{Price} = (\text{physical cost-value created on the other side-value destroyed at the competitor}) + \text{markup}.$$

Competition tends to reduce the markup (as in most markets). In addition the two-sided externality further reduces the prices. A first consequence of the downward pressure brought about by lower opportunity costs is skewed pricing. That is, the margin over physical cost may be very different for the two sides, even negative on one side. In particular the service can be free on one side. For our purpose the main point is that price skewness need not reflect strong market power and is intensified by competition. These 'low' or below physical cost prices are not anti-competitive per se. Negative prices are not an indicator of predatory practices as competition may intensify cross-subsidies.

In general the effect of competitive pressure on two-sided businesses depends on a number of key factors such as:

- Price instruments available/tariffs:
  - How many prices (membership fees, usage fees on all or on a subset of the sides)?
  - Which kind of prices (participation contingent prices/usage, for example, 'per click' contingent prices)?

- Services:
  - Is the service bundled with other goods or services?
  - Is it two-sided or multi-sided?
  - Are the platforms selling complementary products?

- Consumer behavior:
  - Do they rely on one or several outlets?
  - How do they perceive advertising (ad lovers or advert to ads)?
  - Do they have switching costs?

We shall not address all these points but only the issue of end-user behavior, which is crucial to assess the role of competition. The assumption that consumers and advertisers only choose one platform (in jargon 'single-home') is a main driver of the results above. Indeed a key element that affects the analysis of competition with advertising is the extent to which one or the other category of users of the service relies on only one outlet (single-home) or several outlets ('multi-home'). We will address the issue of consumers' behavior when discussing multiple impressions; we focus here on advertisers. Whether advertisers view outlets as competing media between which they must choose or as different channels with different audiences on which they can diversify their campaign may drastically change the nature of competition. The first case corresponds to the situation described above and arises, for instance, when advertisers have limited resources to invest and diversification is too costly. The second case corresponds more to large and well-funded advertising campaigns on outlets with different audiences. In this case, advertisers will consider each outlet separately and their decision to invest in one outlet will depend on its audience only and not on the other outlets. This situation is often referred to as a 'competitive bottleneck' in the two-sided market jargon. This is the canonical model adopted by many influent articles on media competition, such as the work of Anderson and Coate (2005), for instance. In this situation, competition shifts entirely on the consumer side. Platforms do not compete directly to attract advertisers but only through consumers. Indeed once an outlet has succeeded in attracting some 'eyeballs,' it becomes the sole means of access to a these consumers for advertisers and it can sell this access at a monopoly price. Outlets thus receive high revenue per consumer from advertisers but this profit is to a large extent passed on to consumers as outlets compete intensely to attract them. Price skewness becomes maximal with low prices on the consumer side. Although platforms enjoy some form of market power on one side of the market, this is disciplined by competition on the other side of the market. This is one of the main reasons that one cannot analyse the advertising side without considering competition on the consumer side.

9.2.2   Welfare Economics of Two-sided Markets

A first basic challenge faced by antitrust authorities and courts is to adopt a welfare concept to measure industry performance. In most one-sided businesses, practices that foster competition typically increase total surplus. In two-sided businesses, consumer surplus is the sum of the surplus of agents on different sides. The same practices could lead to redistributive effects among end-users. Some anti-competitive practices or agreements that benefit a set of end-users could be overlooked.

Consider, for instance, the consumer surplus as it is inferred from the demand addressed to the firm in standard economic activities. In general when the clients of the firms are also firms that produce and sell goods, the same criterion extends provided that these clients are active in a competitive market (as competition leads them to pass on efficiency gains to final consumers). But this logic is difficult to apply to advertising as it impacts consumption only indirectly, which is often overlooked.

In general how to weight the surplus of different agents is subtle and, as we shall see, even subtler when considering the surplus that derives from advertising. Economists have long had conflicting views on advertising (see Bagwell, 2007 for a survey of the literature). The 'persuasive' view holds that advertising 'shapes' consumer tastes, fostering brand loyalty and spurious product differentiation (Chamberlin, 1933; Robinson, 1933; Kaldor, 1950). This approach suggests that advertising can have serious anti-competitive effects and should not be encouraged. The 'informative' view holds that advertising is a market response to a shortage of information on determinants of consumer choices such as prices, quality, and even mere existence of products and services (Stigler, 1961). As such, advertising could have pro-competitive effects removing frictions that foster market power. A third view holds that advertising can be 'complementary' to consumption (Becker and Murphy, 1993). For instance, network goods need coordination of a sufficiently large base of consumers to deliver any value. Advertising is complementary to the extent that it helps individuals coordinate. 'Signaling goods' (for example, conspicuous consumption) are also examples of goods whose value increases with advertising. Under this view advertising should also be encouraged, as advertisers typically fail to internalize the full extent of consumer surplus.

Advertising can also be a wasteful activity. Waste comes from two sources. Strategic complementarities in advertising choices might trap competing firms into excessive advertising. If a campaign needs to outplay a rival's campaign to be successful, then the firms' incentives to pour resources into advertising can go up even though the individual firm and industry profits go down. Then firms and consumers would be better off without advertising altogether. Furthermore advertising consumes the attention of individuals, which is a scarce resource, increasingly so in the digital world. The lack of a separate market for attention in which consumers register their willingness to pay can lead to inefficient depletion. Advertisers do not internalize consumers' welfare when crafting their campaigns. The option of consumer 'exit' which usually works as a disciplining device of last resort is typically unfeasible and 'ad avoidance' is a costly activity. Fogg-Meade (1901, pp. 231–2) had already pointed out that advertising is 'a subtle, persistent, unavoidable presence that creeps into the reader's inner consciousness.'

Finally, advertising supports the creation of quality content through competition for eyeballs and more generally reduces the entry cost of new content as platforms may be willing to subsidize creation in order to foster their position in the advertising market.

Overall we see that even a simple criterion such as the consumer surplus may be delicate to assess in practical cases, in particular mergers, as it requires taking a stance on the type of advertising considered and its social value.

9.2.3   Market Definition and the Assessment of Market Power

The simple model introduced above is useful for thinking about market definition issues in multi-sided businesses. Suppose, for instance, that the task at hand is to define the relevant market for advertising using a standard tool: the small but significant non-transitory increase in prices (SSNIP) test. The exercise consists in identifying the smallest market such that fully coordinated sellers (a hypothetical monopoly) in this market would find it profitable to increase the price above the current level in a non-transitory way, say by 5 percent. The key question in the case of advertising is how we treat the two sides and the fact that prices on both sides are interrelated.

Suppose we were to adopt a 'naïve' approach neglecting the indirect externalities between readers and advertisers. This means, for instance, evaluating the impact of a price increase on advertisers keeping fixed both the quantity and the price on the readers' side of the market. The estimated impact on profits of an increase of the price of advertising is (approximately) equal to:

$$\Delta P_A * n_A - \Delta n_A * P_A',$$

where P_A' denotes the new, higher price. However, the story is not over. Suppose that some consumers are sensitive to advertising, because of the lower amount of ads, more or fewer consumers would purchase the newspaper at the same price. Changing circulation implies additional revenues equal to $\Delta n_R * P_R$. So the actual impact comprises the additional change in revenues on the readers' side of the market. From this reasoning we can conclude that this 'naïve' incarnation of the SSNIP test on the market for advertising would lead to a systematic overestimation of market size if consumers dislike advertising (underestimation if they like advertising). How big the discrepancy would be between actual and estimated impact depends on the strength of the cross-network externalities. The higher the elasticity of the readers' demand to the advertisers' quantity, the higher the mismatch.

Consider now a more 'sophisticated' version of the test that takes in to account the overall change in revenues resulting from a price increase on the price of advertising: $\Delta P_A * n_A - \Delta n_A * P_A' + \Delta n_R * P_R$. Since the price change affects the willingness to pay on the readers' side the (coordinated) platforms could consider changing[2] the readers' price as well to further boost profits. Clearly the platforms cannot do worse when using a second instrument. So the overall effect of an increase in the advertisers' price would be underestimated. Thus estimated market size would be systematically larger than the market size obtained by considering the full pricing possibilities offered to the platforms on both sides. By how much in turn depends on how sensitive is both own-side demand and cross-side demand to a change in P_R.

Note that not even the sign of the estimation bias is pinned down by the structure of the problem. For example, if we were to conduct the 'naïve' version of the test on the readers' side of the market (that is, increase P_R) then we would end up underestimating the size of the relevant market. The reason being that advertisers like readers and so would react to fewer readers by cutting back on participation. So what looks like a profitable price increase at a first pass could potentially end up reducing profits by helping to identify too narrow relevant markets.

This exercise captures the difficulties that arise in defining markets that are two sided due to the presence of cross-group externalities. In principle the two sides should be evaluated jointly as a single market.

A second observation is that there is no inverse relationship between market power and markups. Reducing prices on one side can be profitable if the resulting revenue losses are more than compensated for by gains on different sides. Redefining the notion of a 'small but significant non-transitory increase in prices' in these markets is a complex task that requires imposing more structure on the problem than the mere existence of well-defined demand schedules.

A final observation when considering the consumer side, either on its own or because it affects the advertising side, is that the current notion of the SSNIP test is inconsistent with markets where the service is free, as is often the case for online services but also for radio stations, free newspapers, or over-the-air TV stations. Here it is necessary to rely on direct or indirect measures of product substitutability. Notice that a free service does not mean there is no competition but that competition relies on non-price dimensions, in particular choice of content and other quality dimensions. Adequate tests should be developed for these markets.

9.3 PART TWO: INTERNET PLATFORMS

The past decade has brought a wealth of new platform businesses that took advantage of new technologies that lowered a range of costs (see

Levin, 2011 on the economics of the Internet). The possibility of tailoring (or customizing) content at the individual user level at no additional cost opened up a wide range of brand new businesses. Search engines, social networking websites, online news outlets, e-commerce websites, portals, and news aggregators are amongst the most successful of these platforms. Most of these markets are 'multi-sided' in the sense that they coordinate more than two sets of users. For example, search engines involve mostly two groups of active users, searchers and advertisers, but also content producers, and e-commerce websites involve buyers, sellers, and advertisers. Understanding the complexities of markets with multi-sided externalities that come in a wide array of forms is a first challenge to academics and practitioners.

The lower costs of monitoring 'interactions' or transactions brought innovation in payments and pricing mechanisms as well. As a result entirely new markets emerged. Search engines charge on a query-by-query basis running real-time (generalized) second-price auctions to sell the ad space on the right-hand side of the results' page. iTunes and its kin Appstore have no membership fees but rather charge for a single piece of content. eBay is able to monitor and tax transactions between otherwise anonymous buyers and sellers.

New market institutions emerged to cope with various market frictions. Feedback systems allow users to solve the old markets-for-lemons problem in a decentralized way. Collecting user information opened up new possibilities for improving the match between members of opposite sides of the market. At the same time it raised privacy concerns.

Lower search frictions significantly changed consumer habits. Internet users have easy access to multiple competing platforms. For example, most online newsreaders often get their news from multiple sources. Buyers can compare prices across a wide variety of stores. Sellers can cross-list on multiple platforms. As we have argued above, it makes a significant difference to outcomes whether groups single-home or multi-home.

9.3.1   Issues for Competition on the Ads

Is Internet advertising on the same markets as newspaper advertising or bill-boards and storefront signage? Online markets reach less people (so far) but allow for better targeting. It is not clear whether the capacity to target advertising enhances (and hence complements) existing offline campaigns or acts as a substitute for them. On the theory side, the prevalent view is that firms substitute between online and offline advertising (for example, Athey and Gans, 2010; Bergemann and Bonatti, 2011). On the empirical side there is preliminary evidence that offline and online ads are negatively related. Goldfarb and Tucker (2011a) study this issue through a randomized trial in the context of advertising on alcoholic beverages. They show that the effectiveness of a ban on alcohol advertising (measured as the likelihood that a given individual purchases alcoholic beverages conditional on exposure type) is significantly reduced when consumers are exposed to online ads. Goldfarb and Tucker (2011b) exploit exogenous variation in the ability of lawyers to solicit customers via traditional media such as direct mail or 'ambulance chasing' behavior. They find that advertising prices per click for search engine advertising are 5–7 percent higher when lawyers cannot use traditional channels. Both pieces of evidence suggest that online advertising substitutes for offline ads. In general the key issue is the extent of multi-homing between online and offline behavior. These results suggest that advertisers use both online and offline resources and that these markets cannot be thought as operating independently. But the extent of substitution/complementarities is still not quantified. Faced with a lack of conclusive evidence, on the public policy side the ongoing view is that these channels are neither complements nor substitutes. The Federal Trade Commission did not consider offline markets in its assessment of the Google-Doubleclick merger. The European Commission explicitly asserted that for antitrust purposes 'on-line advertising is a distinct market from off-line advertising.'[3] The French Autorité de la Concurrence took the same position in an opinion expressed in 2010.[4]

The exercise of market power in online markets takes different, not immediately apparent, static and dynamic forms. A good example of a static distortion is the use of reserve prices in sponsored search auctions (keyword advertising). Search engines often tweak the rules that assign advertisers to particular keyword searches in order to boost profits. This activity, by some dubbed 'market' or 'auction design,' typically leads to higher revenues at the expense of lower advertising surplus. For instance, reserve prices (typically employed by all auctioneers) boost revenues by rationing out of the market advertisers that would have otherwise participated. The employment of these 'shadow' access prices is the reason why many of Google's searches contain few or no ads. (If advertising were costless then it could do no harm to an advertiser to associate its name even to unrelated searches.) A good example of a distortion that results from dynamic considerations is given by display-ad auctions. Many ad networks, such as DoubleClick, allow advertisers to target specific users across websites belonging to the same network. A typical arrangement could condense as follows: 'impress the same user at most x times at a unit-price no higher than z per impression over the course of y days.' In practice display ads (also called banner ads) are auctioned off in real time (thus sequentially) to advertisers who instruct robots to bid on their behalf. A simple strategy is a triple (x,y,z). The fact that users show up on the network multiple times over the relevant advertising period y incentivizes advertisers to 'shade' their bids. ('Bid shading' describes the practice of a bidder placing an offer that is below what he thinks a good is worth.) Suppose that advertisers choosing high price bids (z) also choose a large number of impressions (x). As higher advertiser types reach their target level z their robots drop out of the market for this particular user. So subsequent auctions will have fewer participants with lower bids. The expectation of lower future prices is what induces bid shading. The ad network could increase revenues by cutting back on the number of ads. The lower the expected number of future auctions, the higher the bid for the current one. So even in the absence of static distortions (for example, no reserve prices), there could well be dynamic ones.

As mentioned, Internet fosters multi-homing by consumers (by some called 'switching behavior') via lower switching costs, leading to multi-homing on both sides of the market. This has two main implications. First, in the traditional context of competitive bottleneck, there is little or no competition for advertisers. If outlets are gatekeepers of their customers' attention then they can always insist on charging the monopoly price for accessing that attention. On the contrary, multi-homing by consumers introduces substitutability between platforms: as the fraction of readers who can be reached through multiple outlets goes up, the 'old' Cournot logic kicks in. Individual ad-supply choices affect (common) market prices. These strategic externalities induce lower equilibrium prices (see Ambrus et al., 2011; Anderson et al., 2011).

The second implication is somewhat subtler. Large advertising campaigns can be thought of as stochastic processes. With some probability some of the ads will end up hitting already informed consumers and hence get wasted together with the attention of that particular consumer. Internet platforms react to this problem by introducing tracking technologies that increase allocative efficiency. Although far from being perfect, these technologies reduce within-outlet waste. As switching behavior increases more attention gets wasted as there is no across-outlet tracking. To give a sense of how big the problem is, Athey et al. (2011) provide evidence (based on 30 large recent cross-outlet Internet campaigns) that more than two-thirds of the ads are wasted, hitting the same receivers more than ten times. This fact alone can account for the decline of advertising revenues experienced by newspapers as readership migrates online. Ad networks seeking to build a case for mergers often argue that the merged entity could reduce these inefficiencies by improving tracking through superior information. Athey et al. (2011) show that this need not be the case as profits are not monotonic in consumer switching. Advertisers with a high opportunity cost of missing consumers, the argument goes, increase their demand of ads as a result of switching to make sure they reach their target. Finally, the ability of the merged entity to price-discriminate between different types of advertisers by charging different prices to multiple-outlet and single-outlet campaigns respectively is shown to introduce further allocative distortions.

9.3.2 Illustration with a Simple Model

As an illustration of the issues raised by multi-homing, we develop a very simple model that captures some basic insights of the literature. Consider two outlets 1 and 2 that propose contents to consumers and advertising space. To simplify matters, assume that the audience of each outlet is fixed and independent of the advertising policy. A representative consumer may decide to visit one or both outlets. With probability X_i ($i = 1, 2$) the representative consumer visits only outlet i, while with probability X he visits both outlets. For consistency, $X_1 + X_2 + X$ is smaller or equal to 1. For each advertiser there is a single consumer who is a potential target. A representative advertiser may buy at most one impression on outlet i at price P_i. The outlet then targets the consumer, which results in a probability Q_i that the consumer impressed is the advertiser's target. Q_i thus corresponds to the quality of targeting. If the consumer impressed is not the target the value for the advertiser is zero. If the consumer is the target the value of a first impression is 1, while the value of a second impression is $1-A$ (this occurs if the advertiser buys ads from both outlets and the targeted consumer sees both ads). Thus the value of two impressions is $2-A$, less than the double of the value of one impression. The parameter A can take values between 0 and 1 ($A = 1$ means that a second impression is useless for the advertiser). Proposing an advertising slot costs C.

In this simple model, everything is exogenous except that each outlet chooses the price P_i of its advertising slot. To start the analysis, consider the case where the advertiser must choose only one outlet (single-homing). The expected revenue of the advertiser when choosing outlet i is $Q_i(X_i + X) - P_i$. Assume that outlet 2 is more attractive so that $Q_2(X_2 + X)$ is larger than $Q_1(X_1 + X)$. This could be because it is more efficient at targeting or because it has a larger audience and hence a better chance to be visited by the target. It is then straighforward to see that outlet 1 chooses the price ($P_1 = C$) and outlet 2 sells the ad at price $P_2 = C + Q_2(X_2 + X) - Q_1(X_1 + X)$.

The question now is how does the result change when the advertiser can buy a slot on both outlets? If the advertiser already has a slot on outlet

2, the value of an additional slot on outlet 1 is the difference between the value with two slots and the value with one slot: an extra slot on outlet 1 generates an additional chance of reaching the target $Q_1(X_1 + X)$ but with probability Q_1Q_2X, this consumer receives two impressions, in which case the value is reduced by a factor A (this requires the consumer to visit both outlets and each outlet to succeed in targeting him). Thus the value of the extra slot is $V_1 = Q_1(X_1 + X) - Q_1Q_2XA$. When $V_1 < C$, single-homing by the advertiser prevails. But when $V_1 > C$, it is not sustainable. Indeed the advertiser would be willing to pay the cost of the slot of the second outlet. Suppose that $V_1 > C$. In the equilibrium that emerges, the advertiser buys a slot on both outlets (multi-homing). This implies that an outlet cannot charge a price larger than the incremental value of adding a second slot. Indeed given that he buys the slot on one outlet, the advertiser is only willing to pay V_1 for outlet 1 and, according to the same reasoning, $V_2 = Q_2(X_2 + X) - Q_1Q_2XA$ for outlet 2. In equilibrium outlet 1 sets a price V_1 and outlet 2 sets a price V_2.

Single-homing is more likely when outlet 2 is very efficient (Q_2 is large) and the value of a second impression is small (A is large). Comparing the profits, we find that each outlet obtains a larger profit with multi-homing when it is an equilibrium ($V_1 > C$). This is immediate for outlet 1 as it does not sell with single-homing. For outlet 2, it is due to the fact that it faces a less intense price competition from outlet 1 under multi-homing. Indeed when $V_1 > C$, it can be shown that both prices are higher under multi-homing.[5] Under single-homing outlet 2 must compete with the very low price of the less efficient outlet, while under multi-homing it faces no competition.

Due to lower prices, when $V_1 > C$, the advertiser would obtain a larger profit under single-homing than multi-homing. Thus surprisingly the advertiser does not benefit from the possibility to use both outlets, due to low intensity of competition that offsets the potential benefits of using multiple channels to reach the consumers.

Let us now look at the effect of entry in this context. For this purpose assume that outlet 1 is the sole outlet until some date where outlet 2 enters. Assume that $V_1 > C$. Before entry, outlet 1 is a monopoly and obtains profits $Q_1(X_1 + X)$ by selling the slot (we assume here that entry does not affect the audience of outlet 1). The total industry profit after entry is $V_1 + V_2 - 2C$. Entry may then raise or reduce industry profit (depending on A and C). There are two effects at work here. On the one hand, entry creates new value that is shared between the entrant and the advertiser. On the other hand, entry reduces the value of the first outlet, which depresses profits. This result is similar to that obtained in Athey et al. (2011).

The model also sheds some light on investment. Consider investment in targeting, the return of increasing Q_i under multi-homing is

$(X_i + X - Q_j XA)$, where Q_j is the quality of the other outlet. First, investments in targeting are strategic substitutes (the more the competitor invests, the less the outlet invests). Second, a shift toward more multi-homing by consumers (increasing X at constant audience $X_i + X$) reduces the gains from investment, hence multi-impressions are detrimental to investment. The same conclusion could be derived for investment in content (that raises the audience).

9.3.3   Issues for Competition on the Consumer Side

The importance of advertising for the consumer side online is obvious given that it is a key driver of platform competition for consumers and a key ingredient for most free online services. The importance of advertising raises some new issues for the consumer side.

As pointed out by Crampes et al. (2009), advertising changes the nature of competition for consumers by affecting the nature of returns to scale. Depending on the technology and the type of advertising, it may be the source of increasing returns to scale (when one more consumer helps in increasing the advertising revenues per consumer) or decreasing returns to scale. Decreasing returns may arise if marginal consumers are less attractive for advertisers than infra-marginal consumers. On the Internet, it is often alleged that by exploiting information from a large customer base larger outlets have superior possibilities in targeting leading to increasing returns. Increasing returns to scale would then imply a larger concentration, some level of barriers to entry, and more concerns about anti-competitive practices.

Moreover, in network industries a standard concern for antitrust authorities is that dominant platforms enjoy a competitive advantage because consumers are coordinated or 'locked in' to the platform. This translates into higher barriers to entry, as entrants will have to win over the reluctance of several sides to switch platform in the absence of the other side. A critique to this argument is that 'divide and conquer strategies' in which one side is lured through subsidies (negative prices) that ensure participation for all levels of participation of the other sides can be profitably employed to penetrate the market (see Jullien, 2011). However in online advertising markets, for instance, search engines, the lack of prices on the consumer side make these strategies unfeasible and thus bring back concerns of foreclosure due to coordination The emergence of gatekeepers such as Google's search engines raise concern of foreclosure through prominence, obfuscation, and search diversion. For example, Microsoft repeatedly complained that Google drastically increased the rate for its ads. In September 2007 the cost for placing a 'Windows live' ad next to search results for the keyword 'Hotmail' (Microsoft's own email outlet) allegedly increased from 10 cents to $5 per click. The Federal Trade Commission as of September 2011 is probing this and other increases.[6] A broader issue of course is whether a gatekeeper could favor its own businesses. This could be done in several ways. First, by applying dissimilar conditions to equivalent transactions depending on whether the gatekeeper has a subsidiary in the same market as the advertiser in question. Second, by tweaking on a search engine the 'organic' or 'unsponsored' search results to obfuscate rivals (see Tarantino, 2011). 'Unfair' (whatever that means) ranking of search results could put a firm out of business in a world in which being on page 2 of a search query is pretty much like not existing.[7] Finally, another practice (search diversion) has the gatekeeper favoring some advertisers against the best interest of consumers (see Hagiu and Jullien, 2011a). A basic fact about a sponsored search is that the websites with a higher willingness to pay to reach a consumer are not always the websites that the consumers are looking for when entering their queries. Whenever this mismatch occurs the engine will have an incentive to 'tweak' the results to favor the higher willingness to pay advertisers. A key question is whether competition between platforms is strong enough to discipline them. Consumers, the argument goes, would quickly find another recipient of their queries if they were to find out that results were not packed to suit their needs. The answer seems to rely on the extent of multi-homing in the market, the discipline being effective only if enough consumers single-home (see Hagiu and Jullien, 2011b).

A further challenge is that the forensics for detecting abuses practiced by online businesses has little or nothing to do with its offline counterpart. Detecting or proving the existence of malicious 'tweaks' in the algorithms that determine the outcome of position auctions or search results is a very complex task.

9.3.4   Issues for Competition at the Meta-platform Level (News Aggregators)

News aggregators recently stirred debate on the practice of 'scraping' information on multiple outlets and making it available through one portal. Other examples include meta-search engines such as price-comparison services (Kelkoo, Kayak) and social network aggregators that allow management of multiple social profiles from the same interface (the now defunct Google Buzz service was the most prominent attempt). By reducing outlet loyalty, aggregators somewhat raise the extent of multi-homing, which may be viewed as progress as consumers have more flexibility but also alters competition between outlets.

Moreover, these 'meta-platforms' take away part of the consumers' traffic that would otherwise have visited the target site. The counterpart is that they intercept and drive more traffic to the same sites, since action (that is, reading a full story or purchasing a product) requires a click through a link on the aggregator to the supplier of the content. While the aggregators clearly bring value to consumers, they may raise concerns if they become bottlenecks. Aggregators claim that the option of 'opting out' from the crawler list, that is, the option of not being featured on the aggregator, per se is sufficient to clear the floor from allegations of anti-competitive behavior and violation of intellectual property rights. However the platforms whose content is used by aggregators often claim that they are 'trapped' and that they keep on participating because opting out is not a viable alternative. This issue can be related to several topics within the general area of research on collective action problems and coordination failure (Dixit, 2003 talks in particular about traps). Content producers may face some form of 'prisoner's dilemma' in the sense that collectively they would be better off without the aggregator, but if all others join they have no other choice than to do so or perish. Once coordination on the aggregator occurs, the option of 'opting out' has no value. The issue in analysing such a situation would then be that the aggregator raises the value for consumers in the short run, but may reduce the supply and quality of content in the long run.

9.4 CONCLUSION

The Internet takes on increasing importance in competition policy, due to its impact on the economy and the emergence of global players. Advertising is an essential part of many business models online. As we have illustrated, advertising online raises several issues. Two-sidedness must be accounted for as some practices that seem abusive from one side's perspective may benefit final consumers. Other issues are more specific to advertising, such as the proper welfare criterion for policy makers. Among these is the fact that many online markets involve actors with very diverse business models, for instance, with the coexistence of free and pay services and various mixes of complementary services and bundles. Understanding competition in this complex context requires developing a wider notion of platform than a two-sided market.

A final remark is that the line between consumer protection and competition policy becomes tenuous in online markets. Obfuscation and search diversion by information bottlenecks are examples of practices that could be addressed from both perspectives. Privacy is another major issue. Digital interactions have drastically raised the ability of websites to collect, store, and treat data on individuals, compared to traditional 'brick and mortar.' The use of this information raises ethical issues, but also economic issues related to discrimination and exploitation. In particular increasing concentration may raise concerns for the individuals' control over the use of private data. Evaluating privacy issues and if necessary potential remedies could be done at the merger control stage, which would introduce a dimension different from traditional competition policy considerations such as price-level or market foreclosure.

NOTES

1. Internet Advertising Revenue Report (2011). (Industry Survey Conducted by Price Waterhouse Coopers and sponsored by the Interactive Advertising Bureau (IAB).)
2. Since 'ongoing' prices are not assumed to be optimal, decreasing could also lead to increased profits as discussed at the end of the paragraph.
3. See Article 61, reference case No. Comp/M.5727 – Microsoft/Yahoo! Search business, Regulation (EC) No. 139/2004 Merger procedure. Available at http://ec.europa.eu/competition/mergers/cases/decisions/M5727_20100218_20310_261202_EN.pdf (accessed 9 February 2012).
4. See 'sur le fonctionnement concurrentiel de la publicité en ligne' (10-A-29) 14 December 2010, available at http://www.autoritedelaconcurrence.fr/user/avisdec.php?numero=10-A-29 (accessed 9 February 2012).
5. $V_1 > P_1$ since $P_1 = C$ and $V_2 > P_2$ because $V_1 - P_1 = V_2 - P_2$.
6. http://www.businessweek.com/news/2011-09-21/google-ad-rate-for-microsoft-said-to-be-investigated-by-u-s-.html (accessed 9 February 2012).
7. Jeremy Stoppelman of Yelp (an online search and review of local businesses online) and Jeff Katz, CEO of Nextag Inc., (a price-comparison site) testified along these lines on 21 September 2011 in front of the Members of the Senate Judiciary Subcommittee on Antitrust, Competition Policy and Consumer Rights that discussed issues related to Google's market power.

REFERENCES

Ambrus, A., E. Calvano and M. Reisinger (2011), 'Either or both competition: a 'two-sided' theory of advertising with overlapping viewerships', mimeo, Harvard University, Cambridge, MA.

Anderson, S. and S. Coate (2005), 'Market provision of broadcasting: a welfare analysis', *Review of Economic Studies*, **72**(4), 947–72.

Anderson, S., Ø. Foros and H. Kind (2011), 'Competition for advertisers in media markets', mimeo, Norwegian School of Economics, Bergen, Norway.

Armstrong, M. (2006), 'Competition in two-sided markets', *RAND Journal of Economics*, **37**(3), 668–81.

Athey, S. and J.S. Gans (2010), 'The impact of targeting technology on advertising markets and media competition', *American Economic Review*, **100**(2), 608–13.

Athey, S., E. Calvano and J.S. Gans (2011), 'The impact of the internet on advertising markets for news media', mimeo, Harvard University, Cambridge, MA.

Bagwell, K. (2007), 'The economic analysis of advertising', in M. Armstrong and R. Porter (eds), *Handbook of Industrial Organization*, Vol. 3, Amsterdam: North-Holland, pp. 1701–84.

Becker, G. and K. Murphy (1993), 'A simple theory of advertising as a good or bad', *Quarterly Journal of Economics*, **108**(4), 941–64.

Bergemann, D. and A. Bonatti (2010), 'Targeting in advertising markets: implications for offline vs. online media', Cowles Foundation Discussion Paper No. 1758.

Caillaud, B. and B. Jullien (2003), 'Chicken & egg: competition among intermediation service providers', *RAND Journal of Economics*, **34**(2), 309–28.

Chamberlin, E. (1933), *The Theory of Monopolistic Competition*, Cambridge, MA: Harvard University Press.

Crampes, C., C. Haritchabalet and B. Jullien (2009), 'Advertising, competition and entry in media industries', *Journal of Industrial Economics*, **57**(1), 7–31.

Dixit, A. (2003), 'Clubs with entrapment', *American Economic Review*, **93**(5), 1824–9.

Fogg-Meade, E. (1901), 'The place of advertising in modern business', *Journal of Political Economy*, **9**, 218–42.

Goldfarb, A. and C. Tucker (2011a), 'Advertising bans and the substitutability of online and offline advertising', *Journal of Marketing Research*, **48**(2), 207–27.

Goldfarb, A. and C. Tucker (2011b), 'Search engine advertising: channel substitution when pricing ads to context', *Management Science*, **57**(3), 458–70.

Hagiu, A. and B. Jullien (2011a), 'Why do intermediaries divert search?', *RAND Journal of Economics*, **42**(2), 337–62.

Hagiu, A. and B. Jullien (2011b), 'Search diversion, rent extraction and competition?', mimeo, Harvard Business School, Cambridge, MA.

Jullien, B. (2011), 'Competition in multi-sided markets: divide-and-conquer', *American Economic Journal: Microeconomics*, **3**, 1–35.

Kaldor, N.V. (1950), 'The economic aspects of advertising', *Review of Economic Studies*, **18**, 1–27.

Levin, J. (2011), 'The economics of the internet', NBER working papers, No. 16852.

Robinson, J. (1933), *Economics of Imperfect Competition*, London: MacMillan and Co.

Rochet, J. and J. Tirole (2003), 'Platform competition in two-sided markets', *Journal of the European Economic Association*, **1**(4), 990–1029.

Rochet, J. and J. Tirole (2006), 'Two-sided markets: a progress report', *RAND Journal of Economics*, **37**(3), 645–67.

Stigler, G. (1961), 'The economics of information', *Journal of Political Economy*, **69**(3), 213–25.

Tarantino, E. (2011), 'A note on vertical search engines foreclosure', mimeo, University of Bologna, Bologna, Italy.

Weyl, E. (2010), 'A price theory of multi-sided platforms', *American Economic Review*, **100**(4), 1642–72.

10. Assessing unilateral merger effects in the Dutch daily newspaper market

Lapo Filistrucchi, Tobias J. Klein and Thomas O. Michielsen[1]

10.1 INTRODUCTION

The newspaper market is a typical example of a so-called two-sided market: publishers sell content to readers and advertising slots to advertisers, while taking into account that the demand for advertisements in a newspaper depends positively on its circulation and the demand of readers might be affected by the number (or concentration) of ads in the newspaper (Anderson and Gabszewicz, 2006).

When it comes to assessing a proposed merger, competition authorities are, as a rule, required to establish whether a horizontal merger is likely to raise concerns with respect to unilateral or non-coordinated effects (that is, whether the merger might increase the market power of the merging firms) and with respect to coordinated or collusive effects (that is, whether the merger might make collusion more likely). With regard to the assessment of unilateral merger effects, competition authorities have devised different methods to address the issue. For instance, initial screening has traditionally been based on the analysis of the market shares of the merging parties and of (the changes in) the Herfindahl-Hirschman Index (HHI). Hence mergers among firms with market shares below a given threshold and mergers characterized by a post-merger HHI and a change in the HHI below certain thresholds have been almost automatically approved. For mergers judged to be worthy of further investigation, full merger simulations have only seldom been conducted. More often, preference has been given to a small but significant non-transitory increase in price (SSNIP)-type test, where it is asked whether the merging firms would find it profitable to raise prices post merger by a given threshold, usually 5 or 10 per cent, assuming rivals would not react.[2]

These tools for assessing unilateral merger effects have mainly been developed for single-sided markets. As explained in Wright (2004), analysing a two-sided market as if it were a single-sided market may lead to mistakes and unintended consequences in the application of competition policy. This is mainly because firms' pricing decisions do not only depend on own- and cross-price elasticities of demand on both sides of the market, as they would in a single-sided market with a multi-product firm, but also on the own- and cross-elasticities of demand on one side with respect to demand on the other side, that is, the network effects.

For example, in the newspaper market, when considering to increase the subscription prices after a merger, newspapers will take into account that such an increase will not only have a negative effect on subscription revenues through its negative effect on circulation, but also a negative effect on advertising revenues, as decreased circulation leads to a decline in the demand for advertising. For the same reason, such an increase in price might lead to a decline not only in readers' welfare but also in advertisers' welfare (the former effect is partly offset if readers are ad-averse, and enhanced if instead they are ad-loving). This not only makes a price increase less likely, but it also has an impact on the social desirability of the merger.

The theoretical literature on two-sided markets distinguishes between the price level (roughly the sum of the two prices) and the price structure (roughly their ratio) and shows that, in general, in such a market a merged firm will tend to raise the price level, but it is also likely to change the price structure.[3] In fact, a two-sided market is often defined as a market in which not only the price level, but also the price structure matters for the profits of the firm. Consequently, not only the price level, but also the price structure determines (consumer) welfare. The literature shows that more concentration leads in general to a less efficient price level, but not necessarily a less efficient price structure. As a result, it is not clear whether higher concentration and more market power lead to a welfare loss, not even if one focuses attention on consumer welfare.

Hence, merger assessment in a two-sided market is more complex than the analysis of mergers in a one-sided market. A natural question to ask is thus to what extent traditional methods to assess unilateral effects, albeit adapted, remain valid instruments for competition policy in two-sided markets. In this chapter, we compare different ways to assess unilateral merger effects in a two-sided market by applying them to a hypothetical merger in the Dutch newspaper market. For this, we specify a structural model of demand for differentiated products on both the readers' and the advertisers' side of the market. We use it to recover price elasticities, indirect network effects and, following Filistrucchi et al. (2010), also marginal costs. We then compare, in a typical two-sided setting as the newspaper one, different approaches to the assessment of unilateral merger effects: an analysis based on the HHI, a SSNIP-type test and a full merger simulation based on the structural model.

The empirical literature on mergers involving two-sided platforms is still scarce. Evans and Noel (2008) point out that, as the Lerner pricing formula does not hold in such markets, traditional merger simulation models are wrongly specified if applied without modifications to two-sided or multi-sided platforms. They also perform an analysis of the merger between Google and DoubleClick, which is the first empirical analysis in the literature of a merger in a two-sided industry. They show that relying on conventional methods would have led to significantly different results than using methods that explicitly incorporate the two-sided nature of this market. Nevertheless, they only perform a calibration exercise due to a lack of data. Chandra and Collard-Wexler (2009) assess mergers in the Canadian newspaper market, but their analysis is mainly an *ex post* evaluation of the effects of the merger. They use a two-sided Hotelling model to explain their finding that greater concentration did not lead to higher prices for either readers or advertisers. Yet, they do not build and estimate a structural econometric model and, therefore, their framework cannot be used to simulate mergers.

In our merger simulation, we follow Filistrucchi et al. (2010), who build a structural econometric framework to simulate the effects of mergers among two-sided platforms selling differentiated products and competing à la Bertrand on each side of the market. Their framework extends the supply model of Argentesi and Filistrucchi (2007) to the more general case of a two-sided market with two network effects. For this reason it differs also from Van Cayseele and Vanormelingen (2009), who assume no effect of advertising on readership when analysing mergers in the Belgian newspaper market. Jeziorski (2011) studies instead mergers between US radio stations. In his model, listeners do not pay a monetary price to listen to the radio but advertising generates a nuisance cost. Our model is more general as customers on both sides, readers and advertisers, pay a price to access the platform. Finally, Fan (2011) analyses mergers among US newspapers. Whereas the framework of Filistrucchi et al. (2010) is more general than hers when it comes to analysing merger effects on prices, as it allows for advertising to affect readers, her model allows for endogenous changes in the quality of the newspapers due to the merger. As we do not have data on quality, we abstract from quality changes due to the merger.[4]

This chapter is organized as follows. In Section 10.2 we identify the main features of the Dutch market for daily newspapers. Section 10.3 describes the data set. In Section 10.4, we specify a model of demand for both sides of the market and report estimation results. In Section 10.5, we turn to the hypothetical merger and present results from a concentration analysis, a SSNIP-type test and results from the full merger simulation. Section 10.6 summarizes our findings and concludes.

10.2   THE DUTCH MARKET FOR DAILY NEWSPAPERS

There are eight important national-level newspapers: *Algemeen Dagblad, De Telegraaf, de Volkskrant, Het Financieele Dagblad, Het Parool, NRC Handelsblad, nrc.next* and *Trouw*. In addition, there are two important free newspapers: *Metro* since the second quarter of 1999 and *Sp!ts* since the fourth quarter of 2001.[5]

Since 2009, the publishing company PCM has been the sole owner of the *Algemeen Dagblad* and its regional editions. In the same year, De Persgroep Nederland, also owning *de Volkskrant, Het Parool, NRC Handelsblad, nrc. next* and *Trouw*, bought 51 per cent of PCM. This acquisition needed to be approved by the Dutch competition authority (NMa). The NMa imposed as a condition on De Persgroep Nederland to sell *NRC Handelsblad* and *nrc.next*. Otherwise, PCM would dominate the market for quality newspapers in Amsterdam as it owns *de Volkskrant, Het Parool* and *Trouw*.

In the merger simulation below we first simulate the effect of this remedy and then, starting from this, the effect of a merger between *NRC Handelsblad, nrc.next* and *De Telegraaf, Gooi- en Eemlander, Haarlems Dagblad, Leidsch Dagblad* and *Noordhollands Dagblad*.[6]

10.3   DATA

Our most important data source on the readership side is yearly circulation data at the level of 512 municipalities, which we obtained from Cebuco. These are merged with data on subscription prices. We use subscription prices because, unlike in other countries, almost all of the copies (91 per cent according to our data) are sold in the form of subscriptions.

For the advertising side, we obtained quarterly data from Nielsen on the amount of advertising, which is measured in column millimetres, and the advertising revenues of each newspaper according to list prices. From these, we calculate the (weighted) average list price per column millimetre. Nielsen also provided us with data on the total number of pages of the newspapers, and information on the format, which is measured by the number of column millimetres per page.

We allow the demand for advertising in a newspaper to depend on the characteristics of the readers of this newspaper. For this, we obtained Nederlands Onderzoek Media (NOM) Print Monitor national level data on reach by age, gender, income and wealth, being a breadwinner or not, shopping for groceries or not, as well as reach by region.[7]

The market size is given by the total population over 13 years of age in the Netherlands. Data on this are provided by Statistics Netherlands (CBS). CBS also provided data on the consumer price index, which we use to express prices in year-2002 euros.

10.4   DEMAND ESTIMATION

As argued above, when predicting merger effects in a two-sided market, key inputs into the economic analysis are price elasticities and indirect network elasticities on each side of the market, or equivalently diversion ratios.

Lacking other sources of information on diversion ratios, we proceed to estimate the responsiveness of readership demand to changes in newspaper prices and advertising intensity and the responsiveness of advertising demand to changes in advertising prices and the circulation of a newspaper.

We use a model of demand for differentiated products on each side of the market. The next section introduces a model of advertising demand, the subsequent section then specifies a model of readership demand. Throughout, the superscript 'r' stands for 'readership' (as in the cover price of that newspaper) and the superscript 'a' stands for 'advertisement' (as in the price of an advertisement).

10.4.1   Advertising Demand

We specify advertising demand to be linear in the log of the advertising price per reader. That is,

$$\log q_{jt}^a = \alpha^a \log(p_{jt}^a/q_{jt}^r) + \beta^a x_{jt}^a + \xi_{jt}^a + \varepsilon_{jt}^a,$$

where q_{jt}^a is the quantity of advertising in newspaper j at time t, which is measured in column millimetres, p_{jt}^a is the advertising price per column millimetre and x_{jt}^a are characteristics of the newspaper j that matter to advertisers, such as the demographics of readers of newspaper j at time t.

Such a reduced form is natural in a model in which readers buy at most one newspaper and advertisers buy advertising slots from all platforms. It is similar to the one proposed by Rysman (2004), which is used also by Van Cayseele and Vanormelingen (2009) and Fan (2011), in that it assumes that there are no direct cross-price effects and no direct network effects. So that the decision to advertise in a newspaper only depends on the costs and benefits of advertising in that newspaper and is independent of the decision to advertise in other newspapers. We follow them in impos- ing that the reduced form is of the constant elasticity form and addition- ally assume that the network effect enters the demand function in such a way that it is the price per reader that matters to advertisers.

In our reduced form, the elasticity of demand with respect to the advertising price per column millimetre is equal to α^a, and the elasticity with respect to the number of readers is given by the negative of that, $-\alpha^a$. We use an instrumental variables estimator to estimate α^a, and at the same time control for newspaper fixed effects to capture the effect of unobserved (to the econometrician) characteristics of the newspapers in the eyes of advertisers. We also control for quarter dummies in order to account for changes in overall demand for print advertising. So, to sum- marize, we assume that $\xi_{jt}^a = \xi_j^a + \xi_t^a$. Our instrument is the total number of pages of content in the newspaper, which is related to the endogenous variable, p_{jt}^a / q_{jt}^r, through the increased value of the newspaper to readers, which translates into an increased circulation. It is unrelated to advertising demand if newspaper companies decide on this without knowing the reali- zation of ε_{jt}^a, which is plausible as we already control for time effects and newspaper fixed effects. From the obtained estimate of α^a, marginal effects can be calculated by multiplying it by q_{jt}^a / p_{jt}^a and $-q_{jt}^a / q_{jt}^r$, respectively.

We obtained estimates for four different specifications, which differ by the variables in x_{jt}^a. Throughout, we control for newspaper fixed effects and quarter dummies. Using our preferred specification that we then also use for the subsequent analysis below, we estimate the elasticity of advertising demand with respect to the price per reader to be 0.702, with a standard error of 0.085. We obtain very similar estimates when we control for age, gender, income, region and the fraction of breadwinners and grocery shoppers.

10.4.2 Readership Demand

On the readership side, we estimate a Berry (1994) type logit model of demand for newspapers. However, departing from the usual practice, we do so on the municipality level. The advantage of this is that the substitu- tion patterns that are implied for the national level are much more realis- tic. This is because we add up cross effects over municipalities. If then, for example, two regional level newspapers never compete because there is no municipality in which both are available, then added-up cross effects will be zero, whereas they will not if we use national level data with a standard logit model. In the following, however, we suppress the municipality subscript m, for ease of exposition.

We assume the potential market size to be the population above 13 years of age and that each consumer buys at most one newspaper. The utility from buying a newspaper depends, among other things, on the price of that newspaper and the amount of advertising in that newspaper. Formally, the utility of consumer i from buying newspaper j in t is given by

$$u_{ijt}^r = \alpha^r p_{jt}^r + \beta^r q_{jt}^a + \xi_{jt}^r + \varepsilon_{ijt}^r,$$

where p_{jt}^r is the price of the newspaper, q_{jt}^r is the amount of advertising content in the newspaper, ξ_{jt}^r captures unobserved characteristics and ε_{ijt}^r is the part of the utility derived from buying newspaper j that is specific to individual i at time t. We assume that ε_{ijt}^r is distributed according to the type 1 extreme value distribution independently across j and t. Individuals buy one newspaper or choose the outside good, $j = 0$, buying no newspaper. The outside good yields average utility 0, so that $u_{i0t}^r = \varepsilon_{i0t}^r$.

Under these assumptions, following Berry (1994), we obtain the estimation equation

$$\log(s_{jt}^r) - \log(s_{0t}^r) = \alpha^r p_{jt}^r + \beta^r q_{jt}^a + \xi_{jt}^r,$$

in which the difference between the natural logarithm of the market share of good j and the natural logarithm of the market share of the outside good is equal to the utility from observed characteristics p_{jt}^r, q_{jt}^a and unobserved characteristic ξ_{jt}^r. The left hand side of this equation is observed because s_{jt}^r and s_{0t}^r are observed, and the coefficients α^r and β^r can be consistently estimated if ξ_{jt}^r is uncorrelated with p_{jt}^r and q_{jt}^a. For this to be plausible we control for a flexible time trend by means of year dummies to capture the increased importance of outside options such as online news and free newspapers and also control for newspaper region fixed effects.[8] It is important to allow for different fixed effects per region as a national level newspaper with a focus on Amsterdam, such as *Het Parool*, will be valued differently, on average, in the region around Amsterdam, as opposed to in the south of the country.

We estimate mean utility to decrease significantly in the subscription price (−0.00771 per 2002 euro, with a standard error of 0.00014), to increase in the amount of advertising in the newspaper (0.00918 per million column millimetres, with a standard error of 0.00117) and the amount of content (0.00264 per billion column millimetres, with a standard error of 0.00021), and we find that readers value newspapers of small format (the effect is 0.08838 with a standard error of 0.00346). Following Filistrucchi et al. (2010) we calculate the implied marginal effects and elasticities from the model. The average own-price elasticity is about –1.75 and the average advertising elasticity is about 0.05. This means that readers are ad-loving, but this is not very pronounced. This is plausible in our case as it is possible to skip advertisements, unlike when watching a movie on TV, some advertisements may be informative and hence valued by readers, and the percentage of advertising content is relatively low.

10.5   A HYPOTHETICAL MERGER

As explained earlier, competition authorities are required to assess whether a horizontal merger is likely to raise concerns with respect to unilateral or non-coordinated effects and with respect to coordinated or collusive effects. In order to assess unilateral effects a competition authority needs to predict, at least to some extent, whether prices are likely to rise as a result of the merger.

From the point of view of economics, the correct way to evaluate whether a merger is likely to lead to higher prices is to specify a model of the market in question, estimate demand in order to recover values for the parameters of the model, and then use the models and the estimated parameters to predict the price chosen by the firms post merger. One can then compare the prices, consumer surplus and/or total welfare in the new equilibrium with those in the old equilibrium. In Section 10.5.3, we show the results of such a full merger simulation.

Merger simulation can be very time consuming. As a result, it is often not performed in practice. In many cases a SSNIP-type test is used to predict the effects of a merger. Specifically, such a test is often performed by using Critical Loss Analysis and Critical Elasticity Analysis formulas derived under the assumption of constant marginal costs and either linear or iso-elastic demand. In merger evaluation, the formulas are not used to set an (implicit) benchmark on when substitution across products is enough to consider that they are in the same relevant market (which is what is done for market definition). Instead, they are used to measure the likelihood of a substantial non-transitory increase in price by the merging parties. That means that instead of simulating the effects of a price increase by a hypothetical monopolist above the current (competitive) level, practitioners simulate the effects of a price increase above the current level by the merging parties, assuming rivals do not change their prices and check whether that price increase is profitable or not. In either case, the size of the price increase is given beforehand and is not chosen optimally by the firms.[9] The simplification of the SSNIP test comes at the cost of the assumption that rivals' prices remain unchanged after the merger. We report the results from such a test in Section 10.5.2.

According to the European Union (EU) merger guidelines, a first screening of mergers can be done based on the concentration they lead to in the relevant market. Although requiring market definition as a previous step in the analysis, such an assessment is per se the quickest and easiest one. It is well known, however, that the relationship between market power as measured by the Lerner index and the HHI Index holds perfectly only in case of Cournot competition with homogeneous products. Thus, once again, simplicity comes at the cost of often unrealistic assumptions. We perform a market concentration analysis in Section 10.5.1.

In order to illustrate the different methods to assess unilateral merger effects, we apply them to the analysis of the effects of a hypothetical merger between *NRC Handelsblad* and *nrc.next*, on the one hand, and *De Telegraaf, Gooi- en Eemlander, Haarlems Dagblad, Leidsch Dagblad* and *Noordhollands Dagblad*, on the other hand. Given our data set, we assess the merger as if it were to take place in 2009 and therefore use the market shares, market sizes, prices and ownership structure of 2009 as the pre-merger situation. We do so in the context of the demand model we described in Section 10.4. Again following Filistrucchi et al. (2010), we recover the marginal costs that would rationalize observed behaviour of profit maximizing firms that compete in prices with differentiated products on each side of the market.[10] These estimates are then used for the SSNIP test and the merger simulation. As explained in Section 10.2, we first simulate the equilibrium in what we take as the initial situation in which *NRC Handelsblad* and *nrc.next* are independent after having belonged to De Persgroep.

10.5.1   Herfindahl-Hirschman Index

One of the most common ways to asses market power is to use the HHI, which is given by the sum of the squared market shares in a market (usually multiplied by 10,000 to facilitate the reader). On the advertising side, assuming the relevant product market is the one for advertising in paid daily newspapers in Dutch (thus excluding free newspapers) and the relevant geographic market is the national one, the pre-merger HHI is 2174 and the post-merger one is 2366, which means that the change that is due to the merger ΔHHI is 192.[11]

Likewise, on the readership side of the market, assuming the relevant product market is the one for copies of paid daily newspapers in Dutch (once more excluding the free press) and the relevant geographic market is the whole of the Netherlands, the pre-merger HHI is 2571, the post-merger one is 3099, and hence ΔHHI is 528.[12]

Applying the thresholds of the EU merger guidelines, the merger would thus be investigated because of concerns of unilateral effects on both sides of the market, but particularly on the readers' side.

One of the major criticisms against the use of the HHI in screening mergers is that it is highly dependent on the definition of the relevant market. The above conclusion regarding the readership side may change drastically if we define the relevant geographic market as the municipality one. In our case, concentration is much higher at the municipality level, as indicated by a pre- and post-merger HHI of more than 5000 on average, because many newspapers are regional. Moreover, concentration would change considerably more due to the merger so that the merger would be scrutinized because of competitive concerns in many municipalities.

In addition, the use of the HHI leads to another potential fallacy in a two-sided market, namely the failure to account for the existence of indirect network effects. If these network effects are strong enough, the conclusions drawn from looking at concentration on each side of the market might be wrong even if the market definition on the two sides of the market is the correct one.

10.5.2   SSNIP-type Test

As explained above, the SSNIP test is often used in the assessment of unilateral merger effects. In particular, practitioners use it to simulate a given price increase (usually 5 or 10 per cent) above the current level by the merging parties, assuming rivals do not change their prices, and to check whether that price increase is profitable or not. If the price increase is profitable, it is judged to be likely to take place.

We use the extension of the SSNIP test to two-sided markets developed in Filistrucchi (2008) for market definition. On each side of the market, the SSNIP test asks whether an increase of the subscription prices by the merging parties of 5 per cent is profitable, assuming rivals keep their prices unchanged. The test is modified in such a way as to account for the presence of the indirect network effects in order to correctly assess the competitive constraints faced by the merged firm and therefore the profitability of a price increase. Positive indirect network effects between the different sides of the platform reduce the profitability of any price increase.

We implement both the US and the EU versions of the test and for the EU, implement it either allowing or not allowing the merged firm to optimally adjust the price on the advertising side when the cover price is raised. Throughout, we present the most complete version of the test, using the profit functions to numerically find optimal prices given the prices of the rivals and possibly own prices on one side of the market.[13] As a result, the

Table 10.1   SSNIP test

	Average advertising price	Average subscription price	Profit change
Initial situation	4.42	244.14	0.00
5% increase in p^a, no adjustment of p^n	4.64	244.14	3.05
5% increase in p^n, no adjustment of p^a	4.42	256.35	−2.43
5% increase in p^a, optimal adjustment of p^n	4.64	196.37	8.94
5% increase in p^n, optimal adjustment of p^a	8.83	256.35	35.36
Optimal adjustment of both prices	8.83	157.34	61.99

Note: This table shows results of different variants of the SSNIP test. These are average prices and profit changes when only the merging parties adjust prices. Profit changes are in percentage and relative to the initial situation.

only difference with respect to the full merger simulation is not allowing rivals to react to the price increase.

Table 10.1 shows the results of the different versions of the SSNIP test. It reports (estimated) advertising tariffs, subscription prices and profit changes (in percentages). The first row refers to the status quo, the last row to the US test. The latter shows that performing the US version of the SSNIP test to assess the merger would lead to the merger raising competitive concerns not on the readers' market (as post merger the optimal price is lower), but on the advertisers' market (as the optimal price increase exceeds 5 per cent). Rows two to four refer instead to two different versions of the EU test (with or without the optimal adjustment of the price structure) for each market (advertising and readership). Comparing the second row to the fourth and the third row to the fifth shows that allowing the firms to optimally adjust the price on the other side of the market increases profitability of the price rise. In addition, a comparison of row one to row four and five shows, respectively, that when exogenously forced to raise prices on the reader side of the market by 5 per cent the merged firm would increase prices also on the advertising side of the market, while when forced to raise the advertising tariff by 5 per cent the merged firm would lower the cover price. The latter result moves in the same direction as the US test.

Overall, results from a SSNIP-type test would thus suggest that, contrary to what is predicted by a HHI analysis, the merger raises concerns of

Table 10.2   Effects of the hypothetical merger

	Merged	Not merged
Advertising price	0.000	0.000
Column millimetres sold	−1.713	0.063
Subscription price	1.524	0.052
Circulation	−2.430	0.090
Advertising profits	−1.713	0.063
Readership profits	0.076	0.180
Total profits	−0.604	0.135

Note: This table shows the effects of the merger between the *NRC Handelsblad, nrc.next* and the Telegraaf group. Numbers are percentage changes.

unilateral effects on the advertisers' side of the market and less so on the readers' side of the market.

10.5.3   Full Simulation and Welfare Analysis

As argued above, from the point of view of economics, the correct way to evaluate whether a merger is likely to lead to higher prices would be a merger simulation that uses a model of the market in question and the estimated demand parameters to predict the price chosen by the firms after the merger. If cost data are not available, it is possible to recover estimates for them from the first order conditions of the model, as first proposed by Rosse (1970), and also use these estimates to predict the post-merger prices. One can then compute the change in prices, consumer surplus and/ or total welfare from the pre-merger to the post-merger equilibrium.

In a two-sided market all of the above is possible but there are additional technical complications involved, particularly in the presence of two indirect network effects. We follow Filistrucchi et al. (2010) who propose a framework to recover the marginal costs and simulate the new equilibrium in two-sided markets. Table 10.2 summarizes the estimated effects of the merger on average prices, average quantities and profits. Unweighted averages are taken. The table shows that advertising prices per column millimetre would not be affected by the merger (a result of our specification of advertising demand), while subscription prices would rise by 1.5 per cent.[14] As a result, circulation would decline by 2.4 per cent, which in turn would lower advertising demand by 1.7 per cent. Overall, advertising profits would decline by 1.7 per cent, while subscription profits would only marginally increase.[15] The merging parties would even lose in terms of profits, while outsiders would marginally gain.

Table 10.3 Welfare

	Advertisers	Readers
All newspapers independently owned	0.00	112.55
Ownership as at the end of 2009	−102.88	111.60
As before, only *NRC* and *NRN* independently owned	−81.85	111.94
As before, but *NRC* and *NRN* joined Telegraaf group	−115.48	111.64

Note: This table shows advertiser and reader welfare for different ownership combinations. The former is relative to the situation in which all newspapers are independently owned. Both are measured in euros per year and reader. *NRC* stands for *NRC Handelsblad* and *NRN* stands for *nrc.next*.

Contrary to the results of the HHI-based analysis but consistent with the results of the SSNIP-type test, the merger would seem to raise only modest concerns on the readers' market and a big concern on the advertising market. The latter is due to the fact that as subscription prices are raised after the merger, readership declines and advertisers pay a much higher price per reader, although the price per column millimetre is unchanged. Clearly, the two-sided nature of the market plays a role here. Finally, Table 10.3 shows the effects of the merger on advertisers' and readers' welfare. For the former, we report the sum of the welfare changes, over all newspapers, relative to the situation in which all firms are independently owned. This is given by the negative of the sum of the integral over the demand functions (1), where the integral is taken from the advertising price per reader under the respective ownership situations to the advertising price per reader when newspapers are independently owned.[16] For the readers, we report average welfare per person over 13 years of age per year, as implied by the estimated price coefficient and the well-known log-sum welfare formula for the logit model.

The table shows that readers' welfare is almost unaffected by the hypothetical merger. Overall, results from the full merger simulation suggest that, contrary to what is predicted by a HHI analysis but consistently with a SSNIP-type test, the merger raises concerns of unilateral effects more on the advertisers' side of the market and less on the readers' side of the market.

10.6   SUMMARY AND CONCLUSIONS

We investigate different ways to assess unilateral merger effects in a two-sided market by applying them to a hypothetical merger in the Dutch newspaper industry.

Lacking other sources of information on diversion ratios and profit margins, we first specify and estimate a structural model of demand for differentiated products on both the readership and the advertising side of the market. In particular, we estimate a log-linear demand for advertising slots and a logit demand for newspaper copies. This allows us to recover price elasticities, indirect network effects and marginal costs.

We use these estimates to compare different methods used to evaluate merger effects: a concentration analysis based on the HHI, a SSNIP-type test and a full merger simulation. The results are consistent with the newspaper market being characterized by a positive indirect network effect of readership on advertising demand higher than the positive indirect network effect of advertising demand on readership. In other words, advertisers care more about readers than readers care for advertising. Since raising the newspaper price is likely to lead not only to a loss in readers but also a loss in advertising, the post-merger tendency to increase subscription prices will be lower than in the absence of network effects.

Overall, in our case, the effects of the hypothetical merger on subscription prices and readers' welfare are found to be small. The merger has a larger and negative impact on the advertising side. To this regard, with the exception of market concentration analysis, there does not seem to be a significant difference between the different methods used to assess the unilateral effects of the hypothetical merger we analysed. This is not surprising as we used a SSNIP formula adjusted for two-sided platforms, so that the HHI-based analysis was the only one that did not take the two-sided nature of the market into account.

NOTES

1. This chapter is based on a previous empirical study performed for the Dutch competition authority (NMa). The views expressed are not necessarily the ones of the NMa. We appreciate financial support by the NMa and comments received at seminar presentations in Bergen and Düsseldorf, as well as conference presentations at the 2011 CRESSE conference in Rhodes, at the EARIE conference in Stockholm and at the Media Economics workshop in Moscow. We thank Ron Kemp, Bastiaan Overvest, Lars Sorgard, Frank Verboven and Björn Vroomen for useful suggestions and Pauline Affeldt for her research assistance. For the additional work leading from the above report to this chapter, we acknowledge financial support from a NET Institute (http://www.netinst.org) summer grant and a Microsoft grant to TILEC. Such grants were provided in accordance with the KNAW Declaration of Scientific Independence. All remaining errors are ours.
2. Originally, the SSNIP test was devised for market definition and as such asks the question of whether a hypothetical monopolist would find it profitable to raise the price by 5 or 10 per cent. This is why the test is sometimes called the Hypothetical Monopolist test. Note that in the original context of the test it is somewhat more natural to assume that the prices of the products not owned by the hypothetical monopolists remain unchanged.

3. We use the word 'roughly', because in a two-sided market without a transaction among users of the platform one needs to reduce the two prices to the same unit of measurement by appropriate weights. In a newspaper market, the price level is equal to the per copy revenues from both the readership and the advertising side, while the price structure is the ratio of the revenues from both sides.

4. In practice, although in many circumstances it would probably be relevant, the assessment of unilateral merger effects does not tackle the issue of product repositioning or, if it does, the analysis is mainly qualitative.

5. We model them as part of the outside good when estimating readership demand and allow the value of the outside good to increase with time. Also the increased value of not buying a newspaper and reading news online is captured by the dependence of the value of the outside good on time.

6. *Sp!t*s is also part of the Telegraaf group, but we treat it as part of the outside good for the entire analysis. This is not likely to alter our conclusions on the readership side, as long as it remains a free newspaper. In Section 10.4 we discuss our use of a model for the advertising side in which newspapers do not directly compete with one another. Given that we use this model also, conclusions for the advertising market are likely to be unaffected.

7. Reach differs from circulation in that reach is the number of people reading a newspaper, whereas circulation is the number of copies that are distributed. Circulation can be divided into paid and unpaid circulation. Most of the circulation is paid, and as already pointed out above, most of the paid circulation is paid subscriptions.

8. There are five regions with on average about three million people living in each region. These regions are reasonably small in terms of geographical distance.

9. This is the test in the European Union. In the USA, the formulas are often used to calculate the optimal price increase above the current level by the merging parties keeping rivals' prices constant. Also in the USA, the formulas for Critical Loss Analysis (CLA) or Critical Elasticity Analysis (CEA) assume constant marginal costs and either linear or iso-elastic demand. As with market definition, the difference between the SSNIP and the HM test appears to be very small at first sight and it is a matter of debate whether this difference is in practice relevant or not. In Section 10.5.2 we present the results from both versions of the test.

10. As explained in Filistrucchi et al. (2010), this involves first finding the derivatives of both demands with respect to prices on all sides of the market in order to write the first order conditions, then inverting the set of first order conditions, one for each newspaper and each price. Here, we incorporate the ownership structure in the industry. We find margins to be about 60 per cent on the readership side and 40 per cent on the advertising side. This is somewhat different from Kaiser and Wright (2006) and Song (2011), who find that often margins are negative on the readers' side for German magazines.

11. Here and in the following, we first aggregate the market shares by newspaper company, then square them and finally add them up. This is necessary as newspaper publishing companies are multi-product firms.

12. Absent a price, we do not have a straightforward way to estimate cross-price elasticities or diversion ratios for the free press. Therefore, even though it is straightforward to calculate HHIs without doing so, we prefer to abstract from them also in this section in order to be consistent in our comparison of the different methods for assessing unilateral effects.

13. We constrain the merged firm to set prices that are not negative and that do not exceed twice the prices we observe in our original data. In practice, both in the EU and in the USA, the test is often conducted using formulas derived under the assumption of constant marginal costs and either linear or iso-elastic demand. See Filistrucchi (2008) for a discussion of these formulas and their extension to two-sided markets.

14. Intuitively, the assumption of no direct cross-price effects on the advertising side implies that there are no price effects that could be internalized in addition by the merging parties. At the same time, changes in the optimal subscription prices will affect circulation and this will shift the advertising demand, but because of the constant elasticity specification for advertising demand it is the case that advertising prices will be

unaffected by those shifts in demand, unless there are efficiency gains from the merger on the advertising side. Note, however, that advertising prices per reader will change.
15. Note that the decline in advertising demand and therefore in advertising profits would not take place in the absence of an indirect network effect from readers to advertisers.
16. We do not report absolute levels of welfare here, because the area under the demand function is not finite.

REFERENCES

Anderson, S. and J. Gabszewicz (2006), 'The media and advertising: a tale of two sided markets', in Victor A. Ginsburgh and David Throsby (eds), *Handbook of the Economics of Art and Culture*, Amsterdam: Elsevier, pp. 567–614.

Argentesi, E. and L. Filistrucchi (2007), 'Estimating market power in a two-sided market: the case of newspapers', *Journal of Applied Econometrics*, **22**(7), 1247–66.

Berry, S. (1994), 'Estimating discrete-choice models of product differentiation', *RAND Journal of Economics*, **25**(2), 242–62.

Chandra, A. and A. Collard-Wexler (2009), 'Mergers in two-sided markets: an application to the Canadian newspaper industry', *Journal of Economics and Management Strategy*, **18**(4), 1045–70.

Evans, D. and M. Noel (2008), 'The analysis of mergers that involve multisided platform businesses', *Journal of Competition Law and Economics*, **4**(3), 663–95.

Fan, Y. (2011), 'Ownership consolidation and product characteristics: a study of the U.S. daily newspaper market', mimeo, University of Michigan.

Filistrucchi, L. (2008), 'A SSNIP test for two-sided markets', NET Institute Working Paper No. 08–34.

Filistrucchi, L., T.J. Klein and T. Michielsen (2010), 'Merger simulation in a two-sided market: the case of the Dutch daily newspapers', NET Institute Working Paper No. 10–15.

Jeziorski, P. (2011), 'Merger enforcement in two-sided markets', mimeo, Johns Hopkins University.

Kaiser, U. and J. Wright (2006), 'Price structure in two-sided markets: evidence from the magazine industry', *International Journal of Industrial Organization*, **24**, 1–28.

Rosse, J. (1970), 'Estimating cost functions parameters without using cost data: illustrated methodology', *Econometrica*, **38**(2), 255–75.

Rysman, M. (2004), 'Competition between networks: a study of the market for yellow pages', *Review of Economic Studies*, **71**(2), 483–512.

Song, M. (2011), 'Estimating platform market power in two-sided markets with an application to magazine advertising', The Bradley Policy Research Center Financial Research and Policy Working Paper No. FR 11–22.

Van Cayseele, P. and S. Vanormelingen (2009), 'Merger analysis in two-sided markets: The Belgian newspaper industry', mimeo, University of Leuven.

Wright, J. (2004), 'One-sided logic in two-sided markets', *Review of Network Economics*, **3**(1), 44–64.

11. Leadership in multi-sided markets and dominance in online advertising

Federico Etro[1]

The economics of multi-sided markets has recently attracted a lot of attention among economists (Caillaud and Jullien, 2003; Rochet and Tirole, 2003; Armstrong, 2006; Weyl, 2010; Athey and Ellison, 2011) because it characterizes a number of important markets of the New Economy and generates a number of new intriguing antitrust issues. In particular, wide interest has been focused on the market for search and display advertising, whose dominant firm at the global level, Google, is currently being investigated by a number of antitrust authorities. Analysing this market, it emerges that possible abuses may concern both search and display advertising, with particular reference to manipulation of the opaque bidding system for sponsored links leading to exploitative prices on advertisers, preferential treatment for Google's own services in its free ('universal') search and exclusivity clauses for advertisers leading to exclusion of competing platforms. However, the theoretical debate on the role of market leaders in multi-sided markets is still limited: most of the literature on multi-sided markets is focused on monopolistic pricing and symmetric competition between platforms, not on competition between a potentially dominant platform and its followers.

In this chapter, building on the literature on strategic commitments under different entry conditions (Fudenberg and Tirole, 1984; Etro, 2006) and its recent applications to antitrust and contract theory (Etro, 2010, 2011), we advance some preliminary insights on modeling leadership in multi-sided markets. As usual, the incentives to adopt different strategies or pre-commitments depend on the nature of competition, on the entry conditions, and on the impact of those strategies or pre-commitments on marginal profitability. First of all, we argue that a model of quantity competition between platforms better characterizes the market for search advertising, while a model of price competition better characterizes display advertising. Second, we argue that online advertising can be realistically characterized by a fixed number of players in the short to medium run. And finally, we examine the impact of different pre-commitments on the equilibrium of this multi-sided market. As far as we know, this is the first analysis of asymmetric competition between leaders and followers in multi-sided markets, even if it belongs to a growing body of literature on antitrust issues in multi-sided markets (Evans, 2003a, 2003b; Behringer and Filistrucchi, 2010).

Our analysis suggests that a platform that has reached dominance in search advertising can have an incentive to limit services to consumers to be more aggressive in the competition for advertisers (a 'lean and hungry look' strategy in the classic terminology of Fudenberg and Tirole, 1984), or to exploit its scale in search to build barriers to entry and to adopt price discrimination through opaque click-weighted auctions to manipulate pricing for sponsored links (a 'top dog' strategy in the mentioned terminology). On the other side, a platform that has reached dominance in display advertising may increase the rewards of content providers to increase prices on advertisers (a 'puppy dog' strategy), or may adopt exclusive clauses to marginalize other platforms or even induce their exit.

The chapter is organized as follows. Section 11.1 sets the background of our analysis describing the multi-sided markets of search and display advertising and introduces details of the Google case. Section 11.2 introduces a simplified version of our model of multi-sided markets and applies it to search and display advertising. Sections 11.3 and 11.4 discuss the role of a leader in these markets. Section 11.5 concludes.

11.1 THE STRUCTURE OF THE ONLINE ADVERTISING MARKET

The motivation for this chapter derives from recent attention of the leading antitrust authorities on a prominent multi-sided market, the one for online advertising, which is dominated by Google at the global level. In November 2010 the European Commission started an investigation on potential abuses concerning the preferential treatment for Google services in its free search engine, the manipulation of the pricing system for the sponsored links, and exclusivity clauses or other restrictions for advertisers using Google services. The potential abuse is about lowering the ranking of unpaid search results of competing services (so-called vertical search services) and according preferential placement to the results of its own vertical search services, lowering the 'Quality Score' for sponsored links of these competing vertical search services, imposing exclusivity obligations on advertising partners, and restrictions on the portability of online advertising campaign data. The investigation started with the complaints of some European companies in February 2010: a UK price comparison site (Foundem), a French legal search engine (eJustice), and a comparison shopping site (Ciao!). Later on, Microsoft, one of the main followers in online advertising, also submitted its complaint to the European Commission.[2]

11.1.1   Market Definition

Online advertising is a multi-sided market in which platforms such as Google, Yahoo!, and others attract at the same time Internet users and companies willing to advertise their products to these users. The more Internet users reach a platform, the more effective is an advertising campaign on the same platform. Since Internet users often join the platform with a commercial purpose in mind and use it to find information on products and offers, advertising can be tailored for them in a much more effective way than by other means. Moreover, continuous technological innovations open up new ways for advertisers to be more effective on a platform online. This generates a very limited substitutability between online and traditional advertising, implying the existence of separate markets, which is confirmed by the outcome of multiple investigations.[3] In spite of this, Ratliff and Rubinfield (2010) have advanced the hypothesis that some substitutability between online and traditional advertising could exist because they both serve broad advertising goals. However they have not provided any empirical argument in support of such a view and have neglected two key differences. First, traditional advertising is aimed at building a general brand awareness usually without a specific target audience, while online advertising (especially search advertising) is largely aimed at generating market transactions online. Second, it is not enough to talk loosely about whether or not there is substitutability between two goods or services: there may be substitutability in one direction but not in the other direction, as may be the case here, since online advertising may act as a competitive constraint on offline advertising without offline necessarily acting as a competitive constraint on online. From this perspective, traditional and online advertising are almost always complements rather than substitutes (or at most can be asymmetric substitutes),[4] and for our purposes should be considered separate markets.

Within online advertising, one can also distinguish two markets, search and display advertising. Search advertising is aimed at direct demand fulfillment, as witnessed by the 'text-only' composition and the payments on a cost per click (CPC) basis; moreover, platforms compete to conquer the largest number of visitors (that is, they compete in quantities) and charge advertisers for the clicks they receive on their ads. Display advertising is mainly aimed at brand awareness and directed to a targeted audience (always more so with new technologies allowing for forms of behavioral advertising that are impossible with traditional media): this is witnessed by the advanced graphic/video composition of the ads and the payments on a cost per thousand impression (CPM) basis. Since firms pay exactly for what they value, an impression which gives general brand awareness to the web visitor (and not for a click which may, or may not, lead to a market transaction, as in search advertising), platforms can directly compete in prices for display advertising. In these two markets advertisers not only face different forms of pricing, but they actually buy different goods: clicks leading to market transactions with a certain probability, on the one hand, and impressions that promote a brand on a targeted audience, on the other hand (for one of the first theoretical analyses on market definition in two-sided markets, see Filistrucchi, 2010).

11.1.2 Search Advertising

As well known, Google is the leading search engine in the world. It reached this position through constant innovations that have improved the search experience (think of Google Instant, Place Search, Real-time Search, Social Search, and the Universal Search of course) and provided a wide array of services to Internet users. Beyond this, Google dominates the lucrative business of placing text ads next to search engine results. Google AdWords accounts for more than 70 percent of search advertising revenue worldwide, leaving Yahoo! and Microsoft far behind. All these platforms choose a number of advertisements to be made available in a specific order for any search query. Given the space allocated to these sponsored links, an auction pins down the market clearing price for these advertisements. Payments are based on so-called Vickrey auctions between advertisers on the keywords that match the content of the web pages or searches: charges are typically for each click on the ad, and the highest bid for each keyword association wins, with the price given by the second highest bid. As shown by Vickrey (1961), this tends to force bidders to reveal their true evaluation of the click (for classic works on the theory of auctions, see Myerson, 1981; Riley and Samuelson, 1981; Milgrom and Weber, 1982), which allows the auctioneer to choose the profit maximizing auction mechanism. Contrary to what is usually claimed (see, for instance, Ratliff and Rubinfleld, 2010), these auctions do not necessarily add a competitive element to online advertising, but allow a dominant firm to adopt complex forms of price discrimination aimed at excluding competitors in search advertising or at extracting all the surplus from the bidders (or even both aims at the same time). The auction process for search advertising is made more complex by the different places where the ad can appear on the search page (on these position auctions, see Edelman et al., 2007; Varian, 2007; Agarwal et al., 2009; Athey and Ellison, 2011), and remains largely obscure to advertisers and competitors. More recently, most platforms have introduced forms of click-weighted auctions that weight bids to give priority to ads with a larger chance of being clicked on: this mechanism is aimed at increasing the effective willingness to pay (see Athey and Ellison, 2011 for the most complete theoretical treatment of this issue).[5]

The structure of the market for search advertising depends on a particular form of network externality that is quite different from the one emerging in other markets of the New Economy. This is due to two main reasons. First of all, network effects in search are combined with a form of learning by doing: search engines find more relevant results for each query when there are more queries and the subsequent clicks of the users provide information on what were the most relevant websites associated with particular keywords. Through this feedback mechanism, the same users improve the algorithms that govern the search engine. Therefore, not only more search generates more demand for advertising (as in any market with network effects), but more search also generates the scale needed to improve the search technology and provide more relevant results and ads, which in turn generates more search. This is a key difference compared to other markets with network externalities: in traditional platforms the number of consumers determines the demand of application developers but does not affect the quality of the software platform for a given number of applications, while the number of visitors to a search engine determines not only the demand of advertisers but also the (future) quality of the search engine (in terms of ability to reach the most relevant results). This combination of network effects and learning by doing induces initial increasing returns to scale in this market.

As a consequence of the importance of scale in search, for a platform to enter the search advertising market (or increase its market share) and compete with the leader, it is crucial to rapidly gain scale and close the technological and information gap on the search queries. At the same time, for a leading platform to maintain its market power, it is crucial to protect the information gained through search and limit the scale of the rivals and their learning by doing. Any exclusivity agreement between the dominant firm and hardware or software distributors to install only its search-related product and services or between the dominant firm and advertisers to rely only on its platform may jeopardize any hope of the competitors gaining scale and competing on merit (see Argenton and Prufer, 2011). This may be the case of the exclusivity agreements on the

Google toolbar or on the search default settings between Google and software vendors such as Adobe, hardware vendors like Apple for the iPhone (and others adopting the Android operating system), or browser distributors like Firefox, Safari, and Opera. Moreover, scale requires that any search engine must be able to have full access to all websites and 'crawl' them to find new information to be provided in search queries. Clearly, if the dominant platform obtains a privileged access to some relevant websites and limits the access of competitors, competition is penalized because raising rivals' costs may exclude some of these competitors. In this case, innovation by the followers is penalized as well. This is what may have happened since the acquisition by Google of YouTube, the main website for video contents, to which access by competing search engines does not appear to be as direct and immediate as for Google.

The second reason for which network effects in search are different from the network effects of many other markets is that multi-homing on both sides (by web visitors and advertisers) can easily spread their benefits between different providers. Of course, multi-homing by consumers is key to drive the accumulation of information needed to build scale for a minor search engine. The fact that search engines are free and, most of all, are always 'one click away' (for surfers) on the Internet plays a double role in this context. On the one hand, it allows consumers starting from the dominant search engine to easily try alternative ones to test their capabilities or to perform additional investigations whenever the initial search was not fully satisfactory. On the other hand, multi-homing by consumers allows those who are experimenting with a minor search engine to quickly revert to the dominant one, jeopardizing the chances of the former to develop and protecting the advantage of the latter. Equally important is multi-homing on the advertisers' side. Since advertisers are uniquely interested in the effectiveness of their spending in search advertising, they have good reasons to diversify their investment between alternative platforms in such a way that the marginal returns are equalized. Multi-homing guarantees that different Internet users can be reached with different search engines, typically with a higher budget destined for the leading channel (currently Google AdWord) and a smaller budget shared across the others (as Yahoo! Panama or Microsoft AdCenter). Moreover, data analysis can easily allow for a comparison of the return on investment in each channel to optimize spending. It is clear that multi-homing by many advertisers would contribute to the development of scale and efficiency of minor search platforms. As a consequence, any policy aimed at limiting multi-homing in search advertising (or simply at raising its costs) is going to create obstacles to the creation of network effects. This may be the case for the contracts with which Google prohibits advertisers from using competing platforms, and for the exclusive use by Google of the data on its clients which prevents them from performing data analysis to compare the return on investment of different advertising channels.[6]

11.1.3   Display Advertising

The second field of dominance by Google is in display advertising. Google leads the business of directly placing banner ads on third-party publishers, accounting for three-quarters of the direct channel, that is, the valuable ad inventory that large web publishers directly negotiate with the advertisers. Of course, a lot of the advertising space available on large websites and all of the space available on small websites cannot be sold in direct negotiations. Therefore, most advertising is typically sold through indirect intermediaries that pay a price for the so-called 'remnant' ad inventory from publishers and charge advertisers to fill this space with their ads. Google also plays a major role in this market for intermediation services, providing a vertically integrated platform between online web publishers and advertisers: Google's AdSense reaches more than 80 percent of the ad revenue in the indirect channel with integrated ad networks. The Google platform targets advertising to the relevant websites – so-called contextual advertising (see Athey and Gans, 2010), and pays the web publishers (typically with a percentage of its revenues), but in the absence of any audit or data certification available for the same publishers. Meanwhile advertisers buy inventories from the platform through a bidding system.

Through all the mentioned services, Google controls at least 80 percent of the worldwide market for online advertising, and, as confirmed by the sector inquiry by the French antitrust authority, is protected by high barriers to entry. A first source of barriers to entry is related to the importance of scale in search, and the huge lead time that the dominant player has because of the massive amount of data it can draw on to improve its organic search, which is due to the high volume of the search queries that are made and to the fact that Google is a laggard in the industry with respect to the anonymization of user data. A second source of barriers to entry applies both in search and display advertising. Alternatives to Google can hardly be offered to publishers using Google's services: switching to a different publisher tool involves high sunk costs in terms of substantial investments in software, in training the staff, coding all of the data about keywords' associations, and returns for search advertising, or about publisher's web pages and their statistics for display advertising, managing novel datasets, transferring ad campaigns to the system, and so on, with all the associated business risk.

This leaves space for multiple potential abuses by the dominant firm, including exploitative pricing on advertisers (with negative indirect consequences on all sectors), and aggressive strategies (free services to consumers and free distribution of content produced by third parties), exclusivity clauses for advertisers using Google services, and restrictions that Google can place on advertisers that wish to use the services of competing platforms. The clarification of these mechanisms requires wide theoretical work on the role of leaders in multi-sided markets. In the rest of the chapter we provide some preliminary thoughts on this aspect, focusing on fully fledged multi-sided markets with and without a dominant platform.

11.2 A MODEL OF MULTI-SIDED PLATFORM COMPETITION

In this section we will examine a general model where a platform, as an online advertising platform (say Google or Yahoo!), charges for each interaction (pay per click). Denoting with c the marginal cost of an interaction for a platform, the profit of this platform is:

$$\Pi^i = (p_{ai} - p_{ci} - c_i) A_i C_i,$$

where p_{ai} is the price charged on advertisers per interaction, p_{ci} can be seen as the cost per interaction to attract consumers, that is, the cost of the services freely provided to consumers (in search advertising) or the payment to the content providers (in display advertising), A_i is the number of ads available through the platform, C_i is the number of consumers reached by these ads through the platform, and their product represents (or is proportional to) the number of interactions. The number of consumers reached by an ad for each platform is increasing in p_{ci}, with $C_i = C^i(p_{ci})$. The supply of consumers can also be inverted to obtain $p_{ci} = p^i(C_i)$, which is increasing in the number of consumers. Below we provide alternative microfoundations for this in case of search and display advertising (for further details on search advertising, see Etro, 2012). On the other hand, an advertiser can choose between different platforms on the basis of their prices. We will adopt a reduced form for the number of ads offered to each platform: $A_i = A^i(p_a)$, where p_a is now the vector of prices of different platforms. Analogously we can define the inverse demand of advertising as $p_{ai} = p^i(A)$ where A is now the vector of advertisement choices. In general these relations should depend also on the size of the potential consumers because of network effects, but we leave a full derivation of a microfounded model to a following section and Etro (2012), which discusses the changes occurring in this case.

The profit of platform i can be written as a function of the quantity of advertisements and consumers:

$$\Pi^i = [p^i(A) - p^i(C) - c_i]A_i C_i$$

or as a function of the prices for advertisers and publishers:

$$\Pi^i = (p_{ai} - p_{ci} - c_i)A^i(p_a)C(p_{ci}).$$

Symmetric forms of competition in quantities and in prices have been analysed by Armstrong (2006), Rochet and Tirole (2006), and others in detail. Both of them can be useful to describe the two main forms of online advertising, as shown in the next subsections. In the following sections we will move to the analysis of asymmetric forms of competition where one of the platforms is a market leader.

11.2.1   Search Advertising

As argued earlier, search advertising can be interpreted in terms of quantity competition. On the one hand, each platform decides how many consumers will join the platform, typically providing free services that deliver utility for consumers and can be seen as a price paid to them. Natural search results and a vast array of free applications attract visitors to a search engine, making them available for sponsored search as well. Of course, the number of visitors is constrained by the technology available to the search engine and the exploitation of network effects built over time, but a larger number of visitors can always be obtained at a larger cost. To microfound the number of consumers on the platform, assume that platform i provides services with a cost per interaction given by p_{ci}, and each web visitor k obtains utility $U_k = \theta_k p_{ci} - \bar{u}$ from visiting a platform, where θ_k is a preference parameter, distributed in the population according to a cumulative function $F(\theta_k)$ with density $f(\theta_k)$, and the reservation utility (from visiting other websites) is assumed constant. If total population is N_C, the number of visitors is given by the increasing function $C(p_{ci}) = N_C[1 - F(\bar{u}/p_{ci})]$, which can be inverted to obtain a function increasing in C_i.

On the other hand, each platform decides how many ads will be made available on the search engine (typically above or on the right hand side of the natural search results for each query) and an auction pins down the market clearing price $p_a = p(A)$ for these advertisements. More recently, most platforms have introduced forms of click-weighted auctions that weight bids to give priority to advertisements with a larger chance to be clicked on (see Athey and Ellison, 2011): this amounts to a sophisticated mechanism aimed at increasing the effective willingness to pay, and therefore the total revenues.

Finally, notice that search advertising is characterized by barriers to entry due to the importance of scale in search, and the huge lead time that the dominant player has because of the massive amount of data it can draw on to improve its organic search (which is due to the high volume of the search queries that are made). For this reason, a focus on exogenous rather than endogenous entry appears proper. In our model, quantity competition between an exogenous number of platforms leads to a symmetric Cournot equilibrium satisfying the first order conditions:

$$p^i(A) - p^i(C_i) - c_i + \frac{\partial p^i(A)}{\partial A_i} A_i = 0$$

$$p^i(A) - p^i(C_i) - c_i - \frac{\partial p^i(C_i)}{\partial C_i} C_i = 0,$$

which can be rewritten in terms of a Rochet-Tirole (2003) rule:

$$p_{ai} - p_{ci} - c_i = \frac{p_{ai}}{\varepsilon^i(A)} = \frac{p_{ci}}{\varepsilon^i(C_i)},$$

where the two elasticities at the denominators are, respectively, the elasticity of demand of advertising and the elasticity of supply of consumers. The equilibrium markups for each platform are decreasing in the relevant elasticities and in the marginal cost per interaction, but the relative charge on advertisers increases in the elasticity of demand of advertising and decreases in the elasticity of supply of consumers.

11.2.2 Display Advertising

Display advertising is better described through price competition. On the one hand, each platform decides how much to reward the content providers that make available some space for advertising, choosing a price for each interaction between visitors and ads, or a percentage of the price paid by the advertisers.

More formally, to derive the supply of content as a function of the price offered by a platform, let us consider a content provider that decides C_j for each platform to maximize revenues net of the costs, which are proportional to the number of ads and increasing and convex in the number of consumers reached by them: in practice, we assume that advertising reduces the net utility of the web experience and, through this, the other revenues of the content provider. Therefore, the profits of the content providers are:

$$\pi^C = \sum_j p_{cj} A_j C_j - A_j g(C_j)$$

with the cost function $g(.)$ increasing and convex. Profits are maximized when the following first order condition is satisfied $p_{ci} = g'(C_i)$. This is an increasing function of the number of consumers made available, and provides a direct supply, increasing in the price. For simplicity, we have excluded substitutability between different platforms: this reflects the fact that most content providers adopt a single platform to reach advertisers.

On the other hand, each platform decides the prices for the advertisers, depending on a number of features of the host website and of the same ads. Also in this case, the price of the advertisers is selected by an auction mechanism, but the wide and increasing mechanisms of price discrimination adopted by the online platforms to maximize revenues leads to an outcome that can be generally described in terms of price setting. Given prices, the demand function determines the equilibrium amount of ads (after all, space for ads on websites is unconstrained). Also in display advertising, entry is not endogenous because of substantial barriers to entry: alternatives to Google can hardly be offered to publishers using Google's services (switching to a different publisher tool involves high sunk costs in terms of substantial investments in software, in training the staff, coding all of the publisher's web pages, creating novel datasets, transferring ad campaigns to the system, and so on, with all the associated business risk).

Price competition between platforms leads to a symmetric Bertrand equilibrium satisfying the first order conditions:

$$A^i(p_a) + (p_{ai} - p_{ci} - c_i)\frac{\partial A^i(p_a)}{\partial p_{ai}} = 0$$

$$-C(p_{ci}) + (p_{ai} - p_{ci} - c_i)C'(p_{ci}) = 0,$$

which can be rewritten in terms of a Rochet-Tirole (2003) rule as:

$$p_{ai} - p_{ci} - c_i = \frac{p_{ai}}{\gamma^i(p_a)} = \frac{p_{ci}}{\gamma^i(p_{ci})},$$

where now the elasticities are, respectively, the elasticity of the direct demand of advertising and the elasticity of the direct supply of content. These rules are valid whenever some regularity conditions hold, otherwise extreme pricing rules can easily emerge, with zero price on one of the two sides (see Schmalensee, 2010). The equilibrium markups for each platform are decreasing in the relevant elasticities and in the marginal cost per interaction, but the relative charge on advertisers increases in the elasticity of demand of advertising and decreases in the elasticity of supply of content. Under regularity conditions, an increase in the number of platforms tends to reduce profitability and markups.

Contrary to what has been assumed until now, however, multi-sided markets are often characterized by the leadership of a firm, which creates the case for a strategic rationale behind pricing, to which we now turn in the rest of the chapter. We will consider quantity and price competition in order in the following two sections.

11.3 QUANTITY LEADERSHIP IN SEARCH ADVERTISING

Consider now a situation in which one platform can act as a leader in the choice of a strategic variable and, therefore, pre-commit to it before competition with the other platforms takes place. In this section we examine this possibility in the application to search advertising, that is, assuming that competition in quantities takes place between platforms to conquer ads. As long as the number of platforms is exogenous, we are in the situation characterized by Fudenberg and Tirole (1984) under the assumption of strategic substitutability.

Imagine that the dominant platform 1 can anticipate the choice of how many consumers to attract on the platform, C_1. In other words, in a first stage firm 1 chooses C_1 and in a second stage firms 1 and 2 choose C_2, A_1, and A_2. To verify the incentives of the leader to invest in attracting consumers, we need to look at the equilibrium cross-effect:

$$\frac{\partial^2 \Pi^1}{\partial A_1 \partial C_1} = -\frac{\partial p^1(C_1)}{\partial C_1} < 0.$$

In the terminology of Fudenberg and Tirole (1984), this implies that we are in a 'lean and hungry look' case: a leader has a strategic incentive to restrict or bias the size and quality of services made available on the platform, so as to decrease the utility of the consumers per interaction with the purpose of being more aggressive against the other platforms in the competition for the ads. Examples of this may include underinvestment in new services once dominance has been reached, preferential treatments for the services offered by the platform in the search engine (with limitations on the use of other services), and manipulation of the natural search results to promote objectives of interest for the dominant firm (such as promoting its own services or excluding competitors in particular services). The consequence is that the dominant platform reduces the gains of the consumers but conquers a larger share of total ads.

As an example, assume that there are two platforms and the cost per interaction is the same, c. The optimality conditions derive from the first order conditions for C_2, A_1, and A_2, which implicitly determine how these variables depend on C_1, and from the optimality condition for the pre-commitment variable, which is simplified because C_2 does not directly affect the profitability of the leader, and the impact of A_1 disappears by the envelope theorem. After straightforward manipulation, the equilibrium conditions can be expressed as:

$$p_{a1} - p_{c1} - c = \frac{p_{a1}}{\varepsilon^1(A)} = \frac{p_{c1}}{\varepsilon^1(C_1)} + \frac{\eta p_{a1}}{\zeta}$$

$$p_{a2} - p_{c2} - c = \frac{p_{a2}}{\varepsilon^2(A)} = \frac{p_{c2}}{\varepsilon^2(C_2)},$$

where $\zeta = -p_{a1}/A_2[\partial p_{a1}/\partial A_2] > 0$ and $\eta = (\partial A_2/\partial C_1)C_1/A_2 > 0$. This implies the modified Rochet-Tirole rule:

$$\frac{p_{a1}}{\varepsilon^1(A)} = \frac{p_{c1}}{\varepsilon^1(C_1)\left[1 - \dfrac{\eta \varepsilon^1(A)}{\zeta}\right]}$$

under the regularity condition $\varepsilon^1(A) \in (0, \zeta/\eta)$. A simple comparison of the equilibrium conditions under un symmetric and asymmetric competition shows that the dominant platform manages to increase its profits through an increase of the effective markup $p_{a1} - p_{c1}$, which requires a reduction of the reward of the consumers in terms of both services per interaction (p_{c1}) and size of the market (C_1) and generates an increase of its share of advertising $A_1/(A_1 + A_2)$. Clearly, this is going to reduce consumer surplus compared to the case of symmetric competition. The impact on the advertisers is more complex but the price reduction is likely to end up in gains for this side of the market (the same would happen with free entry; see Etro, 2006).

11.3.1   Scale in Search

Consider now a different pre-commitment of the leader. Suppose that the dominant platform can reduce its marginal cost per interaction through direct investments and through a process of learning by doing in service provision: in search advertising this happens because of the importance of scale in search and because of the huge lead time that a dominant player has because of the massive amount of data it can draw on to improve its organic search. Suppose that the number of visitors improves the search algorithms and reduces the cost of obtaining each click $c(C_i)$, with $c'(C_i) < 0$. As shown by Fudenberg and Tirole (1984), in the presence of barriers to entry, the nature of the incentives depends simply on the equilibrium cross-effect:

$$\frac{\partial^2 \Pi^1}{\partial A_1 \partial C_1} = -\frac{\partial p^1(C_1)}{\partial C_1} - c'(C_1),$$

which is now ambiguous: the first factor is negative as before, but the second is positive because of the gains from scale. If the latter prevails, the dominant firm has an incentive to overinvest to create scale in search and reduce its cost per interaction. Moreover, the leadership is going to strengthen itself automatically as long as it leads to a quicker learning by doing process which reduces costs per interaction and provides an advantage in the conquest of larger market shares in advertising. The first mover advantage can easily lead to conquering the entire market: if it takes time to conquer visitors and improve the search algorithms, this can lock in the market into a monopolistic situation (as in Argenton and Prufer, 2011).

11.3.2 Click-weighted Auctions

Most search platforms have introduced forms of click-weighted auctions that weight bids to give priority to ads with a larger chance to be clicked on (see Athey and Ellison, 2011): this amounts to a sophisticated mechanism aimed at increasing the effective willingness to pay, and therefore the total revenues. Similar systems have been introduced by Google as well as other platforms and represent crucial commercial secrets for this business.

Suppose that the dominant platform can introduce a mechanism of click-weighted auctions that increases the willingness to pay for ads on the platform. The mechanism is indexed by the parameter ϖ, which can be seen as the accuracy in discriminating between valuable and less valuable advertisers, or simply as the cost of development of the mechanism, which should be positively related to its accuracy. The profits of the leading platform are:

$$\Pi^1 = [p^1(A, \varpi) - p^1(C_1) - c_1]A_1 C_1.$$

A higher ϖ increases the inverse demand function for each interaction to $p^1(A, \varpi)$, but this impact is likely to be reduced when the level of advertising on the platform is larger. Therefore, we assume that the elasticity of $\partial p^1(A, \varpi)/\partial \varpi$ with respect to A_1 is less than unitary ϖ, which determines the sign of the following marginal effect:

$$\frac{\partial^2 \Pi^1}{\partial A_1 \partial \varpi} = \left[\frac{\partial p^1(A, \varpi)}{\partial \varpi} + \frac{\partial^2 p^1(A, \varpi)}{\partial A_1 \partial \varpi} A_1 \right] C_1 > 0.$$

This cross-effect suggests that we are in front of a classic 'top dog' strategy in the terminology of Fudenberg and Tirole (1984): a dominant platform should overinvest in the development of a click-weighted auction mechanism. In case of two platforms, the equilibrium conditions would be given by the traditional Rochet and Tirole (2003) rules plus an optimality condition for the choice of the strategic variable ϖ, which compares its marginal cost to the following marginal revenue:

$$\frac{\partial p^1(A, \varpi)}{\partial \varpi} + \frac{\partial p^1(A, \varpi)}{\partial A_2} \frac{\partial A_2}{\partial \varpi}.$$

The second positive term shows that there is a strategic incentive to overinvest in a sophisticated pricing mechanism that manipulates the willingness to pay of the advertisers, because this shifts advertising from other platforms to the dominant one. The higher marginal revenues per click induce the dominant platform to expand both its services to consumers and its space for advertisement, while reducing their counterparts for the competing platforms. Nevertheless, the higher willingness to pay (bid) for advertising induced by the enhanced mechanism may even increase the price charged by the leading platform on advertisers. In this sense, these mechanisms may generate a non-transparent manipulation of the pricing system for the sponsored links, which can limit competition.

Network effects that induce an increase in the willingness to pay for ads on platforms with more visitors can be easily introduced – see Etro (2012) for a microfounded model of quantity competition with network effects that generalizes the one above, and for its solution. Under some additional restrictions, the tendency of market leaders to restrict the services provided to the web visitors (to be more aggressive in advertising) persists. A counteractive force, however, emerges because a larger base of web visitors increases the willingness to pay of the same advertisers on the platform. If network effects and scale in search effects are strong enough, as we would expect given their importance in the market for search advertising, they induce a tendency for the dominant firm to overinvest to conquer visitors and lock in the market into a monopolistic outcome in which followers do not manage to catch up.

11.4   PRICE LEADERSHIP IN DISPLAY ADVERTISING

Let us move to the case of price competition, which is the usual assumption in theoretical models of two-sided markets and allows us to better describe the market for display advertising. As long as the number of platforms is exogenous, we are in the situation characterized by Fudenberg and Tirole (1984) under the assumption of strategic complementarity.

As an example, assume that there are two platforms and the cost per interaction is the same, c. Imagine that the dominant platform 1 can pre-commit to the strategy adopted toward the content providers, that is, the choice of the price for interaction destined to the content providers p_{c1}. In other words, in a first stage firm 1 chooses p_{c1} and in a second stage firms 1 and 2 choose simultaneously p_{c2}, p_{a1}, and p_{a2}. To verify the incentives of the leader, we need to look at the cross-effect:

$$\frac{\partial^2 \Pi^1}{\partial p_{a1} \partial p_{c1}} = -\frac{\partial A^1(p_a)}{\partial p_{a1}} > 0.$$

In the terminology of Fudenberg and Tirole (1984), this implies that we are in a classic 'puppy dog' case: a leader has an incentive to choose a high reward of the publishers for each interaction with the advertisers, with the purpose of softening competition with the other platforms for the advertisers. The consequence is that the dominant platform increases the gains of the content providers, but also increases the price obtained by the advertisers above that of the other platforms.

The equilibrium conditions can be easily rearranged as:

$$p_{a1} - p_{c1} - c = \frac{p_{a1}}{\gamma^1(p_a)} = \frac{p_{c1}}{\gamma^1(p_{c1}) + \vartheta\zeta}$$

$$p_{a2} - p_{c2} - c = \frac{p_{a2}}{\gamma^2(p_a)} = \frac{p_{c2}}{\gamma^2(p_{c2})},$$

where $\vartheta = p_{c1}[\partial p_{a2}/\partial p_{c1}]/p_{a2} > 0$ and $\zeta = -(\partial A^1(p_a)/\partial p_{a2})p_{a2}/A_1 > 0$. This immediately leads to the result that the dominant firm manages to increase its profits through an increase of the reward of the content providers (p_{c1}), and an increase of the price of advertising (p_{a1}). Strategic complementarity leads the other platforms to increase their prices on advertisers as well. Publishers may be better off, but the advertisers will have to pay more for each interaction on every platform, which may ultimately lead to negative consequences for this sector and on the firms paying for the ads.

Let us briefly look at other forms of pre-commitment. In this case, a dominant firm that has reached the leadership would have low incentives to invest to reduce the cost per interaction. However, we can still have the tendency to overinvest in implementing sophisticated pricing schemes aimed at price discrimination toward the advertisers (think of the attempts to introduce forms of pay per action, which is directly associated with the final transactions). To verify this, imagine that demand is increased by ϖ defined as before. The relevant cross-effect is:

$$\frac{\partial^2 \Pi^1}{\partial p_{a1} \partial \varpi} = -\frac{\partial A^1(p_a, \varpi)}{\partial \varpi} + (p_{a1} - p_{c1} - c)\frac{\partial^2 A^1(p_a)}{\partial p_{a1} \partial \varpi},$$

which is positive if the second term is positive or not too negative (which is reasonable). In this case, sophisticated pricing is also aimed at softening competition with other platforms.

Finally, notice that the existence of barriers to entry is crucial for these effects to be at work, since in case of endogenous entry any accommodating practice would be self-defeating for attracting additional entrants (Etro, 2006, 2011).

11.4.1 Mergers

In a context of price competition as the one described above, there is another puppy dog strategy that can be adopted, which takes place through a merger with a rival. This allows the merged entity to increase prices on advertisers and, as long as entry is exogenous, to increase profits.

In our view, this is exactly what happened in the market for display advertising when Google acquired its main rival, DoubleClick, in 2008. As with Google's AdSense, DoubleClick offers an ad serving/management product, DART, for both publishers (DFP) and advertisers (DFA). The publisher tool, in particular, manages the inventory of a website, receives the ads from ad networks, and delivers them in the relevant inventory (according to the behavioral history of Internet users), usually for a percentage of the price charged by the publishers on the advertisers. Before the merger, Google was controlling about half of the global market for display advertising and DoubleClick about a third of it. Today, they jointly control at least 80 percent of the worldwide market. Most important, the merger has led to softer competition. The two services offered by Google and DoubleClick are highly substitutable and, as a matter of fact, many web publishers use both for different inventories in the same website. The high switching costs, together with the difficulty for other companies to build alternative high quality intermediation services (even

Yahoo! and Microsoft had a hard time), represent a substantial limit to endogenous entry of other firms in the short or medium run. The implication is simple. Before the merger, competitive forces kept prices under control: DoubleClick could not increase prices because many consumers would have quickly switched to AdSense, and vice versa. After the merger, these competitive constraints disappeared: Google could increase the price of DFP services, sure that most of the lost customers will switch to AdSense. The profitability of the price increase would be enhanced further because of the high margins and of the network effects that Google could enjoy by increasing its market share.

A similar result is emerging in display advertising for mobile phones, whose largest provider and main rival of Google, AdMob, was acquired by Google in November 2009. Another related case could emerge with the latest acquisition under consideration by Google, the one of ITA Software, a flight information company (whose software is used by some of the leading travel sites such as Travelocity, Orbitz, and others). This may also lead to accommodating strategies in the market for price comparisons on the Internet.

11.4.2   Exclusivity Agreements

What happens if a dominant firm adopts exclusivity clauses toward its advertisers or other restrictions for advertisers using its services? Our model suggests a simple consequence of similar agreements in terms of a standard strategy of entry deterrence. If the dominant platform has a technological advantage (say a lower cost per transaction), exclusivity clauses allow this platform to protect its comparative advantage in attracting both content providers and advertisers. Losing content providers and advertisers, the other platforms may even fail to cover their fixed costs and exit the market, in which case the exclusivity clauses would be predatory. Advertisers, and ultimately consumers, may be worse off, both because the price would increase and because there would be a reduction of variety in the provision of advertising.

11.5   CONCLUSIONS

In this chapter we have analysed the role of leadership in multi-sided markets, with a particular emphasis on online advertising, which is characterized by a single dominant firm in both search and display advertising. The case of quantity competition better characterizes the market for search advertising, while the case of price competition better characterizes display advertising. In both cases the borders of the market should be limited to online advertising, which potentially leads to market transactions (as opposed to offline advertsing). We have shown that a platform that has reached dominance in search can have an incentive to limit services to consumers to be more aggressive in the competition for advertisers or to adopt click-weighted auctions to manipulate the pricing for sponsored links. A platform that has reached dominance in display advertising may increase the rewards of content providers to increase prices on advertisers, or may adopt exclusive clauses to predate on other platforms. Comparing these results with the market for online advertising, it emerges that possible abuses by Google may concern both search and display advertising, with particular reference to exploitative prices on advertisers, preferential treatment for Google's own services in its free ('universal') search, and exclusivity clauses for advertisers. Additional research on the antitrust implications of asymmetric models of competition in multi-sided markets will be fruitful to better understand the structure of these markets and the appropriate antitrust policies.

NOTES

1. I am grateful to Paul Belleflamme, Stephen Behringer, Emilio Calvano, Lapo Filistrucchi, Renato Gomes, William Kovacic, Martin Peitz, Anne Perrot, Michele Polo, Roberto Roson, Richard Schmalensee, Emanuele Tarantino, and other participants to the IV and V Intertic Conferences, to the III Conference on Recent Developments in Antitrust Policy, and to the 2011 CRESSE Conference for useful discussion on the topic.
2. Other complaints have been also filed in front of the US, German, and Italian authorities, mainly regarding unfair competition with publishers and other content providers. The French competition authority has also carried out a consultation, concluding in December 2010 that Google holds a dominant position both in search-related advertising and contextual advertising and that competition law can apply limits to Google's actions and provide a response to the competitive stakes brought to light by the actors, without the need to implement sector-wide regulations. Some constraints to the activity of Google were also decided in Italy in January 2011, but the main antitrust debate will take place at the European Union level.
3. Refer to the Google/DoubleClick investigations by the European Commission and the US Federal Trade Commission and the Microsoft/Yahoo! investigations by the European Commission, the US Department of Justice, and the Australian Competition Commission.
4. Analogously, Amazon may compete with traditional bookstores, but does not compete with traditional advertisers of books (whose services actually promote the business of Amazon rather than being substitutes for it). For a theoretical investigation on the relation between traditional and online advertising, see Athey et al. (2011) and Blasco et al. (2011).
5. The lack of transparency of this pricing and ranking scheme, when implemented by a dominant firm, could easily hide abusive forms of exclusionary behavior, predatory strategies against competing services specialized in providing users with specific online content (price comparisons), price discrimination, or even exploitative pricing toward selected advertisers. For instance, an exclusionary behavior was identified by the French

national competition authority when Google suspended the AdWords account of a French company providing online services (Navx); Google was subsequently forced by the competition authority to re-establish the account.

6. Besides general search engines, some search platforms focus on specific services, such as news, travel information, academic works, finance, videos, maps, and more: since these services offer a deeper information within particular fields, they are usually referred to as vertical search services. To be reached and used (as for any website) these vertical services rely on general search engines such as Google. In the last few years Google has also introduced new services, some of which raise serious concerns not only about antitrust, but also copyright protection (Google Books) and privacy (YouTube and Google Maps with Street View, which emerged ignoring any privacy regulation). This is particularly evident in terms of predatory pricing or free riding against content providers, whose information is freely aggregated and displayed by Google News. On this front, the Italian and French competition authorities have obliged Google to guarantee that press publishers will be able to request and obtain exclusion from Google News, but without being de-listed from the general search. On the antitrust front, the new services of Google have rapidly gained success over competing vertical search services, but possibly with the help of manipulated ranking in the natural search of Google, which ends up marginalizing any competing vertical engine (Tarantino, 2011). As long as a dominant search platform gives priority to its own vertical services and diverts traffic away from its competitors, it is destined to reach leadership in any service provided, hurting competition on merit. Moreover, alternative specialized search engines are the only entry constraints that Google could face in the short and medium run, and protecting their viability is crucial to protect competition.

REFERENCES

Agarwal, N., S. Athey and D. Yang (2009), 'Skewed bidding in pay-per-action auctions for online advertising', *American Economic Review, P&P*, **99**(2), 441–7.

Argenton, C. and J. Prufer (2011), 'Search engine competition with network externalities', mimeo, Tilburg University.

Armstrong, M. (2006), 'Competition in two-sided markets', *RAND Journal of Economics*, **37**(3), 668–91.

Athey, S. and G. Ellison (2011), 'Position auctions with consumer search', *Quarterly Journal of Economics*, **126**(3), 1213–70.

Athey, S. and J. Gans (2010), 'The impact of targeting technology on advertising markets and media competition', *American Economic Review*, **100**(2), 608–13.

Athey, S., E. Calvano and J. Gans (2011), 'The impact of the internet on advertising markets for news media', paper presented at the V Intertic Conference, 11 October.

Behringer, S. and L. Filistrucchi (2010), 'Price wars in two-sided markets: the case of the UK quality newspapers', mimeo, University of Bonn, presented at the IV Intertic Conference, 11–12 October.

Blasco, A., P. Pin and F. Sobbrio (2011), 'Paying positive to go negative: advertisers' competition and media reports', paper presented at the V Intertic Conference, 11–12 October.

Caillaud, B. and B. Jullien (2003), 'Chicken and egg: competition among intermediation service providers', *RAND Journal of Economics*, **34**(2), 521–52.

Edelman, B., M. Ostrovsky and M. Schwarz (2007), 'Internet advertising and the generalized second-price auction: selling billions of dollars worth of keywords', *American Economic Review*, **97**(1), 242–59.

Etro, F. (2006), 'Aggressive leaders', *RAND Journal of Economics*, **37**(Spring), 146–54.

Etro, F. (2010), 'Endogenous market structures and antitrust policy', *International Review of Economics*, **57**(1), 9–46.

Etro, F. (2011), 'Endogenous market structures and contract theory', *European Economic Review*, **55**(4)(May), 463–79.

Etro, F. (2012), 'Google economics', mimeo, University of Venice, Ca' Foscari.

Evans, D. (2003a), 'Some empirical aspects of multi-sided platform industries', *Review of Network Economics*, **2**(3), 191–209.

Evans, D. (2003b), 'The antitrust economics of multi-sided platform markets', *Yale Journal of Regulation*, **20**, 325–81.

Filistrucchi, L. (2010), 'A SSNIP test for two-sided markets: the case of media', mimeo, University of Tilburg, paper presented at the IV Intertic Conference, 11 October.

Fudenberg, D. and J. Tirole (1984), 'The fat cat effect, the puppy dog ploy and the lean and hungry look', *American Economic Review, P&P*, **74**(2), 361–8.

Milgrom, P. and R. Weber (1982), 'A theory of auctions and competitive bidding', *Econometrica*, **50**, 1089–122.

Myerson, R. (1981), 'Optimal auction design', *Mathematics of Operations Research*, **6**, 58–73.

Ratliff, J. and D. Rubinfield (2010), 'Online advertising: defining relevant markets', *Journal of Competition Law and Economics*, **1**, 1–34.

Riley, J. and W. Samuelson (1981), 'Optimal auctions', *American Economic Review*, **71**, 381–92.

Rochet, J.-C. and J. Tirole (2003), 'Platform competition in two-sided markets', *Journal of the European Economic Association*, **1**(4), 990–1029.

Rochet, J.-C. and J. Tirole (2006), 'Two-sided markets: a progress report', *RAND Journal of Economics*, **37**(3), 645–67.

Schmalensee, R. (2010), 'Aspects of multi-sided platforms', mimeo, MIT, paper presented as the IV Stackelberg Lecture at the IV Intertic Conference, 11–12 October.

Tarantino, E. (2011), 'A note on vertical search engines foreclosure', paper presented at the V Intertic Conference, 11 October.

Varian, H. (2007), 'Position auctions', *International Journal of Industrial Organization*, **25**(6), 1163–78.

Vickrey, W. (1961), 'Counterspeculation, auctions, and competitive sealed tenders', *Journal of Finance*, **93**, 675–89.

Weyl, E.E. (2010), 'A price theory of multi-sided platforms', *American Economic Review*, **100**(4), 1642–72.

PART III

Regulation

12. Bargaining and collusion in a regulatory model

Raffaele Fiocco and Mario Gilli[1]

12.1 INTRODUCTION

The aim of this chapter is to examine the possibility of collusion in the regulation of a monopolistic market when a benevolent principal delegates to a regulatory agency two tasks: the supervision of the firm's costs and the negotiation over a pricing policy. In this new setting we investigate the classic questions: which regulatory policy should we expect in such a situation? What are the characteristics of the collusive gains? Which is the best response to collusion? What are the determinants of this response? This chapter is an attempt to derive some preliminary results within this general setting.

We consider a standard model of a three-tier regulatory hierarchy, where the political principal (Congress) directs the activities of a supervisor (the regulatory agency), which in turn oversees the operation of a monopoly (the regulated firm). We innovate the usual approach assuming that the principal delegates to the supervisor a general negotiation with the monopolist on the regulatory policy. The reason for this generalization is that usually regulation does not boil down to a passive enforcement of a policy, but actually involves a negotiation between the regulator and the firm. In other words, regulatory arrangements are generally the result of a give-and-take process rather than of a take-it-or-leave-it offer, since the possibility of pre-committing to a specific offer is unrealistic.

The literature on regulation has long recognized the relevance of introducing general bargaining processes in the interaction between regulator and firm. For example, Kahn (1971) observed that often public utilities represent cases of bilateral monopolies, while Spulber (1989) proposed regulatory models dealing with bargaining processes. Similarly, Scarpa's (1989, 1994) work represents a preliminary attempt to model this aspect of regulatory situations. Finally, Armstrong and Sappington in their survey on optimal regulation have recently recognized that the standard formulation, which ignores negotiations between the regulator and the firm, 'generally is adopted for technical convenience rather than for realism' (2007, p. 1564). Empirical studies also support this idea. Among others, Brotman (1987) reported that negotiations with private firms are a normal way to decide on industry regulation.

In our model a benevolent Congress (interested in the consumer surplus) delegates to a regulatory agency[2] two activities: a supervisory job and a bargaining task.[3] Therefore, the regulator is not only a mere conduit of information about the firm's costs, but it carries out the additional task of negotiating a regulatory settlement with the firm. Congress delegates the full contracting authority to the regulator since it lacks financial resources, skills or expertise to run this task.[4] As usual in collusion models, the agency cannot be trusted to perfectly enforce Congress's intent because it may be self-interested and thus have an incentive to collude with the firm by manipulating its information to Congress in return for a side transfer from the firm.[5] However, different from standard models, side contracting between the agency and the firm is considered as a bargaining process to the negotiations over the regulatory mechanism. The two bargaining stages are modelled using the Nash solution concept (1950, 1953), which we argue is the most effective way to deal with our view.

Our analysis shows how standard results are altered by these two bargaining processes. This does not mean that the approach in this chapter contradicts the classic one. Our set-up turns out to be a generalization of the standard model (Baron and Myerson, 1982; Baron, 1989), which represents the specific case where all the bargaining power is allocated to the agency. In the absence of collusion (Section 12.3), the regulatory mechanism agreed by the agency and the firm maximizes the total gains from trade, which are shared between players according to their bargaining power. However, the introduction of negotiation between the regulator and the monopoly induces a radical change in the collusion stage. While the inefficient firm as usual does not have any interest in cost manipulation, we find that the efficient firm has an incentive to collude only if it is sufficiently weak in the bargaining process. Interestingly, collusion pays off when the firm's revenue from a higher price more than compensates the lower subsidization. Since the latter reduces with the agency's bargaining power, this can be the case only if the agency is strong enough. If the latter could make a standard take-it-or-leave-it offer, the total gains of collusion would be maximized. This implies that bargaining mitigates the incentive to collude.

In the Section 12.4, we focus on the optimal organizational responses to the possibility of collusion. In our setting, incompleteness of contracts arising from institutional constraints prevents Congress from devising a mechanism that perfectly discriminates between the agency's types, and thus the Tirole (1986) equivalence principle does not apply.[6] We assume that Congress can use one of the following three instruments: an incentive reward to the agency, the shutdown of the inefficient firm (of course both intended to deter collusion) or tolerating collusion *tout court*. As long as the probability of facing the efficient firm is low enough and thus the shutdown policy is not convenient, Congress finds it optimal to tolerate collusion in equilibrium if the cost of the incentive reward that induces the agency not to collude outweighs the expected consumer loss from collusion. We explore this condition and show that the players' bargaining powers crucially drive the optimal response to collusion. Interestingly, we find that collusion is optimal if the agency's bargaining power is below a certain threshold. A stronger agency improves Congress's incentives to tolerate collusion in equilibrium. The idea is that such an agency can exact a higher bribe from the firm and thus the incentive reward for not colluding is more expensive. In other words, a high bargaining power of the agency in the negotiation process can make collusion too costly to fight. On the other hand, when the probability of facing the efficient firm is sufficiently high, the shutdown policy may become a valuable option. In this case, Congress never finds it optimal to tolerate collusion and prefers to fight it either by giving the agency an incentive reward or by shutting down the inefficient firm. The latter policy outperforms the former when the agency is strong enough in the bargaining process. This occurs since the expected benefit of allowing the inefficient firm to produce is lower than the incentive reward for not colluding. Clearly these results suggest that the players' bargaining powers in regulatory relationships should deserve careful consideration, since they crucially drive the potential for collusion. The arbitrary limitation to model with all the bargaining power allocated to the regulatory agency may neglect interesting institutional regulatory mechanisms as endogenous best responses to the possibility of collusion.

The chapter is organized as follows. In Section 12.2 we describe the basic structures of the model. Section 12.3 considers the case where collusion is freely possible: in Subsection 12.3.1 we derive the regulatory policy with a benevolent agency, while Subsection 12.3.2 analyses the case of a non-benevolent agency. In Section 12.4 we characterize the optimal institutional responses to collusion. Finally, Section 12.5 is devoted to concluding remarks.

12.2   THE MODEL

12.2.1   The Players

The Congress
Congress is a benevolent principal concerned with consumer surplus only. It hires a regulator that supervises the firm's unknown marginal costs and bargains with the firm over the regulatory mechanism. Full delegation of contracting authority arises from Congress's lack of time, skills or resources to run this task. Congress's problem is to offer a delegation contract that considers both roles of the regulatory agency and provides the compensation $CS \geq 0$ for the supervision and the negotiation over a regulatory policy. The consumers buy a quantity $q(p)$ for the good and pay a two-part tariff, characterized by a unit price p and a fixed amount S. Consumer surplus is equal to the benefit from the marketplace net of the aggregate fixed charges S[7] minus the transfer to the agency T^{CS}, collected through distortionary taxes that impose a shadow cost $\lambda \geq 0$,[8] that is,

$$CS(p,S,T^{CS}) = \int_{p}^{+\infty} q(p^0)dp^0 - S - (1 + \lambda)T^{CS}.$$

For the sake of convenience, consumer demand is supposed to depend linearly on price. Thus, without loss of generality we consider the following simple expression $q(p) = 1 - p$ and consumer surplus reduces to

$$CS(p,S;T^{CS}) = \frac{(1 - p)^2}{2} - S - (1 - \lambda)T^{CS}. \tag{12.1}$$

The firm
The firm's cost function $C(\cdot)$ is affine: $C(q;c_i) = c_i q + K$, where K denotes the fixed costs that are assumed to be common knowledge, while the marginal cost c_i, with $i \in \{L, H\}$, is private information of the firm. The two cost parameters c_L and c_H, with $\Delta c = c_H - c_L > 0$, are drawn with (common knowledge) probabilities v and $(1 - v) \in (0,1)$, respectively. Moreover, we assume that $c_H < 1$ to ensure that production is always first-best efficient.

Therefore the c_i-type firm's profit function is

$$\pi(p,S;c_i) = pq(p) + S - c_i q(p) - K. \tag{12.2}$$

The regulatory agency
The regulator has a twofold role: supervising the firm's unknown marginal costs and bargaining with the firm over the regulatory mechanism.

There are two types of agency: benevolent and self-interested. The benevolent regulator, which is drawn with (common knowledge) probability $\gamma \in (0,1)$, always reports truthfully to Congress the signal received from the surpervisory technology (see below). Moreover, it settles for a transfer T, needed to finance its activity, equal to its reservation value $\hat{T}$ (normalized to zero) and perfectly internalizes Congress's interests during the bargaining process with the firm. Therefore, the utility function of a benevolent agency is

$$V_B = CS. \tag{12.3}$$

A self-interested regulator, which occurs with complementary probability $1 - \gamma \in (0,1)$, has an incentive to forge the informative signal and collude with the firm (see below). Moreover, it internalizes only partly Congress's interests and aims to receive a transfer $T \geq \hat{T}$. The utility function of a non-benevolent agency is given by

$$V_{NB} = T + \beta CS, \tag{12.4}$$

where $\beta \in [0, \bar{\beta}]$, with $\bar{\beta} < 1$, a parameter that captures the regulator degree of internalization of Congress's objectives. If $\beta = 0$, the agency is only interested in its private transfer.[9] A higher β implies that it gives more weight to Congress's aim.

The supervisory technology is characterized by perfect monitoring, so that the signal the agency receives is always informative about the firm's marginal costs. However, the signal is supposed to be soft information, and thus it can be manipulated.[10] This means that the regulator may lie and convey a report $r \in \{c_L, c_H\}$ different from the actual c_i by altering the result of its audit activity. Manipulating information is the agency's degree of discretion: it can announce a wrong cost parameter since this report is never verifiable.

A benevolent agency always reports $r = c_i$ to Congress, while a self-interested agency has an incentive to declare $r \neq c_i$ colluding with the firm.[11]

12.2.2 Timing

The timing of the regulatory game is as follows.

1. Nature draws a type – benevolent or non-benevolent – for the agency with probability γ and $1 - \gamma$ respectively, and privately informs the agency. Nature also draws a type for the firm $c_i \in \{c_L, c_H\}$, with respective probabilities v and $1 - v$, and privately informs the firm.

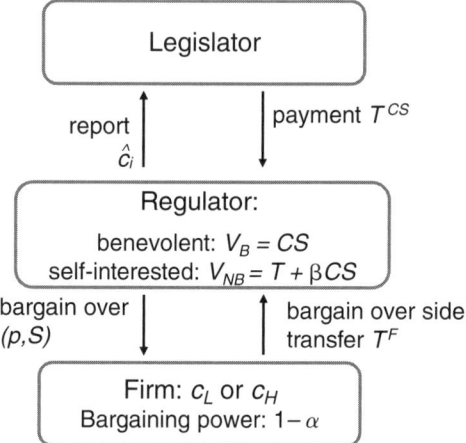

Figure 12.1   The basic structure of the model

2. Congress offers the agency a contract that determines a transfer $T^{CS}(r) \geq 0$ conditional on the report r and delegates the negotiations with the firm about a regulatory mechanism.
3. The contract is signed or rejected by the agency.
4. If the contract is rejected, the game ends. In case of acceptance, the agency performs its audit activity and receives the informative signal. The firm learns the agency's type.[12]
5. Negotiations between the agency and the firm take place on a regulatory mechanism $\{p, S\}$:
    - If it is benevolent, the agency reports $r = c_i$ to Congress.
    - If it is dishonest, the agency has an incentive to collude with the firm and manipulate its information, that is, $r \in \{c_L, c_H\} \neq c_i$. In this case, they bargain over a side transfer $T^F(r)$ as a reward for the agency's report.
6. Contracts are executed and the regulatory policy is implemented.

Figure 12.1 summarizes the basic structures of the model.

12.2.3   Use of the Nash Bargaining Solution

The novelty of this chapter is that the agency negotiates with the firm both on a regulatory mechanism (p, S) and on the split of the collusion gains when the agency is dishonest. Therefore we need to consider a model for both these negotiation processes.

As well known, the outcome of a bargaining game is very sensitive to all the details of the negotiation process as well as to the delay costs of the two players, that is, to all the bargaining protocols. A crucial point in the specification of a bargaining game is whether the players are assumed to commit to their actions, thus providing a specific extensive form. Obviously, in many settings it is difficult to provide a reliable specification of all the possible moves, of their sequence and of the information available to the players during the play. Therefore, instead of describing the specific bargaining procedure in full details, that is, a specific and therefore arbitrary extensive form, we choose to characterize the outcome by a more general approach. The driving idea behind this chapter is to use the cooperative asymmetric Nash model (1950, 1953). We believe there are at least five good reasons to make such a modelling choice:

1. It allows avoiding the specification of a particular extensive form structure.
2. The Nash solution is efficient so that our results do not depend on the unexploited gains from trade in the specific bargaining procedures that can be considered. This means that our approach might underestimate the transaction costs between the colluding parties, but we capture this aspect with a shadow cost of side transfers.
3. The uniqueness of the Nash solution implies that the principal can anticipate the outcome of bargaining to determine its optimal reaction, which is crucial for this kind of collusion models.
4. As we will show, this solution leads to easy calculations but also to interesting and plausible results.
5. As Spulber (1989, chapter 2) emphasizes, a crucial feature of regulatory hearing processes is the direct interaction between players that may result in a consensus, so that the bargaining game can be modelled as a cooperative game.

12.3 REGULATION WHEN COLLUSION IS TOLERATED

12.3.1 The Benevolent Agency

With probability γ a benevolent agency is drawn, which completely internalizes Congress's interest in consumer surplus. Hence, Congress would offer a reward $T^{CS} = \hat{T} \equiv 0$ to the agency, independently of its report r. As long as the regulator is benevolent, it transmits its information truthfully and there is no threat of collusion.

The regulatory policy negotiated between a benevolent agency and a c_i-type firm solves

$$\max_{\{p(c_i),S(c_i)\}} [V_B(p(c_i), S(c_i))]^\alpha \times [\pi(p(c_i), S(c_i))]^{1-\alpha} \text{ s.t.} \quad (12.5)$$

$$V_B \geq 0 \quad (PC_A)$$

$$\pi \geq 0 \quad (PC_F),$$

where the parameters $\alpha \in (0,1)$ and $(1 - \alpha) \in (0,1)$ are, respectively, the agency's and the firm's bargaining power. Notice that this is independent of the benevolence of the agency.

The non-negativity constraints (PC_A) and (PC_F) represent the agency's and firm's participation constraints. A benevolent agency is interested in consumer surplus, which must be non-negative in order to induce the purchase of the good. Similarly, the firm cannot accept to produce by making losses. Hence, also the disagreement payoffs are zero for both bargaining parties.

Substituting Equations (12.2) and (12.3), as defined by Equation (12.1), into Equation (12.5) yields

$$\max_{\{p(c_i), S(c_i)\}} \left[\frac{(1 - p(c_i))^2}{2} - S(c_i) \right]^\alpha \times$$

$$[(p(c_i) - c_i)(1 - p(c_i)) + S(c_i) - K]^{1-\alpha} \text{ s.t. } (PC_A), (PC_F). \quad (12.6)$$

After replacing the choice variable S with π from Equation (12.2) into Equation (12.6), the maximization problem may be rewritten as

$$\max_{\{p(c_i),S(c_i)\}} \left[\frac{(1 - p(c_i))^2}{2} + (p(c_i) - c_i)(1 - p(c_i)) - K - \pi(c_i) \right]^\alpha \times$$

$$[\pi]^{1-\alpha} \text{ s.t. } (PC_A), (PC_F).$$

Ignoring the constraints,[13] from the first-order condition for p it is found that the price agreed by the regulated firm and a benevolent agency is equal to

$$p(c_i) = c_i. \quad (12.7)$$

As the Nash bargaining process is efficient, the negotiated regulatory policy clearly implements the marginal cost pricing, independently of bargaining powers. The agency and the firm do not have any incentive to distort price from marginal cost, since both prefer to maximize the total gains from trade. Not surprisingly, we will see that the firm tries to extract these gains through the subsidy S.[14]

From the first-order condition for π we find

$$\pi(c_i) = (1 - \alpha)\left[\frac{1}{2}(1 - c_i)^2 - K\right] \equiv (1 - \alpha)\,TGT(c_i), \quad (12.8)$$

that is, the profit arising from negotiations is a share $(1 - \alpha)$ of the total gains from trade $TGT(c_i)$ for marginal costs c_i.[15] Note that, even though the agency is benevolent and does not collude, the firm gets a profit that is strictly greater than its reservation value, without any consequence on the allocative efficiency.

Substituting Equations (12.7) and (12.8) into Equation (12.2) yields

$$S(c_i) = (1 - \alpha)\left[\frac{1}{2}(1 - c_i)^2 - K\right] + K = (1 - \alpha)\,TGT(c_i) + K, \quad (12.9)$$

that is, the subsidy covers the fixed costs K and assigns to the firm a share $(1 - \alpha)$ of the total gains from trade $TGT(c_i)$. Obviously, weak agency ($\alpha \to 0$) allows the firm to get a high subsidy, while if all the bargaining power is allocated to the agency ($\alpha \to 1$) as in standard principal-agent models, the firm is hardly able to cover its fixed costs through subsidy ($S(c_i) \to K$) and receives no profit.

The consumer surplus is given by

$$CS(c_i) = \alpha\left[\frac{1}{2}(1 - c_i)^2 - K\right] = \alpha\,TGT(c_i), \quad (12.10)$$

that is, it is a share α of the total gains from trade. The positive relation between α and $CS(c_i)$ clearly shows that consumers benefit from a strong benevolent regulator.

We summarize the main results in the following Lemma.

Lemma 1 If the agency is benevolent, then the negotiated regulatory mechanism maximizes total gains from trade, and in particular

- *applies marginal cost pricing, that is, $p(c_i) = c_i$*
- *gives the firm a subsidy $S(c_i) = (1 - \alpha)\,TGT(c_i) + K$, which is decreasing in the agency's bargaining power α.*

12.3.2 The Self-interested Agency

A non-benevolent agency, which is drawn with probability $(1 - \gamma)$, is interested in consumer surplus and in the private transfer T. This income may come either from consumers, through the taxes they pay, or from the firm, which may give a bribe to the agency for the manipulation of the informative signal.

For the time being, suppose that Congress tolerates the possibility of collusion. Hence, Congress offers a constant reward $T^{CS} = \hat{T}$ to the agency, independently of its report r, so that a non-benevolent regulator has an incentive to collude with the firm.

Proposition 1   Define $\hat{\alpha} \equiv \Delta c/2 - c_H - c_L \in (0,1)$. Then, if $\alpha \in (0,\hat{\alpha}]$ collusion is not attractive for any type of firm. If $\alpha \in (\hat{\alpha},1]$ only the c_L-type firm has a stake in collusion $\Delta\pi(c_H; c_L) \equiv \pi(c_H;c_L) - \pi(c_L)$ from report manipulation which amounts to

$$\Delta\pi(c_H;c_L) = \Delta c(1 - c_H) - (1 - \alpha)(TGT(c_L) - TGT(c_H)). \quad (12.11)$$

Proof   Using Equations (12.7), (12.8) and (12.9), a report $r = c_L$ while the firm's true cost c_H yields an extra profit equal to $\pi(c_L; c_H) - \pi(c_H) = -\frac{\Delta c}{2}[\alpha(2 - c_H - c_L) + \Delta c] < 0$.

The c_L-type firm's extra gain $\Delta\pi(c_H; c_L)$ from forging the agency's report can be written as

$$\Delta\pi(c_H; c_L) = \Delta c(1 - c_H) - (S(c_L) - S(c_H)) =$$

$$\Delta c(1 - c_H) - (1 - \alpha)(TGT(c_L) - TGT(c_H)) =$$

$$\frac{\Delta c}{2}[\alpha(2 - c_H - c_L) - \Delta c],$$

which is positive if and only if $\alpha \in (\hat{\alpha}, 1]$.

While as usual the inefficient firm is never interested in cost manipulation, the efficient firm finds it profitable to collude only if it is sufficiently weak, that is, $\alpha \in (\hat{\alpha}, 1)$. Note from Equation (12.11) that collusion pays off only if the extra gain from a higher market price $\Delta c(1 - c_H)$ more than compensates the subsidy loss $(1 - \alpha)(TGT(c_L) - TGT(c_H))$. Interestingly, the stronger the agency in the bargaining process, the higher the firm's extra profit from pure informational advantage with respect to Congress. This occurs because the agency's bargaining power reduces the subsidy loss from cost manipulation. In fact, we know from Equation (12.9) that a weaker firm can extract a lower subsidization. Since the extra gain from a higher market price is independent of the bargaining power, the stake in collusion increases with a stronger agency. If the latter could make a take-it-or-leave-it offer ($\alpha \to 1$) the total gains of collusion would be maximized. This means that the bargaining process mitigates the firm's incentives to collude.

In line with the main literature, the side contract between the firm (with $\alpha \in (\hat{\alpha}, 1)$) and the self-interested regulator is supposed to be enforceable, even though it is illegal.[16] According to Stigler (1971), collusion is driven by two crucial factors: the stake in collusion and the organization costs. In our setting, the stake in collusion is given by the extra profit $\Delta\pi(c_H; c_L)$ in Equation (12.11) that the c_L-type firm can obtain if its private information is altered before Congress. The firm's costs of organization are represented by transfer costs,[17] which are related to the deadweight loss associated with the side transfer of income from the firm to the regulator.[18] Following Laffont and Tirole (1991), we capture this inefficiency by introducing an exogenous shadow cost of side transfers $\mu \geq 0$. The idea is that a monetary equivalent of one dollar received by the agency costs $(1 + \mu)$ dollars to the firm. This parameter determines the transaction technology between the firm and the agency. If $\mu \to \infty$, the transaction technology is so inefficient that no coalition forms. Otherwise, the transaction technology makes collusion profitable. If $\mu = 0$, then there is no deadweight loss from side contracting.

The regulatory arrangement arising from collusive negotiations allows the c_L-type firm to keep its informational advantage over Congress ($r = c_H$) even though the agency is informed about the firm's costs. The side contract specifies a covert transfer $T^T(r) \geq 0$, which is paid by the firm to the agency only if $r = c_H$ and costs $(1 + \mu)T^T(r)$ to the firm.

We assume that in case of disagreement about the side contract the agency and the firm reach the no-collusion outcome (V_{NB}^D, π_{NB}^D).[19] Thus the solution to this bargaining problem arises from

$$\max_{T^F \geq 0}[V_{NB}(T^F, \cdot) - V_{NB}^D]^\alpha \times [\pi(T^F, \cdot) - \pi_{NB}^D]^{1-\alpha} \text{ s.t.} \qquad (12.12)$$

$$V_{NB} \geq V_{NB}^D \qquad (\text{PC}_A)$$

$$\pi \geq \pi_{NB}^D \qquad (\text{PC}_F)$$

$$\pi = \pi(c_L) + \Delta\pi(c_H; c_L) - (1 + \mu)T^F \qquad (C_\pi^C).$$

The last constraint (C_π^C) indicates the profit of the c_L-type firm under collusion. The rationale is the following. When the collusive agency lies and reports $r = c_H$, we know from Equation (12.11) that the firm's profit from signal manipulation is the sum of the first two addends of (C_π^C). This represents the gross earning of the firm from collusion. The firm spends a part of this gain, equal to $(1+\mu)T^F$, to pay a side transfer T^F to the agency.

We have assumed that, in case of disagreement about the side contract, the agency and the firm continue to negotiate over the regulatory mechanism. In this case, we would be in the same setting as in Subsection 12.3.1 except for the parameter β. The agency would not receive any bribe ($T^F = 0$) and would reveal the truth to Congress ($r = c_L$), which could save the extra profit to the firm ($\Delta\pi = 0$). Hence, the agency's no-collusion utility is equal to the consumer surplus $CS(c_L)$ weighted by β (that is, $V^D_{NB} = \alpha\beta TGT(c_L)$) from Equation (12.10)). The firm's no-collusion profit is given by $\pi(c_L)$ (that is, $\pi^D_{NB} = (1 - \alpha)\beta TGT(c_L)$) from Equation (12.8)). As from Equation (12.10) $r = c_H$ implies that Congress expects $CS(c_H)$, we replace Equation (12.2) and Equation (12.4), as defined by Equation (12.1), into the maximization problem in Equation (12.12), which becomes

$$\max_{T^F \geq 0}[T^F - \alpha\beta(TGT(c_L) - TGT(c_H))]^\alpha \times [\pi - (1 - \alpha)TGT(c_L)]^{1-\alpha}$$

$$\text{s.t. (PC}_A), (PC_F), (C^C_\pi). \tag{12.13}$$

Substituting (C^C_π) into Equation (12.13) and ignoring for the moment the other constraints yields

$$\max_{T^F \geq 0}\left[T^F - \frac{\Delta c}{2}\alpha\beta(2 - c_L - c_H)\right]^\alpha \times$$

$$\left[\frac{\Delta c}{2}(\alpha(2 - c_L - c_H) - \Delta c) - (1 + \mu)T^F\right]^{1-\alpha}. \tag{12.14}$$

After some manipulations the first-order condition for T^F can be written as

$$(1 + \mu)T^F + \frac{\Delta c}{2}\alpha[(2 - c_L - c_H)(\alpha + \beta(1 + \alpha)(1 + \mu)) - \Delta c] = 0. \tag{12.15}$$

From Equation (12.15) in equilibrium the side transfer is given by

$$T^F = \alpha\frac{(2 - c_L - c_H)(\alpha + \beta(1 + \alpha)(1 + \mu)) - \Delta c}{2(1 + \mu)}\Delta c =$$

$$\alpha\frac{\Delta\pi}{1 + \mu} + \frac{\Delta c}{2}\alpha\beta(1 - \alpha)(2 - c_H - c_L). \tag{12.16}$$

Finally, we get the following result.

Proposition 2 Define $\tilde{\alpha} \equiv \Delta c/(2 - c_H - c_L)[1 - \beta(1 + \mu)]$ with $1 - \beta(1 + \mu) \in (0, 1]$. Then, collusion occurs in equilibrium if and only if $\alpha \in (\tilde{\alpha}, 1)$ when Congress tolerates this threat.

Proof Using Equation (12.16) the two bracketed expressions in Equation (12.14) are positive if and only if $\alpha \in (\tilde{\alpha}, 1)$. This implies that (PC_A) and (PC_F) in Equation (12.12) are satisfied.

Note that $\tilde{\alpha} \geq \hat{\alpha}$ since the non-benevolent agency's degree β of consumer surplus internalization reduces its willingness to collude. Only if the agency is completely dishonest ($\beta = 0$) the incentives to collude of both players perfectly align, that is, $\tilde{\alpha} = \hat{\alpha}$. Notice that $\tilde{\alpha} < 1$ as long as $\beta < 2(1 - c_H)/(1 + \mu)(2 - c_H - c_L)$, that is, for β low enough. Otherwise, a dishonest agency will not collude since no bribe can compensate its disutility from lying. Since we are interested in the possibility of collusion, we hereafter focus our attention on the case $\beta < 2(1 - c_H)/(1 + \mu)(2 - c_H - c_L)$.

The bribe that the agency can extort from the firm is increasing in its bargaining power. If $\alpha \to 0$, the regulator does not collect anything ($T^F \to 0$) since it is too weak. If $\alpha \to 1$, all the bargaining power is allocated to the agency and the side transfer tends to

$$\lim_{\alpha \to 1} T^F = \frac{\Delta \pi}{1 + \mu} = \frac{\Delta c(1 - c_H)}{1 + \mu}, \tag{12.17}$$

which is just the maximum extra profit that the firm can obtain from the manipulation of evidence discounted by the shadow cost of side transfers. The side transfer in Equation (12.17) approximates the take-it-or-leave-it call for a bribe taken by the agency.[20]

Using Equation (12.16), we derive after some computations the extra gains from collusion of the agency and the firm. They are given by

$$\Delta V_{NB}^C = \frac{\Delta c}{2} \frac{\alpha}{1 + \mu}[\alpha(2 - c_H - c_L)(1 - \beta(1 + \mu)) - \Delta c] =$$

$$\frac{\alpha}{1 + \mu}\left[\Delta \pi - \frac{\Delta c}{2}\alpha\beta(1 + \mu)(2 - c_H - c_L)\right] \tag{12.18}$$

$$\Delta \pi^C = \frac{\Delta c}{2}(1 - \alpha)[\alpha(2 - c_H - c_L)(1 - \beta(1 + \mu)) - \Delta c] =$$

$$(1 - \alpha)\left[\Delta \pi - \frac{\Delta c}{2}\alpha\beta(1 + \mu)(2 - c_H - c_L)\right].$$

Notice that the parameter β introduces a second source of inefficiency in the collusion process. In fact, a part of the net collusion gains $\Delta \pi / 1 + \mu$ directly finances the share β of the consumer loss internalized by the agency and constitutes a mere waste of resources in the bribing game. An increase in the agency's bargaining power reduces the fraction of the total pie appropriated by the firm, since the agency requires a greater side transfer. Nevertheless, the firm gets an increasing extra rent from collusion over some range. Hence, the benefit for the firm from an increase in the total stake in collusion induced by a outweighs the cost of a reduced bargaining power. When the agency's bargaining power is sufficiently high, the trade-off becomes detrimental to the firm, whose gain from collusion decreases.

12.4   THE INSTITUTIONAL RESPONSES TO COLLUSION

In this section we characterize the institutional responses that Congress should devise to give consumers the highest (expected) surplus. We consider three alternative options:

1.   The Congress deters collusion through an incentive payment to the agency at least equal to the extra gain which is anticipated to arise from side contracting.[21]
2.   The inefficient firm is shut down.
3.   Collusion is tolerated *tout court*.

When choosing option 1, the Congress is supposed to design an incentive scheme that applies to both types of the regulator. This assumption is quite common in the literature and can be justified by institutional settings that allow compensations contingent to agency's report only. Following Laffont (2000, chapter 2), we suppose that incompleteness of contracts arising from institutional constraints prevents Congress from devising an incentive compatible mechanism, which induces the self-selection of regulators according to their type. Collusion literature has shown that removing the screening condition implies that Tirole's equivalence principle does not apply. Starting from this observation, we first derive the conditions that drive the institutional responses to collusion. Then, we show how the players' bargaining powers crucially affect these conditions.

If Congress decides to prevent collusion through an incentive reward to the agency (option 1), the expected consumer surplus is equal to

$$E[CS^I] = \nu CS(c_L) + (1 - \nu) CS(c_H) - \nu(1 + \lambda)\Delta V_{NB}^C. \quad (12.19)$$

In order to get the no-collusion outcome and the associated expected consumer surplus, Congress has to design a bunching mechanism. This scheme gives any type of agency the minimum reward to deter collusion

$T^{CS} = \Delta V_{NB}^C$ in Equation (12.18). The reward is weighted by the probability v that the firm is efficient, since only in this case collusion may emerge (see Proposition 1), and it is paid by consumers through possible distortionary taxes that involve a social cost λ.

If Congress wants to fight collusion through the shutdown of the inefficient firm (option 2), the expected consumer surplus is given by

$$E[CS^S] = vCS(c_L). \tag{12.20}$$

This policy rules out the threat of collusion, as the c_L-type firm's interest in cost manipulation vanishes. However, this occurs at the cost of foregoing production when the firm is inefficient.

If Congress tolerates collusion (option 3), the expected consumer surplus is

$$E[CS^C] = \gamma[vCS(c_L) + (1 - v)CS(c_H)] + (1 - \gamma)CS(c_H) =$$

$$CS(c_H) + v\gamma(CS(c_L) - CS(c_H)). \tag{12.21}$$

Congress expects to receive the consumer surplus $CS(c_H)$ arising with an inefficient firm plus the extra gain in consumer surplus if the agency is benevolent and the firm is efficient, which occurs with probability $v\gamma$.

When designing the optimal response to collusion, Congress compares costs and benefits of any option. We start by comparing the strategy of deterring the collusion through an incentive reward (option 1) with that of tolerating it *tout court* (option 3). Clearly, the latter outperforms the former if and only if the cost incurred to induce the agency not to collude outweighs the expected benefit of deterring collusion. This condition is then formally expounded in the following Lemma.

Lemma 2 Congress prefers to tolerate collusion rather than deter it through an incentive payment if and only if the cost of rewarding the agency for not colluding exceeds the consumer loss from collusion. That is, $E[CS^C] \geq E[CS^S]$ if and only if

$$(1 + \lambda)\Delta V_{NB}^C \geq (1 - \gamma)\Delta CS^C \text{ where } \Delta CS^C \equiv CS(c_L) - CS(c_H). \tag{12.22}$$

Proof Compare Equations (12.19) and (12.21).

As stressed before, the incentive reward ΔV_{NB}^C on the left-hand side of Equation (12.22) costs $(1 + \lambda)\Delta V_{NB}^C$ to consumers, since taxes entail a deadweight loss. The expected consumer loss from collusion ΔCS^C on the right-hand side of Equation (12.22), which represents the benefit of preventing collusion, is weighted by $(1 - \gamma)$, because only the self-interested agency has an incentive to collude.

More importantly, from Equations (12.10) and (12.11) the difference between ΔCS^c and $\Delta\pi$ is after some manipulations

$$\Delta CS^c - \Delta\pi = \Delta c(1 - c_H) - \frac{1}{2}[(1 - c_L)^2 - (1 - c_H)^2] = \frac{(\Delta c)^2}{2} > 0. \tag{12.23}$$

Expression (12.23) shows that the consumer loss from collusion offsets the total stake in collusion. While the impact of side contracting on firm's subsidization constitutes a mere transfer of resources between consumers and firm, the extra gain the firm gets from a higher price is lower than the corresponding consumer loss. In fact, the result in Equation (12.23) stems from the allocative inefficiency due to the price distortion above marginal costs. This implies that collusion does not reduce to a zero-sum game in which the amount of resources extorted from consumers just forms the total pie that can be shared between collusive partners, but it shrinks the total gains from trade and then creates a further distortion in the efficient allocation of resources.

Let us consider now the impact of γ on condition (12.22). As γ increases, the right-hand side decreases. Hence, a raise in the probability of drawing a benevolent agency relaxes condition (12.22) and then allowing collusion is more attractive. The rationale for this result is obvious. Collusion literature has emphasized that if the probability of an honest regulator is sufficiently high, costly measures to eliminate collusion may become unnecessary and the optimal contract may allow collusion in equilibrium.

In this framework, we examine the impact of the agency's bargaining power a on condition (12.22). Notice that ΔV^C_{NB} and ΔCS^c are both increasing in α. A trade-off emerges between deterring and allowing collusion. On the one hand, a stronger agency (α goes up) can extort a higher bribe from the firm. Tolerating collusion becomes more attractive since this allows saving the incentive payment to the agency. On the other hand, the agency's bargaining power increases the consumer loss from collusion and then it makes deterring this threat more desirable. From this trade-off we get the following Corollary of Lemma 2.

Corollary 1   Define $\alpha^* \equiv \tilde{\alpha} + (1 + \mu)(1 - \gamma)/(1 + \lambda)[1 - \beta(1 + \mu)]$, where $\tilde{\alpha}$ is defined in Proposition 2. Then, if $\alpha \in (\tilde{\alpha}, \alpha^*)$ Congress prefers to deter collusion through an incentive reward rather than tolerate it. If $\alpha \in [\alpha^*, 1)$ allowing collusion is more desirable.

Proof Substitute Equations (12.10) and (12.19) into Equation (12.22).

Allowing collusion can be preferred if the interval [α*, 1) is non-empty, which occurs if and only if

$$1 - \gamma < \frac{1 + \lambda}{1 + \mu} \left[\frac{2(1 - c_H)}{2 - c_H - c_L} - \beta(1 + \mu) \right],$$

where the bracketed expression is positive. This is clearly the case when the probability of drawing a non-benevolent agency is low enough. Of course, collusion is not desirable per se, since consumers would be better off if side transfers were infeasible, but it can be allowed when it is too costly to fight. Notice that the parameter β crucially affects the width of the interval $(\tilde{\alpha}, \alpha*)$ where preventing collusion is preferable. A higher β makes this option more attractive. A lower level of corruptibility of the agency (β goes up) increases the desirability of deterring collusion, because the agency internalizes more the surplus loss incurred by consumers and asks for a lower incentive reward (ΔV_{NB}^C in Equation (12.18) decreases). Hence, the agency's interests align with those of Congress, by making collusion less expensive to fight. The same effect emerges when the shadow cost μ increases as side contracting is more inefficient and then easier to prevent.

We have so far neglected the possibility of shutdown. It is well known in the literature that Congress may find it optimal to close up production when facing an inefficient firm.[22] Comparing the strategy of incentivizing the agency not to collude (option 1) with the shutdown policy (option 2) yields the following result.

Lemma 3 *Congress prefers to fight collusion through the shutdown of the inefficient firm rather than through an incentive payment if and only if the cost of rewarding the agency for not colluding outweighs the loss in consumer surplus from shutdown. That is, $E[CS^S] \geq E[CS^I]$ if and only if*

$$v(1 + \lambda)\Delta V_{NB}^C \geq (1 - v)CS(c_H). \tag{12.24}$$

Proof Compare Equations (12.19) and (12.20).

The shutdown policy has the benefical effect of saving the incentive reward to the agency but imposes the cost of closing up the production of the inefficient firm.

We immediately obtain the following result, which represents a Corollary of Lemma 3.

Corollary 2   Define $\alpha^{**} = \tilde{\alpha} + (1 - v)(1 + \mu)[(1 - c_H)^2 - 2K]/v(1 + \lambda)$ $(2 - c_H - c_L)[1 - \beta(1 + \mu)]\Delta c$. *Then, if* $\alpha \in (\tilde{\alpha}, \alpha^{**})$ *Congress prefers to deter collusion through an incentive reward rather than shut down the inefficient firm. If* $\alpha \in [\alpha^{**}, 1)$ *shutdown is more desirable.*

Proof   Substitute Equations (12.10) and (12.18) into Equation (12.24).

We know from Equations (12.10) and (12.18) that both $CS(c_H)$ and ΔV^C_{NB} are increasing in α. Corollary 2 reveals which effect prevails in equilibrium. With a strong agency, that is, $\alpha \in [\alpha^{**}, 1)$, the expected benefit of allowing the inefficient firm to produce is lower than the incentive reward for not colluding, and then the shutdown is preferable. Notice that the interval $[\alpha^{**}, 1)$ is increasing in v. A high probability of facing the efficient firm raises the scope for closing the inefficient firm's production, which creates a low consumer surplus in expected terms. If $v \rightarrow 1$ he shutdown policy is clearly always preferable to paying an incentive reward to the agency ($\tilde{\alpha} \rightarrow \alpha^{**}$), since Congress incurs no expected costs by excluding the inefficient firm.

Comparing the shutdown policy (option 2) with the strategy of allowing collusion (option 3) yields the following result.

Lemma 4   Congress prefers to shut down the inefficient firm rather than tolerate collusion if the probability of facing the efficient firm is sufficiently high. That is, $E[CS^S] \geq E[CS^C]$ *if and only if* $v \in [v^*, 1)$, *where*

$$v^* \equiv \frac{(1 - c_H)^2 - 2K}{(1 - \gamma)(1 - c_L)^2 + \gamma(1 - c_H)^2 - 2K} \in (0, 1).$$

Proof   Compare Equations (12.20) and (12.22) using Equation (12.10).

The shutdown policy is obviously a valuable option only if the firm is sufficiently likely to be efficient.

We are now in a position to summarize our main results.

Proposition 3   With $v \in (0, v^*)$ *the optimal response to collusion exhibits the following features*

- *if* $\alpha \in (\tilde{\alpha}, \alpha^*)$ *collusion is deterred through an incentive payment to the agency;*
- *if* $\alpha \in [\alpha^*, 1)$ *collusion is tolerated* tout court *and Congress never chooses to close up production of the inefficient firm.*

With $v \in [v^*, 1)$ *collusion is deterred*

- *if* α ∈ (α̃, α**) *through an incentive payment to the agency;*
- *if* α∈[α**, 1) *through the shutdown of the inefficient firm, and tolerating collusion is never optimal.*

With α ∈ (0, α̃] *collusion is never attractive.*

Proposition 3 implies that preventing collusion with an incentive scheme is a desirable strategy independently of the *ex ante* distribution of firm's types, as long as the agency is sufficiently weak. On the other hand, Congress views the shutdown policy and the tolerance of collusion as mutually exclusive alternatives. The latter is a valuable option only if the high probability of having an inefficient firm, that is, $v \in (0, v^*)$, makes the former too costly.

The result in Proposition 3 suggests that policy makers should seriously care about some important elements of regulatory relationships like players' bargaining powers in order to evaluate the potential for collusion and the optimal responses to this threat.

12.5 CONCLUDING REMARKS

In this chapter we have examined a monopolistic market, where the regulatory mechanism is the outcome of a bargaining process between the regulatory agency and the regulated firm.

Our analysis has shown how the bargaining process affects the standard results, which turn out to be a specific case of our more general approach. The introduction of a negotiation between the regulator and the monopoly induces a radical change in the collusion stage when the agency is dishonest. We have shown that the efficient firm finds it profitable to collude only if the agency's bargaining power is high enough. Moreover, the total gains of collusion are now lower than those the two partners would appropriate if the agency could make a take-it-or-leave-it offer. In the second part of the chapter, we investigated the optimal organizational responses to the possibility of collusion, in absence of discrimination between the agency's types. We found that preventing collusion through an incentive reward to the agency is optimal if the agency's bargaining power is low enough, independently of the *ex ante* distribution of the firm's types. With a low probability of the efficient firm, a stronger agency improves Congress's incentives to tolerate collusion in equilibrium as this can be too costly to fight. Otherwise, the shutdown of the inefficient firm is the best option. This result has implications of some relevance for the optimal design of regulatory agencies.

We believe that our simple generalization provides useful insights on the role of the bargaining power in institutions or in organizations. Of course, this is just a simple step towards more realistic and complex analysis of the negotiation processes within a hierarchy structure. Our model may be extended in a variety of directions. The supervisory technology may be modified in order to consider the possibility of imperfect monitoring, which implies that the signal received by the agency may be wrong or uninformative. This would allow the study of the bargaining process between the agency and the firm under asymmetric information. Another possibility is to extend the model by introducing the agency's effort to audit, since in practice the regulator can affect the functioning of the supervisory technology and moral hazard turns out to be an important issue.

NOTES

1. We are particularly indebted to Roland Strausz, Helmut Bester, Michela Cella, Michele Grillo and Carlo Scarpa for very helpful comments. We also thank Charles Angelucci, Carlo Cambini, Liliane Karlinger, Bruce Lyons and Alessandro Petretto for valuable insights as well as the seminars' participants at Bari University, University of Milano-Bicocca, Humboldt Universität zu Berlin, Collegio Carlo Alberto of Turin, Politecnico of Milan, tenth INFER, SED 2011 and CRESSE 2011. The financial support from the Deutsche Forschungsgemeinschaft via SFB 649 'Ökonomisches Risiko' is gratefully acknowledged.
2. We use Tirole's (1986) assumption of a unique regulator, which may be justified either by a cost of duplication of the regulatory function or by collusive behaviour between regulators.
3. As in Laffont and Tirole (1990), we assume that regulatory institutions result from a constitution drafted by some benevolent 'founding fathers' or 'social planners', which may be identified with Congress. The latter delegates some activities to a public decision maker, which is represented by a regulatory agency.
4. It seems natural to assume that a legislative assembly does not have the right skills to contract directly with the firm. Of course, this does not mean that full delegation is optimal. The characterization of the conditions under which this is the case is a very stimulating topic, but is outside the scope of this chapter. See on this issue the contribution of Faure-Grimaud et al. (2003).
5. Tirole stresses the importance of reciprocity in the side contracting and states that 'one-sided favors call for reciprocated ones' (1986, p. 185).
6. See Tirole (1992) and Kofman and Lawarrée (1996).
7. The fixed payment S may be thought of as apportioned among consumers in such a manner that no consumer is excluded from purchasing the good.
8. Our results do not crucially depend on the presence of a (strictly) positive shadow cost of public funds, which is considered only for the sake of completeness. This implies that the assumption of non-distortionary fixed charges is (qualitatively) inconsequential.
9. This is the classic case of perfectly non-benevolent agency, see Laffont and Tirole (1991).
10. See Laffont and Rochet (1997) for an analysis of the difference between hard information and soft information models.
11. It is usually assumed in the literature that the firm observes the agency's signal. This can be the case if before signing the collusive agreement the agency must disclose to the

firm the signal it has received. We do not need such an assumption because the signal is always informative and this is common knowledge, hence the firm knows the agency's signal. However, in line with the literature we need to assume that the agency cannot forge the signal against the firm's will. In other words, we require that cost manipulation occurs when it is profitable for both partners. We can imagine that the firm is able to prove before Congress its actual costs. This assumption rules out the possibility of blackmail by the agency in our setting. Khalil and Lawarré (1995) underline the importance for future research of studying this phenomenon.

12. This assumption is made, among others, by Kofman and Lawarrée (1996). The firm can discover the agency's type when it proposes side contracting. A benevolent agency would not accept such a proposal, while a dishonest agency can be willing to collude. Attempted bribery is not punishable, since it is extremely difficult or costly to prove. Alternatively, the agency can show its type, since it is the party that takes the initiative to collude.
13. It can be easily shown that they are satisfied in equilibrium.
14. As well known, a monopolist that maximizes its profit subject to a non-negative consumer surplus constraint sets a price equal to marginal cost and captures all the consumer gains through the subsidy.
15. We assume that the fixed costs K are small enough so that total gains from trade are always positive.
16. Among others, see Laffont and Tirole (1993, chapter 11) for a discussion on this issue.
17. Furthermore, the firm incurs mobilization costs to collect information and intervene in specific regulatory issues. These costs are ignored in our setting.
18. A monetary bribe exposes the parties to the possibility of legal sanctions. Alternatively, the agency's staff values non-monetary side transfers (for entertainment, jobs after the tenure in the agency and so on) less than the monetary expenses incurred by the firm.
19. We follow Tirole's (1986) idea that each party can guarantee itself the no-side contract outcome.
20. See, among others, Laffont (2000, chapter 2).
21. Following Laffont (2000, chapter 2), we assume that limited liability constraints prevent Congress from designing a system of punishments and fines against the agency.
22. See, among others, Laffont and Martimort (2002).

REFERENCES

Armstrong, M. and D.E.M. Sappington (2007), 'Recent developments in the theory of regulation', in M. Armstrong and R. Porter (eds), *Handbook of Industrial Organization*, Vol. 3, Amsterdam: Elsevier Science Publisher B.V., pp. 1557–700.
Baron, D.P. (1989), 'Design of regulatory mechanisms and institutions', in R. Schmalensee and R.D. Willig (eds), *Handbook of Industrial Organization*, Vol. II, Amsterdam: Elsevier Science Publisher B.V., pp. 1347–447.
Baron, D.P. and R.B. Myerson (1982), 'Regulating a monopolist with unknown costs', *Econometrica*, **50**(4), 911–30.
Brotman, S. (1987), 'Achieving consensus at FCC. Two different approaches to cable television policy', *Negotiation Journal*, **3**, 293–96.
Faure-Grimaud, A., J.-J. Laffont and D. Martimort (2003), 'Collusion, delegation and supervision with soft information', *Review of Economic Studies*, **70**, 253–79.
Kahn, A.E. (1971), *The Economics of Regulation: Principles and Institutions*, New York: Wiley.
Khalil, F. and J. Lawarrée (1995), 'Collusive auditors', *American Economic Review*, **85**(2), 442–46.

Kofman, F. and J. Lawarée (1996), 'On the optimality of allowing collusion', *Journal of Public Economics*, **61**, 383–407.

Laffont, J.-J. (2000), *Incentives and Political Economy*, Oxford: Oxford University Press.

Laffont, J.-J. and D. Martimort (2002), *The Theory of Incentives*, Princeton, NJ and Oxford: Princeton University Press.

Laffont, J.-J. and J.-C. Rochet (1997), 'Collusion in organizations', *Scandinavian Journal of Economics*, **99**(4), 485–95.

Laffont, J.-J. and J. Tirole (1990), 'The politics of government decision making: regulatory institutions', *Journal of Law, Economics, and Organization*, **6**(1), 1–31.

Laffont, J.-J. and J. Tirole (1991), 'The politics of government decision-making: a theory of regulatory capture', *The Quarterly Journal of Economics*, **106**(4), 1089–127.

Laffont, J.-J. and J. Tirole (1993), *A Theory of Incentives in Procurement and Regulation*, Cambridge, MA: MIT Press.

Nash, J.F. (1950), 'The bargaining problem', *Econometrica*, **18**, 155–62.

Nash, J.F. (1953), 'Two-person cooperative games', *Econometrica*, **21**, 128–40.

Scarpa, C. (1989), 'Industry regulation when firms have bargaining power', D.Phil Thesis, Nuffield College, Oxford.

Scarpa, C. (1994), 'Regulation as a bargaining process: negotiation over price and cost-reducing investments', *Oxford Economic Papers*, **46**(3), 357–65.

Spulber, D.F. (1989), *Regulation and Markets*, Cambridge, MA: MIT Press.

Stigler, G. (1971), 'The economic theory of regulation', *Bell Journal of Economics*, **II**, 3–21.

Tirole, J. (1986), 'Hierarchies and bureaucracies: on the role of collusion in organizations', *Journal of Law, Economics, and Organizations*, **2**(2), 181–214.

Tirole, J. (1992), 'Collusion and the theory of organizations', in J.-J. Laffont (ed.), *Advances in Economic Theory. Sixth World Congress*, Vol. II, Cambridge: Cambridge University Press, pp. 151–206.

13. Investment and the strategic role of capital structure in regulated industries: theory and evidence

Carlo Cambini, Laura Rondi and Yossi Spiegel

13.1 INTRODUCTION

In the past 30 years, many countries around the world have fundamentally reformed their public utilities sector. Among other things, these reforms included a large-scale privatization of state-owned utilities and the establishment of sector-specific Independent Regulatory Authorities (IRAs) to regulate them. In this chapter, we provide a summary and synthesis of results from an ongoing research project on the effect of privatization and the establishment of IRAs on the capital structure and investments of regulated firms and on regulated prices. In particular, we draw heavily on results from Bortolotti, Cambini, Rondi and Spiegel (2011; henceforth BCRS), Cambini and Rondi (2011, 2012) and Cambini and Spiegel (2011; henceforth CS), although we will also provide some new results on the interaction between the ownership structure of regulated utilities, their investment levels and regulatory independence.

Our research is motivated in part by the fact that investments by regulated firms in infrastructure are crucial for the economy at large (see, for example, Guthrie, 2006) and account for a significant fraction of gross domestic product (GDP). For instance, in 2008, investments of public utilities in infrastructure accounted for 15.24 per cent of GDP on average in the EU 15 countries that were members of the European Union (EU) before the enlargement on 1 May 2004 (see the appendix in CS for details). Another motivation for our research is the fact that at least in the EU, the structural reforms in the public utilities sector were accompanied by a substantial increase in the financial leverage of regulated utilities. This trend, coined the 'dash for debt', has raised substantial concerns among policy markers. For instance, a joint study of the UK Department of Trade and Industry (DTI) and HM Treasury argues that the 'dash for debt' within the UK utilities sector from the mid to late 1990s 'could imply greater risks of financial distress, transferring risk to consumers and taxpayers and threatening the future financeability of investment requirements' (DTI and HM Treasury, 2004, p. 6). Similar concerns were expressed by the Italian energy regulatory agency (see, for example, AEEG, 2008, paragraph 22.13).

The chapter is organized as follows. In Section 13.2 we briefly describe the relevant structural reforms in the EU. In Section 13.3 we present a theoretical model that we use to derive testable hypotheses regarding the leverage and investment levels of regulated firms, and the effect of leverage on regulated prices. Section 13.4 presents our empirical results. Concluding remarks are in Section 13.5.

13.2   STRUCTURAL REFORMS IN THE PUBLIC UTILITIES' SECTOR IN THE EU

Until the early 1990s (or the early 1980s in the UK), public utilities in Europe were largely characterized by vertical integration, state monopoly and public ownership. Regulated prices were mainly set to counterbalance the rise of inflation and utilities were often asked to absorb labour whenever unemployment increased. The result was ill-performing monopolies and inefficiencies (Megginson and Netter, 2001).

The structural reforms of the public utility sector in the EU were promoted by the European Commission through a series of Directives, aimed at redesigning the legal and regulatory framework in order to enhance cost efficiency, service quality and encourage new investments. While the Commission was in favour of privatization of public utilities, the decision about the ownership structure of public utilities was left entirely in the hands of national governments. As of 2010, privatization of public utilities in the EU is far from complete; central and local governments still hold majority (and minority) ownership stakes in many regulated utilities (see Bortolotti and Faccio, 2009).

In order to regulate public utilities and avoid the government's potential conflict of interest in its dual role as an owner and a regulator, the European Commission has been promoting, since the mid 1980s, the delegation of regulatory tasks to IRAs. These tasks typically involve price and quality standard setting, both at the retail and wholesale levels, the definition of entry conditions and the setting of technical rules for the usage of and access to existing infrastructures. Within this set of regulatory rules, utilities are free to make investment and financing decisions at their own discretion.

The implementation of structural reforms varies considerably across countries and sectors. The structural reforms are most advanced in the energy (electricity and gas) and telecommunications sectors. As Table 13.1 shows, sector-specific IRAs were established in all EU 27 countries and most firms are (at least partially) privatized. Yet, despite the reforms, many large utilities are still controlled by the government, particularly in France, Germany, Italy and Portugal, and especially so in the natural gas industry. The structural reforms are less developed in water supply and in transportation infrastructure (docks and ports, airports and freight motorways). With the exception of the UK, most water and transportation utilities are still controlled by central and local governments and still regulated directly by the state rather than by IRAs.[1]

The heterogeneity of institutional structure allows us to examine the effect of private versus state ownership and of regulatory independence on the capital structure and investment decisions of regulated firms and the effect of leverage on regulated prices. It is worth noting that a similar heterogeneity is present in many countries outside Europe. Table 13.2 reports relevant data for selected South American and East Asian countries.

13.3   THE MODEL

This section, which draws on CS, establishes a number of empirical predictions on the effect of regulatory independence and privatization on the capital structure and investments of regulated firms, and on the interaction between leverage and regulated prices. In Section 13.4 we will examine these predictions empirically. The interested reader is referred to CS for more details and for formal proofs.

13.3.1   The Regulated Firm and the Rate Setting Process

Consider a regulated firm, which for simplicity faces a unit demand function. The willingness of consumers to pay, $V(k)$, is an increasing and concave function of the firm's investment, k. Consumers' surplus is given by $V(k) - p$, where p is the regulated price.

The regulated firm is partially owned by the state. The state's stake in the firm's equity is δ. To capture the effect of δ on the firm's behaviour, we adopt the managerially oriented public enterprise (MPE) approach, due to Sappington and Sidak (2003). The key assumption in this approach is that the (partially) state-owned firm's objective function is a weighted average of the firm's profits, π, and revenue, R, and given by $\delta R + (1 - \delta)\pi$. Noting that $\pi = R - C$, where C is cost, we can rewrite the firm's objective function

Table 13.1   The timing of regulation and privatization in the energy and telecommunications sectors in the EU 27 countries

Country	Energy			Telecommunications	
	Date of establishing an IRA	Electricity Ownership (end 2010)	Gas Ownership (end 2010)	Date of establishing an IRA	Ownership (end 2010)
Austria	2000	State (51%)	Partially private (State 31%)	1997	Partially private (State 25%)
Belgium	1999	Partially private (State 49%)	Partially private (State 31%)	1991	State (> 50%)
Bulgaria	1999	State (100%)	State (100%)	2006	Private
Czech Rep.	2001	State (67%)	Private	2005	Private
Cyprus	2003	State (100%)	State (100%)	2002	State (100%)
Denmark	1999	n.d.	n.d.	2002	Private
Estonia	2008*	Partially private	Partially private	2008*	Private
Finland	1995	State (54%)		1987	State (>50%)
France	2000	State (85%)	Partially private (State 37.5%)	1996	Partially private (State 32%)
Germany	2006**	Private (State 2.5%)	Private (State 2.5%)	1996**	Partially private (State 28%)
Greece	2000	State (51%)	n.d.	1992	Partially private (State 10%)
Hungary	1994	Private	Private	2003	Private
Ireland	1999	n.d.	n.d.	1997	Private
Italy	1995	Partially private (State 33%)	Partially private (State 20%)	1997	Private
Latvia	2001***	State	Private	2001***	State (51%)

Lithuania	1997****	State (96.5%)	Partially private (State 30%)	2004	Private
Luxemburg	2000	State (100%)	State (100%)	1997	State (100%)
Malta	2001	State	State	2001	Private
Netherlands	1998	n.d.	n.d.	1997	Private
Poland	1997	State (100%)	Private	2006	Private
Portugal	1995	Partially private (State 26%)	n.d.	2001	Private (State 6%)
Romania	2000	Private	Private	2006	Partially private (State 46%)
Slovenia	2001	State	Partially private (State 31%)	2001	Partially private (State 49%)
Slovakia Rep	2001****	State (51%)	State (51%)	2004	Partially private (State 49%)
Spain	1998	Private	Private	1996	Private
Sweden	1998	Private	Private	1992	State (> 50%)
UK	1989	Private	Private	1984	Private

Notes:

*   Since 1998 regulation is carried on by a branch of the Estonian Competition Authority.

**   The IRA (*Bundesnetzagentun*) was originally in charge of regulating the telecommunications sector but since 2006 it also became in charge of regulating the energy, railway and postal services.

***   The IRA was established with a multi-sector regulatory model (energy, telecoms, transport and water).

****   The regulatory agency is also in charge of regulating the water industry.

Private: fully private company. *State*: majority of shares controlled by state; when data is available we also report the stakes controlled by the central or local governments, in combination with holdings by companies or entities fully owned by the government. *Partially private*: the government's share is below 50 per cent; when available we report the exact residual state's stake. n.d.: no available data.

Source: International European Regulation Network (http://www.iern.net) for energy markets and European Regulators Group (http://www.erg. eu.int/) for telecommunications. For ownership, see http://www.privatizationbarometer.net and http://www.enercee.net (accessed September 2011).

Table 13.2 The timing of regulation and privatization in the energy and telecommunications sectors in selected South American and Eastern Asian countries

Country	Energy			Telecommunications	
	Date of establishing an IRA	Electricity Ownership (end 2010)	Gas Ownership (end 2010)	Date of establishing an IRA	Ownership (end 2010)
Argentina	1993	Partially private and State (100%)*	State (65%)	1990	Private
Brazil	1996	State (52%)**	Private	1997	Private
Chile	1978	Private	Private	1977	Private
Colombia	1994	State	n.d.	1994	State (49%)
Ecuador	1996	n.d.	n.d.	1995	State (100%)
Perú	1996	Private	n.d.	1994	Private
Mexico	1995	State	State	1996	Private
Uruguay	2002***	State	State	2001	State (100%)
Venezuela	n.d.	State (100%)	State (100%)	1991	State owned (renationalized in 2007 after being privatized in 1991)

China	n.d.	State (100%)	State (100%)	n.d.	State (100%)
India	1998	State	State (74%)	1997	State
Malaysia	2001	State (100%)	State (100%)	1998	Private
Philippines	2001	Partially private (State 30%)	n.d.	n.d.	Private
Singapore	2001	State (100%)	State (100%)	1982	State (>50%)
Taiwan	n.d.	State (100%)	n.d.	2006	Partially privatized State (< 50%)
Thailand	2007	State	State	n.d.	State

Notes:

*   Companies in generation and distribution are mostly privatized, while the transmission companies are still fully state controlled.

**   Most of the generating and transport companies are fully state controlled at national or federal level. Privatization occurs for in distributions (64 per cent of the concessionaries are privately controlled). Here the reported percentage is related to Eletrobras, the largest power utility in Brazil.

***   Also operating in the water sector.

Source: International European Regulation Network (http://www.iern.net) for energy markets. Gutiérrez and Berg (1998) and Trillas and Montoya (2011) for telecommunications. See also the IRA's websites. For ownership data on energy, we used the companies' websites.

as $R - (1 - \delta)C$. That is, the firm behaves as if it ignores a fraction δ of its cost. This reflects the idea that managers of MPEs often have considerable interest in expanding the scale or scope of their activities and expand the firm's budget and labour force either for political reasons or due to moral hazard and weak monitoring by the state.

To model the firm's choice of capital structure, we assume that the firm issues debt with face value D, which it needs to cover from its operating income. Due to random cost shocks (for example, fluctuating energy prices), the firm's cost of production, c, is random and distributed uniformly over the interval $[0, \bar{c}]$, where $\bar{c} < V(0)$. If the firm's operating income, $p - c$, is insufficient to cover D in full, the firm incurs a fixed cost of financial distress T. Using $\phi(p, D)$ to denote the probability of financial distress, the total expected cost of the firm is $C = \bar{c}/2 + \phi(p, D)T$, where,

$$\phi(p, D) = \begin{cases} 0 & D + \bar{c} \leq p, \\ 1 - \dfrac{p - D}{\bar{c}} & D \leq p < D + \bar{c}, \\ 1 & p < D. \end{cases} \tag{13.1}$$

Intuitively, as long as $D + \bar{c} \leq p$, the firm can always pay D in full, so $\phi(p, D) = 0$. When $p < D$, the firm cannot pay D in full even when $c = 0$, so $\phi(p, D) = 1$. For intermediate cases, $\phi(p, D)$ is increasing with D and decreasing with p.

We follow Dasgupta and Nanda (1993), Spiegel (1994) and Spiegel and Spulber (1997) by assuming that the regulator chooses the regulated price, p, to maximize a social welfare function defined over consumers' surplus, $V(k) - p$, and the firm's objective function. In line with Levy and Spiller (1994), Gilardi (2002) and Edwards and Waverman (2006), we will assume that a greater degree of regulatory independence improves the regulators' ability to make long-term commitments to regulatory policies.

Specifically, we assume that before the firm invests, the regulator commits with probability ρ to take into account the *ex ante* objective function of the firm, which includes k, and hence sets p by maximizing the *ex ante* social welfare function

$$(V(k) - p)^\gamma (p - (1 - \delta)C - k)^{1-\gamma}, \tag{13.2}$$

where $\gamma \in (0, 1)$ captures the degree to which the regulator is pro-consumer. However, with probability $1 - \rho$, the regulator behaves opportunistically and once k is sunk, he chooses p to maximize the *ex post* social welfare function which ignores k,

$$(V(k) - p)^\gamma (p - (1 - \delta)C)^{1-\gamma}. \tag{13.3}$$

Hence, the parameter ρ captures the regulator's ability to make long-term commitments and therefore serves as our measure of regulatory independence, with larger values of ρ indicating a greater degree of independence.

13.3.2 The Sequence of Events

The game evolves in two stages. In stage 1, the firm chooses k and issues debt with face value D in a competitive capital market. If the funds raised by issuing D exceed k, the firm pays the excess funds as a dividend. If the funds raised by issuing D fall short of k, the firm raises additional funds by issuing equity; to simplify matters, we assume that in this case the state participates in the equity issue to maintain its original stake δ. In stage 2, given k and D, the regulator sets the regulated price p. Finally, the firm's cost c is realized, output is produced and payoffs are realized.

13.3.3 The Regulated Price

In stage 2, the regulator sets p to maximize either Equation (13.2) or (13.3). Let I be an indicator function which equals 1 with probability ρ (the regulator keeps his commitment to take k into account) and equals 0 with probability $1 - \rho$ (the regulator behaves opportunistically and ignores k when he sets p). Then, the regulator's objective function can be written compactly as

$$(V(k) - p)^\gamma (p - (1 - \delta)C - Ik)^{1-\gamma}. \tag{13.4}$$

Maximizing Equation (13.4) with respect to p yields the following regulated price:

$$p^*(D, k, I) = \begin{cases} D_1(k, I) + \bar{c} & D \le D_1(k, I) \\ D + \bar{c} & D_1(k, I) < D \le D_2(k, I) \\ D_1(k, I) + \bar{c} + M(D, I) & D_2(k, I) < D \le D_3(k, I) \\ D_1(k, I) + \bar{c} + \gamma(1 - \delta)T & D > D_3(k, I), \end{cases} \tag{13.5}$$

where

$$D_1(k, I) \equiv (1 - \gamma)V(k) + \gamma(1 - \delta)\tfrac{\bar{c}}{2} + \gamma Ik - \bar{c},$$

$$M(D, I) \equiv \frac{\gamma(1 - \delta)\frac{T}{\bar{c}}(D + (1 + \delta)\frac{\bar{c}}{2} - Ik)}{1 + (1 - \delta)\frac{T}{\bar{c}}},$$

$$D_2(k, I) \equiv \frac{D_1(k, I)(1 + (1 - \delta)\frac{T}{c}) + \gamma(1 - \delta)\frac{T}{c}((1 + \delta)\frac{\bar{c}}{2} - Ik)}{1 + (1 - \gamma)(1 - \delta)\frac{T}{c}},$$

and $D_3(k, I)$ is smaller than the value of D for which $D_1(k, I) + \bar{c} + M(D, I) = D$. Notice that $p^*(D, k, I)$ is (weakly) increasing with D and with I.

13.3.4   The Choice of Capital Structure

Assuming that the capital market is perfectly competitive, the market value of new equity and debt is exactly equal in equilibrium to their expected return. Let $\phi^*(D, k, I) \equiv \phi^*(p^*(D, k, I), D)$ be the probability of financial distress, given $p^*(D, k, I)$. With probability ρ, the regulator is committed and sets a price of $p^*(D, k, 1)$. The resulting probability of financial distress is then $\phi^*(D, k, 1)$. With probability $1 - \rho$, the regulator is opportunistic, so the regulated price and probability of financial distress are $p^*(D, k, 0)$ and $\phi^*(D, k, 0)$. Since the expected cost of the regulated firm is $C = \frac{\bar{c}}{2} + \phi^*(D, k, I)T$ and since the firm ignores a fraction δ of its cost by the MPE approach, the firm's objective function is

$$\begin{aligned}Y(D, k) = &\rho[p^*(D, k, 1) - (1 - \delta)(\tfrac{\bar{c}}{2} + \phi^*(D, k, 1)T) - k] \\ &+ (1 - \rho)[p^*(D, k, 0) - (1 - \delta)(\tfrac{\bar{c}}{2} + \phi^*(D, k, 0)T) - k].\end{aligned} \quad (13.6)$$

The firm chooses its debt level, D, and investment, k, to maximize $Y(D,k)$. In CS we prove the following result:

Proposition 1   In equilibrium, the regulated firm will issue debt with face value $D_2(k, 0)$ if $\rho < \rho^*$, and will issue a higher debt with face value $D_2(k, 1)$ if $\rho > \rho^*$, where

$$\rho^* \equiv \frac{(1 - \gamma)(1 - \delta)\frac{T}{\bar{c}}}{1 + (1 - \gamma)(1 - \delta)\frac{T}{\bar{c}}}.$$

Moreover, holding k fixed, the debt level of the regulated firm is higher the lower is δ.

In what follows, we will say that the regulator is 'independent' if $\rho > \rho^*$ (the regulator is committed to take k into account with a relatively high probability) and 'non-independent' if $\rho < \rho^*$. Proposition 1 implies that the firm issues more debt when it faces an independent regulator. Intuitively, an independent regulator is more likely to be committed, and therefore sets a higher regulated price. This enables the firm to issue more debt.

Proposition 1 also shows that more privatized firms (δ is lower) should issue more debt. The reason is that the firm ignores a smaller part of its cost when δ is lower. Consequently, the regulator, who sets p by taking into account the firm's objective function, will set a higher p. This induces the firm to issue more debt.

In sum, Proposition 1 implies that in a sample of regulated firms that differ only with respect to the values of ρ (how independent their regulator is) and δ (the state's stake in the firm), firms that are regulated by an IRA and are more privatized should be more leveraged.

13.3.5 The Equilibrium Level of Investment

Proposition 1 shows that under a non-independent regulator ($\rho < \rho^*$), the firm issues debt with face value $D_2(k, 0)$ and the regulator sets a price $D_2(k, 0) + \bar{c}$, which ensures that the firm never becomes financially distressed. Substituting these expressions in Equation (13.6), the resulting expected payoff of the firm is

$$Y^{NI}(k) \equiv Y(D_2(k, 0), k) = D_2(k, 0) + (1 + \delta)\tfrac{\bar{c}}{2} - k. \qquad (13.7)$$

When the regulator is independent ($\rho > \rho^*$), the firm issues debt with face value $D_2(k, 1)$. With probability ρ, the regulator is committed and sets a regulated price $D_2(k, 1) + \bar{c}$, which again ensures that the firm never becomes financially distressed. With probability $1 - \rho$, the regulator is opportunistic and sets a price $D_1(k, 0) + \bar{c} + M(D_2(k, 1), 0)$, which leaves the firm susceptible to financial distress with probability

$$\phi^I(k) = 1 - \frac{p^*(D_2(k, 1), k, 0) - D_2(k, 1)}{\bar{c}} = \frac{\gamma k}{\bar{c}\left(1 + (1 - \delta)\dfrac{T}{\bar{c}}\right)}. \qquad (13.8)$$

The overall probability of financial distress is therefore $(1 - \rho)\phi^I(k)$. The expected regulated price under an independent regulator is

$$Ep^*(k) = \rho D_2(k, 1) + (1 - \rho)[D_1(k, 0) + M(D_2(k, 1), 0)] + \bar{c}. \qquad (13.9)$$

Substituting from Equations (13.8) and (13.9) into Equation (13.6), CS show that the firm's expected payoff under an independent regulator is

$$Y^I(k) = Y(D_2(k, 1), k) -$$

$$Ep^*(k) - (1 - \rho)(1 - \delta)\phi^I(k)T - (1 - \delta)\tfrac{\bar{c}}{2} - k. \qquad (13.10)$$

Using $Y^{NI}(k)$ and $Y^I(k)$, CS prove the following result:

Proposition 2   The equilibrium level of investment, k^*, is independent of the degree of regulatory independence, ρ, when $\rho < \rho^*$, but is increasing with ρ when $\rho > \rho^*$. Consequently, the firm invests more when the regulator is independent (that is, $\rho > \rho^*$) than when the regulator is non-independent (that is, $\rho < \rho^*$). Moreover, equilibrium level of investment, k^*, is decreasing with δ.

Proposition 2 implies that the firm should invest more when it faces an independent regulator and when it is more privatized. This result arises since $Ep^*(k)$ is higher when the regulator is independent and when δ is low; consequently, the marginal benefit of investment is higher. The first part of Proposition 2 is consistent with a number of empirical papers that found that regulatory independence is associated with higher investments (for example, Henisz and Zelner, 2001; Wallsten, 2001; Gutièrrez, 2003).

Finally, in CS we prove the following result:

Proposition 3   Taking into account the endogenous choice of investment, the firm's debt and the regulated price are higher when the regulator is independent (that is, $\rho > \rho^*$) than when the regulator is non-independent (that is, $\rho < \rho^*$). Moreover, the firm's debt and the regulated price are both decreasing with the state's ownership stake δ.

Proposition 3 implies that in a sample of regulated firms that differ only in terms of ρ and δ, the firm's debt and regulated price should be positively correlated. Moreover, in our model, debt affects the choice of regulated prices rather than vice versa.

13.4   EMPIRICAL RESULTS

Our empirical analysis is based on an unbalanced panel of 88 publicly traded utilities and transportation infrastructure operators from the EU 15 countries, over the period 1994 to 2005.[2] The interested reader is referred to BCRS for details on the construction of the data set. Descriptive statistics for our main variables are summarized in Table 13.3.

13.4.1   Leverage

Our measure of leverage is market leverage, which is defined as $D/(D + ME)$, where D is total financial debt (both long and short term) in book value and ME is the market value of equity (the number of outstanding

Table 13.3 Summary statistics of 88 publicly listed European regulated firms, 1994–2005

Variable	Mean	Std. Dev.	Min	Max	No. obs.
Market Leverage	0.182	0.169	0	0.881	757
Private Control	0.192	0.735	0	0.881	532
State Control	0.158	0.151	0	0.757	225
Log of Real Total Asset	11.031	1.812	5.694	14.534	876
Tangibility	0.621	0.211	0.034	0.967	876
EBIT-to-Total Asset	0.073	0.099	−1.948	0.299	857
Non-debt Tax Shield	0.052	0.03	0	0.183	876
Investment to Capital Stock	0.111	0.072	0	0.673	703
Cash Flow to Capital Stock	0.135	0.102	−0.936	0.871	719
Sales to Capital Stock	0.742	0.803	0.020	6.191	684
Private Control dummy	0.624	0.484	0	1	876
Regulatory Independence dummy	0.594	0.491	0	1	876
Investor Protection	3.815	1.222	1	5	876
GDP Growth	2.461	1.347	−1.120	10.720	876

shares at the end of the relevant year times the share price at that date expressed in US dollars).[3]

We define firms as 'privately controlled' if the state's ultimate control rights (UCR), which take into account the state's direct stake in the firm, as well as its indirect stake via its holdings in other firms that have stakes in the regulated firm, are below 50 per cent.[4] Otherwise the firm is defined as 'state controlled'. Among the 88 firms in our sample, 42 firms are privately controlled throughout our sample, 25 are state controlled throughout our sample period, and 21 were privatized during our sample period and we therefore observe them before and after their privatization.

Figure 13.1 shows the evolution of market leverage from five years before privatization (year –5) to five years after privatization (year +5) for the 21 firms that were privatized during our sample period (solid line). Of these firms, eight are energy utilities and seven are telecoms. Figure 13.1 shows the evolution of market leverage for these subsamples (the dotted line for energy and dashed line for telecoms).

Figure 13.1 shows that privatized firms increase their market leverage around privatization from 11.3 per cent in the year –5 to 28.4 per cent in the year +5. The bulk of the increase though occurs following privatization, as market leverage increases from 13.8 per cent in year 0 to 28.4 per cent in year +5. The temporary decrease in market leverage from the year

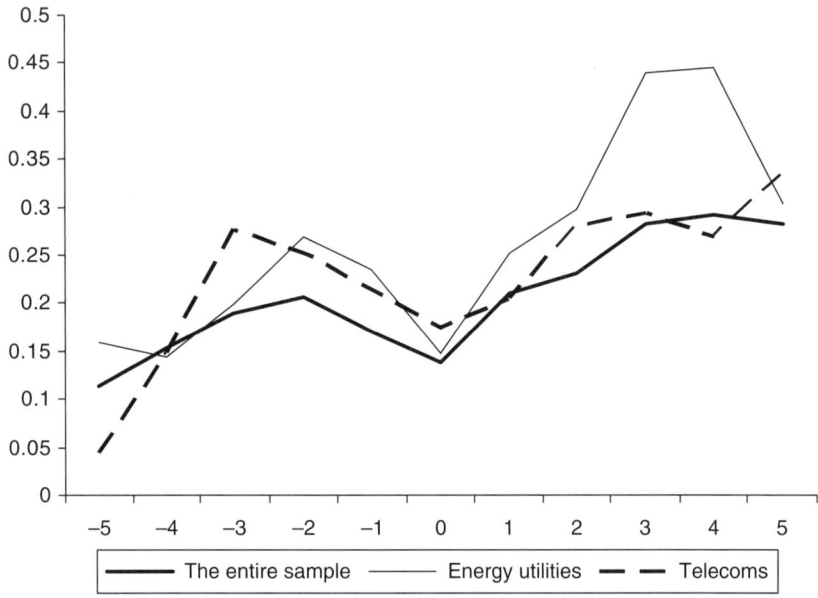

Figure 13.1   Trend of the average market leverage for privatized utilities

–2 to year 0 may be due to the increase in equity during the Initial Public Offering (IPO) in the year of privatization (year 0).

Figure 13.1 is consistent with Proposition 1, which implies that firms should increase their leverage when the government's stake in the firm falls, but it stands in contrast to the findings in Dewenter and Malatesta (2001), Megginson et al. (1994) and D'Souza and Megginson (1999). These papers show that firms typically lower their leverage following privatization and this decrease can often be substantial. However, unlike us, these papers do not focus on regulated firms, and moreover, many of the regulated utilities in their samples were not regulated by IRAs.

We now turn to regression analysis. In BCRS, we estimated a static leverage equation, and found strong support for Proposition 1. Specifically, we found that privately controlled firms tend to have a higher leverage than state-controlled firms, provided that they are regulated by the IRA. We also showed that this result continues to hold when firms are defined as 'privately controlled' if the state holds less than 30 per cent of the UCR instead of 50 per cent, when we use book leverage instead of market leverage, when we take into account the 'golden shares' that some privately controlled regulated firms have which give the state special control rights and when we restrict attention to a subsample of energy utilities.

In this chapter we take a different approach and estimate a dynamic leverage equation that accounts for the possible adjustment process of leverage in response to changes in the exogenous determinants of leverage. This approach allows us to estimate the long-run effects of regulatory independence and privatization. The specification is the following:

$$L_{it} = \alpha_0 + \beta L_{it-1} + \alpha_1 IRA_{it} + \alpha_2 Private\ Control_{it}$$
$$+ \alpha_3 Private\ Control_{it}*IRA_{it} + \alpha_4 X_{it} + \alpha_5\ GDP\ Growth_{it}$$
$$+ \alpha_6 Investor\ Protection_{it} + \eta_i + d_t + \varepsilon_{it}, \tag{13.11}$$

where L_{it} and L_{it-1} are the *Market Leverage* of firm i in the years t and $t-1$, IRA_{it} is a dummy equal to 1 if firm i was subject to regulation by an IRA in year t and equal to 0 otherwise, *Private Control*$_{it}$ is a dummy equal to 1 if firm i was privately controlled in year t and equal to 0 otherwise, X_{it} is a vector of firm-specific controls that may affect the choice of leverage, *GDP Growth* and the *Investor Protection* index reflect time-varying country-specific institutional factors,[5] η_i and d_t are firm and time fixed effects and ε_{it} is an error term.

The vector X_{it} includes the log of real total assets to control for firm size, the ratio of fixed to total assets to control for asset tangibility (more tangible assets may serve as a collateral and lower the cost of debt), the ratio of EBIT (earning before interests and taxes) to total assets to control for 'efficiency' (more efficient firms are likely to have higher earnings with the same assets), and the ratio of depreciation and amortization to total assets to control for tax shields. These variables are commonly used in empirical studies of capital structure (see, for example, Rajan and Zingales, 1995; Frank and Goyal, 2009). We wish to find out if private control and the existence of an IRA affect the choice of leverage even after controlling for these variables.

The effects of ownership and regulatory independence on leverage are captured by the coefficients α_1, α_2 and α_3. The sum $\alpha_1 + \alpha_3$ captures the effect of regulatory independence (IRA versus no IRA) on the leverage of privately controlled firms, while α_1 captures the effect of regulatory independence on the leverage of state-controlled firms. Likewise, $\alpha_2 + \alpha_3$ captures the effect of ownership (private versus State control) on the leverage of firms which are regulated by an IRA, while α_2 captures the effect of ownership on the leverage of firms which are not regulated by an IRA. In the regression below, we will report the values of α_1, α_2, $\alpha_1 + \alpha_3$, and $\alpha_2 + \alpha_3$, and the p-values associated with tests on their significance.

To estimate Equation (13.11), we use the dynamic System-GMM model developed by Arellano and Bond (1991) and Blundell and Bond (1998), which is especially designed for dynamic models where the lagged dependent variable is persistent and the lagged levels of the dependent variables are therefore weak instruments. For the validity of the GMM estimates it is crucial, however, that the instruments are exogenous. We therefore report the two-step Sargan-Hansen test statistic under the null of joint validity of the instruments, as well as an autocorrelation test to control for first- and second-order correlations in the residuals.

Table 13.4 reports the one-step System-GMM estimates. The table shows that the various firm-specific controls are significant and their signs are generally consistent with earlier empirical studies on the determinants of the capital structure. The only exception is the negative and significant coefficient on *fixed-to-total assets* (our proxy for tangibility) which is typically found to be positive, reflecting the fact that tangible assets can serve as collateral and hence lower the cost of debt. However, in our sample, fixed assets are highly firm-specific and non-redeployable (for example, roads, airports, physical electricity or telecommunications networks) and may therefore serve as poor collaterals.

More importantly for us, Column (1) shows that the coefficient on *IRA* is positive and significant: the point estimate shows that on average, IRA is associated with a 4.2 per cent increase in leverage. The coefficient on the *Private Control* dummy is positive but insignificant. Column (2) shows that the coefficient of the *Private Control*IRA* dummy is positive and significant; this indicates that the positive effect of IRA on leverage is significantly larger for firms that are both privately controlled and subject to regulation by an IRA.

Columns (3) and (4) show results for the subsample of firms that remained state or privately controlled throughout our sample period. The positive direct effect of IRA on leverage is even stronger now and equals to 4.8 per cent on average. Column (4) shows that the coefficient of the *IRA*Private Control* dummy is also larger than it is for the entire sample.

Our dynamic specification allows us to estimate the long-run effect of the introduction of an IRA on leverage. In particular, a 1 per cent increase in market leverage in year t translates into a long-run increase of $1 + \beta + \beta^2 + \beta^3 + \ldots = 1/(1-\beta)$ per cent. Columns (1) and (3) show that the introduction of an IRA leads to a long-run increase in leverage by 7.2 per cent for the full sample and by 8.3 per cent for the firms that remained privately or state controlled throughout our sample period. Columns (2) and (4) show that if we restrict attention to privately controlled firms, then the introduction of an IRA is associated with an even larger long-run increase in leverage: 9.2 per cent for all privately controlled firms and 11.9 per cent for firms that were privately controlled throughout (these long-run effects are captured by the values of $(\alpha_1 + \alpha_3)/(1-\beta)$ in Columns (2) and (4)).

Table 13.4   GMM estimates of a dynamic leverage equation

Leverage$_t$	(1) Full sample	(2) Full sample	(3) Privately or state controlled throughout the period	(4) Privately or state controlled throughout the period
Leverage$_{t-1}$ (β)	0.418***	0.361***	0.423***	0.430***
	(0.082)	(0.082)	(0.087)	(0.088)
Log of real total assets	0.012***	0.016***	0.006	0.009
	(0.004)	(0.005)	(0.006)	(0.007)
Fixed-to-Total Assets	−0.099**	−0.108**	−0.088*	−0.099*
	(0.048)	(0.050)	(0.052)	(0.053)
Non-debt Tax Shield	−1.110***	−1.312***	−1.202***	−1.260***
	(0.305)	(0.311)	(0.384)	(0.391)
EBIT-to-Total Assets	−0.249**	−0.247**	−0.249**	−0.250**
	(0.099)	(0.097)	(0.114)	(0.113)
GDP Growth	−0.005	−0.008	−0.007	−0.010
	(0.006)	(0.006)	(0.008)	(0.009)
Investor Protection	−0.013	−0.012*	−0.014	−0.012
	(0.010)	(0.011)	(0.014)	(0.015)
IRA (α_1)	0.042**	−0.018	0.048**	−0.020
	(0.016)	(0.042)	(0.022)	(0.051)
Private Control (α_2)	0.025	−0.028**	0.024	−0.041
	(0.022)	(0.040)	(0.025)	(0.051)
Private Control*IRA (α_3)	–	0.077*	–	0.088*
	–	(0.043)	–	(0.051)

Table 13.4 (continued)

Leverage$_t$	(1) Full sample	(2) Full sample	(3) Privately or state controlled throughout the period	(4) Privately or state controlled throughout the period
$\alpha_1/(1-\beta)$	0.072***	−0.028	0.083**	−0.035
(p-value)	(0.004)	(0.670)	(0.021)	(0.693)
$(\alpha_1+\alpha_3)/(1-\beta)$	–	0.092***	–	0.119***
(p-value)		(0.002)		(0.002)
$\alpha_2/(1-\beta)$	0.043	−0.044	0.042	−0.072
(p-value)	(0.254)	(0.482)	(0.323)	(0.428)
$(\alpha_2+\alpha_3)/(1-\beta)$	–	0.077**	–	0.083*
(p-value)		(0.034)		(0.058)
Arellano–Bond test for AR(1) (p-value)	0.000	0.000	0.001	0.001
Arellano–Bond test for AR(2) (p-value)	0.823	0.739	0.958	0.971
Sargan–Hansen test (p-value)	0.465	0.607	0.683	0.789
N firms [N obs.]	88 [612]	88 [612]	63 [445]	63 [445]

Note: Dynamic panel data estimation, one-step system GMM estimates. Lagged values of right-hand variables used as instruments: lagged levels are used in first-differences equations and lags of first-differenced variables are used in levels equations. All regressions include year dummies. Standard errors in parentheses are robust to heteroscedasticity and to within group serial correlation. AR(1) [AR(2)] tests the null hypothesis of no first-order [second-order] correlation in the differenced residuals.. The Sargan–Hansen statistic tests the null hypothesis that the over-identifying restrictions are valid. ***, **, * denote significance of the coefficients at 1 per cent, 5 per cent and 10 per cent.

By contrast, the introduction of an IRA does not have a significant effect on the leverage of state-controlled firms, as the coefficients of $\alpha_1/(1-\beta)$ in Columns (2) and (4) are not significant.

Columns (1) and (3) also show that in and of itself, private control does not have a significant effect on leverage. Columns (2) and (4), however, show that if we restrict attention to firms that were regulated by an IRA, then *Private Control* does have a positive and significant effect on leverage, and its long-run effect for firms that were regulated by an IRA (captured by the values of $(\alpha_2 + \alpha_3)/(1-\beta)$ in Columns (2) and (4)) are 7.7 per cent for all privately controlled firms and 8.3 per cent for firms that were privately controlled throughout our sample period.

In sum, our estimates indicate that privatization, together with regulation by an IRA, has a positive and significant effect on leverage.

13.4.2   Investment Equation

Next, we estimate a following simple investment equation:

$$(I/K)_{it} = \beta_1(I/K)_{it-1} + \beta_2(CF/K)_{it-1} + \beta_3(S/K)_{it-1} + \alpha_1 IRA_{it-1} + \alpha_2 PrivateControl_{it-1} + \alpha_3 IRA_{it-1}*PrivateControl_{it-1} + d_t + \eta_i + \varepsilon_{it}, \quad (13.12)$$

where $(I/K)_{it}$ and $(I/K)_{it-1}$ are the gross fixed investment (including new plants, property and equipment, and accounting for mergers, acquisitions or divestitures) to capital stock at the replacement value of firm i in the years t and $t-1$, $(CF/K)_{it-1}$ is the cash flow to capital stock ratio of firm i in year $t-1$, $(S/K)_{it-1}$ is the sales to capital stock ratio of firm i in year $t-1$, η_i and d_t are firm and time fixed effects, and ε_{it} is an error term.[6]

Table 13.5 presents the Arellano-Blundell-Bond GMM-System estimates of Equation (13.12). Table 13.5 shows that the coefficient β_1 of lagged investment is positive and significant; this indicates that the adjustment of capital is gradual. The table also shows that the coefficient β_2 of the cash flow term, which is included to reflect capital market imperfections (for example, Hubbard, 1998), is also positive and significant.

More importantly for us, the results show that α_1, which captures the effect of IRA on the investment of state-controlled firms, is positive and significant in all columns. The sum $\alpha_1 + \alpha_3$, which captures the effect of IRA on the investment of privately controlled firms, is not significant however. These results provide support for Proposition 2, but only when firms are state controlled.

Moreover, Columns (2) and (3) show that α_2 and $\alpha_2 + \alpha_3$, which capture the effect of *Private Control* for state-controlled and for privately controlled firms, are both insignificant. One possible reason why

Table 13.5　GMM estimates of a dynamic investment equation

I/K_t	(1) Full sample	(2) Full sample	(3) Full sample	(4) Privately and state controlled throughout the period	(5) Privately and state controlled throughout the period
$(I/K)_{t-1}\,(\beta_1)$	0.307***	0.305***	0.303***	0.384***	0.387***
	(0.082)	(0.087)	(0.090)	(0.046)	(0.049)
$(CF/K)_{t-1}\,(\beta_2)$	0.162**	0.161**	0.162**	0.113	0.116
	(0.074)	(0.073)	(0.073)	(0.086)	(0.087)
$(S/K)_{t-1}\,(\beta_3)$	−0.001	−0.001	−0.001	−0.000	−0.000
	(0.004)	(0.004)	(0.004)	(0.003)	(0.003)
$IRA_{t-1}\,(\alpha_1)$	0.017**	0.017**	0.024*	0.016**	0.015**
	(0.007)	(0.007)	(0.014)	(0.007)	(0.007)
Private Control$_{t-1}\,(\alpha_2)$	–	0.001	0.004	–	0.003
		(0.007)	(0.011)		(0.005)
Private Control$_{t-1}$*$IRA_{t-1}\,(\alpha_3)$	–	–	−0.010	–	–
			(0.019)		

	(1)	(2)	(3)	(4)	(5)
$\alpha_1/(1-\beta_1)$	0.025***	0.025***	0.034*	0.026**	0.025**
(p-value)	(0.006)	(0.006)	(0.063)	(0.022)	(0.025)
$\alpha_2/(1-\beta_1)$	–	-0.022	0.006		0.004
(p-value)	–	(0.835)	(0.693)		(0.581)
$(\alpha_1+\alpha_3)/(1-\beta_1)$			0.020		
(p-value)			(0.124)		
$(\alpha_2+a_3)/(1-\beta_1)$			-0.009		
(p-value)			(0.646)		
Arellano-Bond test for AR(1) (p-value)	0.033	0.030	0.029	0.001	0.001
Arellano-Bond test for AR(2) (p-value)	0.517	0.507	0.512	0.689	0.668
Sargan-Hansen test (p-value)	0.375	0.381	0.410	0.521	0.501
N firms [n obs.]	83 [422]	83 [422]	83 [422]	61 [399]	60 [312]

Note: Dynamic panel data estimation, one-step system GMM estimates. All regressions include year dummies. Standard errors in parentheses are robust to heteroscedasticity and to within group serial correlation. AR(1) [AR(2)] tests the null hypothesis of no first-order [second-order] correlation in the differenced residuals. The Sargan-Hansen statistic tests the null hypothesis that the over-identifying restrictions are valid. ***, **, * denote statistical significance at 1 per cent, 5 per cent and 10 per cent.

state-controlled firms do not invest less than privately controlled firms, as Proposition 2 predicts, might be that governments lean on state-controlled firms to induce them to invest in order to advance their own political agenda. This type of political intervention is not captured by our theoretical model.

The signs and significance of α_1, α_2 and α_3 are broadly consistent with the findings in Cambini and Rondi (2010), who study a panel of energy utilities from five EU states over the period 2000 to 2007, and Cambini and Rondi (2011), who study a panel of 80 regulated firms from the EU 15 states over the period 1994 to 2004.

The value of $\alpha_1/(1 - \beta_1)$ in Table 13.5 shows that the presence of an IRA is associated with a long-run 3.4 per cent increase in the investment rate of all state-controlled firms (Column (3)) and 2.5 per cent for firms that remained state controlled throughout the entire period (Column (5)). These effects are substantial given that Table 13.1 shows that the mean rate of investment (investment to capital stock) in our sample is 11.1 per cent.

13.4.3   Leverage and Regulated Prices

Finally, we use the Granger causality tests to examine whether an increase in leverage is followed by an increase in regulated prices, but not vice versa, as Proposition 3 predicts.[7] In principle, Proposition 3 has three possible alternatives. First, if regulators can make a long-term commitment to regulated prices, then regulated prices will determine the firm's revenues (up to some exogenous demand shocks), so the firm would adjust its capital structure to match its expected revenue stream. Consequently, regulated prices would Granger-cause leverage. Second, leverage and regulated prices may be correlated due to a third variable that causes both of them. A third possibility is that leverage and regulated prices are simply not correlated.

We estimate the following bivariate VAR(2) dynamic model for sector- and country-specific retail price indices and leverage:

$$P_{it} = \alpha^P_{t-1}P_{i,t-1} + \alpha^P_{t-2}P_{i,t-2} + \beta^P_{t-1}L_{i,t-1} + \beta^P_{t-2}L_{i,t-2}$$

$$+ \sum_i \mu^P_i Firm_i + \sum_t \lambda^P_t Year_t + \varepsilon^P_{it}, \tag{13.13}$$

$$L_{it} = \alpha^L_{t-1}P_{i,t-1} + \alpha^L_{t-2}P_{i,t-2} + \beta^L_{t-1}L_{i,t-1} + \beta^L_{t-2}L_{i,t-2}$$

$$+ \sum_i \mu^L_i Firm_i + \sum_t \lambda^L_t Year_t + \varepsilon^L_{it}, \tag{13.14}$$

where P_{it} and L_{it} are the regulated price and market leverage of firm i in period t, *Firm$_i$* and *Year$_t$* are firm and year dummies, and ε_{it}^P and ε_{it}^L are error terms. Our hypothesis that, conditional on individual and time effects, leverage Granger-causes regulated prices, but not vice versa, requires that β_{t-1}^P and β_{t-2}^P are positive and significant, while α_{t-1}^L and α_{t-2}^L are not significant. Moreover, it requires that $L_{i,t-1}$ and $L_{i,t-2}$ contribute significantly to the explanatory power of regression (13.3), while $P_{i,t-1}$ and $P_{i,t-2}$ do not contribute significantly to the explanatory power of Equation (13.14). Since we were unable to find reliable data at the individual firm level, the regulated prices we use are country- and sector-specific retail price indices.[8] All price indices are in constant 2005 prices.

The results of one-step GMM-System estimates of Equations (13.13) and (13.14) are reported in Tables VIII and IX of BCRS. The results show that with the exception of firms that are not regulated by an IRA, or are state controlled, the second lag of market leverage has a significant positive effect on regulated prices. Moreover, Wald statistics tests indicate that the first and second lags of market leverage are jointly significant. By contrast, the lagged regulated prices do not have a significant effect on leverage either individually or jointly.

These results imply that, so long as firms are privately controlled and/or regulated by an IRA, leverage Granger-causes regulated prices, but not vice versa. This is consistent with Proposition 3 and inconsistent with the alternative hypotheses that long-term regulatory commitments to prices induce firms to adjust their capital structure to match their resulting expected revenue stream, or that leverage and regulated prices are driven by a third variable that causes them both.

13.5   CONCLUSIONS

In this chapter we study the effect of privatization and regulatory independence on the capital structure of regulated firms, their investments and the effect of financial leverage on regulated prices. The theoretical predictions in Section 13.3 are that (i) regulated firms should be more leveraged and should invest more when they are subject to regulation by IRAs; (ii) regulated firms should be more leveraged and should invest more when they are more privatized (the state holds a smaller stake in the firm); and (iii) higher leverage should lead to higher regulated prices.

The empirical evidence in Section 13.4 from the EU 15 countries provides strong support for hypotheses (i) and (iii), but much weaker support for hypothesis (ii). Specifically, our estimates reveal that the introduction of an IRA is associated with a long-run increase in leverage by 7.2 per cent for the full sample and 8.3 per cent for the subsample of firms that remained privately or state controlled throughout the period. The long-run effect of an IRA on leverage is even larger if we restrict attention to privately controlled firms: the long-run effect then is 9.2 per cent for all privately controlled firms, and 11.9 per cent for firms that were privately controlled throughout our sample period. Moreover, the introduction of an IRA is associated with a long-run increase of 3.4 per cent in the investment rate of all state-controlled firms and 2.5 per cent for firms that remained state controlled throughout our sample period. These effects are substantial given that the mean rate of investment in our sample is 11.1 per cent.

Our results on privatization are less conclusive: in and of its own, private control does not have a significant effect on leverage or investment. However, when attention is restricted to firms that are regulated by an IRA, we do find a positive and significant effect of private control on leverage, though not on investment. In particular, under an IRA, private control is associated with a long-run increase in leverage by 7.7 per cent for all privately controlled firms and 8.3 per cent for firms that were privately controlled throughout our sample period.

We also find, in line with hypothesis (iii), that so long as firms are privately controlled and/or subject to regulation by an IRA, lagged market leverage has a significant positive effect on regulated prices, but not vice versa. These results are consistent with the main premise of our theoretical model that regulated firms choose their leverage strategically to induce regulators to set higher prices.

Our results indicate that the 'dash for debt' phenomenon observed in many countries is a natural response of regulated firms to the privatization process and the establishment of independent regulatory agencies. Our results also indicate that while the increase in debt is associated with higher regulated prices, it is also associated with higher investments and hence may be welfare enhancing.

NOTES

1. Only recently, the energy IRAs in some new member states (Latvia and Lithuania) started regulating the water sector within a multi-sector regulatory model. And, from 2006, the German IRA (named *Bundesnetzagentun*) started regulating the railways sector.
2. The sample here has only 88 firms while in BCRS there are 92 firms. Since we estimate dynamic models that require us to use lagged variables as instruments, four firms with less than five consecutive observations are dropped from our sample.

3. See Rajan and Zingales (1995) for a discussion of alternative leverage measures.
4. The UCR variables were constructed by Bortolotti and Faccio (2009); the sources used to compute the state's UCR are listed in BCRS.
5. The 'investor protection' index, developed initially by La Porta et al. (1998) and updated by Pagano and Volpin (2005), increases from 0 to 7 as shareholders' rights become more protected. It is conceivable that higher values of this index are associated with a lower cost of equity.
6. See Cambini and Rondi (2011) for details on the construction of the gross investment and capital stock variables.
7. Granger causality tests were also used in a similar context in a number of recent papers, including Alesina et al. (2005) and Edwards and Waverman (2006).
8. Airports, ports and docks are not included in our regressions since their services are considered to be intermediate rather than final services. We believe that given that there is still limited competition in the utilities sector and given that there is little price dispersion, our price indices appropriately reflect the relevant prices for the firms in our sample.

REFERENCES

AEEG (2008), 'Regolazione tariffaria dei servizi di distribuzione e misura del gas per il periodo di regolazione 2009–2012', Deliberation n. 159/08, Regulatory impact assessment analysis, 27 December 2007, Milan, available at http://www.autorita.energia.it (accessed September 2011).

Alesina, A., S. Ardagna, G. Nicoletti and F. Schiantarelli (2005), 'Regulation and investment', *Journal of European Economic Association*, **3**(4), 791–825.

Arellano, M. and S. Bond (1991), 'Some tests of specification for panel data: Monte Carlo evidence and an application to employment equations', *Review of Economic Studies*, **58**(2), 277–97.

Blundell, R. and S. Bond (1998), 'Initial conditions and moment restrictions in dynamic panel data models', *Journal of Econometrics*, **87**, 115–43.

Blundell, R., S. Bond and C. Meghir (1992), 'Econometric models of company investment', in L. Matyas and P. Sevestre (eds), *The Econometrics of Panel Data: Handbook of Theory and Applications*, Dordrecht: Kluwer Academic Publishers.

Bortolotti, B. and M. Faccio (2009), 'Government control of privatized firms', *Review of Financial Studies*, **22**(8), 2907–39.

Bortolotti, B., C. Cambini, L. Rondi and Y. Spiegel (2011), 'Capital structure and regulation: do ownership and regulatory independence matter?', *Journal of Economics and Management Strategy*, **20**(2), 517–64.

Cambini, C. and L. Rondi (2010), 'Incentive regulation and investment: evidence from European energy utilities', *Journal of Regulatory Economics*, **38**, 1–26.

Cambini, C. and L. Rondi (2011), 'Regulatory independence, investment, and political interference: evidence from the European Union', EUI Working Paper, RSCAS no. 42/2011, Florence.

Cambini, C. and L. Rondi (2012), 'Capital structure and investment in regulated network utilities: evidence from EU telecoms', *Industrial and Corporate Change*, **21**(1), 73–94.

Cambini, C. and Y. Spiegel (2011), 'Investment and capital structure of partially private regulated firms', CEPR Discussion Paper No. 8508, August.

Dasgupta, S. and V. Nanda (1993), 'Bargaining and brinkmanship – capital structure choice by regulated firms', *International Journal of Industrial Organization*, **11**(4), 475–97.

Dewenter, K. and P. Malatesta (2001), 'State-owned and privately-owned firms: an empirical analysis of profitability, leverage, and labor intensity', *American Economic Review*, **91**(1), 320–34.

D'Souza, J. and W. Megginson (1999), 'The financial and operating performance of privatized firms during the 1990s', *Journal of Finance*, **54**(4), 1397–438.

DTI and HM Treasury (2004), *The Drivers and Public Policy Consequences of Increased Gearing*, Report by the Department of Trade and Industry and HM Treasury, London.

Edwards, G. and L. Waverman (2006), 'The effects of public ownership and regulatory independence on regulatory outcomes: a study of interconnect rates in EU telecommunications', *Journal of Regulatory Economics*, **29**(1), 23–67.

Frank, M. and V. Goyal (2009), 'Capital structure decisions: which factors are reliably important', *Financial Management*, **38**, 1–37.

Gilardi, F. (2002), 'Policy credibility and delegation to independent regulatory agencies: a comparative empirical analysis', *Journal of European Public Policy*, **9**(6), 873–93.

Guthrie, G. (2006), 'Regulating infrastructure: the impact on risk and investment', *Journal of Economic Literature*, **44**(4), 925–72.

Gutièrrez, L.H. (2003), 'The effect of endogenous regulation on telecommunications expansion and efficiency in Latin America', *Journal of Regulatory Economics*, **23**(3), 257–86.

Gutièrrez, L.H. and S. Berg (1998), *Telecommunications Liberalization and Regulatory Governance: Lessons from Latin America*, Public Utility Research Center, University of Florida.

Henisz, W. and B. Zelner (2001), 'The institutional environment for telecommunications investment', *Journal of Economics and Management Strategy*, **10**(1), 123–47.

Hubbard, G. (1998), 'Capital-market imperfections and investment', *Journal of Economic Literature*, **36**, 193–225.

La Porta R., F. Lopez-de-Silanes, A. Shleifer and R. Vishny (1998), 'Law and finance', *Journal of Political Economy*, **106**, 1113–55.

Levy, B. and P. Spiller (1994), 'The institutional foundations of regulatory commitment: a comparative analysis of telecommunications regulation', *Journal of Law, Economics, and Organization*, **10**(2), 201–46.

Megginson, W. and J. Netter (2001), 'From state to market: a survey of empirical studies on privatization', *Journal of Economic Literature*, **39**(2), 321–89.

Megginson, W., R. Nash and M. van Randenborgh (1994), 'The financial and operating performance of newly privatized firms: an international empirical analysis', *Journal of Finance*, **49**, 403–52.

Pagano, M. and P. Volpin (2005), 'The political economy of corporate governance', *American Economic Review*, **95**(4), 1005–30.

Rajan, R. and L. Zingales (1995), 'What do we know about capital structure? Some evidence from international data', *Journal of Finance*, **50**(5), 1421–60.

Sappington, D. and G. Sidak (2003), 'Incentives for anticompetitive behavior by public enterprises', *Review of Industrial Organization*, **22**(3), 183–206.

Spiegel, Y. (1994), 'The capital structure and investment of regulated firms under alternative regulatory regimes', *Journal of Regulatory Economics*, **6**, 297–320.

Spiegel, Y. and D. Spulber (1997), 'Capital structure with countervailing incentives', *RAND Journal of Economics*, **28**, 1–24.

Trillas, F. and M.A. Montoya (2011), 'Commitment and regulatory independence in practice in Latin American and Caribbean countries', *Competition and Regulation in Network Industries*, **12**(1), 27–56.

Wallsten, S. (2001), 'An econometric analysis of telecom competition, privatization and regulation in Africa and Latin America', *Journal of Industrial Economics*, **49**(1), 1–19.

14. Rethinking regulatory capture

Per J. Agrell and Axel Gautier

14.1 INTRODUCTION

The design of a regulatory process is a challenging task as it involves complex information processing and the participation of many actors: politicians, executives, legislature, supervisors, auditors, regulated firms or industries, customers, taxpayers, trade unions. These stakeholders can be categorized into three groups: (political) decision makers, supervisors, and interest groups. With this distinction in mind, the regulatory process can be represented as a three-layer hierarchy with, on the top, the decision maker (the political principal), in the middle the supervisor (the regulatory agency), and on the bottom the regulated firm (Figure 14.1(a)). In such a hierarchical organization, the bottom layer has privileged access to key information relevant for decision making. Regulated firms, for instance, have private information on firm and industry costs, demand characteristics, and available technologies. This asymmetry of information reduces the effectiveness of the regulatory process. To fill in the information gap,

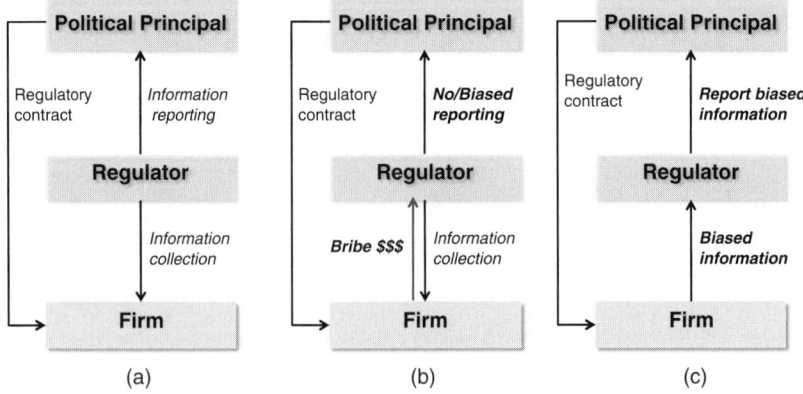

Figure 14.1   *(a) The three-layer hierarchy; (b) Traditional capture; (c) Soft capture*

the political principal appoints a supervisor. The regulatory agency is thus an information gathering intermediate for the political principal who remains in charge of the main regulatory tasks.[1] Performing in this task, the regulatory authority deploys resources, permanent and temporary staff, consultants and experts, in order to collect, process, and produce information for policy making relevant to the regulated sector. Information is valuable for the political principal as it reduces the information rent left to the regulated firm. Improved information quality (precision) reduces the cost of regulating the industry, primarily through a welfare increase by lower downstream prices or higher quality at the expense of (at least some) firms. Effective information gathering by the regulatory authorities is thus essential for an efficient regulatory process.

However, regulatory intervention is not immune to capture. Dal Bó (2006, p. 203) broadly defines capture as 'the process through which special interests affect state intervention in any of its form.' Applied to industry regulation,[2] capture could be more specifically defined as 'the process through which regulated monopolies end up manipulating the state agencies that are supposed to control them' (p. 203). In this chapter, we focus on capture of regulatory agencies by the regulated industry they are charged to monitor.

There are different forms of regulatory capture. Estache and Wren-Lewis (2011) distinguish 'capture of decisions' and 'capture of information'. The former corresponds to situations where a firm or an industry directly tries to influence the decision made. The latter corresponds to situations where the industry tries to manipulate the information on the basis of which the decision is made. This distinction echoes another between 'direct' and 'indirect' capture. Direct capture denotes settings where the regulated firm exerts influence over the regulator itself, while indirect capture denotes situations where the regulated firm influences the regulator indirectly by manipulating decision-making instances[3] that hold power over the regulated agency. When the regulator is solely responsible for filling the information gap between the firm and the decision maker, the two distinctions overlap. If one refers to our three-layer hierarchy, direct capture encompasses all the activities by the regulated firm to manipulate the information collected and reported by the supervisor, hence a form of capture by information, while all the influence activities exerted to modify the principal's behavior are referred to as indirect capture or capture of decision. An additional classification separates 'illegal' (fraud, corruption, extortion) and 'legal' (lobbying, career concerns) influence activity.

Table 14.1 provides some structure to the classifications. Lobbying by organized interest groups to obtain a favorable decision from a politician is both indirect and legal: lobbyists try to obtain favors from the political

Table 14.1   A classification of influence activity

	Indirect	Direct
Legal	Lobbying	Revolving doors, *Soft capture*
Illegal	Corruption	Classical capture

power and not from the regulator by providing information about preferences among the electorate or political alliances. When an interest group uses illegal means, for instance, a bribe, to obtain a favorable decision from a politician, this can no longer be labeled as lobbying but rather as corruption. Evidences on corruption and lobbying are widespread and highly documented.

For the remainder of the chapter, we leave aside indirect capture and focus exclusively on direct capture. In the literature, direct capture has been considered along two complementary lines: the classical view pioneered by the works of Tirole (1986) and Laffont and Tirole (1991, 1993) and the revolving doors approach (Che, 1995). In the classical view, capture consists mainly in bribing the regulator for not reporting or misreporting relevant information to the political principal. Capture is envisaged as a phenomenon based on an exchange of favors. The regulator accepts to be lenient with the firm, for instance, by leaving the price unchanged in a rate review. In return, the firm rewards the regulator, for instance, by offering monetary bribes or any kind of transfer such as access to privileged information (stock/business information) or contracts for services (indirect business). Figure 14.1(b) schematizes the traditional capture.

The classical view on capture is based on reciprocity. Exchange of favors is organized within an explicit or implicit illegal side contract between the regulator and the firm. The revolving doors approach of capture is based on the same premise: offering lucrative post-regulatory employment in the regulated sector (revolving doors) can serve as a mechanism for exchanging favors. The prospect of future employment is never explicit during the regulatory term, nor are the conditions or tasks potentially assigned to the staff. This exchange of favors is hence based on an implicit contract with imperfect enforcement and, as such, it cannot be considered as illegal.[4]

However, these views of direct capture prove to be unsatisfactory. If the theories were complete, we would observe either widespread direct capture through bribes or revolving doors, or institutions designed to prevent capture occuring.[5] But empirical evidence on regulatory capture in the form of corruption is scarce.[6] Likewise, in spite of the open revolving doors most regulators turn out to maintain careers in public service or other sectors. Finally, there is no known example of a high-powered incentive scheme for a sector regulator based on industry rent extraction or welfare gains.[7] We thus have a paradox of capture. Neither capture nor its remedy is observed in practice.

We propose an alternative and more intuitive explanation for regulatory capture (Figure 14.1(c)). To gain influence, the regulated firms do not need to promise a favor to the regulator. Instead, the regulated firms can influence the regulatory outcome by producing pieces of information relevant for the decision makers and transmit this information for free to the regulator.[8] The supervisor receiving a report from the industry has two options: it can either discard it and produce its own report to be transmitted to the political principal or it can copy-paste the industry input and transmit it to the principal. In both cases, the regulator has done its job, but with the latter option, it saves time and resources as the information processing has been made by the industry. We argue that accepting industry input is mutually profitable for the regulator and the firm; the regulator because it saves on the information processing cost (or effort); the firm because it controls the content of information used for decision making. Indeed, a firm would agree to transmit information to the regulator only if the decisions resulting from the use of this information turn out to be more favorable than those expected from the internal information processes of the regulator. Information (if any) transmitted by the firm is necessarily biased.[9]

We thus have another mechanism for direct capture that is not based on exchange of favors but rather on mutual interest. This mechanism is different from lobbying as the regulated transmits information to the regulator and not to the politician as in Austen-Smith and Wright (1992).[10] We will refer to this mechanism as 'soft capture' (Agrell and Gautier, 2010). This approach is both direct and legal and we conjecture that this form of capture is quite common in regulated industries; we illustrate this by looking at the example of the Occupational Safety and Health Administration (OSHA) in the USA in Section 14.4. OSHA can be seen as an example where the regulatory agency develops from an information production intermediary to primarily monitoring in a mechanism based on 'voluntary' or 'self-regulation' by the regulated firms (Shapiro and Rabinowitz, 2000).

14.2   THE PARADOX OF CAPTURE

14.2.1   The Classical Model of Capture

Consider a standard problem of incentive regulation. The regulated firm supplies goods or services to customers on behalf of the political principal but the latter is unaware of the firm's production cost. The principal designs an incentive compatible contract for the firm that specifies a quantity to be produced and a transfer to the firm contingent on a cost report made by the firm; a standard problem (see Laffont and Tirole, 1993). At the optimal contract, the efficient firm receives a compensation above its cost of production, the so-called information rent. This rent is socially costly and, in this framework, the regulator is supposed to mitigate the information advantage of the firm by realizing a costly audit of the firm's private cost parameter.

If the regulator has some discretion when it reports information collected during its audit to the political principal, the firm is ready to bribe the regulator for not reporting rent-reducing information. This mechanism is at the root of the classical model of capture. It is based on two keys elements: regulatory discretion and information rents.

In Tirole (1986) and Laffont and Tirole (1991), the regulator realizes a costly audit of the firm's unknown cost parameter. The auditing technology is imperfect and the cost is observed with some probability lower than one. The information on the firm's cost is 'hard' in the sense that it can be verified by the political principal. Thus, the regulator cannot produce false evidences on the firm's cost but it can hide the relevant piece of information (if any) to the principal. Concealing rent-reducing information is congruent with the regulator's degree of discretion. If the audit is successful and its results reported to the political principal, the regulated loses its information rent. For that reason, the firm may be tempted to bribe the regulator for hiding the results of a successful audit.

The side agreement between the parties may be explicit or implicit but enforcement of the side contract is in any case a non-trivial issue (Tirole, 1986). Administrative rules prohibit monetary transfer from the industry to the regulators, who predominantly are civil servants. Other mechanisms based on trust or reputation (Martimort, 1999) are necessary for the collusion to occur. Such side contracts may thus be costly to write and to enforce which might reduce the scope of capture. In addition, the judicial consequences from detection or delation may be unbalanced between the firm (risking a fine) and the career regulator (risking dishonorable discharge, prison, and ruined public career options) making the acceptance of bribes risky and susceptible to future hold-up by the firm.

Facing the possibility of capture, the political principal must either tolerate capture and consequently rethink the role devoted to the regulatory institution, or design a collusion-proof regulatory process that is immune to capture. In Tirole (1986) the political principal decentralizes its objective to prevent collusion and pays a compensation for a successful audit that is at least as big as the perceived value of the bribe paid by the firm.[11]

Preventing capture is thus costly for the principal as the cost of appointing a supervisor increases. In practice, regulatory institutions do not seem to be designed to prevent the occurrence of this form of capture as, to our knowledge, few regulators are responsible for the regulatory outcome.[12]

Capture is, by definition, a phenomenon that is difficult to estimate empirically. In a rare attempt to test capture with detailed data from regulatory activities, Smith and Söderberg (2010) found no support for the regulatory capture hypothesis. They focus on the treatment of customer complaints by the Swedish Energy Agency (SEA). The resolution of these complaints is delegated to a civil servant that could be either pro-consumer or pro-firm but this information is not known *ex ante*. The SEA can replace the agent if it believes that her (revealed) preferences are incompatible or non-aligned with those of the institution, in which case, the agent is reassigned to another function. Capture in this context would be associated with a higher probability of termination if an agency agent proves to be pro-consumer. The data does not confirm this hypothesis and rather suggests that a bureaucrat that takes pro-industry decisions has a higher probability of being removed compared with a pro-consumer decision maker.

Anecdotical evidence on capture remains relatively rare. Few regulators have been found guilty of corruption though many have shown sympathies with the industry. Evidence of bribed regulators are relatively inconclusive and the traditional view of capture has weak empirical support.

14.2.2 Revolving Doors

The doors between regulatory agencies and the industry are not closed. Many regulators have an industry background (they are coming 'in' the revolving doors). Part of the regulatory staff is also moving 'out' of the revolving doors to a job in industry.[13] Appointing a regulator with an industry background is a way of bringing industry specific knowledge to the regulatory agency. Likewise, expertise of former regulators is valuable to the industry that can then minimize the cost of complying with regulations. Che (1995) and Salant (1995) emphasize the potential incentive effect of the revolving doors that may stimulate acquisition of industry specific human capital. But opening the revolving doors is also a concern as it could bias the regulatory decisions in favor of industry.

Regulators with an industry background may still look at issues with industry eyes and show sympathy for the view expressed by the regulated. Regulators coming in the revolving doors may identify themselves with the industry with, as a consequence, a biased regulation that favors the industry.

Moving out of the revolving doors may also bias regulation. The perspective of posterior employment in the regulated industry may discipline the regulators and lead to pro-industry regulations. Regulators may be lenient in applying rules in order to attract attention from the industry and signal their interest for the industry views with the hope of a later career in the industry.

The possibility of a future job in the industry acts like the bribe in the traditional model. It is the reward paid by the industry in return for favors made by the regulator. There are, however, differences between bribes and post-regulatory employment within the industry. First, there is no need for an explicit contract or agreement between parties. The industry could have the tradition and the reputation to reward regulators that behaved well in the past. Capture is based on an implicit and imperfectly enforceable agreement between parties. Second, unlike bribes, it is not illegal to appoint in the industry someone with regulatory experience. Revolving doors is the legal version of direct capture based on reciprocity.

To our knowledge, there is only one paper that explicitly tests the regulatory bias associated with the revolving doors. Makkai and Braithwaite (1992) collect data on site inspections realized in Australian nursing homes. They test whether the degree of regulatory enforcement depends on prior experience in the industry or an aspiration to leave to a job in the industry. Their study does not confirm the revolving door hypothesis. First, regulatory enforcement records do not depend on prior industry experience. Second, softer inspectors do not have a higher probability of leaving for a job in the industry.

The traditional capture and the revolving doors conjecture do not receive strong empirical support and evidence of regulatory capture based on reciprocity remain scarce and mainly inconclusive. Lack of support for direct capture means that either regulatory institutions are well designed and they effectively prevent capture by special interest groups or that capture takes another, possibly more pervasive, form. We have rejected the first hypothesis and we will now examine the second in more detail.

14.3   SOFT CAPTURE

14.3.1   The Mechanism of Soft Capture

We propose an alternative mechanism for regulatory capture that is not driven by reciprocity but by mutual interest. This mechanism, which we call soft capture, is both direct and legal and it is based on the production of biased information by the firm itself (see Agrell and Gautier, 2010, for a formal model). In the three-layer hierarchy, the regulator acts as an information gathering intermediate and production of information is costly. Now suppose that the regulator receives information from the firm. One option available to the regulator is to endorse the information produced by the regulated firm and present it to the decision maker. In this case, the resources normally devolved to information gathering can be used for another purpose such as monitoring compliance with the rules. A regulator that would use industry input saves resources: the staff that is not used to collect information and drafting reports can be used for other regulatory tasks. Regulators are thus likely to accept industry input as a substitute for in-house produced information. This can take many forms, from making its own an argument put forward by a consultancy financed by the industry to endorsing fully fledged sectorial regulation drafted by the industry itself.[14]

Voluntary disclosure of information by the firm might be strange and counterproductive in a context where the firm benefits from the lack of information of the deciding party. But the alternative consists in having the regulator gathering the information itself, a solution that could be even worse for the firm. Transmission of information to the regulator is a profitable alternative for the firm if (1) regulatory decisions are based on the firm input and (2) information is biased. This last condition is essential for the soft capture mechanism to work. Firms accept to produce and transmit information only if using this information for regulation benefits the firm. In other words, industry inputs must be systematically biased. Being regulated on the basis of information tailored to their need is much more profitable for the industry than being regulated on the basis of independent information. Thus the information transmitted by the firm to the regulator is necessarily biased. Disclosing true information on a voluntary basis would be foolish for firms as the key for successful regulation is access to information.

The soft capture mechanism thus works as follows. The regulated firm transmits biased information to the regulator, the latter endorses it and reports industry input to the decision maker. Regulation is ultimately based on information controlled by the firm rather than on information collected by an independent supervisor, which is beneficial to the firm. The mechanism is also profitable for the regulator that saves on information gathering costs. Moreover, accepting and endorsing industry produced information potentially reduces the conflicts between the regulator and the industry, a behavior that might be compatible with the minimal squawk behavior described by Leaver (2009).

Soft capture is not based on threats and rewards: both parties are better off if the regulator rubber-stamps the information produced by the firm instead of producing its own. The regulator comes to the political principal with information (as it is expected to do). The firm, if it transmits less precise information, increases its information rent. Hence, capture benefits both parties without requiring any form of side contracting nor side payments between parties. Thus, there is no smoking gun when the regulator is softly captured by the firm. For that reason, in Table 14.1, we classified soft capture as a direct and legal mechanism. Financing partisan research and development (R&D) is obviously not illegal and it is somehow beyond the control of the firm if a lazy regulator uses it instead of realizing its own research.

14.3.2   Implications for Regulatory Design

Even if in this mechanism the firm produces information for free and transmits it to the regulator, soft capture is damaging to the political principal and to welfare. Tolerated soft capture indeed decreases the quality of decision making because information is less precise and biased but it leaves unchanged the cost of gathering information. Producing detailed information for a regulatory purpose is profitable for the firm only if the alternative is a more stringent regulation based on the more precise information produced by the regulatory agency. Essential in this mechanism is the presence of the regulator as a 'threat' to extract the biased information from the firm. Should this threat disappear, the firm will no longer produce information.[15]

Maintaining a regulator, even if it only rubber-stamps the industry proposals, is essential to benefit from information for regulatory design. Absent the middle layer in the hierarchy, there is no information at all going from the industry to the top layer. Firms have incentives to softly capture the regulator only if the threat of an independent regulation is sufficiently powerful. When it occurs, soft capture leaves unchanged the cost of the supervision agency but it decreases the quality of information since firms introduce additional bias in their messages. Soft capture thus unambiguously decreases the welfare.

In a formal model of soft capture (Agrell and Gautier, 2010), we show that soft capture might be tolerated at the equilibrium if the quality of the biased information produced by the firm is high enough relative to the quality of information (potentially) produced by the regulator. This implies that the importance of the bias introduced by the firm is directly linked to the treat exerted by the regulator. An understaffed regulator with limited capabilities for gathering and processing information is likely to receive considerably biased industry input. Conversely, a regulator that is able to produce high-quality information, which is highly damaging for the firm's rent, is likely to receive more accurate information (but still biased) from the firm. Maintaining high-level regulators remains important even if the political principal may tolerate capture and participation of the industry in the regulatory process. When the threat exerted by the regulator is not strong enough, the industry may be able to provide information that, at the end, leads to an ineffective regulation.

Facing this form of capture, it is thus essential to have highly skilled regulators. Even if the regulator remains 'a regulator in being,' it forces the firm to produce not too biased information. Multiplying and diversifying the sources of information might be another path to prevent capture. If it is known that regulators are likely to accept cooperative inputs from the industry, additional sources of information might turn out to be useful. Guerriero (2011) documents that rate reviews for regulated US electricity distributors are organized as quasi-judicial hearings where all the interested parties (firms, customers, and so on) have the opportunity to bring information to the Public Utility Commission (PUC). Rate reviews are thus less dependent on the regulator's ability to gather information from the industry. Parties are thus advocates of their interest and multiple sources of biased information may mitigate the problem created by capture.[16]

14.4   AN ILLUSTRATIVE EXAMPLE

The OSHA is responsible for the regulation, monitoring, and enforcement of workplace health and safety in the USA under the Occupational Safety and Health Act of 1970. The economic and social importance of the regulation is paramount, directly affecting about 130 million employees in the USA (in 2010) and the workplace conditions, routines, and equipment at about nine million establishments (in 2009). Despite its importance, the literature only lists a single case of attempted corruption of OSHA inspectors (*US v. Chmielewski*, 1999), the amount of which was modest ($2000).

However, the regulatory endowment has remained constant or even slightly decreased in absolute terms (–12 percent in staff FTE between 1975 and 2009), whereas the numbers of employees and establishments to monitor have increased by 90 percent and 128 percent, respectively. As seen in Figure 14.2, the number of establishments to be regulated vastly outnumbers the staff, radically increasing the potential workload.

The development of new regulations at OSHA is de facto based on re-editing of material as 'national consensus standards,' developed by 'trade or professional associations for the practices, systems, processes, or raw materials of their members' (Hamilton, 1978, note 13). The independent

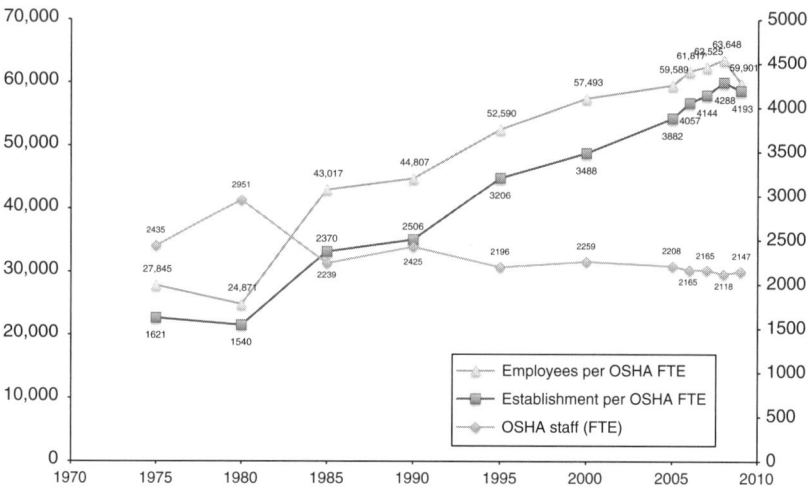

Source: OSHA (2011) and BLS (2005–11).

Figure 14.2   OSHA staff (FTE), employees under OSHA regulation per OSHA staff (FTE), establishments under OSHA regulation per OSHA staff (FTE)

development of safety standards at OSHA is infrequent (two new standards promulgated between 1992 and 2000) and slow (four to seven years, cf. Shapiro and Rabinowitz, 2000). Regulatory rule making in occupational safety at OSHA is based on three analysis steps: determination of significant risk, technological feasibility analysis, and economic feasibility analysis. Given the weak resources for data collection, the initial step is often delayed or ineffective, potentially through the allocation of inspections to sites. The economic analysis is largely based on information provided by regulated firms or industry associations, in essence private standards that are forwarded to be promulgated as regulatory standards.

The underlying information has been found to be systematically biased in an evaluation made by the US Congress (1995), implying adopted standards have more generous thresholds for employers and lower requirements for detection and abatement. For example, in the standards for Vinyl Chloride (4 October 1974, 39 FR 35890), OSHA relied on industry consultants' estimate of $1000 million in compliance costs. Actual spending on equipment and incremental operating cost is around $228–278 million (US Congress, 1995). The report documents similar findings for the exposure regulations for cotton dust, lead, ethylene oxide, and formaldehyde, as well as for the operating regulations for grain handling, mechanical power presses, and powered platforms for building maintenance. In addition, the technical feasibility analysis overestimates the time and number of instances affected by changes, hampering any application. The resulting regulations are not only weaker than those of international counterparts, they are also considerably more difficult to enforce by the regulator. An example for the OSHA enforcement: from 85,539 safety violations in 2003, only 404 were considered 'willful' and eligible for the highest criminal sanctions (Barstow, 2003). The outcome is striking: from a reported 2197 workplace fatalities in 1982–2002, 1242 were investigated by OSHA, thereof finally referring 119 cases for legal prosecution, resulting in nine convictions to prison for the employer. Most investigations were dropped already at reporting, the rest from ambiguities in the regulation (Barstow, 2003). The resulting dismal enforcement record of OSHA, combined with very moderate fines[17] for 'willful' violations of the standards, renders the regulator relatively harmless to the regulated sector.

It is important to note that the highest officer in OSHA, the Assistant Secretary of Labor for Occupational Safety and Health, unlike the administration's staff, is directly appointed by the President and does not benefit from the stature of a civil servant. This specific condition allows a casual test of the 'revolving door' hypothesis, as the direct capture could be exercised by the submitting bodies through later employment in, for example, associations or employers' organizations. However, the evidence is inconclusive: only two of the 12 past Assistant Secretaries since the creation of OSHA have obtained managerial positions in private industry, with five remaining in public service or research (OSHA, 2009). Further, detailed analysis of the rulings from OSHA reveals that the 'soft capture' had already occurred after a few years of existence and was well established in 1978 (Hamilton, 1978). Hence, the continued state of 'soft capture' in OSHA could be seen more as a structural response to a situation where the political endorsement of the regulatory activity is low or uncertain in combination with low independence of the regulatory supervisor. It seems plausible that the regulatory function of OSHA could have been implemented more effectively with similar federal staff numbers if redirected to regulatory design and monitoring and enforcement were left to civil enforcement.[18] However, faced with the prospects of confronting industry with stringent labor regulations and potentially large civil lawsuits, the regulators seem to prefer the self-enforcing industry endorsement in the regulatory design stage while maintaining a relatively undisputed (yet ineffective) monitoring activity as the visible information processing to the political principal.

It remains to be determined whether the 'soft capture' in this case is welfare decreasing. Although the USA naturally benefits from the same occupational safety development as in the rest of the industrialized world,

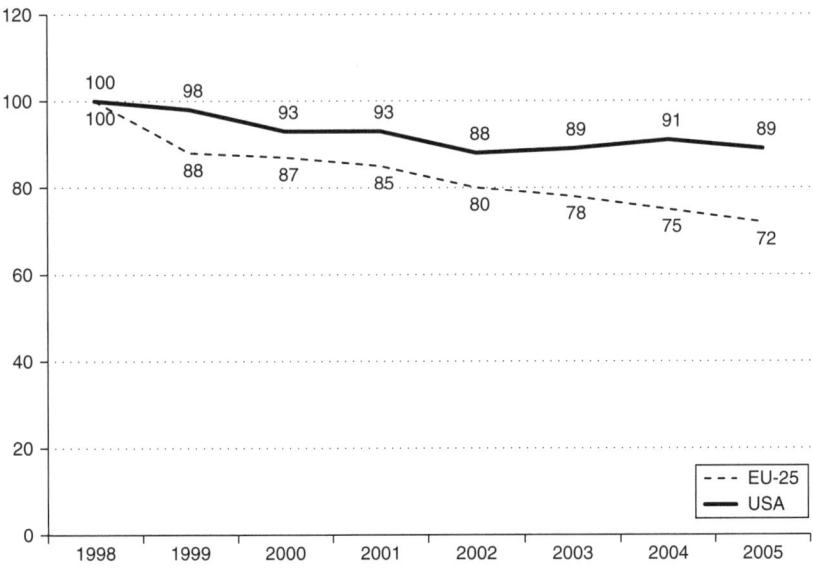

Source: AFL-CIO (2011, p. 72), and EUROSTAT (2011).

*Figure 14.3   Development of the number of fatal workplace accidents per
100,000 employees in the USA and EU-25, 1998 = 100*

data shows (Figure 14.3) that the improvement rate in 1998–2007 was
slower than for a comparative market, EU-25, and stagnated at the end of
the period. The absolute level of fatal accidents per 100,000 employees was
also higher than in EU-25, indicating a continuing problem.

14.5   CONCLUDING REMARKS

Regulatory capture is a composite phenomenon that has multiple expressions and causes. In this chapter we address a specific type, direct legal
capture by the regulated firm, that we claim to be one of the most common
scenarios. Our relatively intuitive model of 'soft capture' is based on self-
enforced collusion between the firm, providing biased information for
free, and the regulator, using this information in its regulation rather than
providing costly internal information processing. It differs from the conventional models of capture in the set-up and the empirical conclusions.

First, whereas the conventional model assumes that the regulator
is offered a monetary award in exchange for blocking information

transmission to the political principal, our model is based on a congruence of interests without side contracting and with information processing in equilibrium.

Second, the positive conjectures resulting from the conventional theories would either predict full capture in the presence of generalized transfers of information rents to the regulators or implementation of collusion-proof mechanisms based on delegation of welfare objectives to the regulator.

Our model predicts a prevalence of soft capture in equilibrium without rent transfer but with transfer of processed information from firms to the regulator. The damages caused by capture are proportional to the cost of information processing for the regulators (or reciprocally, the precision they can obtain for a given budget). The industry is indeed likely to transmit more biased information or more favorable proposals when the regulator has a low capacity to process information by itself.

An analysis of the OSHA, a major federal regulatory agency in the USA, confirms the positive conjectures of our model while no evidence is found for the two conventional conjectures. OSHA operates a regulation where the rule-making is largely done using industry-based material that is biased and results in instructions with weak enforcement power. The regulator has maintained a constant budget since its conception and its resources are foremost devoted to monitoring at the expense of regulation and enforcement. No evidence of high-level corruption, nor of revolving doors between firms and the regulator, has been found. Hence, we have at hand an example of soft capture. Qualitatively, lowered information processing costs, for example, by higher endowment in qualified staff or budgets for external independent experts, would result in lower incidence of soft capture, detected as a more stringent regulation and higher enforcement precision.

The previous 'paradox of capture' has thus found one possible explanation along with several empirically verifiable hypotheses. Further empirical work about regulatory capture, both longitudinal and across sectors, is necessary to fully validate this and alternative models in understanding this socially important phenomenon.

An interesting extension of the model can be made in the case of direct capture by other stakeholders, such as downstream clients, since the regulator merely reacts to submitted information from any source. Although the authors ignore such examples in actual regulatory practice in Europe, plausibly due to problems of information asymmetry and internal cost allocation within the stakeholder collective, the previously mentioned US-type intervenor process at the Public Utility Commissions is analogous. In this manner, an 'information contest' between advocates representing different interest groups might be a more effective way to collect information than a single source of information captured by the industry.[19]

The example notwithstanding, there is no claim of generality emanating from the model. Both the literature (cf. Makkai and Braithwaite, 1992) and the anecdotal evidence above suggest that the relations between the political principal and the supervisor, the independence given to the latter and the implication of the former in the decision making are important in understanding the internal and external functioning of regulation. In particular, for the OSHA case, the implicit acceptance by the political principal (US Government) of the soft capture over a longer time period constitutes, without ever becoming an official endorsement, an indication of indirect capture rigged by the political principal and the regulated firm. Moreover the methodological complexities involved in empirically estimating the overall welfare effects of regulatory capture, yet alone sector regulation and its means, are significant and hamper comparative analysis.

NOTES

1. Note that even if the regulator is endowed with some decisional power, like the right to set a price-cap level, many regulatory tasks remain in the hands of the political power: decisions regarding industrial structure, organization and financing of universal service obligations, the industry safety regulation, the quality regulation, the access regulation in network industries, the procedure to allocate new licenses (for instance, for the 4G cellular technology), to cite a few.
2. Industry regulation encompasses many dimensions such as economic, product, technical, quality, safety, or environmental regulation of sectors and/or natural monopolies.
3. Ministries, other branches of government, legislature, and so on.
4. Notwithstanding, many regulatory authorities have explicit regulations limiting or delaying employment of authority staff in regulated firms, as well as their use of information obtained through their service in the authority. None of these regulations can be said to effectively block the revolving door concerns.
5. A regulatory process is immune to capture when side contracting is non-profitable for the parties. Often, it requires the use of specific incentive schemes for the regulatory intermediate to align its objective with those of the political principal.
6. Note that the difficulty does not primarily reside in the data collection, as the direct capture referred to here only concerns the highest responsible decision maker (the tenured 'regulator'). Bribing subordinate staff to obtain favors is ineffective as the regulatory authorities in both theory and practice organize the internal bureaucracy through limited discretion, job rotation, and team assignments in order to limit the time and depth of repeated industry interaction.
7. In reality, most regulators are civil servants with fixed salaries that are publicly known and under restrictions concerning complementary economic activities.
8. Regulated firms have the legal obligation to transmit data to the regulator. Here we do not consider data transmission but information that has already been processed by the regulated firm such as cost assessments, suggested technical regulations, or methodologies to benchmark industry performance.
9. We disregard the (hypothetical) case of an altruistic firm, for example, under public ownership. First, empirical evidence suggests that such firms frequently are more inefficient than private firms without taking voluntary action. Second, the managers of the public firm may pursue non-altruistic objectives such as budget maximization or effort minimization, but that are consistent with the empirical evidence and refusal to submit

unbiased information. Third, even if there were no internal incentive problems, a rational altruistic firm would not provide unbiased information processing below cost.

10. When the firm transmits information to the regulator, the latter remains the sole source of information for the political principal. Should the firm transmit its information directly to the political principal, it would have two sources of information and it would be able to improve its knowledge of the industry.

11. In most of the models of capture, side contracting is costly meaning that, when the firm pays $1 to the regulator, the latter has less than (the equivalent of) $1 in its pocket. Transaction cost of side contracting reduces the possibility of capture.

12. An exception could be the election of regulators that are thus responsible to the voters (see Guerriero, 2011).

13. Thatcher (2002) provides evidence of the importance of the revolving doors phenomena in selected European countries.

14. In 2001 the Swedish Energy Markets Inspectorate endorsed a detailed voluntary service regulation for the quality of electricity distribution, developed by the sector association.

15. This effect is analogous to the results obtained in lobbying models (cf. Austen-Smith and Wright, 1992): a lobbyist would only invest in costly information transmission provided the regulator enjoys a sufficiently low cost of independent information acquisition, or else the message would be discarded by default as non-informative.

16. Dewatripont and Tirole (1999).

17. The monetary fines have been increased once during 1971–2010. The maximum fine for 'willful' violation of safety standards, potentially leading to death of employees is $7000. The maximum penalty for death caused by willful negligence of workplace safety is $70,000. The average OSHA penalty is $1000; normally even deadly accidents receive small penalties (median initial penalty claimed by OSHA for accidents with death involved was $5700 in 2007) (Testimony by Assistant Secretary David Michels to the US House of Representatives, 16 March 2010).

18. Currently the case for environmental regulation, for example, the Clean Water Act.

19. Dewatripont and Tirole (1999) show that even a non-partisan independent agent may be less effective for collecting information than competing advocates.

REFERENCES

AFL-CIO (2011), *Death of the Job: A National and State-by-state Profile of Worker Safety and Health in the United States*, 20th edn, Washington, DC: American Federation of Labor and Congress of Industrial Organizations.

Agrell, P.J. and A. Gautier (2010), 'A theory of soft capture', Discussion Paper 2010/84, CORE, Université catholique de Louvain.

Austen-Smith, D. and J. Wright (1992), 'Competitive lobbying for a legislator's vote', *Social Choice and Welfare*, **9**(3), 229–57.

Barstow, D. (2003), 'U.S. rarely seeks charges for deaths in workplace', *New York Times*, 22 December.

BLS (2005–11), 'Bureau of Labor Statistics occupational injuries and illnesses report for the years 1994–2010', available at http://www.bls.gov/iif (accessed November 2011).

Che, Y.-K. (1995), 'Revolving doors and the optimal tolerance for agency collusion', *RAND Journal of Economics*, **26**(3), 378–97.

Dal Bó, E. (2006), 'Regulatory capture: a review', *Oxford Journal of Economic Policy*, **22**(2), 203–25.

Dewatripont, M. and J. Tirole (1999), 'Advocates', *Journal of Political Economy*, **107**(1), 1–39.

Estache, A. and L. Wren-Lewis (2011), 'Anti-corruption policy in theories of sector regulation', in S. Rose-Ackerman and T. Soreide (eds), *The International Handbook of Anti-corruption Economics*, Vol. II, Cheltenham, UK and Northampton, MA, USA: Edward Elgar Publishing, pp. 269–99.

EUROSTAT (2011), 'Fatal accidents at work', statistics available at http://epp.eurostat.ec.europa.eu/ (accessed November 2011).

Guerriero, C. (2011), 'Accountability in government and regulatory policies: theory and evidence', *Journal of Comparative Economics*, **39**, 453–69.

Hamilton, R.W. (1978), 'The role of nongovernmental standards in the development of mandatory federal standards affecting safety or health', *Texas Law Review*, **56**(8), 1329–66.

Laffont, J.-J. and J. Tirole (1991), 'The politics of government decision-making: a theory of regulatory capture', *Quarterly Journal of Economics*, **106**(4), 1089–127.

Laffont, J.-J. and J. Tirole (1993), *A Theory of Incentives in Procurement and Regulation*, Cambridge, MA: MIT Press.

Leaver, C. (2009), 'Bureaucratic minimal squawk behavior: theory and evidence from regulatory agencies', *American Economic Review*, **99**(3), 572–607.

Makkai, T. and J. Braithwaite (1992), 'In and out of the revolving door: making sense of regulatory capture', *Journal of Public Policy*, **12**(1), 61–78.

Martimort, D. (1999), 'The life cycle of regulatory agencies: dynamic capture and transaction costs', *Review of Economic Studies*, **66**(4), 929–47.

OSHA (2009), 'Reflections on OSHA's history', US Department of Labor, Occupational Safety and Health Administration (OSHA).

OSHA (2011), 'FY 2012 Congressional Budget justification: Occupational Safety and Health Administration', Washington, DC: US Department of Labor, Occupational Safety and Health Administration (OSHA).

Salant, D. (1995), 'Behind the revolving doors: a new view on public utility regulation', *RAND Journal of Economics*, **26**(3), 362–77.

Shapiro, S.A. and R. Rabinowitz (2000), 'Voluntary regulatory compliance in theory and practice: the case of OSHA', *Administrative Law Review*, **52**(1), 97–155.

Smith, R. and M. Söderberg (2010), 'Public interest versus regulatory capture in the Swedish electricity market', *Journal of Regulatory Economics*, **38**(3), 292–312.

Thatcher, M. (2002), 'Regulation after delegation: independent regulatory agencies in Europe', *Journal of European Public Policy*, **9**(6), 954–72

Tirole, J. (1986), 'Hierarchies and bureaucracies: on the role of capture in organizations', *Journal of Law and Economic Organization*, **2**(2), 181–214.

US Congress (1995), *Gauging Control Technology and Regulatory Impacts in Occupational Safety and Health: An Appraisal of OSHA's Analytic Approach*, Report OTA-ENV-635, Washington, DC: Office of Technology Assessment.

US v. Chmielewski (1999), Case No. 99-1773 in US Court of Appeals, 7th Circuit, F. 3d, Vol. 196, 893.

15. Can structural models be useful to understand the electricity wholesale markets? An application to Spain

Vítor Marques, Adelino Fortunato and Isabel Soares[1]

15.1 INTRODUCTION

The aim of this study is to analyse the behaviour of agents in the Spanish electricity market during the period January 1999 to June 2007 before the Iberian electricity market was started. Our main questions are:

- Did market power occur?
- What kind of long-term strategies have been adopted?

The analysis is carried out in the framework of structural models. This framework is based on the causal relationships between related variables, explained by economic theory. They are, in general terms, expressed by the resolution of a system of equations, thus implying economic equilibrium. Structural models provide a heuristic approach about market economic relationships and they also allow for the answer to other questions, namely the calculation of the price elasticity of demand.

Section 15.2 presents the organization of the Spanish wholesale market. The methodological approaches are presented in Section 15.3. This section includes the survey of the various methodological approaches, and presents the particularities used: the research is carried out through the structural model methodology, and the results are confronted with the direct estimations of the main variables. The structural model has two equations, one for demand and another for profit. The price elasticity of demand is estimated in Section 15.4 through the first equation. The behavioural factor is estimated in Section 15.5 through the profit maximization function. Section 15.6 concludes.

15.2   FRAMEWORK

The former Spanish wholesale market is a Uniform Price Auction (UPA) market. In these markets, the generator that sells the marginal quantity defines the system marginal price. This price is paid each hour to all producers with accepted bids. This market presents a strong regulatory framework. The main regulatory drivers were the stranded costs compensations (CTC) (from 1998 (Ley 54/1997), until 2006 (Real Decreto-ley 7/2006), with a decreasing influence in producers' income over this period).

This market was highly concentrated. Endesa and Iberdrola represented about three-quarters of the supply in the wholesale market. But their importance tended to decrease (75 per cent in 2002 and 60 per cent in 2006).

15.3   METHODOLOGICAL ASPECTS

15.3.1   The Games

The market for power generation is very much like a market with Cournot strategies and capacity constraints (Kreps and Scheinkman, 1983). Within this framework, the quantities correspond to the decision variable. Even when the price is assumed as a strategical variable, the results of the strategies are similar to the Cournot game due to the capacity constraints in that kind of market (see Wolak and Patrick, 1997). Starting with the Nash-Cournot solution and reprising the Cowling-Waterson formula (1976), the Lerner index and the strategies developed by companies can be correlated using the θ^2 index:[3]

$$\frac{(P - \overline{Cmg})}{P} = \frac{\overline{\theta}HHI}{|\varepsilon|} = \lambda, \qquad (15.1)$$

in which $\overline{Cmg}$ is the weighted marginal cost for the industry, HHI the Herfindahl-Hirschman index and λ the factor measuring the level of market power, that is, which corresponds to the Lerner index. In this case, the Lerner index is directly related to the level of concentration and also related to the firms' conjectural variations. In this context, if $\overline{\theta} = 1/HHI$, perfect collusion is verified; when $\overline{\theta} = 1$, Cournot behaviour is verified; and, finally, when $\overline{\theta} = 0$, a perfectly competitive market prevails.

The interpretation of the producers' behaviour done through the conjectural variation methodology presents some particularities. The conjectural variation methodology is a static methodology in which agents act according to expectations regarding the dynamic responses of competitors. Notwithstanding, this methodology can be applied in the present case because the 'games' that occur each hour in a UPA market, like the former Spanish wholesale market, are similar to a repeated game (see Fabra and Toro, 2005). And, as referred to in Perloff et al. (2007, p. 109): 'the theory of repeated games provides a game-theoretic basis for estimating static market conduct for conjectural variation models'.

The issues relating to the interpretation of the value deserve special attention.

15.3.2 The Structural Model

On the basis of the structural models, equilibrium exists in which the economic agents maximise their economic profits taking the demand and cost function into account.

In our case, the chosen model corresponds to the system of equations of monthly demand and supply, in the Spanish wholesale spot market (daily and intra-day) for the specified period. Therefore, the application of the structural model materializes in this present case in the resolution of the following system:

$$\begin{cases} Q_t = \alpha_1 + \gamma P_t + \varphi Z_t P_t + \beta Z_t + \sum_{i=1}^{n} \beta_i D_{ti} + u_{t1} \\ P_t = \alpha_2 + \sum_{j=1}^{m} \beta_j W_{tj} - \theta(\gamma + \varphi Z_t) Q_t + u_{t2}, \end{cases} \tag{15.2}$$

where:

- t, is the time factor related to the month.
- Z_t, is the exogenous variable that allows the demand function to change its slope,

that is, which allow to rotate.

- D_{ti} are explicative variables of the demand function.
- W_{tj}, are exogenous explicative marginal cost variables.
- θ, is the behavioural parameter, interpreted through the conjectural variation methodology: between 0 (Bertrand or perfect competitive strategy) and $1/HHI$ (perfect collusion).

Finally, so as to be able to estimate the Lerner index λ, we apply the following equation based on the derivative of the second equation:

$$\frac{\overline{\theta} HHI}{|\varepsilon|} = \lambda. \tag{15.3}$$

It is important to note that the need to estimate exogenous explicative variables, in the majority of cases underlying economic relations, meant that monthly data had to be used, naturally focussing on the analysis of medium- and long-term equilibriums and strategies.

In order to identify separately the cost component from the strategic component, we have to choose a variable that rotates the demand function in the face of an external shock rather than moving in parallel: $\theta(\gamma + \varphi Z_t)$, Z_t being the rotation variable.

15.3.3   A Model Extension

It has to be highlighted that this methodology was tardily used in wholesale electricity markets (Wolfram, 1999; Hjalmarsson, 2000) due to the fact that assumptions (functional form, economical model, among others) constrain the results (Corts, 1989).

This is the reason why it was given particular attention to the knowledge of the analysed market and to the definition of control methods. Therefore, we use data that makes it possible to estimate with some accuracy the marginal cost incurred. This allows the application of the structural model to obtain market power and to test for the behavioural variable, comparing the results with an almost direct estimate of these variables. Parallel to this, following the work of Genesove and Mullin (1998), the estimation of the price elasticity of demand based on a linear demand function is tested. The demand function is not only expressed as a linear functional form but also expressed as three other functional forms (logarithmic, exponential and quadratic).

Subsequently, the following regression is solved, based on the Lerner index, in order to estimate the behaviour factor λ:

$$P_t = \frac{cmg_t}{(-\lambda + 1)} + \mu_{t4}, \tag{15.4}$$

in which cmg_t represents the marginal cost (that we estimate as an external variable) for month t.

In order to estimate θ, Equation (15.5) is applied:

$$\theta = \frac{|\varepsilon|}{HHI}\lambda. \tag{15.5}$$

15.3.4   A Brief Description of the Market Organization

OMEL[4] is the operator of the wholesale market, which is divided into the daily and the intraday market. In the daily market, the electricity producers submit bids to sell quantities of electricity on an hourly basis for the day after at a minimum price and buyers (distributors, retailers and eligible consumers) submit hourly bids to buy electricity at a maximum price.

The publication of Royal Decree 5/2005 ended the obligation to transact all energy in the market regime on the wholesale market.

In the intraday market the final calculations are made in order to adjust supply and demand. Another source of income for producers comes from compensation for the availability of declared production.

The final price of the electricity traded on the wholesale market, before distribution, comes mainly from the daily and intraday markets that represent 70 per cent to 80 per cent of this price, respectively.

15.3.5 Definition of the Demand Function

Variables of the demand function

Diesel consumption was chosen as the independent variable for the price of electricity because it better reflects the characteristics of the economic activity in Spain in recent years. In addition, the seasonal nature of this variable is very similar to that of electricity consumption. The trend for the consumption of gas, oil and electricity developed in a parallel manner up to February 2006, although diesel fuel consumption appears more volatile.

Electricity and diesel fuel growth rate consumption were higher than growth rate of gross domestic product (GDP) due to the increased purchasing power in Spain and from the absence of any change in the productive structure (Mendiluce et al., 2009). Moreover, some studies have shown that consumption of diesel in Spain evolved differently from that of other fuels, with a much lower price elasticity of demand, a characteristic which it shares with electricity consumption (González-Marrero et al., 2008).

Two variables were chosen reflecting the annual seasonal nature of electricity demand: the number of overnight stays in hotels and monthly temperature difference in comparison with the average monthly figures. In the structural model the last variable was used to 'rotate' the demand function.

The doubts raised by the introduction of this variable led to the use of the Wald test for the deletion of the model explanatory variables, proving that there is a relationship between the variables 'Overnight Stays' and 'Temperature Difference'.

The variables chosen for the electricity demand equation in the daily and intraday markets are:

- Number of overnight stays in hotels each month, 'Overnight Stays'.
- Difference between the average monthly temperature and annual average temperature, 'Temperature Difference'.

- Diesel fuel consumed in each month, 'Diesel'.
- Amount of electricity traded in the daily and intraday markets each month, 'Amount of Electricity'.
- Average price of electricity traded in the daily and intraday markets each month, 'Electricity Price'.

In addition to these variables, a dummy variable must also be considered, which represents the change in the regulatory framework for these markets.

Stationarity of demand function
The stationarity of each variable is tested using the Augmented Dick Fuller (ADF) unit root test, with the order of the test chosen by taking into account the combined analysis of Akaike and Schwartz information criteria.

Seasonal variations are analysed without trend, whilst the remainder are analysed with trend. Given its specific nature, the price variable is analysed with and without trend.

The variables are characterized as follows in terms of integration:

- 'Amount of Electricity' and 'Price of Electricity' are I (1).
- 'Diesel', 'Temperature Difference' and 'Overnight Stays' are I (0).

Since there are two variables I (1) in the model, the stationarity analysis is carried out through testing the existence of a co-integration relationship.

The test for the existence of a co-integration relationship between the variables follows Johansen's methodology (Johansen, 1988).

The statistics[5] enable the H0 hypothesis of the non-existence of a co-integration relationship to be rejected, meaning that the H0 hypothesis for the existence of more than one co-integration relationship also cannot be accepted. Thus, one can consider that the variables 'Price of Electricity' and 'Amount of Electricity' are co-integrated, that is, $Q_t - P_t \sim I(0)$. How those variables can be co-integrated when in the short and medium term the electricity demand and its price varies inversely? The reason is that in the long term, those variables increase proportionally: the demand for electricity has been satisfied by recourse to more expensive production technologies or by conventional fossil fuel technologies that have tended to become more expensive due to the fossil fuel limited reserves.

Instrumental variable
Once the variables incorporated in the demand models have been defined, it is important to ensure the orthogonality of the model. A test for

endogeneity was held in the first equation, since different variables underscored an economic relationship with one another, 'Electricity Price', 'Overnight Stays' and 'Diesel'. 'Temperature Difference' was considered as an exogenous variable.

Moreover, in structural models identification requires compliance with the rank condition. An initial group of instrumental variables must be constituted which respect to the following restrictions: on the one hand, they must not be correlated with the 'Amount of Electricity' dependent variable in the first equation, but with 'Electricity Price'. On the other hand, they will include the exogenous variables in the second equation (see Reiss and Wolak, 2005). The following variables were defined in this group:

- The average monthly price (euros/bbl) of Brent crude 'Oil Price', with three-month lags.
- The average monthly price (euros/t) of coal 'Coal Price', with three- and 12-months lags.
- The average monthly hydroelectrical productivity, 'Hydro'.

In the section related to the definition of the second equation, the reasons for choosing those variables are explained.

A second group of instrumental variables was defined, related to diesel consumption. We chose the instrumental variables that capture the seasonality and the economic activity:

- The 'Diesel' consumption, with 12-month lags.
- The monthly trend for the industrial production index, 'Industrial Production', and the estimated monthly GDP, 'GDP'.

The inclusion of instrumental variables with lags allows us to consider the short-term adjustments, thus taking into account the dynamic nature of the model. The results of the statistical T_2 Wu-Hausman test reject the hypothesis of the non-endogeneity of the model.

Even outside the theoretical framework of structural models, the confirmed existence of endogeneity in the demand function requires the application of the Two-Stage Least Square method. The instrumental variables chosen are those previously referred to.

Bearing in mind the significant number of instrumental variables, the overestimation of the model was tested. The results allowed us not to reject the null hypothesis of all the instrumental variables being exogenous.

15.3.6   The Demand Function in the Structural Model Content

Two events characterized the wholesale electricity market during the period under analysis: the introduction of combined cycle natural gas plants in 2004 and the various changes in legislation that led to a sharp fall in the amounts of electricity traded since March 2006.

Thus, in the application of the structural model as in the other case, the models were tested over four separate periods: January 1999 to June 2007; January 1999 to February 2006; January 1999 to December 2003; January 2004 to June 2007.

The impact of the changes in the framework of the daily and intraday markets since March 2006 onwards is analysed with the inclusion of a dummy variable.

The 'rotation' variable is the 'Temperature Difference' variable.

Therefore, based on Equation (15.2) and assuming a linear demand function, the demand function will be given by (model 1):

$$Q_t = \alpha + \beta_1 P_t + \beta_2 \text{Diesel}_t + \beta_3 \text{DifTemp}_t + \beta_4 \text{Stays}_t + \beta_5 \text{DifTemp}_t P_t + \varepsilon_t, \tag{15.6}$$

where:

- Q_t is 'Amount of Electricity' variable in the month t.
- P_t is 'Electricity Price' variable in the month t.
- Diesel_t is 'Diesel' variable in the month t.
- DifTemp_t is 'Temperature Difference' variable in the month t.
- Dorm_t is 'Overnight Stays' variable in the month t.

However, most of the variables are not significant when the model is presented in this way. Thus, we opted for a model in which the variable 'Temperature Difference' is only included as a rotation variable (model 2):

$$Q = \alpha + \beta_{1a} P_t + \beta_{2a} \text{Diesel}_t + \beta_{3a} \text{Stays}_t + \beta_{4a} \text{DifTemp}_t P_t + \varepsilon_t. \tag{15.7}$$

The chosen model is shaded in grey in Table 15.1. The analyses beyond December 2003 do not present significant results. This is not surprising given that since 2004 the framework of the Spanish electricity market has changed several times, and the market could not be considered, even in a long-term perspective, as being in equilibrium.

The structural model is then applied to 'model 2' for the period between January 1999 and December 2003.

Table 15.1 Comparison of the results of the regression 'models 1 and 2' (January 1999 to December 2003)

	Model 1		Model 2	
	Estimate	t test (Prob.)	Estimate	t test (Prob.)
Constant	3620.7	0.1803 (0.858)	874.3508	0.31121 (0.757)
P_t	−1298.1	−0.3188 (0.751)	−735.5126	−3.1054 (0.003)
$Dorm_t$	4.9648	0.7977 (0.430)	5.6684	1.7674 (0.084)
$Diesel_t$	0.0064399	2.3929 (0.021)	0.0067753	6.4709 (0.000)

From Equation (15.7) two parameters were obtained that are essential for the model as a whole: the inverse of the slope of demand function and the price elasticity of demand. The second parameter stems from the following equation:

$$\frac{\frac{dQ_t}{dP_t}}{\frac{Q_t}{P_t}} = (\beta_1 + \beta_4 \overline{DifTemp}) \frac{\overline{P}}{\overline{Q}}, \tag{15.8}$$

in which $\overline{P/Q}$, is the ratio of the average market prices and quantities traded and $\overline{DifTemp}$, is the average temperature differences. In this case,

$$\frac{\frac{dQ_t}{dp_t}}{\frac{Q_t}{P_t}} = -0.0933.$$

15.3.7 Price Elasticity of Demand Inside and Outside the Structural Model

The demand function is defined outside the structural model in the *sensu stricto*. The functional forms considered in the work of Genesove and Mullin (1998) are presented (linear, exponential, quadratic and exponential). The equations were adapted in order to take into account independent variables other than price.

The general functional form is given by Equation (15.9):

$$Q_{t(p)} = \beta(\alpha \quad P_t)^\gamma \mid \varepsilon_t, \tag{15.9}$$

in which β measures the size of the market demand, α is the maximum willingness to pay, P_t is the price and γ is the convexity index. α tends to infinity and γ/α is a constant.

Results

As in the previous section, the results were only considered whenever the level of significance of the variable price is equal to or less than 5 per cent. For each case, the selection criterion is the degree of significance of the variable 'Price Electricity'.[6]

The figures for the different functional forms are similar, between –0.089 and –0.099. The value calculated for the structural model with a linear equation falls within this interval.

Those values are close to the values generally associated with the elasticity of demand in the electricity sector, around 10 per cent (see Borenstein et al., 1999 or Patrick and Wolak, 1997). For the Spanish electricity sector, and also for hourly data, García-Alcalde et al. (2002) defined 3 per cent as the average elasticity of demand in 1998, and Kühn and Machado (2004) estimated that the elasticity of demand was between 1.5 per cent and 9 per cent in 2001.

15.4   OPTIMAL EQUATION

Due to problems of identification, the optimal equation must include the demand rotation component. Thus, the second equation of the system (15.2) has the following representation:

$$P_t = \alpha_2 + \sum_{j=1}^{n} \beta_j Cmg_j + \beta_8 Q_t - \lambda \left(\frac{1}{(\beta_1 + \beta_4 DifTemp)} \right) Q_t + \varepsilon_t.$$

(15.10)

The Cmg_j variables represent the factors required to calculate the marginal cost. The last variable is the rotation variable for the demand function whose parameters were defined solving the demand equation. The coefficient of this variable corresponds to the behavioural variable. The marginal cost of the system is defined by the production costs of the power plant, which define the closing price of the market.

The power plants with conventional technologies that set the closing price are the coal and fuel oil power plants, natural gas combined cycle power plants and hydro plants. Thus, the variables chosen to estimate the average marginal cost of the system are:

- The average monthly price, euros/bbl, of Brent oil with a three-month lag, which represents the cost of natural gas combined cycle power plants and the cost of fuel oil power plants. It is common practice for natural gas supply contracts to index their prices to the

price of oil or its derivatives, with time lags between three and six months.
- For coal power plants, the monthly average price of coal with a three-month lag, euros/t, in order to reflect the stock management policy.
- Hydro coefficient.

The last variables are exogenous to the model, having been included as instrumental variables in the previous equation. We chose variables that are directly related to a theoretical system marginal cost because this is not necessarily the real marginal cost incurred. In practice, the marginal cost of the system will also depend on technical constraints and company strategies. These factors should be inclu ded into the behavioural variable λ. Thus, Equation (15.10) can be rewritten as follows:

$$P_t = \alpha_2 + \beta_5 Oil_{t-3} + \beta_6 Coal_{t-3} + \beta_7 Hydr_t$$
$$+ \beta_8 Q_t - \overline{\theta}\left(\frac{1}{(\beta_1 + \beta_4 DifTemp)}\right)Q_t + \varepsilon_t, \qquad (15.11)$$

where:

- Oil_{t-3} is the average monthly price of Brent crude lagged three months.
- $Coal_{t-3}$ is the average monthly Coal API # 2 NW Europe lagged three months.
- $Hydr_t$ is the hydro inflows in the month t.
- $\overline{\theta}$ is the behavioural variable.

15.4.1 Stationarity of the Supply Equation

The ADF test perfomed pointed out that 'Hydro Index Inflows' is the only stationary variable that defines the marginal cost.

The variable prices of oil and coal are integrated of order 1. Using the Johansen approach, and a value-at-risk (VAR) model of order 1, as indicated by the information criteria, the statistics[7] allow the rejection of the H0 hypotheses for the non-existence of one and two co-integration relationships, and point out that the H0 hypothesis for the existence of more than two co-integration relationships cannot be accepted.

Thus, two co-integration vectors exist that support the relationship already demonstrated between the price and amount of electricity variables $P_t - Q_t \sim I(0)$; as well as the co-integration relationship between coal and oil prices: $Oil_{t-3} - Coal_{t-3} \sim I(0)$.

Table 15.2   Chosen regression

	January 1999–December 2003		January 1999–December 2003	
	Coefficient	T-ratio (Prob.)	Coefficient	T-ratio (Prob.)
Constant	−4.5369	−0.75148 (0.457)	0.81635	−1.9208 (0.061)
Oil price (−3)	0.010074	0.2825 (0.779)	−0.039856	−1.9571 (0.054)
Coal price (−3)	0.049354	0.3497 (0.728)	0.14786	4.8609 (0.000)
Hydro	−2.3575	−2.4650 (0.018)	0.053211	2.4592 (0.016)
Amount of electricity	0.0006352	1.7757 (0.083)	0.0002727	1.7863 (0.079)
Variable of rotation	0.053596	1.7591 (0.086)	0.053211	2.4592 (0.016)

15.4.2   Instrumental Variables

As part of the structural model, Equation (15.11) is solved with a two-stage least-squares model. The identification of this equation requires that the exogenous variables defined in the other equation should be considered instrumental variables: 'Overnight Stays', 'Diesel' and 'Temperature Difference'. The latter can already be found indirectly in the equation of the demand variable rotation. So instead we used the average monthly temperature. This variable may also serve as an instrumental variable for the hydro inflows.

Testing for the overestimation of the model does not reject the null hypothesis that all instrumental variables are exogenous.

15.4.3   Behavioural Parameter

We tested several models for different instrumental variables. The chosen model presents a level of significance less than 10 per cent for the rotation variable of the demand, which can be interpreted as robust by the statistical tests conducted.

For 48 observations (up to December 2003), the variables are not very significant, especially those related to fuel prices. However, when we extend the series until February 2006 (72 observations), all variables become more significant (Table 15.2). It can equally be observed that considering a longer period of time does not alter the coefficient attributed to the rotation variable, which enables the behavioural factor to be defined. This value lies at around 0.054, indicating a competitive market.

15.4.4   Lerner Index in the Period 1999–2003

Having estimated the behavioural factor for the analysed period (about 0.0535) and the price elasticity of demand (–0.0933), it remains to define the Herfindahl Index, HHI, in order to estimate the Lerner index solving Equation (15.3). The HHI was calculated by an economic group based on data from OMEL and the Ministerio de Industria, Turismo y Comercio. Note that this index was only calculated for conventional producers, that is, the power plants with positive environmental externalities (special regime) were not considered because payment of their production was formed independently of market prices.

The average HHI weighted by the production is equal to 30.5 per cent. Applying Equation (15.3), the Lerner index is 17.4 per cent.

The associated Lerner index is relatively high, despite the fact that the estimation of the producers' behaviour approaches a Bertrand game. We can conclude that given the conditions of the wholesale Spanish electricity market, namely the rigidity of demand and the high concentration, the discretion enjoyed by producers to get a high mark-up is wide.

It is important to note that during the period in the Iberian Peninsula the market structure for energy production did not result from competitive pressures but from the structure of the existing market before liberalization. Furthermore, the technologies for producing electricity are shared by producers, and the efficiency of electricity producers is more dependent on the portfolio of technologies than on the efficiency of the power plants. In this case, it is assumed that there is not an endogenous relationship between market concentration and the marginal costs.

15.5   ESTIMATION OF THE BEHAVIOUR OUTSIDE THE STRUCTURAL MODEL

15.5.1   Marginal Cost Calculation

The definition of marginal cost is one of the main difficulties for the implementation of structural models. This is why we also estimate the cost function outside the model.

The marginal cost of a market can reflect the structure of the production costs for this market or only correspond to the marginal cost of the electricity generating power station that has sold electricity at the highest price, which corresponds to the marginal power station. The latter type of market corresponds to the UPA market and it is the kind of market that has been operating in Spain. In this kind of market, the marginal cost of the market is very close to the cost variable for the power station that sets the market price. In monthly terms, marginal cost corresponds to the weighted average for the amounts traded at any given hour in the marginal cost schedule:

$$
Cmg_t = \frac{\sum_{t=1}^{n} Cmg_t Q_t}{\sum_{t=1}^{n} Q_t} \cong \frac{\sum_{t=1}^{n} Cv_t Q_t}{\sum_{t=1}^{n} Q_t}, \tag{15.12}
$$

in which Cmg_t is the weighted marginal cost of the market in the month t, n is the number of hours h, in the month t, Cmg_t is the marginal cost of the market at the hour h, Cv_t is the cost variable for the marginal power station in the hour h and Q_t is the amount traded on the market in the hour h.

OMEL provides the amounts traded on the daily and intraday markets. In this way, the variable Q_t in Equation (15.12) is known. However, the definition of variable Cv_t is based on a set of assumptions that can be grouped into:

1. Definition of the variable cost function associated with the type of marginal plant.
2. Definition of parameters required to calculate the variable cost.

The information provided by OMEL does not establish with certainty what type of power plant defines the system marginal cost. It was necessary to develop a set of assumptions[8] that allows to associate different technologies and consequently different functions of the variable costs to the nomenclature presented by OMEL for the source of energy that sets the system marginal price (following Wolfram, 1999; Steiner, 2000; Borenstein et al., 2002 among others). In short, in any case, only four types of technology define the market price during the period under review: oil-fired power plant, coal power plants, combined cycle natural gas power plants and hydro plants. In parallel with the technologies that define the market price, it is important to set the variable cost function of marginal technologies.

The variable cost of a thermal power plant will depend on four factors: its load, its efficiency for that load, the heating value of the fuel consumed and the price of the fuel. Assuming that the central i, which sets the market price at full capacity, the function of the variable i, which sets the market price at full capacity, the function of the variable cost at a determined hour, h, of this power plant, Cv_{ti}, is defined as follows:[9]

$$Cv_{ti} = Pcomb_j \times \varphi_{comb_j} \times \eta_i + O\&M \qquad (15.13)$$

where, $Pcomb_j$ corresponds to the price of fuel j, φ_{comb_j} is the calorific value of fuel j, η_i is the efficiency of the power plant and $O\&M$ the maintenance and operation variable costs.

Regarding the price of fuel consumed, this depends largely on the acquisition policy of the producer. Furthermore, we have to refer to the particular case of the coal consumed in Spain. Much of this coal is domestic and less competitive than imported coal, obliging the subsidization of its consumption by the Spanish government.

Meanwhile, the case of hydro power plants must be highlighted. The variable costs of these plants are close to zero, and are merely related to maintenance and operation costs. In periods when the level of reservoirs is automatically reset, that is, in periods of strong hydro inflows, which in the Iberian Peninsula represent some periods of the winter or spring, the value of the water held in reservoirs is almost zero. However, in other periods, it becomes a scarce resource, its value corresponding to the cost of the replaced technology.

There is an important set of unknowns in setting the price of fuel. In order to overcome this situation, we follow three approaches for calculating the monthly variable cost:

1. For production valued at the cost of the conventional power plants, the production costs are calculated on the basis of the average market prices for the fuels and the standard values for O&M costs and efficiency. Production from hydroelectric plants is valued at the production costs for the plants (O&M costs), with the exception of months in which hydro inflows are significantly below the average for the 'dry' period of the water resources year, which are valued at the cost of the fuel oil plants. This approach is referred to as 'marginal cost (a)'.
2. The previous point also applies except for hydroelectric production, which is valued at the cost of the fuel oil power plants, with the exception of months in which hydro inflows are significantly above the average for the 'wet' period, which are valued at the production cost of the hydroelectric plants. This approach is referred to as 'marginal cost (b)'.
3. For production valued at the cost of conventional power plants or combined cycle natural gas plants, the production costs are defined on the basis of costs verified in Portugal for equivalent technologies during the same period. The production of hydroelectric plants is valued as in the first case. This approach is referred to as 'marginal cost Portugal'.

Table 15.3   Variable behaviour for linear demand function for the period
1999–2003

Marginal cost (a)	Marginal cost (b)	Marginal cost (b) without November 2001–February 2002	Marginal cost Portugal
0.119	0.060	0.056	0.126

15.5.2   Behavioural Factor

In this section the regression (15.4) is solved for each cost function in order to estimate the Lerner index λ, and, consequently, in order to define the behavioural factor $\bar{\theta}$, Equation (15.5) is also solved.

Lerner index for 1999–2003

Whatever the cost function considered, periods when the marginal cost of the market approaches the market price succeed to periods when the marginal cost is significantly lower than the market price.[10] This is known and has been already analysed in other studies (see Fabra and Toro, 2005).

The evolution of the Lerner index can easily be associated with various external events. The increase in the Lerner index since 2001 coincides with the threat by the European Union to prevent Spain from maintaining the CTC payments. With the disappearance of this threat, the Lerner index was seen to fall. Later, the entry of the new combined cycle natural gas power plants whose importance can be highlighted from 2004 onwards and that were not governed by the CTCs coincides with a rise in this index.

After solving Equation (15.4), the results point out that the Lerner indexes have high values, between 0.41 ('marginal cost Portugal' cost function) and 0.20 ('marginal cost (b)' cost function) for the 1999–2003 period. Their interpretation requires the resolution of Equation (15.5).

Definition of the behavioural variable for 1999–2003

When we defined the price elasticity of demand for different functional forms, we concluded that only for the 1999–2003 period Equation (15.5) can be solved. In Section 15.4.4 we determined the HHI, being the average value 30.5 per cent. With regard to price elasticity of demand, the estimated values in the Section 15.3.7 are very similar regardless of functional form chosen. We applied the results obtained for the linear functional form: –0.0886 (Table 15.3).

It should be recalled that the closer $\bar{\theta}$ is to 1, the closer we are to finding strategic behaviour of the Nash-Cournot type, whereas when it is closer to 0, the agents are closer to a competitive situation. Therefore, despite the high mark-up, one cannot, apparently, prove the existence of an anti-competitive behaviour, using the conjectural variation methodology.

However, during the period under review the producers of electricity in Spain were framed by CTC, a scheme that was applied whenever the market price was less than 36 euros/MWh. If the market price was higher than 36 euros/MWh, the increased revenue would be deducted from the amounts of CTC established annually.

The CTCs were organized similarly to contracts for difference, whose revenues were defined as functions that decrease with market prices. Therefore, if the CTC was applied to all quantities traded, the profit would not grow with the market prices. To define the function maximizing the profits of a producer i, we reformulated the profit function in a market with CTC given by Fabra and Toro (2005), as follows:

$$\pi_i = P(Q,D)q_i - C_i(q_i, W) + q_{iCTC}(CTC_{ui} + 36 - P(Q,D)), \quad (15.14)$$

where q_{iCTC} are the quantities framed by the contracts and CTC_{ui} the income per MWh produced that are allocated to producer i through the CTC.

If $q_{iCTC} = q_i$, that is, if the quantities traded framed by CTCs, q_{iCTC} are equal to the quantities traded in the market, the maximization of Equation (15.14) results in:

$$CTC_{ui} + 36 = \frac{dC_i(q_i, W)}{dq_i}. \quad (15.15)$$

In this case, any strategy for maximizing profit is independent of the price and we simply need to equate the marginal cost of production at CTC_{ui} added to 36 euros/MWh, which corresponds to the marginal revenue (implicit in the scheme prior to the liberalization) and the marginal cost.

The weight of the power plants framed by CTC in total production fell sharply from 2002, with the entry of new plants (Vives, 2006).

Thus, in practice $q_{iCTC} < q$, that is, the quantities traded framed by CTCs, q_{iCTC}, are lower than those traded in the market that are independent of this mechanism. Assuming q_{iCTC} as a constant, in this case, the profit maximization function result is as follows:

$$P + \theta_i \frac{dP}{dQ}(q_i - q_{iCTC}) = \frac{dC_i(q_i, W)}{dq_i}. \quad (15.16)$$

Rearranging this equation, we obtain the following relationship:

$$(P - Cmg_i) \over P = {\left(s_i - \dfrac{q_{iCTC}}{Q}\right)\theta_i \over |\varepsilon|}. \tag{15.17}$$

This results[11] in the following equation:

$$\frac{(P - \overline{Cmg})}{P} =$$

$$\frac{\left(\sum_i^n s_i^2 - \dfrac{q_{iCTC}}{Q}s_i\right)\theta_i}{|\varepsilon|} = \frac{\overline{\theta}\left(HHI - \sum_i^n \dfrac{q_{iCTC}}{Q}s_i\right)}{|\varepsilon|} \cong \frac{\overline{\theta_{CTC}}HHI_{CTC}}{|\varepsilon|}. \tag{15.18}$$

The parameter HHI_{CTC} is the difference between the market share of each company and the weight of their respective products framed by the CTC in the total production, multiplied by their market shares. Thus, this parameter is the HHI net of the weight of the power plants that give no benefit to producers whenever they developed a strategy to manipulate the market price. It is smaller, the greater the weight of the energy produced by plants covered by the CTC.

We defined an average value for HHI_{CTC} considering, for simplicity, that the production of plants not covered by the CTC is proportional to its capacity as the weight of the production of these plants is the same for all companies. The average value thus found for this parameter was 1.71 per cent. Thus, accepting a broad interpretation of HHI_{CTC} and the relation (15.5), we can apply the following equation:

$$\overline{\theta}_{CTC} = \frac{\lambda|\varepsilon|}{HHI_{CTC}}. \tag{15.19}$$

The obtained values are between those that indicate the existence of Cournot strategies, which correspond to the unit, and those that indicate the existence of pure strategy of collusion, match $1/HHI$ (Table 15.4).

The results obtained now clearly indicate that producers' behaviours are 'somewhere' between the Cournot behaviour and the pure collusive behaviour. This results are consistent with the argument by some authors (see, for example, Vives, 2006) that after the suspicion on the part of producers that from 1999 the payments of CTC could not be made, they may have developed strategies to increase the mark-up implicit in the market price.

Table 15.4   Variable behaviour by cost function considering the CTC period 1999–2003

Marginal cost (a)	Marginal cost (a) (b)	Marginal cost (b) without November 2001–February 2002	Marginal cost Portugal
2.12	1.08	1.00	2.25

15.6   CONCLUSIONS

In the case of the former Spanish wholesale electricity market, the structural methodology allowed for interesting results, similar to those obtained outside this methodological framework and assuming different functional forms.

New Empirical Industrial Organization aims to infer the causes of high levels of market power. However, the capacity to exercise market power and anti-competitive strategies should not be confused, as this study demonstrates in terms of electricity production. They take shape in the form of two related trends that only partially cancel each other out. On the one hand, electricity production can be based on 'anti-competitive' strategies, even at relatively low levels of concentration, due to the price elasticity of demand below the unit, the difficulty in storing the product and the fact that it is a capital-intensive sector. On the other hand, this natural tendency to exercise market power and the fact that electricity is an essential commodity make this sector extremely regulated, including in economies that are more open to private initiatives, limiting the actions of economic agents (sometimes by anticipating the future actions of the regulators).

In that sense, in a pioneering study Wolfram (1999), concludes, in the case of the former English and Wales market at the end of the 1990s, that prices were much higher than marginal costs, demonstrating the existence of market power. However, this difference was less than expected, given the structure of the English market at the time. Fears of State intervention in the wholesale market can explain the 'lower' mark-up. This study also points in this direction. The average Lerner index is high, although it is expected to be much higher considering market structure.

However, at that time the Spanish electricity sector was framed by CTC, which would, nevertheless, turn the average Lerner index lower, since the profit maximization function of the producers was independent from price strategies. The chapter shows that the average high mark-up in the period was very likely due to the implementation of anti-competitive strategies, even though with limited consequences on prices due to the CTC.

Therefore, in the Spanish case, the opening of the market without the prior increase in the number of market players did not, by itself, prevent manipulation.

NOTES

1. The results and comments presented in this chapter are entirely the authors' responsibility and do not reflect the official opinions of ERSE or other institution.
2. See, for example, Just and Chern (1980) and Bresnahan (1982).
3. This equation is based on the assumption that all companies share the same behavioural factor.
4. Before the beginning of MIBEL, OMEL was the acronym for: CompañiaOperadoradel Mercado Español de Electricidad, S.A.
5. Eigen value and trace test statistics.
6. The presentation of the statistical tests is outside the scope of the present chapter.
7. Eigen value and trace test statistics.
8. Is has to be higjlighted that the assumptions were made in order to not underestimate the variables costs and, therefore, overestimate the mark-up. The presentation of these assumptions is outside the scope of this chapter.
9. During the analysed period, CO_2 costs were not yet recovered.
10. The presentation of the evolution of the Lerner indexes is outside the scope of the present chapter.
11. The development of this deduction is outside the scope of this chapter.

REFERENCES

Borenstein, S., J. Bushnell and C. Knittel (1999), 'Market power in electricity markets: beyond concentration measures', *Energy Journal*, **20**(2), 65–88.

Borenstein, S., J. Bushnell and F. Wolak (2002), 'Measuring market inefficiencies in California's restructured wholesale electricity market', *American Economic Review*, **92**(3), 1376–405.

Corts, K. (1999), 'Conduct parameters and the measurement of market power', *Journal of Econometrics*, **88**(2), 227–50.

Cowling, K. and M. Waterson (1976), 'Price-cost margin and market structure', *Economica*, **43**(171), 267–74.

Fabra, N. and J. Toro (2005), 'Price wars and collusion in the Spanish electricity market', *International Journal of Industrial Organization*, **23**(3–4), 155–81.

García-Alcalde, A., M. Ventosa, M. Rivier, A. Ramos and G. Relaño (2002), 'Fitting electricity market models: a conjectural variations approach', available at http://www.iit.upcomillas.es/docs/02AGA01.pdf (accessed 10 March 2010).

Genesove, D. and W. Mullin (1998), 'Testing static oligopoly models: conduct and cost in the sugar industry, 1890–1914', *RAND Journal of Economics*, **29**(2), 355–77.

González-Marrero, R., R. Lorenzo-Alegría and G. Marrero (2008), 'Fuel consumption, economic determinants and policy implications for road transport in

Spain', Documento de trabajo 2008-23, available at http://www.fedea.es/pub/papers/2008/dt2008-23.pdf (accessed 5 March 2010).

Hjalmarsson, E. (2000), 'Nord pool: a power market without market power', Working Papers in Economics, Department of Economics, Göteborg University, available at http://econpapers.repec.org/paper/hhsgunwpe/0028.htm (accessed 5 March 2010).

Johansen, S. (1988), 'Statistical analysis of cointegration vectors', *Journal of Economic Dynamics and Control*, **12**(2–3), 231–54.

Just, R. and W. Chern (1980), 'Tomatoes, technology, and oligopsony', *Bell Journal of Economics*, **11**(2), 584–602.

Kreps, D. and J. Scheinkman (1983), 'Quantity precommitment and Bertrand competition yield Cournot outcomes', *Bell Journal of Economics*, **14**, 326–37.

Kühn, K. and M. Machado (2004), 'Bilateral market power and vertical integration in the Spanish electricity spot market', CEPR Discussion Paper No. 4590.

Mendiluce, M., I. Pérez-Arriaga and C. Ocaña (2009), 'Comparison of the evolution of energy intensity in Spain and in the EU15: why is Spain different?' Center for Energy and Environmental Policy Research Working Papers, available at http://web.mit.edu/ceepr/www/publications/workingpapers/2009-011.pdf (accessed 5 March 2010).

Patrick, R. and F. Wolak (1997), 'Estimating customer-level demand for electricity under real time pricing', available at ftp://zia.stanford.edu/pub/papers/rtppap.pdf (accessed 19 March 2010).

Perloff, J., L. Karp and A. Golan (2007), *Estimating Market Power and Strategies*, 1st edn, New York: Cambridge University Press.

Reiss, P. and F. Wolak (2005), 'Structural econometric modeling: rationales and examples from industrial organization', available at http://www.stanford.edu/~preiss/makeit.pdf (accessed 15 July 2010).

Steiner, F. (2000), 'Regulation, industry structure and performance in the electricity supply industry', Economics Department Working Papers No. 238, OCDE.

Vives, X. (2006), 'El reto de la competencia en el sector eléctrico', Occasional Paper No. 06/13, IESE SP, available at http://www.iese.edu/research/pdfs/OP-06-13.pdf (accessed 18 March 2010).

Wolfram, C. (1999), 'Measuring duopoly power in the British electricity spot market', *American Economic Review*, **89**(2), 805–26.

PART IV

Financial regulation

16. Rebuilding international financial regulation and Basel III

Kern Alexander

16.1 THE FAILINGS OF THE INTERNATIONAL STANDARD SETTING BODIES TO CONTROL RISK PRE-CRISIS

The financial crisis that began in 2007 demonstrates how international financial standard setting bodies, such as the Basel Committee on Banking Supervision, failed to develop regulatory and supervisory standards to limit excessive risk-taking in structured finance markets and in Over-the-Counter (OTC) derivatives markets and to provide adequate loss-absorbent capital in the banking sector. These regulatory and supervisory weaknesses were manifest in the practices of the leading Basel Committee members, such as the USA and the UK. US and UK regulators and policymakers failed to grasp how the so-called shadow banking system would fail to self-regulate itself and the potential social costs of this failure for their national financial systems and the impact this would have on global financial markets and the world economy. During the 1980s to 2000s, in the most advanced financial systems (the G10 countries), financial markets were undergoing significant changes involving a shift away from a bank-based model of finance to a wholesale capital market model of finance; this had brought diversification and increased liquidity to financial markets, but also had introduced systemic risks to the financial system, which international standard setting bodies, such as the Basel Committee, the Joint Forum on Financial Conglomerates and the Financial Stability Forum had failed to identify and recommend adequate controls. Specific types of financial innovation – such as securitization and credit default swaps – that began in the early 1990s, partially in response to regulatory requirements such as Basel I, had changed the nature of financial risk-taking and systemic risk. The development of the structured finance market and in particular the role of securitization in decomposing and distributing credit risk to wholesale institutional investors who were seeking higher yield in a low inflation environment was crucial in transforming the way that risk is measured and managed. Moreover, the dramatic growth of the OTC credit derivatives market made it possible for enhanced corporate balance sheet management, but it also allowed traders to take excessive risks on the underlying assets in these contracts. And the role of technology and statistical theory in the use of value-at-risk (VAR) models in risk management, which allowed financial firms to calculate how much they expected to lose if the markets turned sharply against them, substantially understated the frequency and severity of financial shocks (so-called 'fat-tailed events'). Other factors contributed to the crisis, including the incentives of rating agencies to provide AAA ratings to complex debt instruments and their failure to use adequate risk measurement methodologies to assess the underlying risks embedded in these instruments.

These flawed methods of assessing and managing risk, combined with financial product innovation and structural changes in financial markets, provided the ingredients that allowed risk to be under-priced and shifted around the financial system. Regulators and policymakers believed that this spreading of risk created a more resilient and robust financial system based on the enlightened assessment of risks by banks and other financial firms. Instead, this regulatory 'light touch' approach failed to monitor the build-up of risk in the financial sectors and its potential impact on the economic and financial system.[1]

16.2   FINANCIAL RISK-TAKING IS A CONCERN OF FINANCIAL REGULATION

Financial risk-taking is a concern of public law because associated with the risk-taking actions of individuals there are externalities, that is, costs and benefits accruing to the society that are external to the calculations of the individual investor, and not accounted for in the market place.[2] A major financial failure imposes costs on society going far beyond the losses suffered by the immediate investors. In an economy where there are important externalities, competitive markets will be socially inefficient. The task of public law and policy, in this case of financial regulation, is to attempt to mitigate these market failures.

Both US and UK policymakers and financial supervisors adhered to a 'light-touch' approach to prudential regulation that was premised on the assumption that bankers, investors and other market participants had the expertise and incentives to control excessive financial risk-taking. As it turned out, they had neither the expertise nor incentives to do so. Indeed, the Financial Stability Forum observed in an April 2008 report (before Lehman Brothers collapsed) that the 2007 credit crunch was the result of massive failings in risk management in some of the largest and most sophisticated financial institutions. Executive compensation contributed to excessive risk-taking at banks and other financial firms, while institutional shareholders failed to exercise an effective stewardship role to curb the excessive risk-taking of senior management at leading financial institutions. Moreover, the legal foundation of this so-called shadow banking sector was largely built on a private law system of contracts and property law: the public law of financial regulation had little role to play in providing effective supervision over the development of the securitization markets and the OTC derivatives market. Policymakers and regulators had permitted major weakness in financial contracts to fester that allowed counterparties to enter OTC derivatives transactions that shifted much of the risk they had created away from themselves onto the market at large. This type of financial dumping was facilitated by lawyers devising contracts that aimed to reduce transactions costs for their clients, but had the effect of imposing huge negative externalities onto the economy and financial system. Lawyers also failed to appreciate or understand the externality risks of the structured finance market and in particular to understand the extent of the risks of their clients' leveraged positions in the mortgage-backed securities market and the OTC credit default swap market. This contributed to destructive speculation that fuelled the market bubble and exacerbated the fallout when the markets inevitably collapsed. Essentially, lawyers devised contracts that allowed risk to be under-priced and shifted onto the broader economy, which resulted in much of the economic slowdown in what has become known as the 'great recession'.

The shadow banking system was unable to cope with a liquidity crisis because, among other things, of the unregulated nature of the contracts that governed the structured finance markets. The private law framework that governs wholesale capital market transactions and bank trading practices merit closer supervisory oversight along with tighter regulatory controls of the contracts themselves. Left to its own devices, the operation of the structured finance markets became too complex and opaque with the result that the risks to which investors were exposed (credit, market and liquidity risks) were substantially under-priced with the result that too much of it was created and the financial system itself did not have the regulatory infrastructure to monitor and control it. The financial system was thinly capitalized, had excessive leverage and market participants had serious conflicts of interests.[3] Any review of the role of lawyers in exacerbating the crisis should consider what role public law should play in developing sound regulatory and supervisory frameworks. Indeed, the role of law reform in financial markets should not be constrained to the national level, but should also look to enhancing the role of international financial regulation in controlling excessive financial risks in liberalized and globalized financial markets.

16.3   THE PRESSURES ON STATES TO COMPLY WITH INTERNATIONAL FINANCIAL SOFT LAW

International financial regulation is primarily a system of 'international soft law' – meaning standards, guidelines, interpretations and other statements that are not legally binding or enforceable according to formal techniques of international law, but nevertheless are capable of exerting powerful influence over the behaviour of countries, public entities and private parties.[4] International financial soft law has had a hard impact in a number of areas including prudential bank regulation, anti-money laundering and terrorist financing law because it has been adopted and implemented into the domestic legal and regulatory regimes of most countries with functioning financial markets. Many of the organizations and other bodies that produce international financial regulatory standards are themselves 'soft' in the sense that they are networks of informally constituted international bodies consisting of public regulatory officials, or private sector consisting of industry representatives.[5] However, these informally constituted international bodies have enormous influence on State behaviour and compliance with international financial soft law norms. In contrast to international economic organizations such as the World Trade Organization (WTO), the IMF or the World Bank, international financial standard setting bodies are not entities with separate legal personality created by States, but rather informal associations of State representatives and/or professionals that address specific problems and identify technical issues of concern. Because of their informal institutional status, they are not subject to the same rules of procedural accountability and principles of institutional legitimacy as are the formal international economic organizations, such as the WTO or the World Bank.[6] Indeed, proponents of these soft institutional bodies argue that it is their flexible institutional structure that makes it possible for these international bodies to devise effective technical regulatory standards that address the complexities of global finance.

Other international pressures on States to comply with international financial soft law standards come from organizations formally established by international treaty.[7] The IMF and the World Bank provide examples of so-called official sector actors who oversee and pressure States to implement international financial standards through their Article IV surveillance programmes and most significantly through their Article V conditionality programmes that often make reference to the Fund's Financial Sector Assessment Programmes (FSAPs) that provide a checklist of the extent to which IMF member states comply with international financial standards.[8] Indeed, the IMF has been described as the 'vehicle through which international financial soft law is implemented and as the main instrument by which to disseminate new standards and codes globally and monitor their observance'.[9] This type of international institutional pressure has the effect of supplementing traditionally soft international standards with soft (yet potentially powerful) enforcement.

In addition, there are pressures on States from non-official sector sources to comply with international financial soft law. A State's compliance with 'best practice' international standards can result in lower funding costs for its sovereign debt and more favourable financing terms for its financial institutions. Similar market incentive-related reasons may lead banks and other regulated firms to adopt soft international standards, even though the country in which they are based has not implemented them, because they will want to signal to the global market that they adhere to the latest, most sophisticated models, and which have received the approval of the FSB and other international bodies.[10] International soft law can therefore be highly influential by serving as 'best practice' regulatory standards to which market participants adhere for a range of motives from the perceived prestige of complying with globally recognized standards to the more immediate need of placating investors' demands in order to obtain lower funding costs. These examples illustrate another aspect of soft law's flexibility that can be viewed critically, namely that the standard setters can include bodies and groups that have no capacity to make treaties or other forms of hard law; and that under certain circumstances this can lead to regulatory capture, resulting in suboptimal regulatory standards for market participants.

Nevertheless, for the foreseeable future, international soft law remains as an important instrument of international financial regulation. As discussed below, it has become an important instrument for the G20 and FSB in the international reform agenda.[11] Even though emergency situations can open the door to radical ideas, proposals for new treaty-based rules or institutions have not gained momentum in the immediate post-crisis period.[12] Rather, the focus has been on reforming the soft law system to make it more effective and more representative. Despite the various imperfections and limitations of softer methods, in the area of international regulatory reform it appears to be accepted that no better option is politically acceptable in the immediate future and that the soft law approach will continue to dominate international standard setting.

16.4   BASEL COMMITTEE AND INTERNATIONAL FINANCIAL REGULATION

The Basel Committee on Banking Supervision consists of Central Bank Governors and senior financial supervisors of the countries who are represented on the FSB.[13] The Committee is responsible for the Basel Capital Accord – probably the most important and influential international financial regulatory agreement – that sets regulatory capital standards for banking institutions and for establishing the principle of consolidated supervision based on home country control and mutual recognition as set forth in the Basel Concordat.[14] It is presently engaged in deliberations over the Basel III agreement, which has more or less been agreed to in principle, but with several outstanding issues to be resolved.[15]

At the time of its adoption, Basel II was viewed to be one of the most important regulatory innovations in global finance because it allowed supervisors to create incentives for banks to improve their risk management by creating the incentive that if they could prove to supervisors that they managed their risk effectively based on the use of probability of default and loss given default data incorporated into VAR models, they would then be permitted to hold a lower level of regulatory capital that more closely approximated the economic capital that they were already holding. It is not surprising that this model-based approach for determining regulatory capital led to significantly lower levels of regulatory capital for the largest banking institutions.

The Basel Committee was often praised for its informal decision-making structure and ability to meet on short notice and often away from public scrutiny to assess market developments and react quickly and flexibly to changing circumstances, which in rapidly evolving financial markets was viewed to be a valuable attribute. Indeed, the institutional features of the Basel Committee in the 1980s and 1990s, when it developed the Basel Capital Accord (Basel I, 1988) and the Market Risk Amendment (1996) for calculating regulatory capital for banks' trading books, demonstrated a coherence in focus and flexibility in institutional decision making that was generally considered by policymakers and the banking sector to be an advantage in developing international norms for banking regulation. These early successes of the Basel Committee suggested that international soft law could serve as a mechanism in international financial policymaking that was superior to hard law-making processes by achieving regulatory objectives whilst providing a more harmonized supervisory framework for overseeing cross-border banking operations. The Basel I decision-making process showed how responsive and adaptable international regulatory standards could be to ever-changing and highly complex financial markets. However, this adaptability and flexibility was not always apparent in the negotiations over the Basel II process, which took place over seven years (1999–2006) and after being amended several times failed to address liquidity funding risks and trading book risks that banks faced and related systemic risks in financial markets.

Another important aspect of Basel II (and also Basel III) concerns its process-based regulatory framework, which involves regulators interacting with banks on an individual basis to assess their risk controls and approve the regulatory capital models they have devised based on their own internal risk-based data and calculations. If the regulator is happy with the bank's methodology for managing and measuring risk, it can approve the bank's model with the result that the bank's regulatory capital level can be reduced from the higher regulatory capital level that the regulator would have imposed according to the regulator's risk-based formula. Instead, banks have the option to devise an internal risk-based model (the Advanced Internal Ratings-Based (AIB) approach or the Foundation Approach), which, if approved by the supervisor, can result in a significantly lower level of regulatory capital. In theory, the Basel II process (also incorporated into Basel III) provides an incentive for banks to improve their risk management by offering them a lower level of regulatory capital if they can prove to the regulator that their risk-based model adequately controls the risks the institution faces. Indeed, much of the Basel capital adequacy framework is quite detailed in stipulating 'risk-based process frameworks', that is, a set of principles, standards and rules for regulators to measure the particular risks that financial institutions face.[16]

Although Basel II was not formally adopted in Europe until January 2007 and not fully implemented for all banks in the USA, the flawed model-based approach for measuring and managing risk on which Basel II was based had become an industry standard for most large western financial institutions several years before Basel II was actually implemented into European Union (EU) law. The model-based approach to measuring risk was already in use by financial institutions in the 1990s to determine their economic capital. The economic capital models of these institutions were premised on the notion that volatility was a proxy for risk. This was based on conventional portfolio management theory[17] utilized by most large western financial institutions that involved the widespread use of volatility-based models, such as VAR. As it turned out, these standardized

VAR models massively underestimated the likelihood of significant falls in asset prices based on external shocks and failed to take into account the likelihood of numerous aftershocks. The use of these volatility-based (or VAR) models for determining bank economic capital were the basis for the development of Basel II, and remains the essential basis for measuring risk under Basel III. This model-based approach for assessing and managing risks requires the supervisor to review the bank's models and risk management practices and, more generally, its corporate governance standards in deciding whether or not to approve the amount of regulatory capital that the bank proposes based on the calculations of its internal risk-based model.[18] The results of allowing banks to use their own internal risk-based models to set their regulatory capital standards were adumbrated by the Basel Committee's five quantitative impact studies (QISs) conducted between 2002 and 2005. The five QISs provided a trial run for banks to estimate what the potential impact might be on their capital requirements if they were to implement Basel II. The results consistently showed that most banks, especially the largest banks, across many jurisdictions, would be required to hold much less regulatory capital under the Basel II AIB and Foundation approaches than if they had stayed on a modified version of Basel I. As a result of these studies, protracted and extended negotiations developed over the minutiae of Basel II until final agreement was reached in 2006.[19]

Basel II embodied some of the major weaknesses with the current international financial standard setting approach. Basel II was initially proposed to fill some of the gaps and loopholes that existed in the Basel I Capital Accord.[20] This led to riskier bank balance sheets. However, it was also a response by policymakers and regulators to banking industry lobbies that demanded that regulatory capital charges should more closely approximate the economic capital that banks were already holding based on their economic capital models. The banks argued, and central bankers and regulators agreed, that global financial markets had become more resilient and robust in the late 1980s and 1990s because of securitization and other forms of structured finance and the growth of the OTC derivatives market: in particular the massive growth of OTC credit derivatives had allowed parties to hedge risks from their balance sheets and to shift risk to those most capable of absorbing risk. The economic capital models used by banks were accepted by regulators as being valid reference points for the calculation of regulatory capital. This market-based approach to measuring and managing risk disproportionately focused on the risk facing the individual firm, and not the risk that the firm faced from a malfunctioning financial system. The economic capital models that were accepted by regulators under Basel II failed to anticipate macro-prudential risks – that is, drying up of liquidity in the wholesale funding markets – and utilized risk sensitive techniques that, in the face of extreme events, could exacerbate systemic risks, with the potential to precipitate a crisis. Essentially, Basel II embodied the failure of financial policymakers and regulators to incorporate systemic risks into the design of regulatory institutions and of risk management.

The major lesson to be drawn from the current crisis is that a rebalancing is urgently needed. An important aspect of this rethink is determining the right balance between liberalized and liquid financial markets and adequate legal and regulatory controls to curb the social costs of excessive financial risk-taking. Unfortunately, Basel III essentially builds on the edifice of Basel II by incorporating many of its weaknesses, while only strengthening prudential regulation in limited ways by, for example, increasing the level of Tier One capital and making it more loss absorbent and imposing certain liquidity requirements, and by requiring banks to hold more liquid assets and decrease the maturity mismatch in their wholesale funding. As argued, this fails to address the externality problem posed by financial institutions that requires a more holistic approach to regulation that addresses the liquidity risks on the liability side of a bank's balance sheet and the risk of moral hazard generated in part by the enormous indirect subsidy that banks gain through lower funding costs in the capital markets.

16.5   REFORMING THE INTERNATIONAL FINANCIAL ARCHITECTURE

The FSB[21] is the international body that has been given the responsibility by the G20 to develop international financial standards that control systemic risk and provide more effective oversight of the global financial system.[22] The FSB has adopted 12 key standards for sound financial systems, all of which are legally non-binding soft law but nevertheless are expected to be incorporated into the national regulatory regimes of all countries.[23] The FSB is composed of senior representatives of national financial authorities (central banks, regulatory and supervisory authorities and ministries of finance), international financial institutions, standard setting bodies and committees of central bank experts from leading developed countries and some large developing countries, including the so-called BRIC countries, Brazil, Russia, India and China.[24] The FSB's membership includes significantly more countries than the traditional membership of the G10 committees, which, according to some observers, enhances its accountability and legitimacy.[25]

Membership carries with it obligations to pursue the maintenance of financial stability, to maintain the openness and transparency of the financial sector, to implement international financial standards and to submit to periodic peer reviews.

The FSB is part of a new drive to devise more effective international regulatory frameworks that durably link micro-prudential supervision with broader macro-prudential systemic concerns.[26] Indeed, a major shift in regulatory focus is occurring from micro-prudential to macro-prudential regulation. The focus on macro-prudential regulation involves, among other things, devising regulatory standards to measure and limit leverage levels in the financial system as a whole, requiring financial institutions to have enhanced liquidity reserves against short-term wholesale funding exposures, and, more generally, counter-cyclical capital regulation whereby capital requirements are linked to points in the macro-economic and business cycle. This move to a more macro-prudential regulatory regime has been a major focus of the Basel Committee adopting Basel III.

Since its establishment, the FSB has been addressing a diverse range of regulatory issues. For example, it has taken some of the work of the Financial Stability Forum forward by overseeing reviews of the system of supervisory colleges to monitor each of the largest international financial services firms.[27] It has developed guidance notes and draft bank recovery and resolution plans to assist with its advice to national authorities for implementing the FSB Principles for Cross-Border Cooperation on Crisis Management.[28] It has established Principles for Sound Compensation Practices,[29] and has coordinated with other international financial bodies such as IOSCO to develop a consistent regulatory framework for the oversight of hedge funds.[30] It is also overseeing the emergence of national and regional frameworks for the registration, regulation and oversight of credit rating agencies and encouraging countries to engage in bilateral dialogues to resolve home-host country issues, involving inconsistencies and disagreements that may arise because of different regulatory approaches.[31] In pursuit of this broad agenda, the FSB issued a paper in 2009 proposing guidelines for use by national authorities to assess whether a financial institution, a market or an instrument is systemically important. Nevertheless, as of August 2011, the FSB has been criticized for not achieving any significant regulatory agreements: other than agreeing to the work of the Basel Committee in adopting Basel III, its other regulatory initiatives have lost momentum and its ambitious agenda has been subordinated to the EU and US regulatory and supervisory reforms.[32]

However, the FSB has made some progress by working with the IMF in collecting data and performing surveillance of individual country financial systems as well as the global financial system by issuing early warnings.[33] In broad terms, there are similarities between some of the functions that the FSB performs at the global level and those that will be entrusted to national systemic risk oversight committees, such as the Bank of England's Financial Policy Committee and the US government's newly established Financial Stability Oversight Committee chaired by the Federal Reserve. The FSB-IMF have undertaken collaborative early warning exercises to strengthen assessments of systemic risks and to identify possible regulatory controls and supervisory practices as a response to the changing face of systemic risk in financial markets.[34] These exercises are aimed at providing policymakers with policy options and, as such, they add to the data-gathering, analysis and evaluation work and information-sharing activity that the IMF already conducts with a view to preventing crises by identifying policies to control macro-economic and systemic risks.[35] It is argued that the combination of the IMF's macro financial expertise with the FSB's micro regulatory perspective will provide an important link in building a more effective macro-prudential supervisory perspective.[36] These exercises are expected to be incorporated into the IMF's surveillance activities and this could serve as a way by which findings and policy recommendations may acquire more concrete effect.

As discussed above, the FSB is a soft law body with no authority to adopt legally binding international standards. Its primary role is to facilitate the adoption of international standards by the existing international standard setting bodies, such as the Basel Committee. In that respect, the FSB itself is merely an additional institution added to the already overcrowded community of international financial standard setters. Moreover, there is a concern regarding the FSB's continued use of soft law instruments to implement financial regulatory reform initiatives. The success (or lack thereof, as demonstrated by Basel II) in terms of practical effectiveness raises concerns about the effective accountability and legitimacy of the standard setting process.[37] Indeed, the attention that the FSB is attracting on this front could be viewed as an indirect sign of its growing capacity to exert real power and influence. Mervyn King, the Governor of the Bank of England, has raised important questions regarding the accountability and legitimacy of FSB standards for countries not represented in the G20. He observed that 'the legitimacy and leadership of the G20 would be enhanced if it were seen as representing views of other countries too'.[38] Close collaboration between the FSB and the IMF is a step towards addressing this concern. However, the involvement of the IMF does not address fully the existing weaknesses in the international financial architecture because the IMF itself has been subject to extensive criticism on legitimacy grounds, most recently because of its allocation of Special

Drawing Rights and the related allocation of weighted voting rights. Also, the recent appointment of Christine Lagarde as Managing Director perpetuates the image that the IMF is governed by and for the interests of the G10 advanced economies. The IMF's Executive Board should therefore develop a new multilateral mandate that recognizes the importance of it adopting internal governance reforms to enhance its accountability and legitimacy and to reorient its financial policy advice towards a more holistic approach to financial regulation that takes account of macro-prudential risks and the differential impact of regulatory structures on different financial systems and economies.[39]

16.6   CONCLUSION

The financial crisis has triggered intense efforts internationally, regionally and nationally to enhance the monitoring of systemic stability and to strengthen the links between macro- and micro-prudential oversight. This chapter has examined some of the practical policy and legal issues involving the operation of international soft law in the context of the Basel II agreement, and the implications of these weaknesses for the effectiveness of international financial regulation more generally. Basel II's market-based approach to measuring and managing risks had become the banking industry's gold standard prior to the crisis without any built-in safeguards against wholesale market liquidity risks and undercapitalization of banks. These lessons have not been completely learned as demonstrated with the Basel III proposals. The creation of the FSB has not yet demonstrated that it is a meaningful institution for enhancing the macro-prudential focus of international financial regulation. Although the FSB has been engaged with micro-prudential reform issues, its efforts so far do not inspire confidence that more adequate macro-prudential measures are being adopted at the international level.

This chapter suggests that future international regulatory reform must be built on a more holistic approach to financial regulation and supervision that involves linking micro-prudential supervision of individual banks with broader oversight of the financial system and to macro-economic policy. Not only should regulation focus more on macro-economic factors, such as liquidity risks and leverage requirements for banks, but it should also develop capital adequacy standards that have linkages and reference points in the broader macro economy, such as counter-cyclical capital ratios. Macro-economic prudential regulation will necessarily require a more rules-based approach to regulation in order to be effective. Effective international regulatory reform will require a more

macro-prudential approach to regulation, supervision and crisis management that will necessarily require enhanced measures to control excessive
risk-taking whilst mitigating and paying for the tremendous social costs
imposed by financial crises.

NOTES

1. The UK Financial Services Authority (FSA) supported the light touch regulatory
   approach that allowed firms to decide for themselves what regulatory controls they
   should use. See FSA (2007, p. 7) stating '[the FSA] believe that, in many circumstances,
   the economic and business interests of firms' senior management and their Boards
   and shareholders can be aligned more effectively with our regulatory goals through
   a principles-based approach. In practice this means giving firms increased flexibility
   to decide more often for themselves what business processes and controls they should
   operate.'
2. There are a number of other important market failures in the financial sector that attract
   the concerns of public policy, most notably the asymmetry of information between individual savers and market professionals that is the motivation of consumer protection
   legislation. This chapter, however, addresses only the market failure manifest in systemic
   risk, and the international regulatory standards (such as Basel II) that exacerbate it.
3. See discussion in Burns (2011), chapter 3.
4. International legal scholarship also recognizes the concept of soft provisions within
   treaties or other binding legal instruments. Since international treaties relating to international financial regulation are insignificant, this type of soft law need not be considered in this chapter. But see Gold (1996) discussing how soft law emerges in the gaps of
   the International Monetary Fund (IMF) Articles of Agreement.
5. See Alexander et al. (2006), chapters 2 and 3. See also Köndgen (2002), pp. 27 ff.
6. See in greater detail Köndgen (2002), pp. 27 ff.
7. The organizations that provide the key standards listed by the FSB include international treaty-based associations (World Bank, IMF), less formally constituted
   public sector groups (such as the Basel Committee, the International Organization for
   Securities Commissions (IOSCO) and the Organization for Economic Cooperation
   and Development (OECD)) and groups that have significant private sector representation (such as the International Accounting Standards Board (IASB)). The Financial
   Stabilities Board (FSB) itself performs a standard setting role (compensation packages,
   cross-border cooperation in crisis management).
8. On the IMF/World Bank FSAP and Reports on Observance of Standards and Codes
   (ROSCs), see http://www.imf.org/external/NP/fsap/fsap.asp (accessed November 2009).
   See also Gola and Spadafora (2009). Another example of soft enforcement is provided
   by the Financial Action Task Force (FATF), which operates a mutual evaluation
   process to promote implementation of its anti-money laundering and counter-terrorist
   financing. Each member jurisdiction is evaluated in turn by a team made up of other
   FATF members. FATF views evaluation exercises as a key component of its work.
   For a general report on evaluation methodologies and a report on recent exercises, see
   Financial Action Task Force (2009), pp. 12–15.
9. See Gola and Spadafora (2009).
10. Alexander et al. (2006), chapter 3.
11. The IOSCO *Code of Conduct Fundamentals for Credit Rating Agencies* (2004) (updated
    2008) is an example of an international code aimed at influencing industry practice.
12. See Report of the High Level Group on Financial Supervision in the EU, chaired by
    Jacques de Larosière (Brussels: EU Commission) (25 February 2009), para. 230 for a
    suggestion that, over the medium term, thought might be given to establishing a full

international standard setting authority, established by a treaty. See also the reflections of Mervyn King (Bank of England) discussed below and surrounding text.

13. The most recent embodiment of an international financial soft law institution is the FSB. The FSB consists of 26 member countries and the IMF, whose representatives consists of central banks, regulatory and supervisory authorities, ministries of finance, international financial institutions, standard setting bodies and committees of central bank experts. See http://www.financialstabilityboard.org/about/overview.htm (last accessed 14 August 2011).

14. See Alexander (2009) and Walker (2000).

15. The Basel Committee reached agreement on Basel III in September 2010, which was approved by the G20 in November 2010. Basel III requires increases in the level of Tier One regulatory capital to 7.5 per cent (including a capital conservation buffer), a tighter definition of Tier One capital to include mainly ordinary common equity shares, an additional 2.5 per cent counter-cyclical capital ratio (yet to be determined for implementation); and liquidity requirements that include a ratio for stable wholesale funding, liquidity coverage ratios and an overall leverage ratio. Recently the Basel Committee has agreed on an additional capital charge of up to 2.5 per cent regulatory capital for large and interconnected systemically important financial institutions (SIFIs).

16. In the case of bank capital adequacy, this often leads to different bank capital rules for individual banks depending on which risk measurement process they use (that is, AIB approach or Foundation approach and so on), which can vary between large and small banks and between different lines of banking business. This is also the case with MIFID because it applies a set of principles and rules (that is, best execution) to measure the most efficient or lowest cost trading process for customers.

17. Indeed, the proliferation of economic capital and other risk management models over the last 30 years was based on the ideas espoused by Professor Harry Markowitz of the University of Chicago, who won a Nobel Prize based on his seminal article in 1952 that articulated the linkages between volatility and risk that became known as modern portfolio theory.

18. These model-based approaches to measuring and managing risk were adopted by other international financial bodies under the aegis of the Joint Forum on Financial Conglomerates, which oversaw the supervisory standard setting processes in the International Association of Insurance Supervisors and the International Organisation of Securities Commissions.

19. The Basel Committee has run one quantitative impact study under Basel III with similar results, showing a large drop in regulatory capital from 11.7 per cent under Basel II to 5.8 per cent under Basel III. See Freeland (2011).

20. For instance, Basel I was relatively insensitive to the riskiness of bank's assets, requiring them to hold the same (more or less) level of regulatory capital for high risk and low risk assets. This created an incentive for banks to sell or securitize less risky assets off their balance sheets and retain higher risk assets.

21. The FSB is an institutional continuation of the Financial Stability Forum (FSF) and has continued more or less to follow similar financial policies and regulatory approaches that are market based and sensitive to the needs of the major international banks.

22. The FSB was formally created in April 2009 by the G20 Heads of State, See G20 Heads of State (2009), para. 15.

23. The list is published at http://www.financialstabilityboard.org/cos/key_standards.htm.

24. The FSB consists of representatives from the central banks and national supervisory authorities of the following countries: Argentina, Australia, Brazil, Canada, China, France, Germany, Hong Kong SAR, India, Indonesia, Italy, Japan, Korea, Mexico, Netherlands, Russia, Saudi Arabia, Singapore, South Africa, Spain, Switzerland, Turkey, UK, USA, and non-State representatives including the European Central Bank, international financial institutions, international standard setting bodies and committees of central bank Experts. See FSB (2010), Press Release, Annex, 9 January.

25. See Alexander (2009), pp. 865–6. The Basel Committee has also attempted to enhance the accountability and legitimacy of its international standard setting process by increasing its membership to 26 jurisdictions, with the addition of Australia, Brazil, China, India, Korea, Mexico and Russia as full-voting members.
26. Micro-prudential supervision focuses mainly on the solvency and risk management practices of individual financial institutions, depositor protection and protecting bank investors. In contrast, macro-prudential supervision involves assessing the aggregate risks developing in the financial system, the financial system infrastructure, and the linkages between financial institutions and markets and the risks of common shocks in the financial system (see Trichet, 2009).
27. See G-20/FSB protocol to establish colleges of supervisors for all major cross-border financial institutions September Report, (see FSB, 2009b, pp. 2–3 and November Report, p. 13).
28. FSB (2009b) November Report, p. 14.
29. FSB (2009a).
30. FSB (2009b) November Report, pp. 11–12.
31. Ibid., p. 13.
32. See Freeland (2011).
33. IMF (2009a).
34. Ibid.
35. The IMF's *Global Financial Stability Reports* and *World Economic Outlook Reports* are its 'flagship' global surveillance publications.
36. IMF (2009c).
37. Alexander et al. (2006), chapters 5 and 10.
38. King (2010), p. 8.
39. See IMF (2009b). This committee was established by the IMF to review its governance. Follow-up to this review is ongoing. Quota and voice reforms to make quotas more responsive to economic realities by increasing the representation of fast-growing economies and to give low-income countries more say in the IMF's decision making have been adopted and are in the process of being accepted by member countries: (see *IMR Quotas* in IMF, 2009a). The G20 has supported governance reform to deliver an IMF with more credibility.

REFERENCES

Alexander, K. (2009), 'Global financial standard setting, the G10 Committees, and international economic law', *Brooklyn Journal of International Law*, **34**, 861.

Alexander, K., R. Dhumale and J. Eatwell (2006), *Global Governance of Financial Systems: The International Regulation of Systemic Risk*, Oxford: Oxford University Press.

Burns, T. (2011), 'The role of law and the shadow banking sector', in K. Alexander and R. Dhumale (eds), *The Research Handbook of International Financial Regulation*, Cheltenham, UK and Northampton, MA, USA: Edward Elgar Publishing, pp. 48–71.

Financial Action Task Force (2009), *Annual Report 2008–2009*, Paris: OECD.

Financial Services Authority (FSA) (2007), *Principles-based Regulation – Focusing on the Outcomes that Matter*, London: Financial Services Authority, April.

Financial Stability Board (FSB) (2009a), *Principles for Sound Compensation Practices: Implementation Standards*, Basel: BIS, September.

Financial Stability Board (FSB) (2009b), *Reports of the Financial Stability Board to G20 Finance Ministers and Governors, Overview of Progress in Implementing the London Summit Recommendations for Strengthening Financial Stability*, FSB September Report, pp. 2–3 and FSB November Report, p. 13, Basel: BIS.

Freeland, C. (2011), 'Calibrating capital requirements programmes', paper presented at New Challenges in Financial Regulation and Supervision, Christ's College, Cambridge, 21 September.

Gola, C. and F. Spadafora (2009), 'Financial sector surveillance and the IMF', Working Paper 247, IMF, Washington, DC.

Gold, Sir Joseph (1996), *Interpretation: The International Monetary Fund and International Law*, London: Kluwer International Law.

G20 Heads of State (2009), 'London Statement', 2 April.

International Monetary Fund (IMF) (2009a), 'IMF-FSB early warning exercise', IMF Factsheet, IMF, Washington, DC.

International Monetary Fund (IMF) (2009b), Committee on IMF Governance Reform, *Final Report*, IMF, Washington, DC, March.

International Monetary Fund (IMF) (2009c), 'Initial lessons of the crisis for the global architecture and the IMF', IMF Strategy, Policy and Review Department, available at http://www.imf.org/external/np/pp/eng/2009/021809. pdf (last accessed 15 August 2011).

International Organisation of Securities Commissions (IOSCO) (2004), *Code of Conduct Fundamentals for Credit Rating Agencies* (updated 2008), available at http://www.iosco.org/library/pubdocs/pdf/IOSCOPD271.pdf (accessed November 2009).

King, Sir Mervyn (2010), Speech at the University of Exeter, 19 January.

Köndgen, J. (2002), 'Regulation of banking services in the European Union: a comparative view', in J. Basedow, H. Baum, K.J. Hopt, H. Kanda and T. Kono (eds), *Economic Regulation and Competition: Regulation of Services in the EU, Germany and Japan*, The Hague and London: Kluwer Law, pp. 27–74.

Trichet, J.C. (2009), 'Macro-prudential supervision in Europe', Text of the 2nd City Lecture, available at http://www.ecb.int/press//key/date/2009/html/sp091211_2.en.html (last accessed 15 August 2011).

Walker, G.A.E., (2000), *International Banking Regulation: Law, Policy, and Practice*, Boston, MA: Kluwer Law International.

17. The shock of the old: the first financial crisis of the twenty-first century

Geoffrey Wood[1]

17.1 INTRODUCTION

The first banking crisis of the twenty-first century came towards the end of the first decade of that century. It was a surprise almost everywhere, and nowhere was it a greater surprise than in Britain. For the Bank of England, with the guidance of a few outsiders, had learned how to prevent crises by the third quarter of the nineteenth century. There had been no financial crisis in Britain – even at the outbreak of wars – since then. Much the same can be said of most of the countries that had learned from the Bank of England and followed its crisis-preventing procedures.

But crisis there was. What had changed between the nineteenth and twenty-first centuries to allow this to happen? And what is worth changing now so as to make such events less likely in the future? Probably there are many things that would help. But in this chapter it is argued that one change was crucial. That change allowed individual failure to lead to crisis. Reversing it is essential to prevent banking crises recurring.

It is necessary first to be precise as to what is meant by a banking crisis. Once that is done discussion of how they were prevented in the past naturally follows. That enables identification of the crucial difference between the nineteenth and twenty-first centuries. It is then possible to proceed to consider how to remove this difference.

17.2 WHAT IS A BANKING CRISIS?

In her 'Real and pseudo financial crises' (1986), Anna Schwartz considered this question.

> A widely held belief in the United States and the world financial community is that the default of major debtors – whether companies or municipalities

or sovereign countries – could lead to bank failures that would precipitate a financial crisis. The remedy proposed by those propagating this view is that major debtors therefore must be rescued from the threat of bankruptcy to avert the projected dire consequences for banks and for the stability of the financial system. I shall argue that (a) the debtor whose affairs have been mismanaged should be liquidated or reorganised under new management; (b) default by major debtors need not result in bank failures; (c) if defaults do result in bank failures, so long as the security of the private sector's deposits is assured, no financial crisis will ensue. (Schwartz, 1986, p. 11)

Her argument was in three parts. First, there was a brief comparative history of crises in England and of episodes when they did not occur in England but did in the USA, and an explanation for the differences. This is followed by an examination of the frequently expressed views of Charles Kindleberger (for example, 1978) that 'manias' and crises are inextricable. And third, she argues that the belief that 'financial distress' triggers financial crises is based on a misunderstanding of history.

The individual episodes she considers were 1866, 1873, 1890, 1907, 1914 and 1931. 1866 was the famous Overend-Gurney crisis. In 1873 there were, after a sharp fall in stock prices in Vienna, a series of such declines across Europe. Britain experienced only a series of increases in Bank rate over four weeks, followed by a reversal over the subsequent ten weeks. In contrast, the USA experienced a 'real' crisis. 'By 22 October, the currency was virtually unobtainable at par' (Schwartz, 1986, p. 4). In 1890 there were stock price falls in the USA, and in London the failure of Barings, but no financial crisis occurred in either country. In 1907 there were serious problems in New York. There was a restriction of payments by banks, and currency went to a premium over deposits; but in London there was no panic, only three increases in bank rate, intended and sufficient to restore gold stocks after shipments to New York. 1914 saw panic in both countries, and a severe liquidity squeeze, with the outbreak of war; but crisis in neither. 1931, Britain's abandoning of gold, is often said to have been a crisis. But internally there was no crisis; indeed, all the consequences were benign. Schumpeter's description is characteristically vivid:

> In England there was neither panic nor – precisely owing to the way in which the thing had been done or, if the reader prefer, had come about – loss of 'confidence' but rather a sigh of relief. (Schumpeter, 1939, p. 956)

Why the contrasts between these various episodes? Schwartz explains as follows:

> The reasons may now be summarised, accounting for financial crises that did or did not occur in the past. In both cases the setting is one in which the

financial distress of certain firms became known to market participants, raising alarm as creditors became concerned about the value of their claims not only on those firms but also firms previously in sound condition. Banks that were creditors of the firms in distress became targets of suspicion by the depositors. *When monetary authorities failed to demonstrate readiness at the beginning of such a disturbance to meet all demands of sound debtors for loans and of depositors for cash, a financial crisis occurred. A financial crisis per contra could be averted by timely predictable signals to market participants of institutional readiness to make available an augmented supply of funds.* The sources of the funds supplied might have been inflows from abroad – attracted by higher domestic than foreign interest rates – or emergency issues of domestic currency. The readiness was all. Knowledge of the availability of the supply was sufficient to allay alarm, so that the funds were never drawn on. (Schwartz, 1986 p. 21) [Emphasis added]

17.3   CRISIS PREVENTION

Britain started to learn how to prevent banking crises in 1793, when war was declared between France and Britain.

That dreadful calamity is usually preceded by some indication which enables the commercial and monied men to make preparation. On this occasion the short notice rendered the least degree of general preparation impossible. The foreign market was either shut, or rendered more difficult of access to the merchant. Of course he would not purchase from the manufacturers; ... the manufacturers in their distress applied to the Bankers in the country for relief; but as the want of money became general, and that want increased gradually by a general alarm, the country Banks required the payment of old debts. . . . In this predicament the country at large could have no other resource but London; and after having exhausted the bankers, that resource finally terminated in the Bank of England. In such cases the Bank are not an intermediary body, or power; there is no resource on their refusal, for they are the *dernier resort*. (Baring, 1797, pp. 19–23)

Thus did Francis Baring, writing in 1797 of the dramatic events of 1793, introduce the notion of the Bank of England as the 'last resort' of the banking system.

Very soon after that use of the term *dernier resort*, Henry Thornton (1802) provided a statement of what the role was, why it was necessary and how it should operate. This statement was essentially a complete description of the lender of last resort role as it worked up to the beginning of this century. His statement was made in a particular institutional context; it is useful for subsequent clarity to describe what that context was.

There were many banks in England all (except the Bank of England) constrained to being partnerships of six or fewer. The joint stock form was not generally allowed until 1826, and limited liability not until 1858. Even with the care unlimited liability brought, failures were common. Here the Bank of England comes in.

> If any bank fails, a general run upon the neighbouring banks is apt to take place, which if not checked in the beginning by a pouring into the circulation of a very large quantity of gold, leads to very extensive mischief. (Thornton, 1802, p. 182)

And who was to 'pour in' this gold?

> if the Bank of England, in future seasons of alarm, should be disposed to extend its discounts in a greater degree than heretofore, then the threatened calamity may be averted. (Thornton, 1802, p. 188)

This was not incompatible with allowing some individual institutions to fail.

> It is by no means intended to imply that it would become the Bank of England to relieve every distress which the rashness of country banks may bring upon them: the Bank by doing this, might encourage their improvidence. . . . The relief should neither be so prompt and liberal as to exempt those who mis-conduct their business from all the natural consequences of their fault, nor so scanty and slow as deeply to involve the general interests. (Thornton, 1802, p. 188)

Concern should be with the system as a whole.

And the reason a 'pouring into the circulation' (to use Thornton's phrase) would stop a panic and stabilize the system was described with great clarity by Bagehot in 1873:

> What is wanted and what is necessary to stop a panic is to diffuse the impression that though money may be dear, still money is to be had. If people could really be convinced that they would have money . . . . Most likely they would cease to run in such a herd-like way for money. (Bagehot, 1873, pp. 64–5)

In the kind of banking system which Britain had by the mid to late nineteenth century, a system based on gold but with the central bank the monopoly supplier of notes, the responsibility for diffusing 'the impression that . . . . Money is to be had' clearly rested with the central bank. Exactly why was set out by Bagehot in 1848:

> It is a great defect of a purely metallic circulation that the quantity of it cannot be readily suited to any sudden demand; it takes time to get new supplies of

gold and silver, and, in the meantime, a temporary rise in the value of bullion takes place. Now as paper money can be supplied in unlimited quantities, however sudden the demand may be, it does not appear to us that there is any objection on principle of sudden issues of paper money to meet sudden and large extensions of demand. It gives to a purely metallic circulation that greater constancy of purchasing power possessed by articles whose quantity can be quickly suited to demand. It will be evident from what we have said before that this power of issuing notes is one excessively liable to abuse because, as before shown, it may depreciate the currency; and on that account such a power ought only to be lodged in the hands of government . . . . It should only be used in rare and exceptional circumstances. But when the fact of a *sudden* demand is proved, we see no objection, but decided advantage, in introducing this new element into a metallic circulation. (Bagehot, 1848, p. 192, emphasis in original)

That summarises nineteenth-century theory on the subject. Because the central bank was the monopoly note issuer, it was the ultimate source of cash. If it does not supply that cash in a panic, the panic will continue, get worse and a widespread banking collapse will ensue, bringing with it a sharp monetary contraction. What was nineteenth-century practice?

Sterling returned to its pre-war gold parity in 1821. The first subsequent occasion for emergency assistance from the Bank was in 1825. There had been a substantial external drain of gold, and there was a shortage of currency. A panic developed, and there were runs on banks. The type of bills the Bank would normally discount soon ran out and the panic continued. If a wave of bank failures were to be prevented, the banks would have had to borrow on the security of other types of assets. On 14 December the Bank of England suddenly deviated from its normal practice, and made advances on government securities offered to it by the banks instead of limiting itself to discounting commercial bills. Of that change of policy Jeremiah Harman, a Director of the Bank, spoke as follows when giving evidence before a Parliamentary Committee in 1832. The Bank had lent money 'by every possible means and in modes we had never adopted before; we took in stock on security, we purchased Exchequer bills, we made advances on Exchequer bills, we not only discounted outright but we made advances on the deposit of bills of exchange to an immense amount, in short by every means consistent with the safety of the Bank, and we were not on some occasions over nice.'

As Hawtrey wrote of these now famous remarks, 'In reality the advances he describes were of a highly conservative character' (1932, p. 122). But to continue the quotation from Hawtrey: 'The importance of the change in practice was that it admitted a class of borrowers on irreproachable security, who had nevertheless been barred by the previous limitations. The concession was a real one, and it stayed the panic.'

The next step was taken in 1866, with the Overend, Gurney Crisis.

Overend, Gurney, and Co. originated with two eighteenth-century firms, the Gurney Bank (of Norwich) and the London firm of Richardson, Overend and company. By the 1850s the combined firm was very large; its annual turnover of bills of exchange was in value equal to about half the national debt, and its balance sheet was ten times the size of the next largest bank. It was floated during the stock market boom of 1865 but by early 1866 the boom had ended. Bank rate had been raised from 3 per cent in July 1865 to 7 per cent in January 1866. After February, the bank rate started to ease, but on 11 May Gurney's was declared insolvent.

To quote the *Bankers' Magazine* from June 1866, 'a terror and anxiety took possession of men's minds for the remainder of that and the whole following day'. The Bank of England for a brief time made matters worse by hesitating to lend even on government debt. The Bank Charter Act (which, among other things, restricted the note issue to the extent of the gold reserve plus a small fiduciary issue) was then suspended, and the panic gradually subsided.

The failure in 1878 of the city of Glasgow Bank was much less dramatic. The bank had started respectably, subsequently was managed fraudulently, and then failed. There was fear that the Bank Charter Act would have to be suspended again (see Pressnell, 1968), but no major problems appeared.

In 1890 came the (first) 'Baring Crisis'. When this bank got into difficulties, although there was some switching of bills of exchange into cash there was no major panic and no run on London or on sterling. The impact on financial markets was small.

Why the great difference between the first of these episodes and the second and third? The Bank of England had both learned to act as lender of last resort (LOLR) and had made it clear that it stood ready so to act. What the Bank had done wrong in 1866 was to lend 'hesitatingly, reluctantly, and with misgiving . . .' (Bagehot, 1873). The Bank learned the appropriate action quickly; H.H. Gibb, Governor of the Bank from 1875 to 1877 described the 1866 crisis as 'the Bank's only real blunder in his experience'; but he did not criticize the then Governor, for 'the matter was not as well-understood then as it is now . . .'.

The lesson learned in Britain was that a banking crisis could be stopped by prompt LOLR action. This lesson was learned also overseas; a good example is provided by the Banca d'Italia, which in its 1910 report and accounts referred to 'The Bagehot Principle', and said that it would henceforward act as LOLR. Its doing so stabilized Italian banking.

17.4 WHY SHOCK AND DISORDER?

Since what to do to prevent a banking crisis had been so well established in the nineteenth century, why was there such shock and disorder when one threatened in the twenty-first century?

The start of the crisis in Britain was with the problems of a bank called Northern Rock. Northern Rock had been created by the merger of two 'building societies', the Northern Counties and the Rock, on 1 July 1965. Building societies were mutuals, owned by their depositors and their borrowers. Their deposits came primarily from retail customers, and their major (essentially sole) lending activity was to individuals to buy their residences. In the 1990s these organizations were allowed to demutualize, and 'convert' (in the term of the time) to banks. Most of the large societies converted. Northern Rock was among them. It demutualized on 1 October 1997.

All the demutualized societies grew, and many were taken over by or merged with previously existing banks. Northern Rock remained independent. Aside from that, two features of its post-demutualization behaviour were distinctive. It grew very rapidly. At the end of 1997 its assets (on a consolidated basis) stood at £15.8 billion. By the end of 2006 its assets had reached £101.0 billion. But it never departed from its traditional focus on residential mortgage assets, which by end-2006 were £86.8 billion, that is, about 86 per cent of total assets. Even so, at the end of the second quarter of 2007 these mortgage loans were only 8 per cent (by value) of the stock of mortgage debt in the UK, and therefore only about 5 per cent of total bank lending, while Northern Rock deposits were only about 2 per cent of sterling bank deposits. It was not an enormous institution.

The second feature relates to its liabilities. While on the asset side of the balance sheet it remained close to the traditional building society model, concentrating on lending on mortgage to individuals wishing to buy their own home, there were dramatic changes in the structure of its liabilities. It adopted an 'originate to distribute' model of funding, using securitization, the issue of covered bonds (bonds issued by banks and collateralized against property), and direct borrowing in the wholesale markets, to finance its lending.

This dependence on wholesale markets for the large majority of its funding was what most distinguished Northern Rock from other UK banks. Retail deposits (and other classes of retail funds) did grow, but not nearly as rapidly as wholesale funds. Retail funds fell as a proportion of the total liabilities and equity of Northern Rock from 62.7 per cent at end-1997 to 22.4 per cent at end-2006.

When the wholesale money markets essentially closed in autumn 2007 it is unsurprising that Northern Rock experienced difficulties. That this was a shock is understandable. There had been no such problems in the UK since 1866. In another way of course it is not understandable, for it reflected a major failure by the supervisors of Northern Rock, and to an extent in the supervisory system; these failures are discussed in Milne and Wood (2009) and *The Run on the Rock*, the report of the House of Commons Treasury Select Committee into the affair.

But what is important from the point of view of the present chapter is not these failures, but the reaction to the problems of Northern Rock. The Authorities (the term for the collective of the Bank of England, the Financial Services Authority (FSA) and the Treasury) did not follow the traditional, well-tested and shown to be robust nineteenth-century approach. They could have considered whether the troubled institution was of sufficient importance that its failure would have damaged the reputation of London, as they did in the case of Barings in 1890, and if it failed that test it would have been allowed to sink or swim, and liquidity would have been provided to the rest of the banking sector as needed to calm any subsequent panic.

Northern Rock was not allowed to sink or swim. There was a determined attempt to keep the institution going, or to find a rescuer for it. This can certainly not be justified by the size or reputation of Northern Rock. It was not a particularly large institution, and even its greatest admirer would not claim that it was a bank of international renown similar to that of Barings in 1890. Why, then, did the Authorities act as they did?

A range of factors probably mattered. First and most obviously is that the problem came as a shock, and one to previously untested regulatory and money market regimes. Then there are some essentially political factors about which it is only possible at this time to speculate. These are discussed in Milne and Wood (2009).

But there were also 'economic' reasons why the traditional course was not followed. There was an aspect of the Bank's money market operations, and then, more fundamentally, the nature of interbank linkages. These latter made it extremely difficult to subject a commercial bank to a normal corporate insolvency procedure. And finally, the nature of retail bank deposits in the twenty-first century differed from that in the nineteenth century, and in a way that made even orderly closures of a bank difficult both politically and economically.

Detailed discussion of money market operations would take us too far from the main line of analysis; but briefly, the problem was that while the system did allow for banks to obtain additional liquidity from the Bank of England, it also made it highly likely that receiving such assistance would be interpreted as a sign of problems. That of course created problems even if none more serious that a trifling error in forecasting liquidity needs had until then existed.[2]

The nature and extent of interbank linkages create a problem with the 'sink or swim' option in the following way. When Northern Rock got into difficulties there was no separate legal framework for handling bank insolvency; it would have been subject to the normal law of corporate insolvency. Its transactions, its assets and its liabilities would be frozen. A court-appointed liquidator would try, avoiding a 'fire sale', to dispose of the assets at the best possible price, taking quite possibly some time to do so in order to minimize the loss for creditors. This would of course cause problems for a modern banking system, as it could leave many transactions uncompleted for months or even years.[3]

Northern Rock's failure thus highlighted the absence in the UK of any regime for handling bank insolvency, which was available in some other countries.

Finally, on the reasons for the Authorities' actions, when 'sink or swim' was the course of action retail depositors differed in two ways from their modern-day counterparts. They were more prosperous than the average citizen, and they did not rely to the same extent on bank transactions for day to day living – banking services were not as crucial to functioning in nineteenth-century society as they are now. In Britain today the politicians, who make the ultimate decision over bank closure, could not tolerate bank customers, especially poor ones, losing both money and access to banking services. Indeed, aside from any questions of protecting savings, loss of access to banking services would impede economic efficiency in many ways, by, for example, forcing reliance on cash and unwarrantedly destroying credit ratings.

Britain does have a deposit insurance scheme supposedly intended to deal with these things, but despite changes since Northern Rock (an increase in the amount covered) it remains significantly defective. There are no practical arrangements for ensuring that insured depositors are paid out in any reasonably short time period; they could have to wait months for the money that is due to them.

It might so far appear that all that is needed to restore stability, through allowing the nineteenth-century approach of providing general liquidity and not bailing out individual institutions, is to improve deposit protection and have a special insolvency regime for banks. These are at least in outline straightforward measures. Are they really all that is needed? To clarify, a wider look at the crisis is necessary.

Before taking that wider look it should be remarked that there have already been some changes in the UK. It is now possible to take a bank away from its shareholders and management while it is still solvent, and keep it running so that all who transact with it can continue doing so. The bank can then be sold on, in an orderly way, in whole or in parts, to buyers who will keep it running and restore it to financial health. The proceeds from the sale are used to settle the bank's debts, and anything left goes to the shareholders.

Such a facility, which has existed for some years in the USA, was proposed in the UK by the Treasury Select Committee of the House of Commons, and the proposal was implemented in the Banking Act (2009). The procedure has already been successfully used to carry out the closure of the Dunfermline Building Society in 2009.

17.5   A WIDER LOOK AT THE CRISIS

The problems so far examined were capable of being solved, at any rate in principle, very simply. Bring in a means of orderly bank closure, and, together with provision of liquidity to prevent that closure's damaging other banks through contagion, the problem is solved. Is that really all that would have been needed to make the recent crisis a non-crisis? Certainly not. There remain four other problems. First, that solution can deal only with shortage of liquidity. Second, internationally diversified banks may fall between jurisdictions. Third, there is no approach in that framework for closing investment banks in an orderly way. And fourth and last, there is a presumption that the closure rules can function for all (non-investment) banks, even ones bigger than the Dunfermline Building Society.

Let us take these in turn.

17.5.1   Liquidity or Capital

The classic origin of a banking crisis is a liquidity crisis. One bank for some reason cannot meet all its payment obligations. In consequence other banks experience runs, they too get into difficulties because, by the nature of fractional reserve banking, they cannot immediately pay out on all deposits, and in the extreme the entire banking system collapses like a row of dominoes.

The other possible cause is when there is a sharp decline in the value of a bank's capital. This could come about, for example, if one large loan suddenly collapsed in value, or if a whole group of loans collapsed. As bank balance sheets are opaque to customers (and apparently often to management too if recent experience is anything to go by) this leads to fears about the solvency of other banks, runs take place on them, and in the extreme the whole system fails.[4]

Of course if either is allowed to persist shortages of both capital and liquidity emerge; but there are two possible originating factors.

It was a liquidity crisis that LOLR emerged to contain. How it does so, and how it emerged, was described above.

The archetypal capital crisis also occurred in England. This episode, as it turned out, was confined to one bank, and thus was not a banking 'system' crisis, but it could easily have spread to the entire system, and indeed perhaps beyond. This was the 'Baring Crisis' of 1890.

Barings was then a bank of high and long-standing reputation, but it had become somewhat complacent. Driven by competition to seek higher returns, it invested substantially in Argentina. Then, in April 1890, the Argentinean government did not pay the bulk of interest then due on its debts. Partly in consequence, the Argentinean national bank suspended interest payment on its debts. This precipitated a run on the Argentinean banking system and there was a revolution on 26 July. Barings had lent heavily in Argentina. By November it became clear to its directors that it could not survive unaided, and on 8 November it revealed its problems to the Bank of England. The Bank was horrified, fearing a run on the British banking system, and perhaps on sterling, if Barings defaulted. After a hurried inspection of the books of Barings, it was decided that the situation could be saved by a substantial injection of capital. A consortium was organized – the Bank was too small to have sufficient funds on its own – and Barings was saved. There was some anxiety briefly in the London markets when news of the rescue leaked (as such news tends to), but no more than a tremor. The episode was contained to an individual firm.

That is a perfect example of a capital crisis. A firm is short of capital and cannot pay its debts. If this brings down other banks, or if depositors in the original bank lose their deposits, a system-wide liquidity crisis may start. It may start because depositors are (inevitably) unclear about the state of the balance sheet of their bank, so fear for it when another bank previously believed to be sound appears to be in difficulties. But the injection of capital can stop the crisis short. Note that central bank provision of liquidity would not suffice, for, to continue with the example of Barings, Barings did not have sufficient short-term assets to offer in exchange for the liquidity. The Bank would have had to accept some of Barings' long-term assets as collateral, and not only would this have been against a recently settled policy but the Bank's balance sheet was too small to let it assume the risk.

A comparison between the 2007–09 crisis, the first major banking crisis of the twenty-first century, and the crisis of 1929–33, the first major banking crisis of the twentieth century, is now helpful.

What was the main cause of 1929–33? The US economy started to decline after the 1929 Stock Market Crash. But the decline of 1929–30 was not the end of the decline. There were three further years, by which time money income in the USA had fallen by 53 per cent and real income by 36 per cent. There had been wave after wave of bank failures, which did not end until the closure of all banks by President Roosevelt and the suspension of gold shipments abroad on 6 March 1933. Why these waves of bank failures?

The two explanations are banking practices of previous years, with banks getting into securities dealing, and, in competition with that, the behaviour of the Federal Reserve. The first explanation has been examined by Peach (1941), Benston (1990) and Kroszner and Rajan (1994), among many others. All found that securities dealing did not bring the banks down. The cause of their collapse was substantial pressure on bank liquidity, unrelieved by Federal Reserve action. Banks were forced to sell their holdings of government bonds at a deep discount, thus adding shortage of capital to shortage of liquidity. But the cause of failure was the Federal Reserve's behaviour. It had lent as Walter Bagehot had criticized the Bank of England for in the 1866 crisis in London; 'hesitantly, reluctantly, and with misgiving'. As Bagehot went on, 'to make large advances in this faltering way is to incur the evil of making them without incurring the advantage . . .'.[5]

That, then, was manifestly a liquidity crisis at least in its origins. How did it spread across the world? As the monetary approach to the balance of payments leads one to expect, the monetary squeeze in the USA affected those countries pegged to the US dollar (through gold, in this case) but left countries without such a link substantially unaffected. Countries such as Sweden and the UK, which broke early from the gold standard, escaped the consequences of the US problems, while those that stayed on gold, such as France, experienced banking strains and severe recessions.[6]

Some have argued – notably Tim Congdon (2009) – that the recent crisis was also triggered by liquidly shortage. He has maintained that Northern Rock could have been kept functioning in the private sector had the Bank of England been willing to accept its assets as collateral for the provision of liquidity. And the same point could apply by extension to all banks that received capital injections from taxpayers. The claim is arguable – would the provision of liquidity on the scale required and by the method then in use (see Milne and Wood, 2009) have triggered fears about the solvency about Northern Rock and indeed other banks? And there is a further point. Once Northern Rock's problems had emerged, had the Bank of England provided liquidity against the assets Northern Rock could offer there would have been a downside for the Bank limited only by the size of Northern Rock's balance sheet, but upside limited by the extent of the haircut taken and the proportion of the assets that came good. The same would apply to the assistance given to every other bank. In contrast, injections of capital gave a potentially substantial upside for the taxpayer, so the risk was not so skewed. It is fair to conclude that the problems were so substantial that a liquidity injection might not have worked, and would certainly have been irrational from the point of view of the liquidity provider.

The conclusion that capital shortage was the essence of the recent crisis is reinforced by considering how it spread. Here the contrast with 1929–33 could not be sharper. It spread between countries whose exchange rates were floating – the USA and the UK, for example. And it did not spread across all of an area that used a single currency, the extreme case of fixed exchange rates – some countries in the Eurozone found their banking systems either unaffected, or affected only trivially, Finland, for example.

It can be concluded that the first crisis of the twenty-first century was a capital crisis, not a liquidity crisis. Banks suddenly found themselves with insufficient capital to reassure their creditors.

Therefore it would appear that to ensure an individual bank's failure cannot lead to a general banking crisis there must be a mechanism for the injection of capital as well as one for the injection of liquidity. To this it may be objected that such a mechanism is only needed if there is no mechanism for orderly bank resolution, necessitating by its absence the need to keep insolvent banks alive by restoring their solvency. That objection is simply noted here, and considered more fully after the discussions of international and investment banks. The mechanism is also discussed subsequently.

17.5.2 International Banks

For international banks there is no difficulty so long as the problem is shortage of liquidity – a normal LOLR operation is what is required. But as considered immediately above, banks can also fail because of loss of capital.

The USA, where failures have been relatively common, has tried to construct a system where the incentives to restrict losses are compatible across the parties involved. However, as soon as we look across borders, various countries' national systems are ill matched. Indeed in many cases they are explicitly contradictory. If each country attempts to minimize the losses in the event of a cross-border bank within its own jurisdictional powers it will almost certainly be doing so at the expense of losses in another jurisdiction. While the European Union (EU) has been alert to these problems and has tried to construct the arrangements for handling failures so that the cross-border bank is treated as a single entity under the Winding Up Directive[7] and all creditors and debtors within its jurisdiction are treated equally according to priority, irrespective of their nationality or residence, there remain major gaps in the system (Lastra and Wood, 2011).

Outside the EU the problems are greater because there is no explicit drive to try to create an effective single financial market. Even in Australia and New Zealand, between which countries economic integration is more developed than in the EU, each country is currently trying to make sure that it can apply as near a national approach as is possible so that it can control the impacts on its own country.

The problem is particularly severe for a small country. If much of its banking system is foreign-owned then it may effectively be dependent upon the decisions of the authorities in other countries both for the avoidance of problems and for their resolution. If, on the other hand, like Switzerland, it is home to large multinational banks whose main operations are abroad, it may not have the resources to handle a major failure on its own.[8] (Sweden is facing the prospect of having both problems by being the home country for Nordea, which has the large majority of its operations abroad, and host to Danske Bank, which is growing to systemic proportions in Sweden.)

If the cross-border bank chose to operate entirely through branches (as has been proposed for Nordea under the European Company Statute) then such a scheme could be administered by the home country authorities. As in the USA they would be the insurer of the deposits across the whole group. Where the arrangement is more mixed, some national authorities may be prepared to see subsidiaries close because they are not of systemic importance, while others would wish to apply the bridge bank or an equivalent technique.

This implies that some joint arrangement needs to be established, and one that can operate swiftly according to some predetermined guidelines. To summarize then, international banks present considerable problems, not least that interests may well conflict as between national jurisdictions. This is not a problem for economists to solve, but only for them to highlight.

17.5.3 Investment Banks

There is no problem with investment banks in the traditional sense of the term – organizations that provided advice and assisted with raising capital. But such firms are now rare. Most so-called investment banks now not only provide advice and help with raising finance, but lend funds in their own right and are continually engaged in transactions across a range of markets either to assist customers or to make profits directly on their own account.

A fundamental difficulty is to decide what a trigger point for takeover by an administrator would be for such a firm. Further, such firms are viable only so long as other firms think they are viable. Could a firm taken over for the sake of maintaining financial stability persuade other firms of its viability? Someone would have to stand behind it. This suggests that there may need to be a government agency, an 'investment bank of last resort', charged with running such institutions.

17.5.4   Too Big to Close?

A special insolvency law for banks is yet to be adequately tested in many jurisidictions. Such a law not only allows but compels a bank to be taken over by some administrator before it becomes insolvent. It is taken over as it approaches some predetermined threshold. The bank is then run no longer in the interests of the shareholders, but in the interests of financial stability. Its activities are run down or sold off in an orderly manner. In principle there is such a law for banks in Britain already. It has been applied, and worked – for the Dunfermline Building Society, for example. That is an important example as it highlights how untested the law is for serious events. It points to the urgency and importance of every bank developing a 'living will'.

The term 'living will' comes from a development in English law relating to individuals and their wellbeing. When an individual dies, if they leave a will which is legal then whatever property they leave on death is disposed of according to their wishes, subject to taxes and any challenges from parties who think they were entitled to a bequest (or a bigger bequest). A 'living will' does very much the same thing, but for an individual who although incapacitated is not dead. The 'will' appoints 'attorneys', who can take decisions for the individual who can no longer do so, either according to instructions given in the 'living will' or if discretion has been given then according to what they think best for the individual. These decisions can appertain either to medical treatment (including its withdrawal or withholding) or to financial matters, or both.

The idea is then that banks draw up an analogous document. What would the document do?

Large banks could, quite simply, be beyond the capacity of the liquidators to understand and wind down in a reasonable period of time. That is the problem 'living wills' are designed to deal with. They would tell an outsider how the bank worked. They would clearly assign different assets and liabilities to different subdivisions of the bank. They would provide an accessible list of counterparties, and their associated transactions. They would clearly describe provisioning and write-off procedures that had been adopted in particular cases and were adopted as general rules. In short, just as a person's living will lays out what should be done when they can no longer do it for themselves, so would a bank's living will provide all the information needed for someone to intervene when it was in trouble and run it down (or otherwise dispose of it) in a prompt and orderly manner.

These living wills would thus be important in two ways. First, they would ensure that when some institution, however large or complex, got into difficulties, it could be handled without major collateral problems. That in itself is a good argument for them. Second, and associated with that, these wills would make future crises less likely. For they would ensure that no bank was ever again 'too big to fail'. The 'brooding presence' (Bucheit, 2009) of the risk of failure would once again make bankers act in a prudent way.

17.6   CONCLUSIONS

A market system cannot function unless it is possible for firms to fail. This failure must be orderly. This is essential for all but the smallest of organizations, and even then its absence is a nuisance and impedes the efficiency of the capital market. For banks, with their importance to monetary policy and their links throughout the economy, its absence would be a disaster. Hence only when there is a system to allow orderly closure of banks, including large ones international ones and investment banks, is there no danger of chaotic bailouts again in the future.

That is the main conclusion of this chapter. More can of course be done. Admirable proposals for capital requirements were laid out in Haldane (2011). These proposals are simple, transparent and enforceable – in clear contrast to more elaborate schemes.

Two matters remain. The proposals above are designed to deal with individual banks. What if an entire banking system is hit simultaneously? If that were really to happen, no alternative to taxpayer support exists. But it should be noted that individual prudence will do much to diminish the likelihood of such events. And one other unresolved question. Should there be a mechanism for the orderly injection of capital, such as that described in Wood (2012, forthcoming), lest there are doubts about the robustness of the insolvency mechanism for some bank? The proposed mechanism involves depoliticizing the process, as LOLR was depoliticized in the nineteenth century by having the Bank of England take the initiative over any necessary suspension of the gold standard. The problem is of course that the existence of a mechanism makes it more likely it will be used.

On these two notes of uncertainty, surely appropriate in a world that suffers from uncertainly as well as risk, this chapter concludes.

NOTES

1. I am greatly indebted to Dr Ali Kabiri of Cass Business School and the University of Buckingham for his assistance and suggestions on this chapter.
2. See Milne and Wood (2009) for details.
3. In an insolvency REPO borrowing (financing through an initial sale of a security and its later repurchase at a slightly higher price) is closed out, in a similar way to over the counter (OTC) derivative transactions, but unsecured borrowing such as Northern Rock relied on, because it lacked eligible collateral for REPO finance, must be left finally to be resolved through the insolvency procedure.
4. These runs may well, in modern circumstances, be what are called 'silent runs'. These are runs by relatively well-informed participants in wholesale markets, who can often 'run' simply by declining to roll over their loans. These runs can but need not be well founded, for a bank's balance sheet is to an extent opaque also to its banking counterparties.
5. The classic study of the 1929–33 episode is of Friedman and Schwartz (1963), chapter 7.
6. A brief overview of the years can be found in the introductory essay to *Critical Writings on the Great Depression* (Capie and Wood, 2011).
7. Directive 2001/24/EC of 4 April on the reorganization and winding up of credit institutions OJ 2001 L 125/15.
8. In Switzerland, for example, the authorities have announced that there will be a cap of four billion CHF on the payout associated with any single institution, thus limiting the liability of the insurance fund but leaving open the prospect of some residual disturbance to the financial system at home and abroad.

REFERENCES

Bagehot, W. (1848), 'The currency problem', *Prospective Review*, 297–337.

Bagehot, W. (1873), *Lombard Street*, London: Henry King.

Baring, F. (1797), *Observations on the Establishment of the Bank of England and on the Paper Circulation of the Country*, New York: A.M. Kelly, facsimile reprint 1967, ed. F.A. Hayek, pp. 19–23.

Benston, G.J. (1990), *The Separation of Commercial and Investment Banking. The Glass-Steagall Act Revisited and Reconsidered*, London and New York: ONP and Macmillan.

Bucheit, L. (2009), House of Lords Economic Affairs Committee, oral evidence.

Capie, F.H. and G. Wood (2011), *Critical Writings on the Great Depression*, London: Routledge.

Congdon, T. (2009), *Central Banking in a Free Society*, London: Institute of Economic Affairs, chapter 6.

Friedman, M. and A.J. Schwartz (1963), *A Monetary History of the United States (1867–1960)*, Princeton, NJ: Princeton University Press.

Haldane, A. (2011), 'Capital discipline', Speech given to the American Economic Association, Bank of England, 9 January.

Hawtrey, R. (1932), *The Art of Central Banking*, London: Longmans, Green & Co.

Kindleberger, C.P. (1978), *Manias Panics and Crashes*, New York: Basic Books, Kroszner.

Kroszner, R.S. and R.G. Rajan (1994), 'Is the Glass-Steagal Act justified? A study of the U.S experience with universal banking reform before 1933', *American Economic Review*, **84**(4), 810.

Lastra, R. and G. Wood (2011), 'The crisis of 2007–2009: nature, causes, and reactions', *Journal of International Economic Law*, **13**(3), 531–50.

Milne, A.K. and G. Wood (2009), 'Shattered on the rock? British financial stability from 1866 to 2007', *Journal of Banking Regulation*, **10**(2), 43–62.

Peach, N. (1941), *The Security Affiliates of National Banks*, Baltimore, MD: Johns Hopkins University Press.

Pressnell, L. (1968), 'Gold reserves, banking reserves, and the Baring crisis of 1890', in C.R. Whittlesey and J.S.G. Wilson (eds), *Essays in Money and Banking in Honour of RS Sayers*, Oxford: Oxford University Press, pp. 167–228.

Schumpeter, J.A. (1939), *Business Cycles*, New York and London: McGraw Hill.

Schwartz, A.J. (1986), 'Real and pseudo financial crises', in F.H. Capie and G.E. Wood (eds), *Financial Crises and the World Banking System*, London: Macmillan, pp. 11–40.

Thornton, H. (1802), *An Enquiry into the Effects of the Paper Credit of Great Britain*, reprinted 1978 (with an introduction by F.A. Hayek), Fairfield, NJ: Augustus Kelly.

Wood, G. (2012), 'Relationships with governments and bankers', in C. Jones and R. Pringle (eds), *Central Banking in the 21st Century*, London: Central Banking Publications, pp. 43–54.

18. Fixing finance: are we there yet?

Thomas F. Huertas[1]

Crises are costly. The crisis that started in August 2007 has already cost society over six trillion euros in lost output, and it will cost trillions more. Output in most industrialized countries remains significantly below the level that it would have reached had the pre-crisis trend rate of growth continued. The crisis also poses a threat to the public finances in the USA, the UK and, most significantly, in the Eurozone, and failure to address these problems could cause the world economy to plunge once again into turmoil.

It will be many years, if ever, before the economy again reaches the pre-crisis trend line. According to a World Bank forecast global gross domestic product (GDP) in 2015 will still not have caught up to the level of GDP that it would have reached had the pre-crisis trend rate of growth continued (Figure 18.1). The present value of that future output shortfall is 8.5 trillion euros; so the total cost of the crisis is likely to be on the order of 15 trillion euros or over 30 per cent of the level of pre-crisis global GDP. These losses will magnify if the recovery stalls or a double dip occurs (Huertas, 2011a, pp. 1–2).

That could well occur if governments cannot bring sovereign debt back under control. Accordingly, there is some possibility that we may

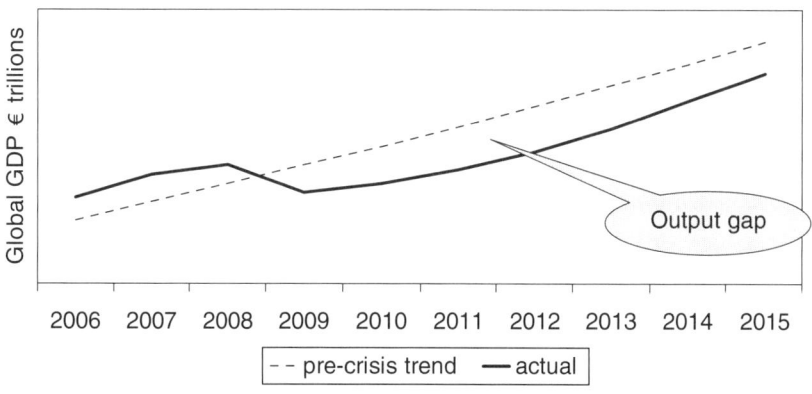

Figure 18.1   Crisis Depresses Global GDP

never again reach the level of output that we would have attained had the pre-crisis trend rate of growth continued. In other words, there is the possibility that the crisis will leave a permanent scar on the world economy. Should that occur, the costs of the crisis could rise to 50 per cent or more of pre-crisis GDP.

So, fixing finance has high priority. Are we there yet? No. But we have made a strong start. Policymakers have reformed regulation and improved supervision. They have strengthened deposit guarantee schemes. They have also revised resolution regimes and laid the foundations to end 'too big to fail'. All these measures point to financial institutions that are more resilient and to a financial system that is more resistant to crises.

But that does not preclude crises. Crises need not always emanate from finance. Crises can also originate elsewhere. Indeed, as this chapter is being written (November 2011), sovereign debt is posing strong challenges to financial stability – well before the end of the transition period envisioned by the architects of the new finance.

18.1   REFORMING REGULATION

Regulation has received a complete overhaul. The Basel Committee on Banking Supervision has revised capital regulation and introduced for the very first time a global standard for liquidity regulation. And, at the prompting of the G-20 and the Financial Stability Board (FSB), countries have agreed for the first time to regulate remuneration.

The so-called Basel III framework will significantly increase – over a transition period lasting until 2019 – the amount of capital that banks need to hold against the risks in their portfolio (BCBS, 2010a) (Figure 18.2). Trading book risks will be measured more accurately. Assets such as goodwill will no longer count towards capital; and financial institutions will no longer be able to double count investments in other financial institutions as part of their own capital. The minimum amount of capital will increase, from 2 per cent of risk weighted assets to 4.5 per cent and banks will have to maintain an additional capital conservation buffer equal to 2.5 per cent of risk weighted assets if they wish to retain complete flexibility to pay dividends and make distributions. In addition, central banks may impose a countercyclical capital buffer to prevent banks overheating the economy by expanding credit too rapidly. Finally, the new regime includes a leverage ratio (ratio of capital to assets (not weighted for risk)) as a backstop to the risk-based regime.

Systemically important financial institutions (SIFIs) will face a surcharge of 1 per cent to 2.5 per cent of risk weighted assets as an addition

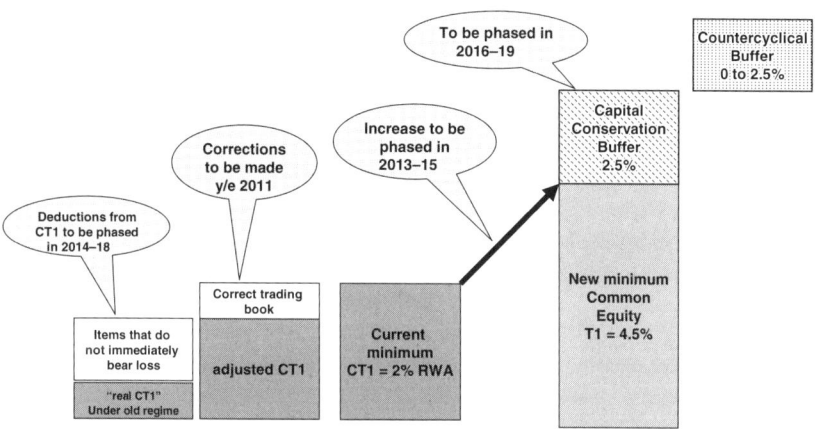

Figure 18.2   The amount of capital will increase

to their capital conservation buffer (BCBS, 2011a). This recognizes that the world economy is running what amounts to a concentration risk on such large and/or complex and interconnected institutions. Considering the damage that the failure of such an institution could cause to financial markets and to the world economy, policymakers considered it prudent to take a step that would reduce the probability that a global SIFI could fail as well as raise the cost to the global SIFI itself of its becoming ever larger or more complex.

In addition to increasing the amount of capital, the new Basel framework will improve its quality. Although the minimum total capital requirement remains at 8 per cent of risk weighted assets, three-quarters of this amount (6 per cent of risk weighted assets) must be Tier I capital, and fully three-quarters of Tier I capital (4.5 per cent of risk weighted assets) must be common equity Tier I capital. In addition, to continue to qualify as capital, non-core Tier I and Tier II capital must contain provisions that make such instruments subject to conversion or write down at the point at which the bank becomes non-viable in private markets (that is, the point at which the regulator intervenes (BCBS, 2011b)). Together these measures assure that all capital instruments bear loss either whilst the bank is a going concern (common equity Tier I) or at the point of non-viability (non-core Tier I and Tier II). This facilitates the reform of resolution (see below) so that private investors, rather than the taxpayer, will bear loss in the event a bank fails.

With respect to liquidity, the Basel Committee has broken new ground. It has introduced for the first time a global standard for liquidity regulation (Figure 18.3). This has three aspects: a requirement that banks measure the

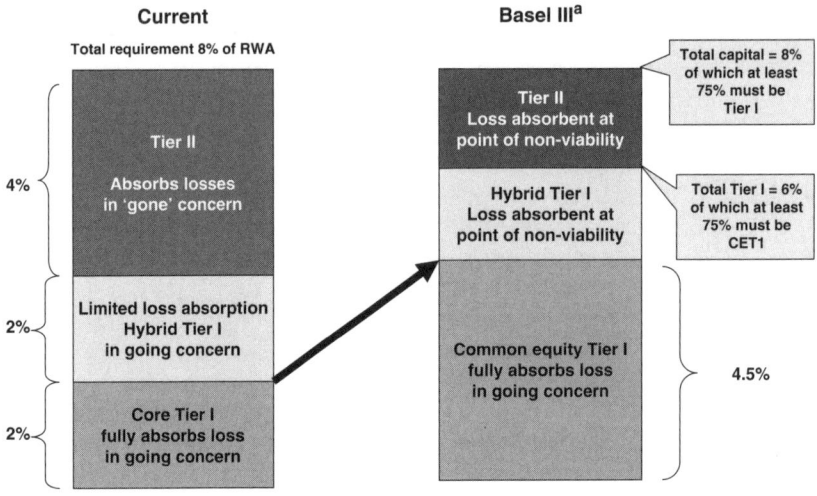

Note: ᵃ Excludes capital conservation and countercyclical buffers.

Figure 18.3   The quality of capital will improve

liquidity risks to which they are exposed; a requirement that banks hold a buffer of liquid assets against the short-term liquidity risks that they run; and a requirement that banks fund themselves in a stable manner. These changes are to be phased in over the next five to eight years (BCBS, 2010b).

With respect to remuneration, banks are now required to structure remuneration so that it promotes effective risk management. This entails limits on the percentage of bonus that can be paid immediately and limits on the percentage of bonus that can be paid in cash. Bankers must defer 40 per cent to 60 per cent of their variable compensation, and bankers must take at least 50 per cent of their variable compensation in forms, such as equity, that depend on the ongoing performance of the firm. Additionally, banks must demonstrate that the amount of cash paid in variable compensation does not compromise the bank's ability to accumulate the capital that it will require to support its business (FSB, 2009).

18.2   STRENGTHENING DEPOSIT GUARANTEE SCHEMES

In addition to reforming regulation policymakers have strengthened deposit guarantee schemes (Huertas, 2011a, pp. 145–56). Limits have been raised (in the European Union (EU) to 100,000 euros per person per insured bank). Co-insurance has been eliminated so that depositors have full coverage for the headline amount. Authorities have also taken steps to improve the ability of schemes to pay out promptly in the event a bank fails. Finally, authorities have taken steps to assure that deposit guarantee schemes are adequately funded, including where necessary granting such schemes lines of credit from the central bank and/or finance ministry. This has greatly improved the capability of deposit guarantee schemes to do what it says on the tin: pay out insured deposits promptly in the event that a bank fails.

18.3   IMPROVING SUPERVISION

Supervision is also improving. In response to the crisis, supervisors have intensified their review of individual institutions (micro-supervision). In addition, macro-prudential supervision is being introduced. Its task is to identify threats to financial stability, issue warnings and assure that steps are taken to mitigate the risks identified.

Supervision of individual institutions is now more forward-looking, more proactive and more intrusive (Huertas, 2011a, pp. 184–92). A good example is the introduction of stress testing as a means of determining whether or not banks are capable of meeting the challenges that a more troubled economic environment might pose, and requiring the banks that are not to put in place remedial measures before the hypothesized stress actually materializes. In addition, supervisors have started to demand that banks write recovery and resolution plans (Huertas and Lastra, 2011). In the recovery plan, the bank has to document how it could cope under extreme stress and subject this to supervisory review. If the supervisor determines that the bank would not be resilient under such stress, the supervisor can demand that the bank take steps to improve its resiliency.

Micro-supervision is also undergoing reorganization. The EU has established a European System of Financial Supervision with three pan-European authorities (European Banking Authority, European Securities and Markets Authority and European Insurance and Occupational Pensions Authority) to assure that there is a single rule book in the EU and that the actual supervision of firms improves and converges towards that higher standard.

Policymakers have also introduced a new category of supervision, macro-prudential supervision. To this end, the EU has established the European Systemic Risk Board; the USA, the Financial Stability Oversight Council; and the UK, the Financial Policy Committee. Each of these groups has the responsibility to consider the financial system as a whole. The task facing such groups is akin to finding and removing the needle in the haystack before the sunlight ignites a spark that will set the stack and the stable ablaze. The trouble is that the 'needles' that are easy to find are generally politically sensitive and therefore difficult to remove (for example, use of Fannie Mae and Freddie Mac to promote sub-prime mortgages, excessive budget deficits in Eurozone countries), whilst the ones that can be removed may be difficult to find (Huertas, 2011b).

18.4 REVISING RESOLUTION REGIMES; ENDING TOO BIG TO FAIL

Finally, policymakers have made significant progress in revising resolution regimes and are moving towards ending too big to fail (Huertas, 2012). The USA, the UK, Germany and several other countries have introduced or strengthened special resolution regimes for banks. The EU is also proposing to introduce such measures. Under such regimes, the trigger for putting a bank into resolution is a finding by the bank's supervisor that the bank no longer meets threshold conditions (generally this results when the bank is no longer viable in private markets, and that results when the bank no longer has adequate liquidity and/or capital).

The regimes empower a resolution authority to take rapid measures to deal with the failed bank. Generally, the special resolution regime empowers the resolution authority to select a resolution method from a predefined 'tool box' that best meets the authority's statutory objective (for example, to minimize social costs or costs to the deposit guarantee fund). The tool box generally includes five techniques (liquidation/deposit pay-off, deposit transfer, bridge bank, bail-in and temporary public ownership) that may be used singly or in combination. The objective is to be able to resolve even the largest and most complex banks – if they were to fail in a manner that limits social and economic costs and removes the need for the taxpayer to provide solvency support.

To realize this objective, resolution authorities have to be able to act extremely quickly. If a bank fails, there is a very limited window of time – generally no longer than 48 hours over a weekend – for the resolution authority to select and implement a resolution method, if disruption to financial markets is to be avoided. To enable the resolution authorities to meet such a deadline, supervisors are requiring banks to provide data to the authorities as part of their living wills that will enable the authorities to draw up a resolution plan for the institution. Such resolution plans amount to financial continuity plans for the institution, and it is intended that each plan be in place for each global SIFI by the end of 2012 (FSB, 2011a).

This revision to resolution promises to end 'too big to fail' and to make banks 'safe to fail'. In combination special resolution regimes and resolution plans will allow, if a bank fails, the resolution authority to effect what amounts to a pre-pack recapitalization. This will effectively restructure the bank's investor capital. Non-core Tier 1 capital, subordinated debt and possibly unsecured senior debt will either suffer a stay, be written down or converted into common equity. This will expand the bank's loss-bearing capacity beyond its common equity, whilst allowing customer obligations such as deposits to continue to be serviced in a timely fashion. That minimizes social costs and avoids recourse to the taxpayer.

18.5   WHAT REMAINS TO BE DONE?

In concept, the new architecture makes banks less likely to fail and makes banks safe to fail. Whether this will be enough to deter future crises depends on three factors:

1.   Whether the concept is complete.
2.   Whether the concept is implemented.
3.   Whether and when other shocks may occur.

18.5.1   Completing the Concept

Although the concept covers the main areas that require reform, there are three unfinished elements that still require attention. The first is financial infrastructures. They need to be made robust. The second is shadow banking. This needs to be controlled. The third area requiring attention is sovereign debt. This is not risk-free, and regulation needs to recognize this.

Financial infrastructures are payment, clearing and settlement systems, including the clearing houses through which derivative transactions are to be channelled. Such clearing houses will reduce systemic risk if and only if they are robust, that is, able to withstand the simultaneous failure of two or more of their largest participants. This demands that the clearing house have appropriate risk management policies, procedures and systems, that the clearing house require adequate margins from its counterparties, that the clearing house have an adequate default fund and that the clearing house itself be adequately capitalized. Anything less poses massive systemic risk. Indeed, the failure of a major clearing house to meet its commitments would adversely affect practically all major financial institutions and potentially impair the ability of one or more such institutions to meet their obligations to other financial infrastructures. To limit such contagion, policymakers and financial institutions need to assure that financial infrastructures are robust (Huertas, 2012; Tucker, 2011). That is exactly what the Committee on Payment Settlement Systems (CPSS) and the Technical Committee of the International Organization of Securities Commissions (IOSCO) (CPSS-IOSCO, 2011) standards are designed to do, and the Basel Committee only accords lower capital requirements and/ or exemption from large exposure limits to exposures to clearing houses that meet the CPSS-IOSCO standards (BCBS, 2011c).

Shadow banking refers to essentially two different things: banks operating in the shadows, and non-banks acting as if they were banks. Both need to stop if financial stability is to be maintained (Huertas, 2011a, pp. 206–10). The FSB (FSB, 2011a, 2011b) has set in motion a process to do just that.

Regulators have already made progress in stopping banks from operating in the shadows. Prior to the crisis banks built up an extensive range of vehicles such as structured investment vehicles that they managed and to which they provided liquidity commitments, but which they did not consolidate onto their balance sheets. New regulations force banks to consolidate such vehicles and subject them to capital and liquidity requirements as well as to official supervision.

Similar steps need to be taken to limit the ability of non-banks to operate as if they were banks. In particular, limits need to be placed on the ability of US money market mutual funds to market their obligations as deposit equivalents and to commit to investors that the fund will maintain a unit value of $1. Although regulations aim to assure that funds diversify their investments and restrict the extent of maturity transformation, such limits do not preclude the possibility that a fund would have to 'break the buck'. If one fund did so, this would create the possibility that runs would occur on all money market mutual funds. This poses significant systemic risk. To limit this, money market mutual funds should either stop promising to provide a fixed unit value, or sponsors should be required to hold capital and liquidity sufficient to provide a backstop to the fund. The FSB will conduct work in this area.

Under current regulation in the EU sovereign debt occupies a privileged position. If held in the banking book, sovereign debt carries a zero risk weight and is effectively free from capital requirements. It is also exempt from large exposure limits. There is a presumption that such debt is liquid, and that such debt is suitable for inclusion in the bank's liquidity buffer. The difficulties that several Eurozone countries are currently experiencing undermine the basis for such a privileged position. The architecture of the new regime needs to take the risk of sovereign debt into account (Hannoun, 2011).

The proposed liquidity regime already takes a step in the right direction. For the purpose of calculating the liquidity buffer assets are valued at market prices, not book values. This assures that the value of the buffer is approximately equal to the amount of cash that the bank could realize if it had to sell the assets in the buffer.

The treatment for capital requirements needs to be brought into line, particularly if sovereign debt is to continue to enjoy an exemption from large exposure limits. One way to do this would be to require that all sovereign debt be held in the bank's trading book (where it would be marked to market and subject to capital requirements for interest rate risk and for default risk). Alternatively, if the bonds continue to be held in the banking book, they should not carry a zero risk weight, they should be classified as 'held for sale', and a reserve should be made for any unrealized losses (that is, the bonds would effectively be held at the lower of cost or market). This will help assure that banks calculate their capital in a conservative manner and therefore allow banks to raise liquidity more readily through the sale of sovereign debt (as they would not have to be concerned that the sale itself would crystallize an incremental loss and deplete the bank's regulatory capital).

18.5.2   Implementing the Concept

For this broad reform of regulation to be effective as a bulwark against future crises, the EU, the USA and other principal jurisdictions must actually implement what has been agreed around global conference tables in Basel, at the Financial Stability Board and at the G-20 summits.

It is vital that the new regime be implemented in full. That will assure that banks have adequate capital and adequate liquidity and reduce the likelihood that the crisis could recur. It will also help create a level playing field. Indeed, for those truly interested in a level playing field, the cry should be to implement the global standard. Each tweak in the standard to accommodate local business practices creates a pothole in the global standard. Once potholes proliferate, the playing field will no longer be level.

18.5.3   Other Shocks

Building a defence against crises is akin to designing a building code. One wants the buildings to be strong enough to stand on their own and to withstand foreseeable shocks. Once implemented, the international agreements relating to capital, liquidity and resolution will greatly reduce the probability that problems in finance will cause a crisis as well as the probability that a fragile banking system would magnify shocks emanating elsewhere into a crisis.

But the world won't necessarily wait until 2018 or 2019 before presenting further shocks to the economy and the financial system. Indeed, as this chapter is being written, the world must grapple with a number of actual and potential shocks, above all the threat to financial stability posed by troubled Eurozone sovereigns (that is, sovereigns that are having trouble financing themselves in private markets).

Such debt poses a threefold challenge to the banking system:

1. Banks are directly exposed to loss if they hold the debt of the troubled sovereign.
2. Banks are indirectly exposed to loss on their exposures to consumers and corporates in the jurisdiction of the troubled sovereign as a result of slower economic growth or recession caused by the austerity measures that the troubled sovereign will have to take.
3. The troubled sovereign can no longer act as an effective backstop to the banks headquartered in their jurisdiction.

The start to a remedy is to separate the banking problem from the sovereign problem. This can be done first, by forcing banks, as recommended above, to mark sovereign debt to market and to hold capital and/or reserves against that debt; second, subjecting the banks to a stress test that takes into account the possibility of a deep recession as a result of the austerity measures that troubled sovereigns may introduce; third, forcing banks to meet the new capital standards within a short time frame; and fourth, – as the new resolution regimes are not yet fully in place – providing a supranational (for example, Eurozone) mechanism to serve as a backstop provider of capital to banks that are not able to bring their ratio into line with the new requirements before the deadline. This is essentially the programme agreed by Eurozone Heads of State (2011) in October 2011. It envisages that EU banks will – after marking their holdings of sovereign bonds to market – reach a core Tier 1 capital ratio greater than or equal to 9 per cent of risk weighted assets by mid-2012. In other words, the EU banks will accelerate the implementation of the new capital Basel capital regime. Together with the backstop from member states and the European Financial Stability Fund (EFSF), this should enhance market confidence in EU banks.

The separation of the banking problem from the sovereign problem should allow the Eurozone countries to tackle the sovereign problem more directly. This has to be done on two levels: first, the troubled sovereign has to take measures that will bring its budget deficit under control (back within the Maastricht criteria) within a limited time period, and second, the Eurozone has to finance the troubled sovereign during its transition back to a more sustainable budget outcome. The two elements go hand in hand. Indeed, without some assurance that the troubled sovereign is actually taking measures to bring its budget deficit under control, the 'financing' provided by the Eurozone member states to the troubled sovereign would effectively be a transfer rather than a loan. To prevent this, the Eurozone must impose conditions on the troubled sovereign and the troubled sovereign must agree to monitoring and surveillance by the EU/Eurozone.

Whether such a programme can work depends on the level of debt relative to GDP in the troubled sovereign as well as the amount of resources that the Eurozone sets aside to backstop troubled sovereigns during the transition phase. In the case of Greece, the debt:GDP ratio was so high that budget reform alone would not have restored the debt to a sustainable level. For this reason, the Eurozone heads of state secured an agreement in principle with the private holders of Greek sovereign debt that the latter would accept a 50 per cent reduction in their claims on the Greek sovereign.This increases the probability that Greece will be able to avoid a damaging debt-deflation downward spiral and be able to actually repay the remaining debt.

The position of other troubled Eurozone sovereigns (Ireland, Portugal, Spain and Italy) is significantly better than that of Greece. The debt: GDP ratio is lower and/or the budget deficit is smaller relative to GDP. Provided the member state takes measures to bring down its deficit, there is the prospect that the troubled sovereign – with sufficient transitional financing – can ultimately finance itself in private markets at a sustainable cost without requiring private creditors to reduce their claims on the troubled sovereign. The question is whether the aggregate demand for transitional financing will exceed the resources allocated by Eurozone member states to the EFSF for that purpose. The answer depends on whether the troubled sovereigns in general and Italy in particular take the necessary measures, and whether means can be found to lever the effectiveness of the EFSF. The Eurozone Heads of State (2011) clearly recognized this in the October 2011 communiqué. Indeed, they went further and reached a consensus that preventing such problems in the future would require a closer fiscal union, at least within the Eurozone.

18.6 CONCLUSION

In sum, policymakers have designed a framework that has the potential to fix finance. The reform of capital and liquidity requirements will make banks less likely to fail. The reform of resolution will make banks 'safe to fail'. Together these reforms will make banks more resilient and the financial system more resistant to crises.

But to achieve financial stability countries must actually implement the reforms. That will limit the shocks that the financial system can pose to the economy. But countries also need to limit the shocks to which the financial system could be exposed. They need to create a macro-economic environment conducive to growth and price stability. In particular, sovereigns themselves need to assure that they remain creditworthy.

NOTE

1. The author presented a preliminary version of this chapter to the CRESSE conference in Rhodes on 2 July 2011. At the time the author was a member of the Executive Committee, Financial Services Authority (FSA) (UK) and Alternate Chair, European Banking Authority (EBA). He is currently a partner in the risk practice at Ernst & Young. The opinions expressed in this chapter are the author's own and do not necessarily represent the views of the FSA, the EBA or Ernst & Young.

REFERENCES

BCBS (Basel Committee on Banking Supervision) (2010a), 'Basel III: a global regulatory framework for more resilient banks and banking systems', available at http://www.bis.org/publ/bcbs189.pdf (accessed 9 November 2011).

BCBS (Basel Committee on Banking Supervision) (2010b), 'Basel III: international framework for liquidity risk measurement, standards and monitoring', available at from http://www.bis.org/publ/bcbs188.pdf (accessed 9 November 2011).

BCBS (Basel Committee on Banking Supervision) (2011a), 'Global systemically important banks: assessment methodology and the additional loss absorbency requirement – consultative document', available at http://www.bis.org/publ/bcbs201.pdf (accessed 9 November 2011).

BCBS (Basel Committee on Banking Supervision) (2011b), 'Basel Committee issues final elements of the reforms to raise the quality of regulatory capital', available at http://www.bis.org/press/p110113.pdf (accessed 9 November 2011).

BCBS (Basel Committee on Banking Supervision) (2011c), 'Capitalisation of bank exposures to central counterparties', available at http://www.bis.org/publ/bcbs206.pdf (accessed 9 November 2011).

CPSS-IOSCO (2011), 'Principles for financial market infrastructures', available at http://www.bis.org/publ/cpss94.pdf (accessed 9 November 2011).

Eurozone Heads of State (2011), 'Statement', 26 October, available at http://www.consilium.europa.eu/uedocs/cms_data/docs/pressdata/en/ec/125644.pdf (accessed 9 November 2011).

FSB (Financial Stability Board) (2009), 'FSB principles for sound compensation practices: implementation standards', available at http://www.financialstability-board.org/publications/r_090925c.pdf (accessed 9 November 2011).

FSB (Financial Stability Board) (2011a), 'Key attributes of effective resolution regimes for financial institutions', available at http://www.financialstability board.org/publications/r_111104cc.pdf (acessed 9 November 2011).

FSB (Financial Stability Board) (2011b), 'Shadow banking: strengthening oversight and regulation', available at http://www.financialstabilityboard.org/publications/r_111027a.pdf (acessed 9 November 2011).

Hannoun, H. (2011), 'Sovereign risk in bank regulation and supervision: where do we stand?', available at http://www.bis.org/speeches/sp111026.pdf (accessed 9 November 2011).

Huertas, T.F. (2011a), *Crisis: Cause, Containment and Cure* (2nd edn), London: Palgrave Macmillan.

Huertas, T.F. (2011b), 'Forecasting, warning and preventive policy: the case of finance', in C. de Franco and C.O. Meyer (eds), *Forecasting, Warning and Responding to Transnational Risks*, London: Palgrave Macmillan, pp. 217–26.

Huertas, T.F. (2012), 'Resolution requires reform', in P.S. Kenadjian (ed.), *Too Big to Fail – Brauchen Wir ein Sonderinsolvenzrecht für Banken?*, Berlin: de Gruyter, pp. 63–84.

Huertas, T.F. and R.M. Lastra (2011), 'Living wills', *Bank of Spain Financial Stability Review*, November, 23–39, available at http://www.bde.es/webbde/Secciones/Publicaciones/InformesBoletinesRevistas/RevistaEstabilidadFinanciera/11/ref0221%20.pdf.

Tucker, P. (2011), 'Central counterparties: the agenda', available at http://www.bankofengland.co.uk/publications/speeches/speaker.htm#tucker (accessed 29 October 2011).

Index